TEACH YOURSELF
EXCEL 4.0

by

Phyllis Romanski

and

Susan Rothenberg

First Edition—1992

ISBN 1-55828-208- 4

Printed in the United States of America.

10 9 8 7 6 5 4 3 2

MIS:Press books are available at special discounts for bulk purchases for sales promotions, premiums, fund-raising, or educational use. Special editions or book excerpts can also be created to specification.

For details contact: Special Sales Director
MIS:Press
a subsidiary of Henry Holt and Company, Inc.
115 West 18th Street
New York, New York 10011

Trademarks

dBase II, dBase III, and dBase IV are trademarks of Ashton-Tate Corporation

IBM PC/AT is a trademark of International Business Machines, Inc.

IBM Personal System/2 is a trademark of International Business Machines, Inc.

Lotus and 1-2-3 are trademarks of Lotus Development Corporation

Macintosh is a trademark of Apple Computer, Incorporated

Micro Channel Architecture (MCA) is a trademark of International Business Machines, Inc.

Microsoft Excel is a trademark of Microsoft Corporation

Microsoft Windows is a trademark of Microsoft Corporation

MS-DOS is a trademark of Microsoft Corporation

Multiplan is a trademark of Microsoft Corporation

Spelling checker is a trademark of Soft-Art, Inc.

VisiCalc is a trademark of Lotus Development Corporation

Dedication

This book is dedicated to Uncle Joe, who "Excels" above all others.

Acknowledgments

We would like to thank all of the people who helped to make this book happen:

Joy and John Tortorici, who gave us a hand when we really needed one.

Lois Karp, for her love and support.

Eli Hertz, of Hertz Computer Corp., who provided the superb hardware we used to test the program and write the book.

Ken Cuite, of Hertz Computer Corp., who didn't read this book either, but was helpful in other ways.

Paul Landsman and Joe Gruner, of Landsman and Gruner—good lawyers, good friends, and good guys.

Matt Wagner, of Waterside Productions, who keeps us in mind when interesting projects come along (and who always Fed-Ex's our checks!).

Steve Berkowitz, our publisher, who traded our pandemonium for his during the last week of production.

Elizabeth Gehrman, our editor, for her patience and flexibility. She handled nonexistent icons, oversized worksheets, and last-minute rushes with total equanimity.

Liz Misch, our associate production editor, for her time and effort.

And, last but not least, our clients, who put up with being put off while this book was being written.

CONTENTS

CHAPTER 8: WORKING WITH CALCULATIONS

CHAPTER 9: USING PRINT ENHANCEMENTS WITH WORKSHEETS

INTRODUCTION

Microsoft Excel is one of the most popular spreadsheet packages in the world. Its flexibility and array of features exceed those of all other spreadsheet packages available today. With Excel 4.0, Microsoft has taken a great leap forward. Even if you are a seasoned Excel user, you will be thrilled with the exciting new features offered by the program. Beginners will love that it is so user-friendly. Either way, you are in for an exhilarating experience when you begin to work with this program.

This book is written for beginner and intermediate-level users. Even if you are a complete novice on computers, you will be able to master Excel comfortably and painlessly. The approach used in this book reflects the hundreds of hours of training we have done in Excel. We have anticipated the most common questions and problems, and have presented the material in a logical, easy-to-master format. The book starts with the basics and gradually builds up to the more complex features. We have focused on Microsoft Excel only; this book does not delve into the mysteries of Q+E and the Dialog Editor.

Readers who are familiar with another version of Excel will be able to use this book to learn the new features in Excel 4.0.

A Word About Mice

You can operate Microsoft Excel without a mouse, but the program really is designed to be used with a rodent. If, like many people, you have an aversion to rodents, this may be a problem. We strongly suggest that you force yourself to use the mouse as much as possible in the beginning. Eventually, you will find it faster and easier than the keyboard.

Exciting New Features in Excel 4.0

There are so many exciting new features in Excel 4.0 that it would be impossible to list them all here. We will have to be content to enumerate just a few.

Toolbars

Excel 4.0 has many new built-in toolbars, as well as a wide selection of new tools to make even the most complex tasks possible with just a flick of a click.

Workbooks

Workbooks are a great way to organize groups of documents and keep related information together. Binding documents into a workbook provides easier file management and security, and allows you to quickly move between documents, control window display and placement options, and edit groups of documents with ease.

On-Screen Slide Shows

This is one of the most exciting new presentation features in Excel 4.0. You can now create slide shows from worksheets, charts, and graphics. You can even include sound notes with the slide show. All you need to give a polished presentation is a monitor and Excel 4.0.

Spell Checking

You can now check the spelling in your worksheets, macro sheets, and charts.

AutoFill

You can create a series of sequential numbers, dates, and mixed text using the new AutoFill feature. For example, if you type *January* into a cell, AutoFill will extend the series to include February, March, and so forth.

Shortcut Menus

By clicking the right mouse button you can display a shortcut menu with commands appropriate to whatever task you are working on at the time. Plus, lots of new editing and formatting features will enhance your documents, stimulate your imagination, and make document production a breeze.

How this Book Is Organized

This book is basically organized into two parts. Chapters 1 to 10 cover the basics through the intermediate level. You will learn basic information about your computer and how it interacts with Excel. You will create several worksheets and learn how to use basic and advanced editing and formatting features, as well as working with multiple documents, linking worksheets, building formulas, creating trends and analyses, and learning other features necessary for a solid foundation in worksheet production and enhancement.

Chapters 11 to 15 cover more advanced features, and will take you through creating charts and databases and integrating graphics into your documents. You will also learn how to customize Excel, and a special section on Microsoft Windows will help you learn how to switch between applications and use the Windows Program Manager.

Each chapter begins with a list of what you will learn in the chapter. At the end of the chapter are review exercises to reinforce what you have learned. Following the review exercise is a "Before You Go On..." section, which details all of the features you should know before you move on to the next chapter.

Additional Information

Key combinations on the PC keyboard are indicated with a plus sign. For example, *Shift+F1* means that you should hold down the Shift key while pressing the F1 function key.

Throughout the book there will be sections that require special attention. The following icons will be used to mark these sections.

Indicates that you should take note of the information. This symbol may indicate a helpful hint or a special condition.

Indicates that you can perform an action more quickly by using shortcut keys or by following the suggestion in the text.

Indicates cautionary information or warnings. This symbol often provides a warning that you may lose data if you perform an action incorrectly.

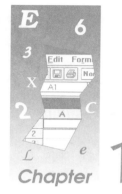

Chapter 1

GETTING STARTED

What You Will Learn in This Chapter

- ◆ How to identify the parts of your computer
- ◆ How the parts of your computer interact
- ◆ Why DOS is necessary
- ◆ Some facts about Windows
- ◆ How to start Excel
- ◆ How to identify and use parts of the Excel application window
- ◆ How to work with a mouse
- ◆ How to use the numeric keypad

An Introduction to Your System

If you have never worked with a computer before, you might find it somewhat intimidating. We hope this chapter will put your mind at ease and answer some of your questions. We will cover the bare-bones basics about hardware and software. For more detailed information about how your computer works, we suggest you read *Welcome to Personal Computers,* by Kris Jamsa (MIS:Press), available at your local bookstore.

A computer system consists of two basic elements: **hardware** and **software**. The hardware consists of the physical components of the system. These components break down and decode instructions. The software consists of the programs that transmit instructions to the computer. There are many different software programs available for your computer. Excel is one of them.

The **disk operating system (DOS)** is a software program that acts as a link between the hardware and software. In a sense, it is the brain of the computer and is responsible for translating software instructions into language that will be understood by the hardware. DOS is explained in more detail later in this chapter.

About Hardware and Software

It helps if you can identify all of the basic parts of your computer and understand what they do (see Figure 1.1).

Figure 1.1. A typical PC.

Let's start with the big box, otherwise known as the **chassis**. The chassis contains most of the parts necessary to make the computer work. If you open it up (see Figure 1.2) you will see several **boards**, or cards containing futuristic-looking paraphernalia called **chips** and **circuits**.

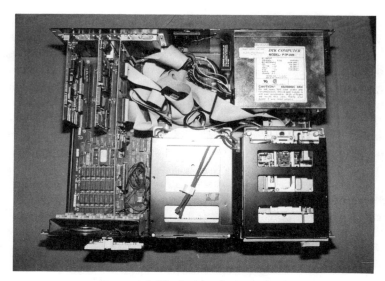

Figure 1.2. The inside of a typical PC.

These are plugged into a master board, appropriately called the **motherboard**. Also on the motherboard is the **central processing unit** chip, or CPU. This is the most important chip in the computer. The CPU controls the operation of the computer and is the part of the computer that performs logical operations and decodes and executes instructions. The circuitry on this chip also determines, to a large extent, the speed of your computer.

In the chassis you will also see a bunch of cables that look like wide ribbons and twisted-pair wire. These connect the battery, floppy disk drive(s), hard drive, power pack, and other peripherals to the motherboard, either directly or through another board. These basic parts are essential to the operation of your computer, but they operate in the background, so to speak, and it is rarely necessary for a user to have to deal with them directly.

Also in the chassis are your **hard drive** and **floppy disk drive(s)**, and these parts are of more interest to you because you must work with them directly. The hard drive is really a large, high-capacity storage device used to store software and data. It is sometimes called the **fixed drive** because, unlike floppy disks, it is screwed down inside the chassis of your computer and is not movable. The hard drive has many advantages over floppy disks. The most obvious advantage is that it can hold much more data. Also, it is not as subject to damage as floppy disks. Hard drives come in many sizes, but most hold anywhere from 20 megabytes (20 million characters) to several hundred megabytes. On a really large system, you might have a hard drive that can store hundreds of gigabytes (billions of characters). Like any large space, hard drives must be organized to work efficiently. Chapter 10 explains how to organize your hard drive into directories for easier management.

On one or more of the boards inside the chassis are chips known as **RAM chips**. These chips determine how much information can be held at a time in a temporary buffer called **random-access memory (RAM)**. Usually when you execute a program (such as Excel), all of the instructions necessary to operate the program are loaded into RAM, as is the data you are creating while using the program (such as documents). If you have enough RAM, you can operate more than one program at a time. Programs like Windows create a shell that allows the user to execute more than one program at a time and then switch back and forth between them. Or, you could have a program running in the background (for example, indexing a database) while concurrently operating another program such as Excel. This is known as **multitasking**. The key elements in this type of operation are speed and RAM. If you are using Excel 4.0, you should have at least 2 megabytes (2 million bytes) of RAM in your computer. This allows enough space to accommodate DOS, Windows, and Excel 4.0, all of which are in use at the same time. Additional RAM can be added to a computer by purchasing more RAM chips or, in some cases, a RAM board (refer to your computer manual for information on how to add RAM to your computer). The more programs you plan to operate concurrently, the more RAM you will need. Information loaded into RAM is temporary. When you exit a program, all information relating to that program is deleted from RAM. When you reboot or turn off the computer, all information of any kind is deleted from RAM.

Floppy drives are accessible to the user from outside of the chassis. They are the small slots into which you can insert your floppy disks. Floppy disks are storage devices used to store software and data. They hold much less data than a hard drive. There are two sizes of floppy disks in most computer systems: 5.25-inch and 3.5-inch (see Figure 1.3).

Figure 1.3. 3.5-inch (left) and 5.25-inch (right) floppy disks.

The larger, 5.25-inch floppy disks are available in two densities: **high density** (sometimes called **quad density**) and **low density** (often called **double density**). High-density 5.25-inch floppy disks hold approximately 1.2 megabytes (or 1,200,000 bytes) of information. Low-density 5.25-inch disks hold approximately 360 kilobytes (or 360,000 bytes) of information. If you have a 5.25-inch floppy disk drive on your computer and your system is a 286 or higher, you probably have a high-density disk drive. You may have a 3.5-inch disk drive on your computer. The 3.5-inch disks also come in high and low density, holding approximately 1.4 megabytes (1,400,000) and 720 kilobytes (720,000) of information, respectively.

Floppy disks must be **formatted** before they can be used. Formatting initializes the floppy disk so that it will be recognized by DOS. Different versions of DOS require different instructions to format floppy disks. Refer to your DOS manual for the correct instructions for your system.

When you turn on your computer, several lights appear on the front of the chassis. One of these lights is usually attached to the power pack, and indicates that power is being received by the computer. Another light is attached to the hard drive, and indicates that the hard drive is receiving power from, and is recognized by, the system. The remaining lights are attached to the floppy disk drive(s), and indicate that they are receiving power from, and are recognized by, the system.

Another peripheral attached to the computer by a cable is the **monitor**. This is sometimes called the **CRT**, or **cathode ray tube**. This is a scientific term for how patterns are actually formed on the monitor. Although there are other types of monitors, the term CRT has become so widespread that it is frequently (although incorrectly) used to describe all monitors.

Monitors come in many different sizes and can be monochromatic, monochromatic with gray tones, or color. The clarity, or **resolution**, of the monitor depends on the type of monitor you are using and the video interface card it is plugged into. If you are using a color monitor, you will be able to configure your software to reflect your personal color preferences (within the color limitations of your monitor). Some monitors have knobs or wheels for adjusting brightness and contrast as well as horizontal and vertical position and size. Refer to your manual for information on how your monitor works.

Keyboards are the most common input device—the most common way to send instructions to the computer. They are plugged into the chassis and are used to transmit text and instructions to the computer. There are two basic styles of keyboards used with IBM or IBM-compatible computers: standard and enhanced. The standard keyboard usually has eighty-eight keys and contains ten function keys located on its left side. The enhanced keyboard usually has 101 keys, with twelve function keys located across its top. The type of keyboard you use is a matter of personal preference.

The **mouse** is another kind of input device. A mouse is extremely desirable for working in a Windows environment. Unlike the keyboard, where you "key in," or type, instructions, the mouse is a pointing device. You point to an instruction or **icon** (picture) on the screen and then click a button on the mouse to execute the command represented by the icon. Some mice have two buttons, some three. Like the different types of keyboards, the number of buttons on the mouse is a matter of personal preference.

You probably also have a **printer** plugged into your computer. The printer is an output device for printing text and graphics sent to it from the computer. Instructions are transmitted from the computer to the printer through parts of programs called **printer drivers**. Most software programs come with their own printer drivers, which allow you to configure the software to communicate with your particular printer. Appendix A, *Installation of Excel*, explains how to configure Excel for your printer. There are many different printers available, from inexpensive dot matrix printers to expensive laser printers. The type of printer you choose will depend upon your needs and budget.

You should refer to the manuals that came with your computer and printer for information on their maintenance and use. If you take good care of your equipment and use it properly you will avoid expensive repairs.

About Your Disk Operating System (DOS)

When you purchased your system, you probably also purchased a software program called DOS. DOS is essential to the operation of your computer. It is the bridge between your hardware and software programs. DOS is available in different versions and for different hardware systems. This book is written for users with an IBM or IBM-compatible computer, so your computer has IBM or Microsoft DOS. People with Apple computers would have a different type of DOS. Software written for your computer is also written to interface with your DOS. When you purchase a software program, check to be sure it is compatible with the version and type of DOS you are using.

Different versions of DOS (such as DOS 3.x, 4.x, or 5.x) have slightly different command languages and may interface a little differently with other software. If DOS has been properly installed on your system, this should be no problem.

DOS is not a user-friendly program, which makes it difficult for beginners. With most versions of DOS the command language must be memorized and typed in at the DOS prompt. Since DOS is essential to the operation of your computer, a certain amount of user interface cannot be avoided. Windows minimizes this problem by providing a user-friendly program to perform DOS functions from within Windows.

About Windows

Windows is a program developed by Microsoft, Inc., to make your computer much easier to operate. In addition to providing an easy way to perform DOS functions (such as formatting a floppy disk or copying files), Windows provides a way for you to run more than one program at a time and switch easily between them. Because it is a highly visual program, beginners find it much easier to use. Accessing programs, or **applications**, is much easier in Windows. People who are intimidated by computers are delighted to find that tasks can be accomplished by simply clicking with a mouse on an icon. Experienced computer users can get into the advanced features. Windows is a program for all users.

Windows got its name because it runs programs in separate windows. You can switch back and forth between full-screen windows, and you can reduce the size of the windows and view different programs on one screen.

While working in Windows, think of the computer screen as your desktop. Each window on the screen or desktop represents a different project or task. You can switch back and forth between windows or tasks just as you would while working at your desk. If you think of Windows in these terms you will have a better understanding of what is happening on your screen.

While Windows can run regular DOS programs, there is no question that programs specifically designed to work with Windows have a number of advantages. For one thing, because they have similar screens and commands, Windows programs are easier for a person who already knows Windows to learn. Excel is produced by the same company that produces Windows (Microsoft), and is designed to be used in a Windows environment.

It is important to note that while Windows can do away with the need to interface directly with DOS, it does not replace DOS. You must install DOS before you can install any other software program, including Windows.

Windows Inputting Devices

The Mouse

In Excel you will be working with two methods of input: the keyboard and the mouse. Although instructions can be sent to the computer using the keyboard, it is used primarily for entering data—that is, typing text. The mouse is used primarily for inputting commands; Excel is designed to be used with a mouse. If you have never used a mouse before, it may take some getting used to, but it is well worth the effort. Using a mouse will allow you to operate Microsoft Excel at maximum efficiency.

Mice have either two or three buttons. As with different types of keyboards, the choice of which style to use is a matter of personal preference. In this book we will focus primarily on the left button to perform the clicking and dragging functions.

All instructions is this book are for right-handed mouse users. If you are a left-handed mouse user, the left and right buttons are swapped. To change your mouse to a left-handed mouse, so that all functions listed in this book as performed by the left mouse button can be performed by the right mouse button, see your Microsoft Windows manual. Excel will pick up the

N O T E   configuration from Windows.

How to Hold the Mouse

Much of the difficulty beginners have with using a mouse is caused by holding the mouse improperly. It is important to have a secure grip on the mouse, otherwise the pointer will continue to move before you have a chance to click or begin dragging. To hold the mouse securely, use your thumb to grasp its left side. Your index finger should securely rest on, but not press, the left mouse button. Your middle finger should rest on, but not press, the right mouse button. Your ring finger and pinky should securely grasp the right side of the mouse.

Clicking

You **click** with the mouse to select an item or bring the insertion point to a new location. An instruction to click means that you should click only once with the left button.

An instruction to double-click means that you should click the left button twice very quickly. If there is too much time in between clicks, Excel will think that you have clicked only once.

An instruction to triple-click means that you should click the left button very quickly three times.

An instruction to quadruple click means that you should click the left button very quickly four times.

Dragging

You **drag** the mouse to select blocks of data or program commands. To drag with a mouse, bring the mouse pointer to where you want to begin selecting information. Then press down on the left button and, while keeping the button down, drag the mouse in the direction you need to move to select the data or command. When you release the button, the data or command will remain highlighted.

Mouse Pointer Shapes

In Excel 4.0, the mouse pointer takes on different shapes depending on where it is in a window. Throughout this book, wherever necessary, changes in mouse pointer shapes will be indicated with a description of the new shape.

The Keyboard

As explained earlier in this chapter, we will be using the mouse throughout this book to input commands. In instances where we feel it is more efficient than the mouse for a particular command, we will provide you with a keyboard shortcut. A list of all keyboard commands and shortcuts can be found in Appendix E. You can use either the mouse or the keyboard movement keys to move around in documents. When using the keyboard, movement keys vary depending upon the type of document you are working with. We will list the movement keys for each of the document types in the appropriate sections of the book. A list of all movement keys for all document types can be found on the command card included with this book.

The Numeric Keypad

The numeric keypad is usually located on the far right of your keyboard. The configuration of the keys on the numeric keypad corresponds to that of an electronic calculator. When you are typing a lot of numbers, you will probably find that using the numeric keypad is more efficient and easier than using the number keys at the top of the keyboard. To use the numeric keypad to type in numbers, the Num Lock key located directly above the keypad must be turned on (when the Num Lock key is turned on, the indicator light is on). When the Num Lock key is turned off, the keys in the numeric keyboard become movement keys.

Installing Excel 4.0 and Windows

Excel 4.0 is designed to be used with Windows. Therefore, Windows should be installed before Excel is installed. Refer to your Windows manual for instructions on how to install Windows. Instructions for the installation of Excel 4.0 can be found in Appendix A.

Starting Excel from Windows

Once you have properly installed Windows and Excel, you are ready to begin operating the program. To start Excel:

1. Start Windows, following the instructions in your Windows manual. You should end up in the Windows Program Manager.
2. Once in Windows, look at the bottom of the screen for the Microsoft Excel 4.0 group icon (see Figure 1.4). Double-click to access the Microsoft Excel 4.0 program group.
3. Double-click on the Microsoft Excel program icon. It may take a minute or so to execute the program (a small hourglass should appear on the screen, indicating that Windows is executing a command). The Microsoft Excel application window and a worksheet document window will be displayed (see Figure 1.5).

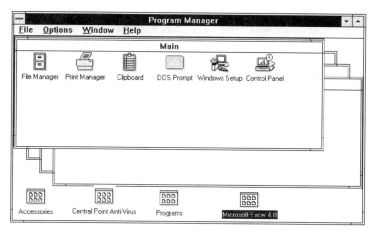

Figure 1.4. Microsoft Excel 4.0 group icon.

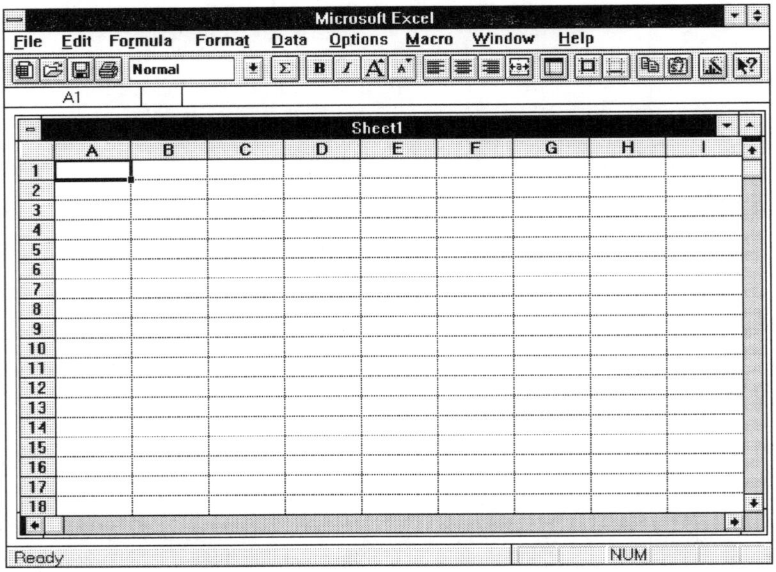

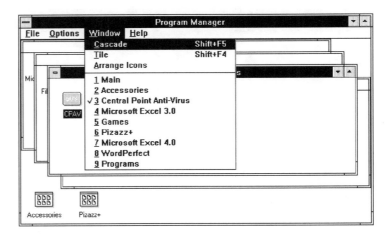

Figure 1.5 Microsoft Excel application window and worksheet document window.

If the Microsoft Excel 4.0 group icon does not appear on the screen while you are in the Windows Program Manager, the Microsoft Excel 4.0 program group may already be on the screen. If you have more than one program group on the screen, you may not see the Microsoft Excel 4.0 program group—it might be hidden behind another program group. You can bring it to the front by following these steps:

Figure 1.6 The Windows Program Manager Window menu.

1. While in the Windows Program Manager, click once on the Window menu item in the menu bar. A list of program groups appears (see Figure 1.6).

2. Click once on Microsoft Excel 4.0. The Microsoft Excel 4.0 program group will be displayed.

3. Double-click on the Microsoft Excel 4.0 program icon. The Microsoft Excel application window and a worksheet document window will be displayed (see Figure 1.5).

Understanding Excel Windows

Microsoft Excel has two types of windows: an application window and a document window. The **application window** displays the parts necessary to operate the program without a document, and provides the workspace for documents used within the application. The **document window** appears in the workspace provided in the application window, and displays the parts of the document with which you are working. When you start Excel, the application window is automatically displayed with a worksheet document window, as shown in Figure 1.5. Figure 1.7 displays the application window *without* a document window open.

If you are not familiar with Microsoft Excel for Windows, you should take some time to learn the various parts of the application window. Figure 1.7 labels the basic parts of the window. The worksheet document window shown in Figure 1.5 is covered in Chapter 2.

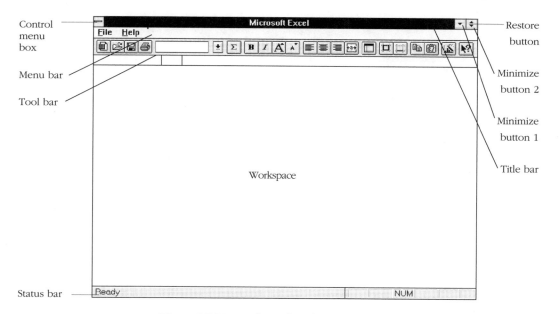

Figure 1.7 Microsoft Excel application window.

Parts of the Application Window

The Title Bar

The title bar appears at the top of the application window and contains the name of the program or application you are running in that window. The title bar of the application window in Excel 4.0 displays the name *Microsoft Excel*. The title bar also serves another purpose: when more than one window is displayed, it indicates which one is **active** by changing the color (or intensity, on monochrome monitors) of the active window.

The Menu Bar

The menu bar appears right under the title bar. The menu bar contains a row of words called **menu names**. The menu bar in the application window contains only two menu names: File and Help. When you select a document type, the menu bar changes to accommodate the document type you have chosen. Figure 1.5 shows the menu bar for a worksheet document. For purposes of illustration, we are going to work with this menu bar.

There are two ways to open a menu. The best way is to click once on the menu name with the left mouse button. You can also open a menu by holding down the Alt key and pressing the underlined character in the menu name. For example, the File menu can be opened by typing Alt+F. To close a menu, press Esc or click anywhere outside of the menu.

When you open a menu in a menu bar a new menu appears. For example, if you click on File, the menu shown in Figure 1.8 appears.

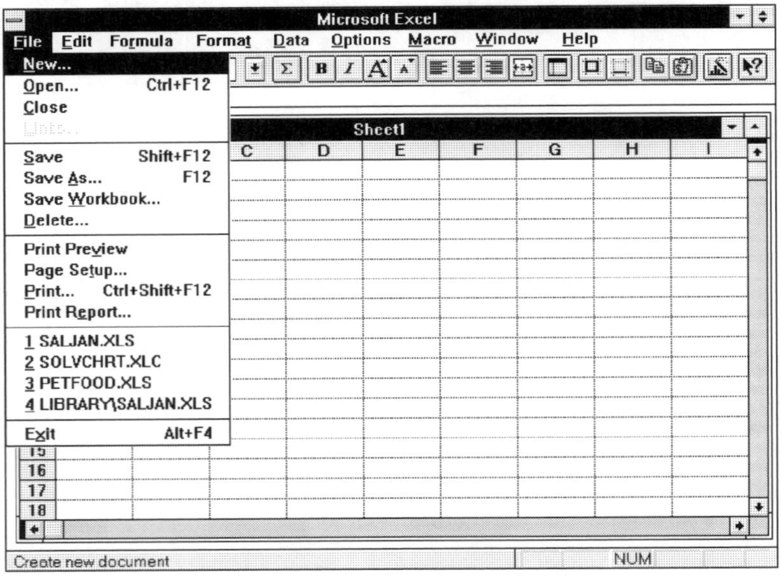

Figure 1.8 Worksheet file menu.

The new menu contains menu commands, which can be selected:

1. By clicking on the menu command name.
2. By typing the underlined letter in the menu command name.
3. By using the Up Arrow (↑) and Down Arrow (↓) movement keys to highlight the menu command, and then pressing Enter.

Some menu commands (such as Close or Save) perform functions immediately. Other commands appear with certain menu indicators, which have special meanings.

A Dimmed Menu Item

When a menu item is dimmed it means that this choice is not currently available to you. This usually occurs because there is no logical use for the menu item at that particular time. For example, if there you have not copied or cut information, the Paste command in the Edit menu, which inserts copied or cut information, will be dimmed.

An Ellipsis

Menu items followed by an ellipsis (...) open a dialog box, which asks the user to provide additional information. Dialog boxes are explained in greater detail later in this chapter.

A Checkmark

A menu item preceded by a checkmark (✔) indicates that the item is a currently activated toggle. A toggle item is turned on or off each time you select it. It works like a toggle light switch. If you select an item that currently has a checkmark, the item will be deactivated. To reactivate the item, select it again.

Shortcut Keys

Some menu commands are followed by shortcut keys in parentheses. These are keystrokes that can be used to choose a menu command instead of using the mouse to open the menu and choose the command. For example, the menu command Open in Figure 1.8 is followed by the shortcut key Ctrl+F12. Throughout this book instructions will be given using the mouse, except where keystrokes are necessary. However, if you wish to use shortcut keys, refer to Appendix E.

Dialog Boxes

As explained above, a menu command followed by an ellipsis (...) opens a **dialog box**. A dialog box appears in the window when Excel requires information to complete the command (hence the name "dialog"). You may be requested to supply a name or make choices from a list. Some dialog boxes contain subboxes or submenus. You will notice that the menu command Open in Figure 1.8 is followed by an ellipsis. If you choose this command, the dialog box shown in Figure 1.9 will be displayed.

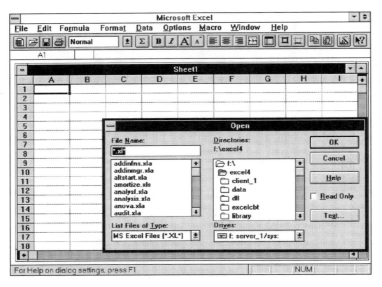

Figure 1.9 The Open dialog box.

Most dialog boxes have more than one section. There are three ways in which you can move between the sections:

1. Click on the section.
2. Hold down the Alt key while pressing the underlined letter to access the section.
3. Use the Tab key to move between sections.

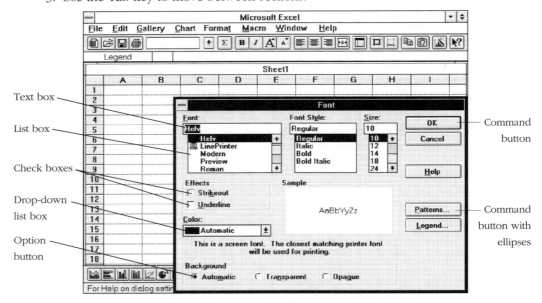

Figure 1.10 Parts of a dialog box.

There are six basic sections found in a dialog box: a text box, a check box, an option button, a command button, a list box, and a drop-down list box. All of these sections are labeled in the Font dialog box shown in Figure 1.10. Not all sections are found in all dialog boxes. Information is supplied differently in the different sections.

Text Boxes

In a text box you are asked to type the required information. When you open a dialog box there is usually text already typed in the text box. If the text is correct, leave it as it is and go on to the next section. If the text is incorrect, click on the section, backspace to delete the old text, and type in the new text.

Check Boxes

Check boxes are squares with x's marked in them. These are used to allow you to select more than one item. For example, in Figure 1.10 you might want to select strikeout or underline print, or both. To select a check box click on the square. An x will appear. To deselect a check box, click on the box again. The x will disappear.

Option Buttons

Option buttons work differently than check boxes in that you can select only one option at a time. For example, in Figure 1.10 you may select only one background option. You select an option by clicking on the desired button or circle, filling it. Only one button can be filled at a time. If you click on another button, an already-selected option button will be deselected.

Command Buttons

Command buttons are commands found inside rectangular boxes. Clicking on a command button executes the command immediately. The most common command buttons are Cancel and OK. If a command button is followed by an ellipsis (see the Patterns command button in Figure 1.10), clicking on it will open a new dialog box.

List Boxes

List boxes are lists of items you can choose. For example, Figure 1.10 contains a list box with a list of fonts. To make a selection click on the item in the list. If you are using the keyboard, use the arrow keys to highlight the item and press Enter to select it. If the list is too long to fit in the list box, use the scroll bars to see all the selections (scroll bars are explained in Chapter 2).

Drop-Down List Boxes

Drop-down list boxes have a small arrow in a box to the right of the option (see the Color box in Figure 1.10). By clicking on the arrow you open a list. You can select an item on the new list by clicking on it. Drop-down list boxes are used when there are too many selections to fit in the dialog box.

Shortcut Menus

Shortcut menus are an alternative to using the menu bar for most editing and formatting commands. To display a shortcut menu, position your mouse pointer on a cell, chart, or any object in the window, and click on the right mouse button. The shortcut menu is displayed at the mouse pointer, as shown in Figure 1.11. Select a shortcut menu command the same way you select any other menu command. (You can also press Shift+F10 to display a shortcut menu. The menu will appear in the upper-left corner of the window.) To close a shortcut menu, press Esc or click anywhere outside the menu.

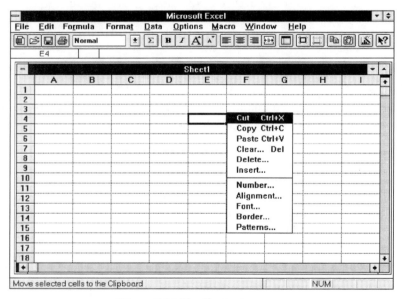

Figure 1.11 The Shortcut menu.

Minimize Buttons

Your application window (see Figure 1.7) contains two Minimize buttons. Clicking on Minimize button 1 allows you to shrink the window to an icon. This is useful when you are working in more than one application. (Remember, Windows allows you to **multitask**; that is, work with more than one program at a time.) To restore the icon to a window, double-click on the icon. Clicking on Minimize button 2 reduces the size of the window.

The Restore Button

Click on this button to restore the application window to the size it was before it was minimized using Minimize button 2.

The Control Menu Box

The application window Control box displays the following menu items: Restore, Move, Size, Minimize, Maximize, Close, Switch To, and Run. If you have used Minimize button 2 (see above), clicking on the Restore command will restore the window to normal size. Clicking on the Maximize command will return your window to normal size if you have shrunk it using Minimize button 1. Clicking on the Minimize command will reduce your window to an icon. The rest of the commands will be covered in later chapters.

The Tool Bar

Tool bars contain **icons** (or pictures) on which you can click to execute a command quickly. Excel comes with nine tool bars. You can have as many tool bars as you wish showing on your window. Each icon on a tool bar represents a **tool**. If you click on the tool represented by the printer icon, you will print out your active document. You can create new tool bars or customize existing ones. You can add and delete tools from any bar. To see a description of a tool, point to the tool while you are holding down the left mouse button. Continue to hold the mouse button down. A description of the action that tool performs will appear in the status bar. To cancel the tool without performing the action, move the mouse pointer off the tool and then release the mouse button. Tool bars are covered in detail in Chapter 11.

The Status Bar

The status bar is the bar across the bottom of the application window. The left side of the status bar displays information about the operation in progress or the status of the currently selected command. The right side of the status bar indicates whether a keyboard mode (such as ADD) is turned on.

Exiting Excel

To exit from Microsoft Excel:

1. Click on File.
2. Click on Exit. You have exited Microsoft Excel and are back in Windows.

Review Exercises for Chapter 1

- ◆ Identify the parts of your computer.
- ◆ Start Microsoft Excel 4.0 for Windows.
- ◆ Identify the parts of the application window.
- ◆ Open a dialog box. Identify its sections and close the dialog box.
- ◆ Using the mouse, open and close a shortcut menu.
- ◆ Practice dragging and clicking with the mouse.
- ◆ Exit from Excel.

Before You Go On...

Before you continue on to the next chapter, you should be able to start Microsoft Excel 4.0 for Windows and exit from the program. You should be able to identify the parts of the application window and the parts of a dialog box. You should know how to access the shortcut menus and how to use a mouse.

Chapter 2

CREATING A WORKSHEET

What You Will Learn in This Chapter

- ◆ The definition of a worksheet
- ◆ How to identify and use the parts of a worksheet window
- ◆ The definition of constant values and formulas
- ◆ How to enter constant values and formulas into a worksheet
- ◆ How to build formulas
- ◆ How to copy formulas

What Is a Worksheet?

You are probably familiar with the term **spreadsheet**. In Excel, a spreadsheet is called a **worksheet**. A worksheet is simply a table of numbers and text arranged in rows and columns, as shown in Figure 2.1. It can be likened to an old-fashioned ledger sheet in appearance. However, since a worksheet is an electronic tool, it has certain advantages over the old-fashioned method of using paper and pencil to organize data. Worksheets can be used for a variety of purposes, ranging from simple addition of figures to complex projections and analyses. It is in employing these applications that the advantage of using Excel over manual methods becomes apparent.

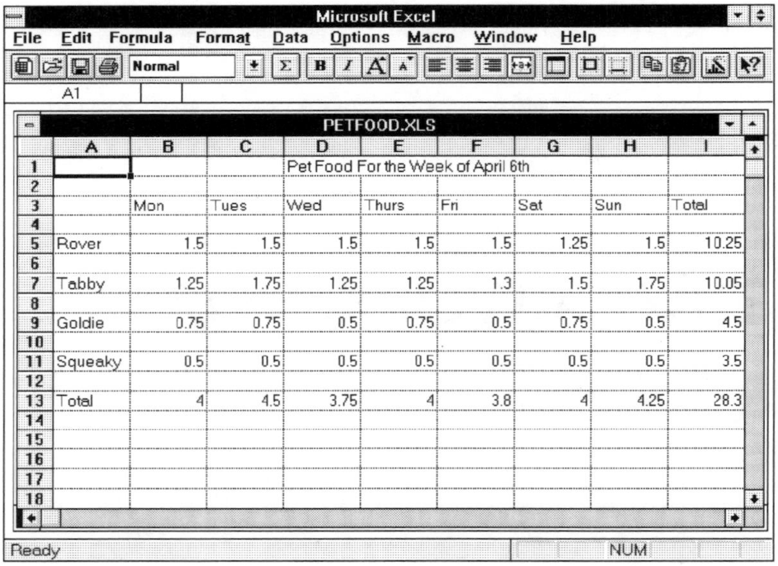

Figure 2.1. A worksheet.

For example, if you change a figure on a ledger sheet, you must recalculate the entire row and column for a new total, then you must change the grand total of all the rows and columns. If you change a figure in an Excel worksheet, all of the figures will be recalculated automatically by the program. Another example of the superiority of Excel over the old-fashioned method is its ability to copy data from one worksheet to another. For example, a common occurrence in bookkeeping (one of the more popular uses for a worksheet) is the need to combine the totals from one or more worksheets to create a new worksheet. You might want to combine the totals from an income worksheet and an expense worksheet to create a new worksheet concerned with both income and expense. To do this with paper and pencil, you would have to manually enter all of the text and totals from the old worksheets into the new one.

Not only will Excel copy information for you, it will allow you to link the copy to the original. Using the old-fashioned method, if you make a change on one of the old worksheets, you must then make the change on the new worksheet and recalculate the rows and columns and grand totals. If you use Excel's linking feature, all of the changes made on the old worksheets are automatically carried through to the new worksheet, and the totals of all worksheets are recalculated by the program.

The uses for worksheets are innumerable and limited only by your imagination. Worksheets can be used to organize any kind of information or data into tables for the purposes of presentation, calculation, comparison, projection, and analysis.

In this chapter, you will set up a sample worksheet for the accounting department of a small boutique called Frills and Thrills, which sells women's clothing and accessories. You will learn how to enter information into a worksheet and set up simple formulas for calculations. As you continue through this book, you will create additional worksheets for the accounting department of Frills and Thrills.

The Worksheet Document Window

Now that you know a little about the uses of worksheets, you are ready to take a closer look at the parts that comprise the worksheet document window.

1. Turn on your computer and access Windows.
2. Double-click the Microsoft Excel 4.0 group icon to open the Microsoft Excel 4.0 program group. (See "Starting Excel from Windows" in Chapter 1 for more detailed information on icon groups.)
3. Double-click the Microsoft Excel 4.0 program icon. The Microsoft Excel application window and worksheet document window are displayed on the screen; see Figure 1.5 for a depiction of these windows.

Inside the application window is the document window. The document window contains either a worksheet, a chart, a macro sheet, a workbook, or slides. In this chapter we are covering only worksheets; other document types will be covered later in the book. When you execute Excel, the document window defaults to a worksheet. A worksheet consists of the Control Menu box, the title bar, the menu bar, the reference area, the worksheet, the Select All box, the formula bar, the Maximize and Minimize buttons, the status bar, scroll arrows, scroll bars, scroll boxes, split boxes, column headings, row headings, cells, and the active cell, as shown in Figure 2.2, on the next page.

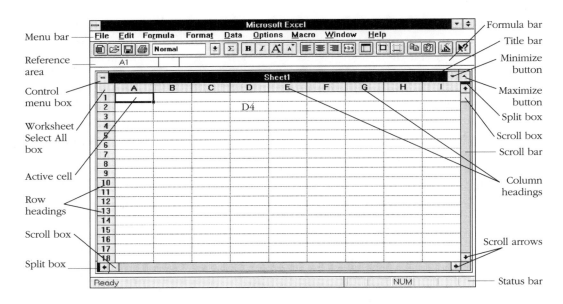

Figure 2.2. Worksheet document window.

The Control Menu Box

Clicking on the Control Menu box opens a menu listing the Restore, Move, Size, Minimize, Maximize, Close, Next Window, and Split Menu commands. The Minimize command will reduce your worksheet to an icon. To restore the worksheet, double-click on the icon. The Maximize command will enlarge the worksheet to its maximum size, as shown in Figure 2.3. To restore the worksheet to normal size, click on the Restore button, also shown in Figure 2.3. The rest of the menu commands are explained in detail in future chapters.

The Title Bar

The title bar in the worksheet window contains the name of the worksheet. If the worksheet has not yet been named, it will be called Sheet1, Sheet2, and so on, depending on the number of unnamed worksheets you have open.

The Worksheet Select All Box

The worksheet Select All box selects all of the cells in the active worksheet. This can be used to perform certain tasks (such as printing or calculating) for the entire worksheet, as opposed to performing these tasks for selected portions, or **ranges**, of a worksheet. Ranges will be explained in Chapter 4.

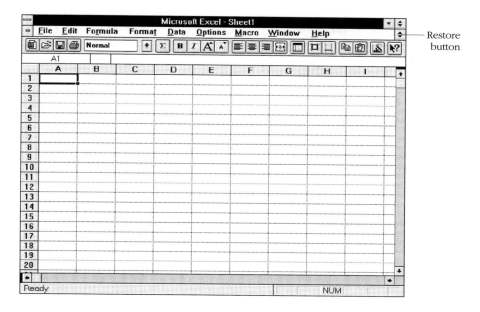

Figure 2.3. Maximized worksheet with Restore button.

The Reference Area

The reference area of a worksheet displays the location of the active cell (cells are explained later in this chapter), and displays the percent of progress during a worksheet operation (such as sorting or calculating).

The Formula Bar

The formula bar displays the data in the active cell. This is the part of the worksheet window where you edit information in a cell.

The Maximize Button

The maximize button works the same way as the Maximize command in the Control Menu box. It enlarges the worksheet to its maximum size, as shown in Figure 2.3.

The Minimize Button

This is actually two buttons with different uses. The Minimize button shown in Figure 2.2 works the same way as the Minimize command in the Control Menu box. It turns the worksheet into an icon. To restore the worksheet to normal size, double-click on the icon. If the worksheet has been maximized, a Restore button, as shown in Figure 2.3, is displayed. To restore the worksheet to its normal size, click on the Restore button.

The Status Bar

The status bar is the bar across the bottom of the window. Its left side displays information about the operation in progress or the status of the currently selected command. The right side of the status bar indicates whether a keyboard mode is turned on.

Scroll Arrows

The scroll arrows are used to scroll up, down, left, or right in the worksheet. By clicking on a scroll arrow, you will move one column or row at a time. If you position the mouse pointer on a scroll arrow and hold down the left button, you will quickly scroll through the worksheet in the direction of the arrow.

Scroll Bars and Scroll Boxes

Dragging through a scroll bar will move you quickly through a worksheet. By clicking above or below the vertical scroll box or to the left or right of the horizontal scroll box, you can move the worksheet one screen at a time.

The scroll boxes show you the position of your current location relative to the whole worksheet. For example, if you move the vertical scroll box to the middle of the scroll bar, it will bring you to the row in the middle of the entire worksheet. Figure 2.4 contains a worksheet with 100 rows.

The vertical scroll box has been positioned in the middle of the scroll bar, which brings the scroll box to row 50 of the worksheet. As you scroll through the worksheet, the scroll boxes also move to reflect the change in location.

	A	B	C	D	E	F	G	H	I
42					900			750	750
43	100					500	750		
44			650		300		800		
45	350		750	350			900	750	750
46	400				450				
47		350		500		350		800	800
48		800	800				350		
49		900		750		350			350
50	800				800		865	900	
51				800		200			200
52		600			900			850	
53	750			750			850		850
54					350	900			
55			650					750	750
56	250			750			975		
57			800		800	900		750	
58					900				900
59				600			800		

Figure 2.4. Vertical scroll box in middle of scroll bar.

The Split Boxes

Split boxes divide a worksheet into panes, or sections, so that you can view different sections of the worksheet simultaneously. Splitting windows into panes will be covered in Chapter 6.

Column Headings

Columns are separated by vertical lines on the worksheet. **Column headings** are the row of letters across the top of the worksheet that identify each column. Column headings range from column A (the first column) to column IV (the last possible column). You can have a maximum of 256 columns in a worksheet.

Row Headings

Rows are separated by horizontal lines on the worksheet. **Row headings** are the numbers down the left side of the worksheet that identify each row. They range from 1 (the first row) to 16,384 (the last possible row).

Cells

Cells are the boxes that are formed by the intersection of the horizontal and vertical lines that make up rows and columns. Cells are the basic units of a worksheet. You enter information such as text, figures, and formulas into the cells. Each cell is identified by its column and row location. For example, to locate cell D4, first find column D at the top of the worksheet, then locate row 4 on the left side of the worksheet. The point where column D and row 4 intersect is cell D4, as shown in Figure 2.2.

Active Cell(s)

The **active cell** is the one in which you are currently working. It is usually highlighted or set apart from the other cells by a heavy border. Any information you type will be entered into this cell, and any command you choose will be applied to it. You can select more than one active cell. When you do this, any commands entered will apply to all of the selected cells.

Creating a Worksheet

Now that you are familiar with the parts of the worksheet window, you are ready to create your first worksheet. This is going to be a salary worksheet for Frills and Thrills, as shown in Figure 2.5. We are going to enter figures for salaries paid in January 1992. Business was so good that Clarisse had to employ temporary help to accommodate the work flow. Clarisse would like to find out if using temporary help costs more than hiring a new full-time employee.

We will break down the month into four weeks, which will be listed across the top of the worksheet. We will divide the employees into two categories: Perm, for permanent

		Salaries for January, 1992				
		Week1	Week2	Week3	Week4	Total
Perm						
Joy		500	500	500	500	2000
Amy		550	550	550	550	2200
Temps						
Linda		300		250		550
Marie		175	275		400	850
Sue		230		150		380
Sub T						
Perm		1050	1050	1050	1050	4200
Temps		705	275	400	400	1780
Total		1755	1325	1450	1450	5980

Figure 2.5. Salary worksheet for Frills and Thrills.

employees, and Temps, for temporary employees. These will be listed down the left side of the worksheet. We will then type in the salaries for each employee for each week. Finally, we will calculate our subtotals and grand totals. We will calculate a weekly subtotal for each group of employees and a weekly grand total for all employees. We will also calculate the monthly subtotal for each group of employees, the monthly grand total for each employee, and the monthly grand total for all employees.

Constant Values and Formulas

Two basic types of data can be entered into a worksheet: constant values and formulas. A **constant value** is information you type into the cell. Constant values do not change unless you change them by editing the information in the cell. There are four types of constant values: date, time, text, and numeric. Table 2.1 illustrates the kind of information contained in each of the four values. Values will be discussed in greater detail in Chapter 8.

Type	Format	Appearance
Text values: Text values can contain any alphabetical characters, any combination of alphanumeric and punctuation characters, and numeric characters preceded by a single quotation mark ('). A cell can contain up to twenty-five text characters.	ABCD abcd TC2v4 R&R '12345	ABCD abcd TC2v4 R&R 12345
Numeric values: Numeric values can contain numeric characters and specific special characters: $+ - (\ )\ ,\ /\ \$\ \%\ .\ E\ e$	67.22E+12 −450 $123.45 12,345 (450) 1/2 8.5%	67.22E+12 −450 $123.45 12,345 (450) 1/2 8.5%
Date values: Date values are identified as numbers in Excel and usually follow one of the following built-in formats, where *m* represents month, *d* represents day, and *y* represents year. You can type either uppercase or lowercase letters in dates.	m/d/yy dd-mmm-yy dd-mmmm mmmm-yy	03/31/92 31-Mar-92 31-Mar Mar-92
Time values: Time values are identified as numbers in Excel and follow one of the listed formats. If you do not specify AM or PM, Excel will display the time using the 24-hour clock (military time). Time formats are not case-sensitive—you can use either uppercase or lowercase AM or PM.	h:mm AM/PM h:mm:ss AM/PM h:mm h:mm:ss	5:23 PM 5:23:35 PM 17:23 17:23:35

Table 2.1. Types of constant values.

A **formula** is a series of instructions entered into a cell that calculates a new value from existing values. If you change the existing values, the new value calculated by the formula will also change. For example, in our salary worksheet we will enter names and figures. These are constant values—they will not change unless we change them by editing the data in the cells. After we enter the constant values, we will enter instructions, or formulas, into certain cells to add the figures. The formula will add the existing figures (constant values) and enter a new figure in the same cell in which the formula was typed. If we change one of the existing figures, the figure in the formula cell will also change.

Entering Constant Values

Let's enter the constant values in our worksheet. You should be in Excel 4.0 and the document window should have a blank worksheet with Sheet1 in the title bar (see "Starting Excel from Windows" in Chapter 1 if you don't remember how to start Excel). Enter information using the following steps. Notice as you type that the data you are typing also appears in the formula bar. In addition, the reference area displays the location of the cell in which you are typing. If you make a mistake while typing information in the cell, backspace over it and retype the information.

1. First we will type in the headings for the weeks of January. We will leave the first two rows of the worksheet blank for now. Later, we will add the overall worksheet heading. Use the mouse pointer to move to cell C3 and click to select the cell, as shown in Figure 2.6. Now type *Week1*.

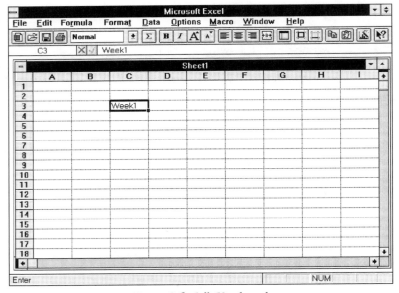

Figure 2.6. Cell C3 selected.

2. Click on cell D3 and type *Week2*, click on cell E3 and type *Week3*, click on cell F3 and type *Week4*, then click on cell G3 and type *Total*. Your worksheet should look like Figure 2.7.

3. Click on cell A4 and type *Perm* to represent permanent employees. We will list our permanent employees under this heading.

4. Now click on cell A6 and type *Joy*, then click on cell A7 and type *Amy*.

5. Click on cell A9 and type *Temps* to represent temporary employees. We will list our temporary employees under this heading.

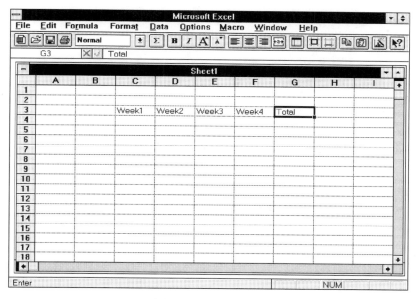

Figure 2.7. Worksheet with one row of data entered.

6. Click on cell A11 and type *Linda*, click on cell A12 and type *Marie*, then click on cell A13 and type *Sue.*

7. Click on cell A15 and type *Sub T* to represent subtotals. We will calculate the subtotals for all of the permanent and temporary employees under this heading.

8. Click on cell A17 and type *Perm*, click on cell A18 and type *Temps.*

9. Click on cell A20 and type *Total.* These figures will be the grand totals for each week for all employees and the grand total for the month of January for employees. You are now ready to enter the weekly salaries for each employee.

10. Click on cell C6 and type *500.* You will notice that when you click on the next cell, the number in cell C6 will automatically **right justify** (the numbers are aligned so that they are flush against the right side of the cell). Numbers automatically right justify in a cell and text automatically left justifies. Click on cells D6, E6, and F6, and type *500* in each of them. Leave the cell in the Total column, cell G6, empty. It will be used to calculate Joy's total salary for the month of January.

11. Click on cells C7, D7, E7, and F7, and type *550* in each of them. Once again, leave the cell in the Total column (cell G7) empty.

12. Click on cell C11 and type *300.* Click on cell E11 and type *250.* You have entered the salary for Linda for weeks 1 and 3 of the month of January.

13. Click on cell C12 and type *175,* click on cell D12 and type *275,* and click on F12 and type *400.*

14. Click on cells D13 and E13 and type *230* and *150,* respectively. All of the salaries paid by Frills and Thrills for the month of January have now been entered.

We are now ready to go to our next step, which is entering formulas in certain cells of our worksheet to add our figures.

Building Formulas

A formula always starts with an equal sign (=). This tells Excel that a formula will follow. Formulas are composed of operators and operands.

Operators are the parts of the formula that specify or identify the type of operation. There are four types of operators in Excel: arithmetic, text, comparison, and reference. In this chapter we will work only with the arithmetic addition operator. In Chapter 8 we will fully develop the use of all operators and discuss the scope of their applications. Table 8.1 contains a list of operators and how they are used.

Operands are the values on either side of the operator on which the operator performs the operation. For example, in the formula *A1+B1,* the operator is the + symbol, and the operands are A1 and B1. The formula is instructing Excel to add (which is the action performed by the + operator) the values of the cells A1 and B1 (the operands).

The arithmetic operator performs basic mathematical operations and uses numeric values to produce numeric results. The arithmetic functions and operators are:

◆ Addition: +
◆ Subtraction (negative number if used with only one operand): -
◆ Division: /
◆ Multiplication: *
◆ Percentage (one operand only): %
◆ Exponentiation: ^

For example: =100/2*10% divides 100 by 2 and then multiplies the result by .10 for a final result of .5

Entering a Formula into a Cell

We are now going to enter a formula in cell G6 that will add Joy's salary for weeks 1, 2, 3, and 4 to show the total of her monthly salary for January 1992. Click on cell G6 and enter the following formula:

```
=C6+D6+E6+F6
```

This formula adds the value of cell C6 (500) + the value of cell D6 (500) + the value of cell E6 (500) + the value of cell F6 (500), and enters the sum in cell G6.

Copying a Formula

We'll need the same formula, but with different cell designations, to get a total of the monthly salaries for each employee. We can retype the formula for each employee, but it is much easier to copy Joy's formula for each employee. Excel will automatically change the cell designations in each formula to reflect the new location of the formula. To copy a formula:

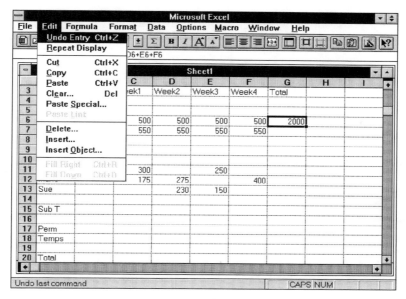

Figure 2.8. The Edit menu.

1. Click on cell G6.
2. Click on Edit in the menu bar to open the menu shown in Figure 2.8
3. Click on the Copy command. The status bar will show the following prompt:

   Select designation and press ENTER or choose Paste.
4. Click on cell G7.
5. Click on Edit in the menu bar to open the menu shown in Figure 2.8.
6. Click on the Paste command to paste the formula in cell G7. If you look at the formula bar, you will notice that the formula has changed to reflect its new location. It now reads: =C7+D7+E7=F7
7. Repeating steps 4 to 6 above, paste the formula into cells G11, G12, G13, G17, G18, and G20. Note that cells G17, G18, and G20 show a 0 value. This is because there are no values yet in the cells these formulas are adding.

You can use the shortcut key Ctrl+V to paste.

SHORT CUT

Our next step is to insert a formula to subtotal the salaries for Week1 for the permanent employees. We will then copy this formula to get the subtotals for Week2, Week3, and Week4.

8. Click on cell C17 and type the following formula:

   =C6+C7

9. Now copy this formula to cells D17, E17, and F17. You will notice that G17 now has a total.

Our next step is to insert a formula to subtotal the salaries for Week1 for the temporary employees. We will then copy this formula to get the subtotals for Week2, Week3, and Week4.

10. Click on cell C18 and type the following formula:

    =C11+C12+C13

11. Now copy this formula to cells D18, E18, and F18. You will notice that G18 now has a total.

We will now enter formulas to add the subtotals for the permanent employees and the temporary employees to produce a grand total for all employees for Week1. We will then copy this formula for Week2, Week3, and Week4.

12. Click on cell C20 and type the following formula:

    =C17+C18

13. Now copy this formula to cells D20, E20, and F20. You will notice that G20 now has a total.

14. Finally, we will enter the heading for our worksheet. We usually do this last because we want to enter the heading in a location that is aesthetically pleasing in relation to the rest of the worksheet, and it is easier to make this determination once the worksheet is completed. Excel has many formatting features to accomplish this, but for now we will just do it by eye. Click on cell C1 and type *Salaries for January, 1992.* Notice that as you type, the words scroll to the left of the cell. When you are finished typing, click on a different cell, or press Enter, and all of the text in the heading will be visible. Cell C1 expands to accommodate the text you have just entered. Your worksheet should now look like the one shown in Figure 2.5.

Congratulations! You have just completed your first Excel worksheet. You are now ready to save the worksheet and exit Excel.

Saving the Document and Exiting Excel

Chapter 3 will cover the various commands and features pertinent to saving a document. We will end this chapter very simply by saving our worksheet and exiting Excel.

To save your worksheet:

1. Click on File in the menu bar to open the File menu.
2. Click on Save. The Save As dialog box appears, as shown in Figure 2.9.
3. In the Save As text box, type *SALJAN*.
4. Press Enter or click on OK.
5. The worksheet has now been saved with the name SALJAN.XLS (Excel automatically inserts the extension .XLS to the names of all worksheets).

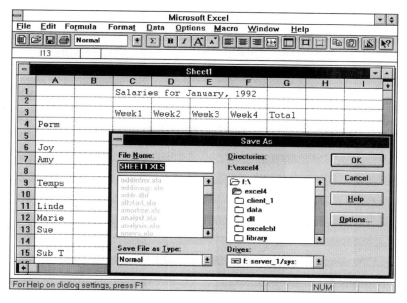

Figure 2.9. The Save As dialog box.

To exit Excel and return to the Windows Program Manager:

1. Click on File in the menu bar.
2. Click on Exit.

Review Exercises for Chapter 2

◆ Create a worksheet summarizing your expenses for the week. Leave a few empty rows at the top of the worksheet for the title. List the days of the week across the top of the worksheet, and the expenses down its left side. Abbreviate the expenses (up to five characters) so that they fit in the cell (for example, "Trans" for transportation, "Laund" for laundry, and so on). You should list at least five but no more than ten expenses. Enter the word *Total* in the column immediately following the last day of the week and the row immediately following the last expense entry (you may skip one row if you wish).

◆ Enter the constant values into the worksheet.

◆ Enter the necessary formula to total the first expense for the week.

◆ Copy the formula into the appropriate cells to total each of the remaining expenses for the week. Be sure to also copy the formula into the row for Total.

◆ Enter the necessary formula to total all of the expenses for the first day of the week.

◆ Copy the formula to the appropriate cells to total all of the expenses for each of the remaining days of the week.

◆ Go back to the first row and type a brief title for the worksheet (for example, "Weekly Expenses").

◆ Identify as many parts in the window as you can.

◆ Practice minimizing, maximizing, and restoring the worksheet window.

◆ Practice scrolling through the worksheet using the scroll buttons, scroll bars, and scroll boxes.

◆ Save your worksheet with the name *WEEKLY,* and exit Excel.

Before You Go On...

Before you continue on to the next chapter, you should be familiar with the parts of the Excel worksheet document window. You should know how to minimize, maximize, and restore the worksheet window. You should be able to scroll through the worksheet. You should understand the difference between constant values and formulas. You should be able to create a worksheet and enter constant values and simple formulas into it, and copy the formulas into other cells.

Chapter 3

SAVING, RETRIEVING, AND PRINTING DOCUMENTS

What You Will Learn in This Chapter

- ◆ How to save your documents
- ◆ How Excel interacts with your computer to store data
- ◆ How to create an automatic backup of your documents
- ◆ How to close your document and your document window
- ◆ How to open (or retrieve) an existing document
- ◆ How to create a new document
- ◆ How to print your documents
- ◆ How to exit Excel

Features Covered in This Chapter

Each of the commands reviewed in this chapter opens its own dialog box, but we will not cover all of the features found in the dialog boxes just yet. As we progress through the book, we will gradually integrate the rest of the features. In this chapter, we will focus on the basics of saving and retrieving.

Saving Documents

You must understand the importance of saving your documents, and the means by which Excel interacts with the computer to retain permanent copies of your work.

Saving is the process of writing your document to a permanent storage device such as a hard drive or floppy disk. If you wish to retain a permanent copy of your work, you must save it. If you do not save your document, you will lose it when you clear the window or exit Excel. In order to fully understand the importance and mechanics of saving, you must understand how Excel interacts with the computer to store documents.

While you are creating or editing a document in Excel, your document is being held temporarily in a **buffer**, or holding area, called RAM (random access memory). It is only when you save the document that it is physically written (stored) on a floppy disk or hard drive. Once you exit Excel or clear the document from the window, the document is deleted from RAM. This means that if you do not save the document before clearing the screen or exiting Excel, the document will be lost.

N O T E

You should save your documents frequently while you are working to avoid losing work in the event of a power interruption or hardware problem.

When a document has been stored to a floppy disk or a hard drive, it remains there unless it is deleted by a user. Opening a document does not remove it from the drive. This means that if you open a document, but make no changes to it, the document does not have to be saved again.

Naming Documents

When you save your document you must give it a **filename**. The following rules and restrictions apply when naming a file.

1. You may use up to eight characters, followed by a period (.) plus up to three more characters (called an **extension**). If you do not give the filename an extension, Excel will automatically append one. Each document type has its own extension. For example, worksheets have an .XLS extension. If you allow Excel to append the

extension to your document, you will find it easier to identify the type of document a file contains.

2. Do *not* use the following extensions: .EXE, .COM, .BAT, .PIF. You should also avoid extensions used by Excel program files because you may accidentally overwrite a program file. Again, you can avoid this problem by allowing Excel to automatically assign the appropriate extension to your filename (for example, .XLS for worksheets) or to store your files in directories other than the one in which your Excel program files are stored (see Chapter 10, *System and Document Management,* for a discussion on directories).

4. You may use all letters and numbers and any of the characters permitted by your current DOS version (refer to your DOS manual to determine which characters are valid; it varies). Excel refuses to accept any other characters, and you may *not* use spaces.

5. You may use uppercase or lowercase letters when typing in a filename.

The following would be valid filenames: JANUARY.XLS, SALES.FEB, and FEBRUARY.BDT.

You cannot have more than one document with the same filename in a directory. This means that if you edit a document that has already been saved, the new version automatically overwrites the old version when it is saved again. When you overwrite the old version of the document with the edited version, the original version will no longer be stored on the hard drive or floppy disk. If you want to retain the original version of the document, you must use the Save As command (explained below) to save the document with a different filename.

Once you have given your document a filename, the new name replaces the default one in the title bar. For example, Sheet1 would be replaced by the worksheet name.

It is important to be consistent and logical when naming documents. Eventually you will have hundreds of documents stored on your computer, and locating files will be very difficult if you do not use an organized naming system.

N O T E

The Save As Command

Save As is used to name a document and save it for the first time, and to save an existing file to a new name or directory.

If you are using the Save As command and you try to save a file to a filename that already exists, an Excel dialog box will appear asking if you want to replace the existing file. If you choose Yes, the existing file will be overwritten. If you choose No, you will have to give the new file another name.

N O T E

Let's save a worksheet using the Save As command.

1. Create the worksheet shown in Figure 3.1.

	A	B	C	D	E	F	G	H	I
1			Pet Food For theWeek of April 6th						
2									
3		Mon	Tues	Wed	Thurs	Fri	Sat	Sun	Total
4									
5	Rover	1.5	1.5	1.5	1.5	1.5	1.25	1.5	10.25
6									
7	Tabby	1.25	1.75	1.25	1.25	1.3	1.5	1.75	10.05
8									
9	Goldie	0.75	0.75	0.5	0.75	0.5	0.75	0.5	4.5
10									
11	Squeaky	0.5	0.5	0.5	0.5	0.5	0.5	0.5	3.5
12									
13	Total	4	4.5	3.75	4	3.8	4	4.25	28.3

Figure 3.1. A Sample worksheet, PETFOOD.XLS.

2. Click on File in the menu bar to open the menu shown in Figure 3.2.

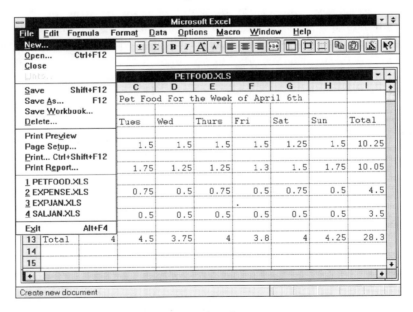

Figure 3.2. The File menu.

3. Click on Save As. The Save As dialog box, shown in Figure 3.3, is displayed. The insertion point is in the File Name text box.

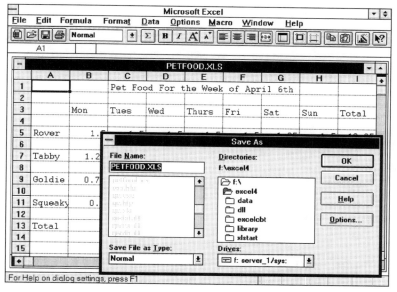

Figure 3.3. The Save As dialog box.

4. Type in the filename PETFOOD.

5. Press Enter or click on the OK command button. The worksheet has now been saved with the filename PETFOOD.XLS (Excel automatically assigned the .XLS extension to the filename).

Note that the worksheet is still in the window, and that the default name, Sheet1, in the title bar has been replaced by the name of the worksheet. The worksheet will remain in the window until you close it or exit Excel. If you decide to make any changes in the worksheet, you must save it again using the Save command, or you will lose your edits.

The Save Command

Once a document has been saved using Save As, use the Save command to save changes to the same directory and filename. Let's edit PETFOOD.XLS and save it again. If the file is not open, follow the instructions in step 1 to open it. If the file is still in the window, go to step 2.

1. Click on File in the menu bar, then click on Open to display the Open dialog box. Double-click on PETFOOD.XLS in the file list box (use the scroll buttons if necessary to move the list up or down). The worksheet is displayed in the window.

2. Edit the worksheet as follows: Click on cell C7 and type *1.5*. The old figure will be replaced by the new figure. Tabby's amount for Tuesday has been changed from 1.75 to 1.5. Change Rover's amount for Sunday to 1.25. Notice that the totals update to reflect the new figures as soon as you click on another cell.

3. Click on File in the menu bar to open the File menu.

4. Click on Save. The edited file is saved.

5. Close the window by clicking on File in the menu bar and then clicking on Close.

If the file has never been saved before, you can use the Save command to display the Save As dialog box and give the file a name. However, once the file has been saved, use the Save As command only to save it to a new name or directory.

Do not cancel the Save As or Save process after it begins. If you do, you may lose data.

WARNING

The Close Command

The Close command closes the window when you are finished working with a document. Unless you have a reason to work with more than one document at a time (you will learn how to work with multiple documents in Chapter 7), you should close the window before you open another file. If you have modified the document in the window (and have not yet saved it), you will be asked if you want to save the document before the window is closed. The Close command is a quick way to save a file and clear the window in one operation.

Let's open the worksheet named PETFOOD.XLS, edit it, then save the document and close the window in one operation using the Close command.

1. Click on File in the menu bar, then click on Open. Double-click on PETFOOD.XLS in the dialog box's file list box. The worksheet is displayed in the window.

2. Briefly edit the worksheet.

3. Click on File in the menu bar to open the File menu.

4. Click on Close.

5. The Microsoft Excel dialog box, shown in Figure 3.4, is displayed asking if you want to save your changes.

    a. Choose Yes to save the document and close the window.

    b. Choose No to close the window without saving the document.

    c. Choose Cancel to cancel the Close process.

6. If you choose Yes and the document has been saved previously, it will be saved again to the same filename. If you choose Yes and the file has not been saved previously, the Save As dialog box is displayed and you must name the file.

You can also use the Close command in the document window Control menu box to close a document.

1. Click on the Control menu box in the document window.

2. Click on Close.

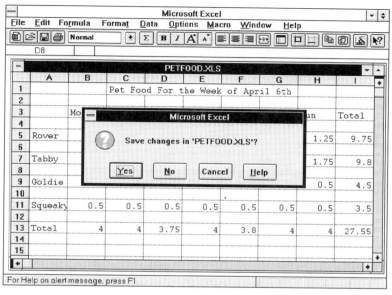

Figure 3.4. The Microsoft Excel dialog box.

If you close all open documents, you will be in the application window with an empty space for a document window, as shown in Figure 3.5. Use the Open command in the File menu to open an existing document, or the New command in the File menu to create a new document. Both of these commands are covered later in this chapter.

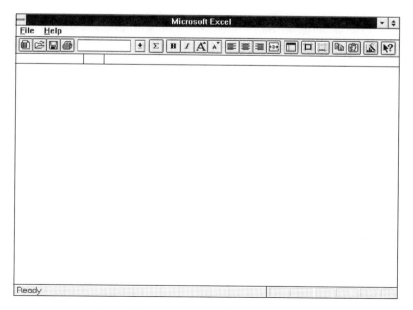

Figure 3.5. An empty application window.

The Exit Command

The Exit command is used to exit from Excel and return to the Microsoft Windows Program Manager. The Exit command allows you to save any modified open files before exiting from the program. To exit from Excel:

1. Click on File in the menu bar to open the File menu.
2. Click on Exit. If there are no unsaved open files, you will exit from the program. If you have any modified open files, the Microsoft Excel dialog box shown in Figure 3.4 is displayed. New documents that have never been saved are identified as [Document Type]1, [Document Type]2, and so forth. You will be prompted with the name of each open modified file and asked if you want to save the file.
   a. If you choose Yes, the document(s) will be saved and you will exit from the program.
   b. If you choose No, the document(s) will not be saved and you will exit from the program.

You can also exit Excel using the Close command in the application window Control menu box:

1. Click on the Control menu box in the application window.
2. Click on Close.

Creating a Backup File

As discussed above, when you replace a document with another document of the same name, the original document is overwritten. The Create Backup File option allows you to save both the original document and the new document with the same name. It does this by renaming the original document to the same filename with a .BAK extension (e.g., BUDGET.BAK). Every time you replace the document, the .BAK file is replaced with the new original file. This means that if you are using the Create Backup File option and you accidentally overwrite a file, you will be able to restore the original version by retrieving the file with the .BAK extension. To create an automatic backup file:

1. Click on File in the menu bar to open the File menu.
2. Click on Save As to open the Save As dialog box.
3. Click on the Options command button to open the Save Options dialog box, as shown in Figure 3.6.
4. Select the Create Backup File check box.
5. Click on OK.

The Create Backup File option works on a document-by-document basis. Selecting this option for one document will not automatically select it for any other document.

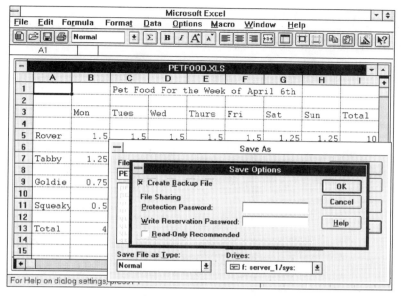

Figure 3.6. The Save Options dialog box.

 Files with the same filename but different extensions use the same backup filename. If you have a file named BUDGET.JAN and one named BUDGET.XLS, they will both use the backup filename BUDGET.BAK. Therefore only *one* of the files (the last one you saved) will end up with a backup file. If you use the Create Backup File feature, be sure that all of your files have different filenames, not just different extensions.

N O T E

To recover a backup file, open the file and save it again (using the Save As command) with a filename that does not have a .BAK extension.

A disadvantage of using the Create Backup File option is that it doubles the amount of space required to store your documents, since each document is saved twice. If you wish to use the Create Backup File option, be sure that you have enough storage space on your hard drive, and that you periodically delete unnecessary .BAK files (see Chapter 10 for a discussion on how to delete files).

Retrieving Documents

Once you have saved your documents, they are permanently stored on your hard drive or floppy disk. If you want to edit the document, you must retrieve it to a window. This is done by opening the file.

This chapter will teach you how to retrieve files in the current directory only. For information on how to retrieve work stored in other directories or on floppy disks, see Chapter 10, *System and Document Management*.

When you retrieve a file to a window, the document remains stored on the hard drive or floppy disk, but is also loaded into RAM. Any changes made to the document are held in RAM only. If you want to store the edits, you must save the document before clearing it from the window.

N O T E

The Open Command

The Open command is used to open an existing file in a new window. If you have a document already opened in one window, and you use the Open command to open another document, it will be opened in a new window. See Chapter 7 for more information about working with multiple documents. To open an existing document in the current directory:

1. Click on File in the menu bar.
2. Click on Open to display the Open dialog box, as shown in Figure 3.7. The files located in the current directory are listed in the file list box. If you cannot view all of the files at once, you can use the scroll buttons on the right side of the list box to scroll through the filenames.

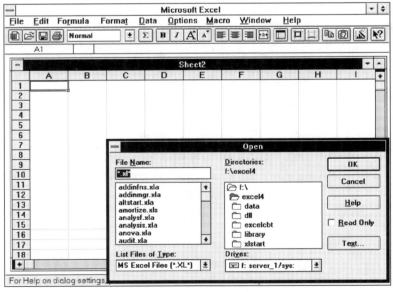

Figure 3.7. The Open dialog box.

3. To open a file, type the filename in the File Name text box and click on the OK command button. **Or,** click on the filename in the file list box (the filename will appear in the File Name text box) and click on the OK command button. **Or,** double-click on the filename in the file list box.

Opening Recently Used Files

At the bottom of the File menu, Excel displays a list of the last four files that were opened. To open one of these four:

1. Click on File in the menu bar.
2. Click on one of the four files listed at the bottom of the menu.

The New Command

The New command is used to create a document in a new window. Excel automatically opens a new worksheet when you start the program. You should use the New command when you have a document in the current window and you want to create a new document in another window, or when you want to create a document type other than a worksheet, or when you have closed all documents and only the application window is displayed, as shown in Figure 3.5. To use the New command:

1. Click on File in the menu bar to open the file menu.
2. Click on New to open the New dialog box, as shown in Figure 3.8.

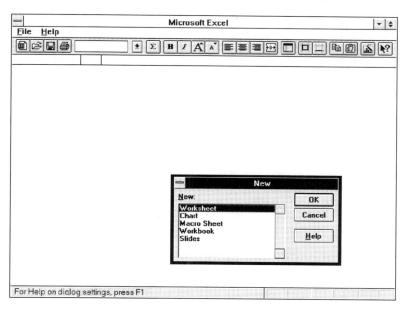

Figure 3.8. The New dialog box.

3. Double-click on the type of document you want to create (in this case, a worksheet), or select the type of document you want to create and then click on OK.

4. You can switch back and forth between open documents by clicking on Window in the menu bar to open the Window menu. All of the opened documents will be listed. The active document has a check mark next to it. To switch documents, click on the document you want to switch to.

5. Remember to close every open document before you exit Excel.

Printing

Once you have typed a document, you will probably want to print it. Printing a job involves transmitting to your printer the file(s) to be printed as well as the necessary printer codes. Different printers require different codes or instructions, which are contained in the part of the Microsoft Windows program called **printer drivers**. Fortunately, Excel makes transmitting printer instructions very easy. When you install Windows, you tell the program what printers you will be using. You can also add printers in the Windows program by using the Windows Control Panel. When you install a printer in Windows, the Windows printer driver for that printer is used by Excel. Excel sends instructions to the Windows Print Manager and the Print Manager handles the chore of transmitting the instructions to the printer. This frees up Excel and allows you to continue to work in the program while Windows handles the process of printing your file. Working on a file while Windows prints is a very simple example of **multitasking**, or working with two applications or programs at the same time.

This chapter will cover only the basic elements involved in printing a worksheet. For information on how to use advanced printer enhancements or change printer settings in Excel, see Chapter 9. Refer to your Windows manual or Appendix A in this book for information on how to install printers.

The Print Command

The Print command opens a dialog box that controls most of the features involved in printing a document. Let's use this command to print the file named SALJAN.XLS.

1. Open the worksheet named SALJAN.XLS. The document is in the active window.
2. Click on File in the menu bar.
3. Click on Print to open the Print dialog box, shown in Figure 3.9.
4. Choose OK. The Now Printing dialog box is displayed. This dialog box shows the name and page of the document currently being processed. To cancel the print job, select Cancel.

The Print dialog box automatically defaults to the All option in the Print Range option box. The All option will print the entire worksheet.

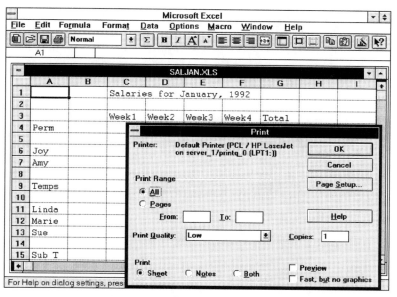

Figure 3.9. The Print dialog box.

Printing Selected Worksheet Pages

You may want to print individual pages or groups of pages, rather than a whole document. To print selected pages:

1. The document should be in the active window.
2. Click on File in the menu bar.
3. Click on Print to open the Print dialog box, as shown in Figure 3.9.
4. Choose the Pages option in the Print Range option box.
5. Enter the appropriate page numbers in the From and To text boxes.
6. Choose OK. The specified pages will print.

Printing Multiple Copies

Excel automatically prints one copy of a document unless you instruct it otherwise. To print multiple copies of a document:

1. The document should be in the active window.
2. Click on File in the menu bar.
3. Click on Print to open the Print dialog box, as shown in Figure 3.9.
4. Select the appropriate option from the Print Range option box (All, or Pages.)
5. Click on the Copies text box and type in the number of copies you want to print.
6. Select OK. The specified number of copies will print.

Selecting a Different Printer

If you have more than one printer, and you want to use a printer other than the one currently selected, you will have to select the printer:

1. Click on File in the menu bar.
2. Click on Page Setup to open the Page Setup dialog box, as shown in Figure 3.10.

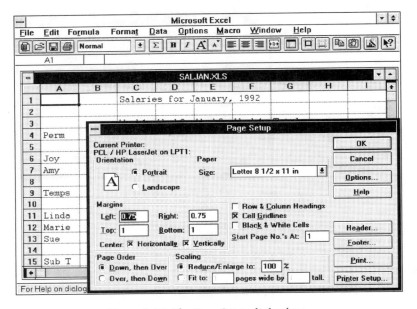

Figure 3.10. The Page Setup dialog box.

3. Click on the Printer Setup button to display the Printer Setup dialog box, as shown in Figure 3.11. This dialog box lists all of the printers installed on your system.
4. Select the printer you want to use.
5. Click on OK to exit the Printer Setup dialog box and return to the Page Setup dialog box.
6. Click on OK to save your printer selection and exit the Page Setup dialog box.

The new printer remains selected until you select another printer.

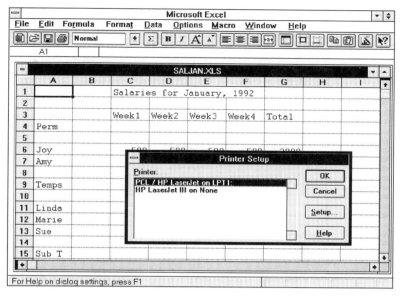

Figure 3.11. The Printer Setup dialog box.

Review Exercises for Chapter 3

- ◆ Create a brief worksheet and save it using the Save As command.
- ◆ Save the same worksheet to a different name using the Save As command.
- ◆ Close the document.
- ◆ Open an existing worksheet.
- ◆ Edit the worksheet and save it again.
- ◆ Print two copies of the worksheet.
- ◆ Save the worksheet and exit from Excel using the Exit command.

Before You Go On...

Before you continue on to the next chapter you should be familiar with the basic procedures for saving and retrieving documents in Excel. You should know how to open an existing document and how to create a new document. You should know how to use the Save and Save As commands to save new and edited documents. You should be able to print simple documents.

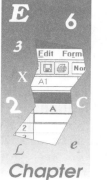
NAVIGATING AND EDITING YOUR WORKSHEET

What You Will Learn in This Chapter

- ◆ How to select cells and ranges
- ◆ How to use GoTo and Autoselect
- ◆ How to use functions
- ◆ The definition of relative and absolute references
- ◆ How to edit, replace, and delete data in a cell
- ◆ How to clear information in ranges
- ◆ How to insert and delete cells and ranges
- ◆ How to insert and delete rows and columns
- ◆ How to move and copy data within a worksheet
- ◆ How to undo and repeat a command
- ◆ How to search for and replace specific data in a worksheet

In this chapter, you will learn how to move around in your worksheet and how to perform basic editing operations. You will also be introduced to functions. You will need to create a worksheet to accomplish this. Create the worksheet shown in Figure 4.1. This is a worksheet for the accounting system of Frills and Thrills, detailing the expenses incurred by the company for the month of January. You will notice as you type that some of the column and row titles do not fit in the cell (for example, *Inv. 100* or *Print Cartridge*). Don't worry—the data is all there, as you can see by looking in the formula bar. It just doesn't fit in the cell display. In addition, you will notice that some numbers have decimals and some do not. Do not add decimals to the whole numbers. We will deal with all of these problems in our next chapter when we format our worksheet. When you have finished typing in all of the information, save the worksheet. Call it EXPJAN.XLS.

N O T E

If you have a laser printer, do not attempt to print this worksheet without first referring to Chapter 9. A number of changes will have to be made to accommodate longer paper in landscape orientation. In addition, our worksheet is not yet properly formatted. It is not necessary to print the worksheet in order to accomplish any of the tasks in this chapter.

The Totals columns and rows are blank. Up until now, you have used only one type of formula to add the values of cells. In this chapter you are going to learn a faster way.

Selecting Cells in a Worksheet

In order to work with a cell in a worksheet you must first select it. You have learned how to select a single cell simply by clicking on it. The selected or active cell is surrounded by a dark border. In this chapter you are going to learn how to select groups of cells (or **ranges**). This is necessary if you want to perform a command or action on a range rather than on a single cell. When you select a group of cells, the selected cells are highlighted, except for the active cell, which remains unhighlighted and surrounded by a heavy border.

You can select cells using the mouse, the keyboard, or a combination of the two. Most users prefer the mouse or mouse/keyboard combination. However, the most efficient method for you is the one you are most comfortable with. We suggest you make a copy of the EXPJAN.XLS worksheet and use the copy to practice the movement and selection features listed in tables 4.1 and 4.2, until you feel comfortable navigating and selecting. Since you will be working with a copy, don't worry about corrupting the worksheet—that's what it's there for. You can copy the worksheet by saving it to a different name:

1. Open the EXPJAN.XLS worksheet.
2. Click on File in the menu bar.
3. Click on Save As to open the Save As dialog box.
4. In the File Name text box, type in the new name PLAY.
5. Choose OK. The worksheet PLAY.XLS is now in the active window. (Don't worry about the original worksheet—it is still on the hard drive, and can be opened later.)

	A	B	C	D	E	F	G	H	I	J	K	L	M	N	O	P	Q	R	S
1			Inv. 100	Inv. 101	Inv. 102	Inv. 103	Off. 200	Off. 201	Off. 202	Rent	Phone	Electric	Salaries	Tax FICA	Tax Fed	Tax State	Tax City	Tax Dis	Totals
2	Inventory																		
3	Dresses		500	350	222.77	105.46													
4	Skirts		345.65	400	234.5	225													
5	Blouses		200.6	98.99	430	300													
6	Slacks		315	375	250	210.45													
7	Jackets		435	378	287.45	175													
8	Suits		250	788	300	325													
9	Coats		750	925	400	1000													
10	Handbags		150	75															
11	Earrings					150													
12	Bracelets					100													
13	Belts				175														
14	Hair Bows					50													
15	Office																		
16	Paper						55												
17	Clips							10											
18	Pens							25											
19	Print Cartridge							100											
20	Stamps								50										
21	Constant																		
22	Rent									2500									
23	Phone										375.23								
24	Electric											305.78							
25	Salaries												5980						
26	Taxes													598	700	400	150	75	
27	Totals																		

Figure 4.1. Worksheet for Frills and Thrills.

You can make three kinds of selections in a worksheet: a single cell, a range of cells, or multiple nonadjacent cells. Nonadjacent selections are single cells or groups of cells that are not next to each other. Figure 4.2 illustrates a single cell selection, Figure 4.3 illustrates a range selection, and Figure 4.4 illustrates multiple, nonadjacent selections.

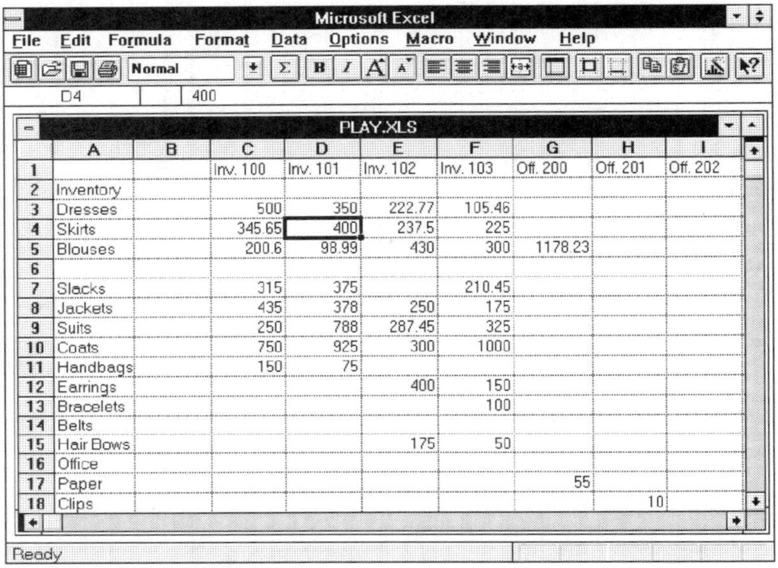

Figure 4.2. Single-cell selection.

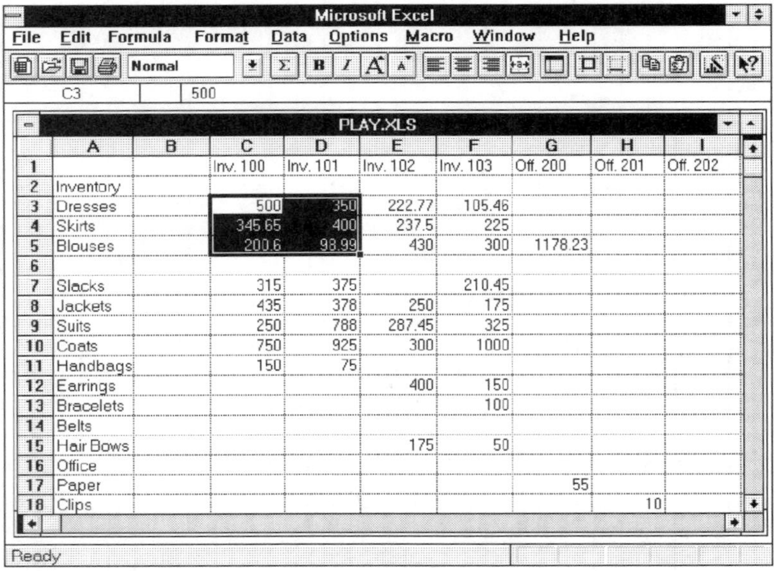

Figure 4.3. Range selection.

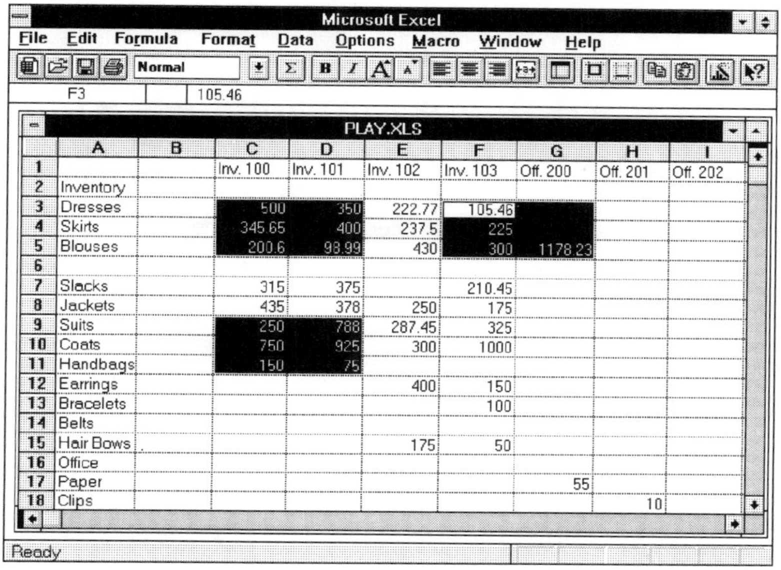

Figure 4.4. Multiple nonadjacent selections.

Selecting a Single Cell

To select a single cell using the mouse, click on the cell you want to select. Using the keyboard, press the movement keys as shown in Table 4.1, shown on page 56, to move to the cell you want to select. Table 4.2, shown on page 57, shows the actions you can select using a mouse.

Selecting a Range

To select a range using the mouse:

1. Point to the first cell you want to select.
2. Drag the mouse through the remaining cells you want to select.

Or,

1. Click on the first cell you want to select.
2. Hold down the Shift key and click on the last cell in the range you want to select (the click-shift-click method).

To select a range using the keyboard:

1. Press the movement keys to move to the first cell in the range you want to select.
2. Press the movement keys to extend the selection to the range you want to select. For example, to extend the selection to the beginning of the row, press Shift+Home.

To	Use
Move to and select one cell	Up, down, left, and right arrow keys
Select a range of cells	Shift+Arrow key
Select a block of cells	Ctrl+Shift+Arrow key
Move to beginning of row containing active cell	Home
Extend selection to beginning of row	Shift+Home
Move to end of row containing the active cell	End
Extend selection to end of row containing active cell	Shift+End
Select entire row containing active cell	Shift+Spacebar
Select entire column containing active cell	Ctrl+Spacebar
Move to and select cell at upper-left corner (beginning) of worksheet	Ctrl+Home
Extend selection to cell at upper-left corner of worksheet	Ctrl+Shift+Home
Move to and select cell at lower-right corner (end) of worksheet	Ctrl+End
Extend selection to cell at lower-right corner of worksheet	Ctrl+Shift+End
Move to and select cell at upper-left corner of window	Home (Scroll lock on)
Extend selection to cell at upper-left corner of window	Shift+Home (Scroll lock on)
Move to and select cell at lower-right corner of window	End (Scroll lock on)
Extend selection to cell at lower-right corner of window	Shift+End (Scroll lock on)
Select the entire worksheet	Ctrl+Shift+Spacebar
Reduce selection to a single cell	Shift+Backspace

Table 4.1. Using the keyboard to select.

To	Do this
Select a single cell	Click on the cell you want to select.
Select a range of cells	Click on the first cell you want to select and drag through the rest of the cells you want to select. **Or,** click on the first cell you want to select, hold down the Shift key, and click on the last cell in the range you want to select.
Select an entire row or column	Click on the row or column heading of the row or column you want to select.
Select several rows or columns	Click on the first row or column heading you want to select and drag through the row or column headings to the last row or column you want to select. **Or,** click on the first row or column heading you want to select, hold down the Shift key, and click on the last row or column heading you want to select.
Select the current array	Hold Ctrl+Shift and double-click on any cell in the range.
Select the entire worksheet	Click on the blank rectangle at the top of the row headings and to the left of the column headings (Select All).
Make multiple selections	Drag through the first selection, then hold down the Ctrl key as you drag through each additional selection. **Or,** click on the first cell you want in the first selection, hold down the Shift key, and click on the last cell in the first range you want to select. Hold down the Ctrl key and click on the first cell in each additional selection, hold down the Shift key, and click on the last cell in each additional range you want to select.
Select a block of text (autoselect)	Click on the first cell in the block, hold down the Shift key, and double-click on the border of the first cell (left, right, top, or bottom) in the direction of the block that you want to extend the selection.

Table 4.2. Using the mouse to select

Making a Multiple Nonadjacent Selection

To make a multiple nonadjacent selection using the mouse:

1. Select the first cell or range.
2. Hold down the Ctrl key as you select each additional cell. To select an additional range, hold down the Ctrl key as you select the first cell in the range. Then select the rest of the range. Repeat step 2 for each additional cell or range you want to select.

To make a multiple nonadjacent selection using the keyboard:

1. Press the movement keys to move to the first cell in the range you want to select.
2. Press the movement keys to extend the selection to the range you want to select.
3. Press Shift+F8 to keep the current selection. The *ADD* prompt appears on the right side of the status bar.
4. Press the movement keys to move to the first cell of the next range you want to select.
5. Press F8. The *EXT* prompt appears on the right side of the status bar.
6. Press the movement keys to extend the selection to the range you want to select.
7. Press Shift+F8 to keep the current selection.
8. Repeat steps 4 through 7 for each selection you want to add.

Moving Within a Selection

When you select a range or make an additional nonadjacent selection, you can move the active cell within the selection while retaining the selection. Simply hold down the Ctrl key and click the cell in the selection you want to become the active cell. Or use the keyboard commands listed in Table 4.3.

To move	Use
Down one cell	Enter
Up one cell	Shift+Enter
Right one cell	Tab
Left one cell	Shift+Tab
Right within a single selected row	Tab or Enter
Left within a single selected row	Shift+Tab or Shift+Enter
Down within a single selected column	Enter or Tab
Up within a single selected column	Shift+Enter or Shift+Tab
To next corner of range	Ctrl+Period
To next range in a multiple nonadjacent selection	Ctrl+Tab
To previous range in a multiple nonadjacent selection	Ctrl+Shift+Tab

Table 4.3. The keys used to move the active cell in a selected range.

Using the GoTo Command

You can use the GoTo command to find and select cells and ranges. This is particularly useful when working with large worksheets.

Using GoTo to Select a Specific Cell or Range

You can use the GoTo command to find and select a cell or range quickly. It is also possible to assign names to cells, ranges, and formulas and then use the GoTo command to find them. Naming is covered in Chapter 6. To use the GoTo command to select a cell or range:

1. Click on Formula in the menu bar.
2. Click on GoTo. The GoTo dialog box is displayed, as shown in Figure 4.5.
3. In the Reference text box, type a cell or range reference (such as *C3:F3*), or select a name from the list.
4. Choose OK.

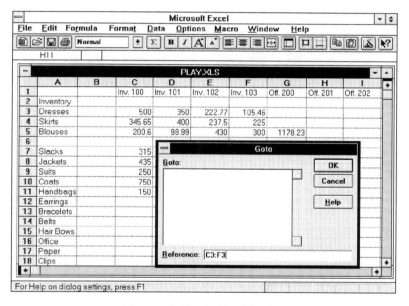

Figure 4.5. The Go To dialog box.

Using GoTo to Return to a Previous Location

After you have used the GoTo command to go to another location in the worksheet, you can use it to return to any of your last four locations. To return to a previous location:

1. Click on Formula in the menu bar.
2. Click on GoTo. The GoTo dialog box is displayed. Your last four locations are listed.
3. Select a location and choose OK.

Using GoTo to Extend a Selection

You can use the GoTo command to extend a selection from the active cell:

1. Click on Formula in the menu bar to open the Formula menu.
2. Click on GoTo. The GoTo dialog box is displayed.
3. In the Reference text box, type a cell or range reference (such as *C3:F3*), or select a name from the list.
4. Hold down the Shift key when you choose OK.

Using GoTo to Add a Nonadjacent Selection

You can use the GoTo command to turn the selected area into a nonadjacent selection.

1. Click on Formula in the menu bar.
2. Click on GoTo. The GoTo dialog box is displayed.
3. In the Reference text box, type a cell or range reference (such as *C3:F3*), or select a name from the list. This area will become a nonadjacent selection.
4. Hold down the Ctrl key when you choose OK.

An alternative method is to press the toggle Shift+F8, *ADD,* then click on the cell you want to add the selection to.

Using GoTo to Select a Named Area in Another Worksheet

You can use GoTo to find and select a cell or range from another opened worksheet.

1. Click on Formula in the menu bar.
2. Click on GoTo. The GoTo dialog box is displayed.
3. In the Reference text box, type the name of worksheet, an exclamation point, and a cell or range reference or a name (such as *SALJAN.XLS!C6*).
4. Choose OK. The worksheet and the cell or range you have selected are now in the active window.

Selecting Cells by Content

You can select cells by content in a worksheet or in a selected range of a worksheet. For instance, you can select all of the cells in a worksheet or range that contain formulas or that contain constant values. We have not yet covered all of the types of contents for which you can select cells; you will encounter them as we progress through the book.

To select a cell or range containing a specific type of contents:

1. Select a single cell to search the entire worksheet. Select a range of cells to limit the search to a specific area of the worksheet.
2. Click on Formula in the menu bar.
3. Click on Select Special to display the Select Special dialog box, shown in Figure 4.6.
4. Select the option that contains the search criterion you wish to select. In this case, select Blanks.
5. Choose OK. All of the blank cells in your worksheet are highlighted.

To cancel your selection, click on any cell.

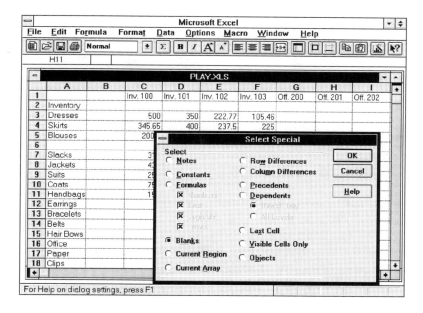

Figure 4.6. The Select Special dialog box.

To move within your selection using the mouse, hold down the Ctrl key then click on the cell you wish to be active within the selection. To use the keyboard to move within the selection, refer to Table 4.3.

Table 4.4, on the next page, contains the specific types of cell contents you can select.

Cell type	Useful for
Notes	Quickly finding comments
Constants	Selecting data to be cleared
Formulas	Finding formula errors
Blanks	Finding cells that should contain data but don't
Current region or array	Selecting the region or array to which the active cell belongs
Row or column differences	Finding cells that are different in the same row or column
Precedents or dependents	Tracing the connections between cells
Last cell	Finding the end of your worksheet
Visible cells	Selecting visible cells in an outline
Graphic objects or text boxes or buttons	Finding all graphic objects on your worksheet

Table 4.4. Cell types and reasons to select them.

Using Autoselect for Blocks of Cells

The autoselect feature is most useful in large worksheets to move around in or select **blocks**, which are groups of cells surrounded by blank cells. When you use autoselect you do not have to know the exact cell locations to move to or extend the selection to the end of a block. Autoselect will find the end of the block for you. Let's experiment with autoselect. If the PLAY.XLS worksheet is not in your document window, open it now.

Using Autoselect to Move Within a Block of Cells

You can move to the left, right, top, or bottom of a block of cells by double-clicking on the border of a selected cell. Position the mouse pointer (it should be in the shape of an arrow) on the border of the cell. If you double-click on the top, you will move to the first adjacent cell in the column. If you double-click on the bottom of the border, you will move to the last adjacent cell in the column. If you double-click on the left border, you will move to the first adjacent cell in the row. If you double-click on the right border, you will move to the last adjacent cell in the row. Let's move to the last adjacent cell in row 3 in PLAY.XLS.

1. Select cell C3.
2. Double-click on the right border of the cell.
3. Your active cell is now F3.

Using Autoselect to Move Between Blocks of Cells

You can move from one block of cells to another in a row or column by selecting a cell on the edge of a block and double-clicking on the top, bottom, left, or right border of the cell, depending on the position of the block you wish to move to. For example, if you double-click on the bottom of the cell, you will be moved to the last cell in the column of the next block. If you have blank cells between blocks, you will be moved to the last blank cell in the row or column.

Using Autoselect to Select a Block of Cells Within a Row or Column

You can select all of the cells to the left, right, top, or bottom of a block by pressing Shift and double-clicking on the border of a selected cell. If you press Shift and double-click on the top or bottom of a selected cell, you will extend the selection to the first or last adjacent cell in the column. If you press Shift and double-click on the left or right border of a selected cell, you will extend the selection to the first or last adjacent cell in the row.

To extend the selection from cell C3 to the last cell in the block:

1. Select cell C3.
2. Press Shift and double-click on the right border of the cell.
3. You have selected all of the adjacent cells in the row. If the row extends beyond the current screen, your worksheet will scroll to the point where you can see the end of the selected block.

Using Autoselect to Select Multiple Blocks

The autoselect feature allows you to extend a selection to include multiple blocks separated by blank cells. To extend a selection to include multiple blocks, select the first block of text. Your next selection will extend the block to include all of the blank cells, and your final selection will extend the selection to include the next block of text. To select multiple blocks of text:

1. Select a block of text.
2. Press Shift and double-click on the left, right, top, or bottom border of the cell in the direction of the next block you wish to select. (The cell should be on the edge of the block).
3. You have extended the selection to include the blank cells between the blocks of text.
4. Repeat step 2 until you have extended the selection to include all of the blocks of text you want to select.

Scrolling Through the Worksheet

When you are working with worksheets that are too large to fit in one window, you must be able to scroll through the worksheet and locate sections quickly. This can be done using the keyboard movement keys listed in Table 4.1, or using the scroll bars.

Scroll bars, scroll arrows, and scroll boxes allow you to scroll vertically and horizontally through the worksheet. This allows you to see information that cannot fit into the window. When you scroll through a worksheet, only the window display changes; the active cell or selection does not change. Refer to Figure 2.2, which labels the scroll bars, scroll arrows, and scroll boxes in a worksheet window.

If you click on a scroll button, the worksheet will move vertically or horizontally one column or row at a time. If you hold the mouse button down on a scroll button, the columns or rows will scroll continuously.

The scroll boxes are the little empty boxes in the scroll bars. The entire length of the scroll bars represents the entire vertical or horizontal data areas of the worksheet. The scroll boxes show your current location relative to the whole worksheet. For example, if you move the vertical scroll box to the middle of the scroll bar, it will bring you to the row in the middle of the worksheet. You can move a scroll box by dragging it with the mouse.

You can scroll through your document one window at a time by clicking in the scroll bar on either side of the scroll box. For example, clicking above the scroll box in the vertical scroll bar will move the window up one screen.

Working with Functions

A function is a different way of constructing a formula. In Chapter 2 we created formulas to add our columns and rows. For example, we used the following formula to add cells C6 through F6:

```
=C6+D6+E6+F6
```

In this chapter we are going to learn how to use a more sophisticated formula—a **function**—to produce the same result. A function consists of a built-in formula (or function name) and a value (or group of values) that performs the specified calculation ordered by the function name and produces a result.

The values you insert into a function are called **arguments**. The values that the calculation produces are called **results**. For example, in the following function:

```
=SUM(6,5,3)
```

SUM is the built-in formula or function name, and the values 6, 5, and 3 are the argument. The result of the function is 14 (the sum of 6+5+3=14). In this function, SUM is replacing the operator +.

Excel has fourteen categories of functions. Each of these categories contains numerous functions. As we progress through this book, we will introduce additional functions where appropriate. In Chapter 8 we will discuss functions in greater detail.

All functions employ the same basic **syntax**. If the syntax of your function is incorrect Excel displays a message informing you that there is an error in the formula. The basic syntax of a function is as follows:

```
=FUNCTION NAME(value or values)
```

Like any formula, a function always begins with an equal sign (=). This is followed by the function name, in this case, SUM. The function name is followed by the argument, which consists of a value or values enclosed in parentheses. As a rule, you should not use spaces in functions. You may use uppercase or lowercase when typing a function.

Values in an argument can be expressed differently. Nonsequential values are separated by commas. For example, in the following functions:

```
=SUM(5,6,3)  and  =SUM(C6,C9,C15)
```

the values are separated by commas.

Values consisting of sequential groups of cells (ranges) are separated by a colon (:). (Periods (.) are used in Lotus 1-2-3 and can also be used in Excel 4.0.) For example, the values that represent cells C5 through C12 are separated by a colon (:) in the function:

```
=SUM(C5:C12)
```

Let's return to our example of the formula we used in Chapter 2 to add cells C6 through F6:

```
=C6+D6+E6+F6
```

A more efficient way to construct this formula would be to use the SUM function:

```
=SUM(C6:F6)
```

Let's insert a function into our expense worksheet.

1. Open the worksheet named EXPJAN.XLS (if PLAY.XLS is still open, close it first).
2. Select cell S3.
3. Type the function =SUM(C3:R3), and click on another cell.
4. Cell S3 now shows the result, 1178.23, which is the sum of cells C3 through R3.

We now have a total for row 3. Next we will need to calculate the sums of all of the values in rows 4 through 26.

Copying a Formula to a Group of Cells Using Copy and Paste

In Chapter 2 you learned how to copy a formula and paste it into another cell. Though this method works well with one or two cells, it is not the most efficient way to work with groups of cells. In this section you are going to learn how to copy a formula to a group or range of cells.

1. If the worksheet named EXPJAN.XLS is not open, open it.
2. Click on cell S3, which now contains the function =SUM(C3:R3). We are going to copy this function to a range in order to calculate the sums of the values in rows 4 through 26.
3. Click on Edit in the menu bar to open the Edit menu.
4. Click on Copy.
5. Using the mouse or keyboard, select cells S4 through S26.
6. Click on Edit in the menu bar to open the Edit menu.
7. Click on Paste. The function is copied to each cell in the range. The value of each argument has been changed to reflect its new cell location. For example, if you click on cell S4 and look in the formula bar, you will see that the function has been changed to read =SUM(C4:R4).

Let's insert a formula to calculate the sum of the values in cells C3 through C26.

1. Select cell C27.
3. Type the function =SUM(C3:C26), and click on another cell.
4. Cell C27 now shows the result, 2946.25, which is the sum of cells C3 through C26.

We now have a total for column C. Next we will need to calculate the sums of all of the values in columns D through S.

1. Click on cell C27, which contains the function =SUM(C3:C26). We are going to copy this function to a range in order to calculate the sums of the values in columns D through S.
3. Click on Edit in the menu bar to open the Edit menu.
4. Click on Copy.
5. Using the mouse or the keyboard, select cells D27 through S27.
6. Click on Edit in the menu bar to open the Edit menu.
7. Click on Paste. The function is copied to each cell in the range. The value of each argument has been changed to reflect its new cell location.

Your worksheet should now look like Figure 4.7. Save and close the worksheet.

References

A **reference** identifies a cell or range: it is a cell or range address, based on the column and row headings the cell or range is in. For example, the reference for cell A1 is A1. The reference for cells A1 through A20 is A1:A20. References tell Excel which cells to look in to find the values for use in formulas. Using references, you can create a formula that will use values contained in cells in different parts of the worksheet. For example, the formula =A1+D1+F1 uses the references A1, D1, and F1 to add the data contained in those cells.

	A	B	C	D	E	F	G	H	I	J	K	L	M	N	O	P	Q	R	S
1																			
2	Inventory		Inv. 100	Inv. 101	Inv. 102	Inv. 103	Off. 200	Off. 201	Off. 202	Rent	Phone	Electric	Salaries	Tax FICA	Tax Fed	Tax State	Tax City	Tax Dis	Totals
3	Dresses		1200	780	875	210													2865
4	Skirts		500	750	675	550													2475
5	Blouses		375	550	600	450													1975
6	Slacks		425	500	620.67	210.45													1756.12
7	Jackets		1224	750	500	778													3252
8	Suits		450	788	300	325													1863
9	Coats		2200	1050		1800													5050
10	Handbags		150	75	400														625
11	Earrings				500	150													650
12	Bracelets					100													100
13	Belts				175														175
14	Hair Bows					50													50
15	Office																		0
16	Paper						55												55
17	Clips							10											10
18	Pens							25											25
19	Print Cartridge							100											100
20	Stamps								50										50
21	Constant																		0
22	Rent									2500									2500
23	Phone										375.23								375.23
24	Electric											305.78							305.78
25	Salaries												5980						5980
26	Taxes													598	700	400	150	75	1923
27	Totals		6524	5243	4445.87	4623.45	55	135	50	2500	375.23	305.78	5980	598	700	400	150	75	32160.13

Figure 4.7. The worksheet with totals.

You can also use references to use the values of one cell in several formulas. For example, if in cell G1 you create the function =SUM(A1:F1), and in cell A6 you create the function =SUM(A1:A5), you have used the reference in A1 in two formulas. Actually, you have been using references for several chapters. You just didn't know they were called references. There are two types of references: relative references and absolute references.

Relative References

A **relative reference** is one in which the value of a formula changes when the formula is copied, in order to reflect the value of the new location. For example in EXPJAN.XLS, when we copied the function =SUM(C3:R3) to a range, the value of the function in each cell of the range changed to reflect each cell's new location. You can confirm this yourself. In the worksheet, click on cell S4 and note the function in the formula bar. Now click on cell S5 and note the function in the formula bar. In each case, the value in the function automatically changed to reflect the location of the formula. Excel automatically assumes relative references unless you tell it you want a reference to be absolute.

Absolute References

An **absolute reference** is one in which the value in a formula remains constant even when moved or copied to a new location. To indicate to Excel that a formula contains an absolute reference, precede the column references and row numbers with dollar signs ($).

For example, look at Figure 4.7. Cells D4 and D5 each have a value of 20. If we enter the formula =$D$4+$D$5 in cell D6, the result will be 40. When we copy that formula to cell E6, the formula will not change, even though it has been copied to a new location. The result will still be 40 even though the values of cells E4 and E5 are not the same as the values of cells D4 and D5.

Figure 4.8 shows the type of document that would require a formula with an absolute reference. We entered a formula with an absolute reference in cell C10 for Total Income and one in cell C18 for Total Expenses. We then copied the formula for Total Income from cell C10 to cell D20, and copied the formula for Total Expenses from cell C18 to D21. Since we used a formula with an absolute reference, the result remained the same after the formulas were copied.

N O T E

You cannot move (cut and paste) a formula with a relative reference. If you do, the formula will not change to reflect the new cell designation. You can move or copy a formula with an absolute reference.

```
┌────────────────────────────────────────────────────────────┐
│ Income and Expense Report for January, 1992                  │
│                                                              │
│ Income                                                       │
│                                                              │
│ Books                             700                        │
│ Papers                            200                        │
│ Pens                              400                        │
│ Pencils                           223                        │
│                                                              │
│ Total Income                              1523               │
│                                                              │
│ Expenses                                                     │
│                                                              │
│ Rent                              300                        │
│ Phone                              76                        │
│ Electric                           98                        │
│                                                              │
│ Total Expenses                             474               │
│                                                              │
│ Total Income                                      1523       │
│ Less Total Expense                                 474       │
│                                                              │
│ Total Net Income                                  1049       │
└────────────────────────────────────────────────────────────┘
```

Figure 4.8. Worksheet using absolute reference.

Editing Your Worksheet

A major advantage of using an electronic spreadsheet package is that you can edit information after it has been entered. Some of the basic editing features you can perform include editing information in a cell, inserting and deleting columns and rows, moving and copying information, searching for and replacing data, and sorting data. In this chapter we will learn how to perform these editing operations using menu commands.

Editing, Replacing, and Deleting Data in a Cell

You may want to edit, replace, or delete information that has been entered into a cell.
To edit the information in a cell:

1. Select the cell you want to edit. The information in the cell will appear in the formula bar.
2. Click in the formula bar at the location where you want to edit the information. The edit and cancel check boxes, shown in Figure 4.9, are displayed. This indicates that you are editing information in the formula bar.
3. Edit the information in the cell.
4. When you are finished editing, press Enter or move to another cell.

	A	B	C	D	E	F	G	H	I
1			Inv. 100	Inv. 101	Inv. 102	Inv. 103	Off. 200	Off. 201	Off. 202
2	Inventory								
3	Dresses		500	350	222.77	105.46			
4	Skirts		345.65	400	237.5	225			
5	Blouses		200.6	98.99	430	300	1178.23		
6									
7	Slacks		315	375		210.45			
8	Jackets		435	378	250	175			
9	Suits		250	788	287.45	325			
10	Coats		750	925	300	1000			
11	Handbags		150	75					
12	Earrings				400	150			
13	Bracelets					100			
14	Belts								
15	Hair Bows				175	50			
16	Office								
17	Paper						55		
18	Clips							10	

Figure 4.9. Edit and cancel boxes in formula bar.

To delete all of the information in a cell:

1. Select the cell in which you want to delete information. The information in the cell will appear in the formula bar.
2. Press the Backspace key once. All of the information in the cell will be deleted.

To replace the information in a cell:

1. Select the cell in which you want to replace the information.
2. Type in the new information. As soon as you enter the first character of the new information, all of the old information will be deleted.

Let's delete, replace, and edit information in cells in the PLAY.XLS worksheet. Leave the worksheet open so you can practice editing with it.

1. Open the worksheet PLAY.XLS.
2. Select a cell and press the Backspace key to delete the information from it.
3. Select another cell with a figure in it. Type in a new figure. The old figure will be replaced with the new one.
4. Select cell A18. Click on the *P* in *Pens* in the formula bar and edit the cell to read *Red Pens.*

Clearing Ranges

You can clear or delete all of the information in the cells in a range or in multiple, nonadjacent ranges.

1. Select the range or multiple, nonadjacent ranges in which you want to clear information.
2. Click on Edit in the menu bar to open the Edit menu.
3. Click on Clear. The information in the selected range or ranges has been cleared.

Let's practice clearing a range in the PLAY.XLS worksheet.

1. Select a range of three cells in any part of the worksheet.
2. In the Edit menu, click on Clear to clear the information in the cells in the selected range. Notice that the information in the other columns has not been affected. (However, if you have entered formulas in this worksheet that reference the cleared cells, the results of those formulas will update to reflect the fact that the cells have been cleared.)

Deleting and Inserting Cells and Ranges

When you delete the information in a cell or a range, the empty cell or cells remain in place. There will be times when you want to delete not just the information in the cell or range, but the cells themselves. For example, suppose you entered information in an entire row of cells in row 3 and then discovered you started with column C when you meant to start with column B. If you delete cell B3, you will be able to move the entire row to the right of cell B3 one column to the left, so that cell B3 rather than cell C3 will be the first cell containing information. When you delete a cell or range you must close up the space that was taken by the deleted cell or range. You can do this by moving the adjacent cells either left or up. The adjacent cells will move left or up the same number of columns or rows that were deleted. For example, if you delete cells B3 and B4, the rest of the column beginning with cell B5 will move up two rows.

To delete a cell or range:

1. Select the cell or range(s) you want to delete.
2. Click on Edit in the menu bar to open the Edit menu.
3. Click on Delete to open the Delete dialog box, as shown in Figure 4.10.
4. Select either the Shift Cells Left or the Shift Cells Up option.
5. Choose OK.

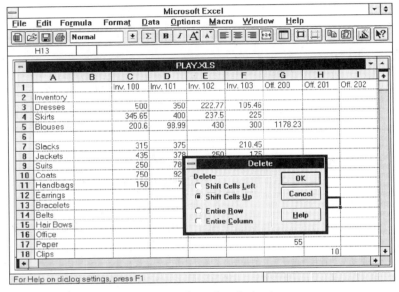

Figure 4.10. The Delete dialog box.

WARNING

If you delete cells that are referenced in a formula, the formula will not be able to find the referenced cells and you will receive a *#REF* error message. To correct this you will have to adjust the formula. Notes attached to cells will be deleted with the cells they are attached to. Delete cells with caution!

Let's delete a cell in the PLAY.XLS worksheet.

1. Select cell C3.
2. Click on Delete in the Edit menu. Select the Shift Cell Left option to move the rest of the cells in the row, starting with cell D3, one column to the left.
3. Choose OK. Notice that all of the cells in row 3 starting with cell D3 have moved one column to the left.

When you insert a cell or range, the columns or rows shift to the right or down to accommodate it. For example, if you insert a new cell in the location F7, either the remaining cells in the F column will move down one row, or the remaining cells in row 7 will shift one column to the right. If you insert more than one cell, the remaining cells in the column or row will move either down or to the right to accommodate the exact number of new cells.

To insert a cell or range:

1. Bring your pointer to the cell where you want to insert a new cell, and click. If you want to insert more than one cell, extend the selection down to include an additional cell for each additional cell you want to insert.

2. Click on Edit in the menu bar to open the Edit menu.

3. Click on Insert to open the Insert dialog box, shown in Figure 4.11.

4. Select either the Shift Cells Right or the Shift Cells Down option.

5. Choose OK.

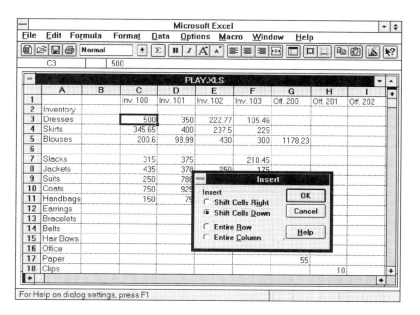

Figure 4.11. The Insert dialog box.

Let's insert a range in the PLAY.XLS worksheet.

1. Select cells C3 and D3.

2. Click on Insert in the Edit menu. Select the Shift Cell Right option to move the rest of the cells in the row two columns to the right.

3. Choose OK. Notice that the remainder of the cells in row 3 to the right of the inserted cells have moved two columns to the right.

Inserting Rows and Columns

There will be times when you will want to insert entire rows or columns in your worksheet. You may want to add a row between your title and the following information, or you might want to set off your first column from the rest of the spreadsheet with a blank column.

To insert a row or rows:

1. Bring your pointer to any cell in the row where you want to insert a new row, and click. If you want to insert more than one row, extend the selection down to include an additional cell for each additional row you want to insert.
2. Click on Edit in the menu bar to open the Edit menu.
3. Click on Insert to open the Insert dialog box.
4. Select the Insert Entire Row option.
5. Choose OK.

A new row has been inserted in the worksheet. All existing formulas will change to reflect the additional rows.

To insert a column or columns:

1. Bring your pointer to any cell in the column where you want to insert a new column and click. If you want to insert more than one column, extend the selection to the right to include an additional cell for each additional column you want to insert.
2. Click on Edit in the menu bar to open the Edit menu.
3. Click on Insert to open the Insert dialog box.
4. Select the Insert Entire Column option.
5. Choose OK.

A new column has been inserted in the worksheet. All existing formulas will change to reflect the additional column.

Let's insert a few rows in the EXPJAN.XLS worksheet.

1. Close PLAY.XLS and open EXPJAN.XLS.
2. Click on cell A1.
3. Extend the selection to cells A2 and A3.
4. Click on Edit in the menu bar to open the Edit menu.
5. Click on Insert to open the Insert dialog box.
6. Select the Insert Entire Row option.
7. Choose OK. You have inserted three rows at the top of your worksheet.
8. Insert rows between Inventory and Dresses, Hair Bows and Office, Office and Paper, Stamps and Constant, Constant and Rent, and Taxes and Totals. Your worksheet should now look like the one shown in Figure 4.12. Save and close your worksheet.

	A	B	C	D	E	F	G	H	I	J	K	L	M	N	O	P	Q	R	S
			Inv. 100	Inv. 101	Inv. 102	Inv. 103	Off. 200	Off. 201	Off. 202	Rent	Phone	Electric	Salaries	Tax FICA	Tax Fed	Tax State	Tax City	Tax Dis	Totals
1																			
2																			
3																			
4																			
5	Inventory																		
6																			
7	Dresses		1200	780	675	210													2865
8	Skirts		500	750	875	550													2475
9	Blouses		375	550	600	450													1975
10	Slacks		425	500	620.67	210.45													1756.12
11	Jackets		1224	750	500	778													3252
12	Suits		450	788	300	325													1863
13	Coats		2200	1050		1800													5050
14	Handbags		150	75	400														825
15	Earrings				500	150													650
16	Bracelets					100													100
17	Belts				175														175
18	Hair Bows					50													50
19																			
20	Office																		0
21																			
22	Paper						55												55
23	Clips							10											10
24	Pens							25											25
25	Print Cartridge							100											100
26	Stamps								50										50
27																			
28	Constant																		0
29																			
30	Rent									2500									2500
31	Phone										375.23								375.23
32	Electric											305.78							305.78
33	Salaries												5980						5980
34	Taxes													598	700	400	150	75	1923
35																			
36	Totals		6524	5243	4445.67	4623.45	55	135	50	2500	375.23	305.78	5980	598	700	400	150	75	32180.13

Figure 4.12. Worksheet EXPJAN.ELS with rows inserted.

Deleting Rows and Columns

Sometimes you will need to delete rows or columns in your worksheet. For example, if your worksheet has several blank rows or columns and will not fit on one page, you might want to delete some of the blank rows or columns to shorten the worksheet.

To delete a row:

1. Bring your pointer to any cell in the row you want to delete and click. If you want to delete more than one row, extend the selection down to include an additional cell for each additional row you want to delete.

2. Click on Edit in the menu bar to open the Edit menu.

3. Click on Delete to open to Delete dialog box.

4. Select the Delete Entire Row option.

5. Choose OK.

A row has been deleted from the worksheet.

To delete a column or columns:

1. Bring your pointer to any cell in the column you want to delete and click on the cell. If you want to delete more than one column, extend the selection to the right to include an additional cell for each additional column you want to delete.

2. Click on Edit in the menu bar to open the Edit menu.

3. Click on Delete to open the Delete dialog box.

4. Select the Delete Entire Column option.

5. Choose OK.

A column has been deleted from the worksheet.

WARNING

If you delete rows or columns that contain cells that are referenced in a formula, the formula will not be able to find the referenced cells and you will receive a *#REF* error message. To correct this you will have to adjust the formula. Notes that are attached to cells in deleted columns or rows will be deleted with the cells they are attached to. Delete columns or rows with caution!

Let's practice deleting a column in PLAY.XLS.

1. Open the PLAY.XLS worksheet.

2. Select a cell in column H.

3. Click on Edit in the menu bar to open the Edit menu.

4. Click on Delete to open the Delete dialog box.

5. Select the Delete Entire Column option.

6. Choose OK. Column H has been deleted from the worksheet. All of the columns to the right of column H have shifted over one column.

Moving and Copying Cell Contents

When you move the contents of a cell, you cut them from one location and paste them to another. Unless you specify otherwise, the entire contents of the cell, including data, notes, formats, and formulas, are moved (copying or moving cell attributes will be covered in Chapter 6). Moving data is a two-step process: first you cut the contents of the cell(s), then you paste the contents to another location.

When you copy the contents of a cell, you duplicate the data in a new location without removing it from its original location. As with moving the contents of a cell, unless you specify otherwise, the entire contents of the cell, including data, notes, format, and formulas, are copied. Copying data is a two-step process: first you the copy the contents of the cell(s), then you paste the contents to another location.

N O T E

When you move or copy the constant values of a cell or range, the values in the formulas referencing those cells are automatically changed to reflect the new location. When you *move* a formula with a relative reference, the formula will not change to reflect the new location. When you *copy* a formula with a relative reference, the formula *will* change to reflect the new location. Moving or copying has no effect on absolute cell references.

Cutting the Contents of a Cell or Range

When you cut the contents of a cell or range they are removed from their original location in the worksheet and placed in the **Windows Clipboard**. This is a special holding pen in Windows for information that will be used again. When you cut or copy data again, the new selection replaces the old selection in the Windows Clipboard. To cut the contents of a cell or range:

1. Select the cell or range you want to cut.
2. Click on Edit in the menu bar to open the Edit menu.
3. Click on Cut. The contents of the cell(s) are placed in the Windows Clipboard.

Copying the Contents of a Cell or Range

When you copy the contents of a cell or range they remain in the same location and are placed in the Windows Clipboard. To copy the contents of a cell or range to the Windows Clipboard:

1. Select the cell or range you want to copy.
2. Click on Edit in the menu bar to open the Edit menu.
3. Click on Copy. The contents of the cell(s) are placed in the Windows Clipboard.

Pasting the Contents of a Cell or Range

When you paste data into a cell or cells, you are retrieving data that has been cut or copied and placed in the Windows Clipboard and inserting it into the selected paste area (the **paste area** is the area to which you are moving the contents of the cut or copied cells).

You can designate the paste area by selecting a single cell. If you are moving or copying the contents of more than one cell, select the upper-left cell of the paste area and Excel will expand the paste area to accommodate all of the data.

When you insert data into the paste area Excel will automatically replace the existing contents in the paste area with the new data. To avoid replacing the existing contents in the paste area, you can use the Insert Paste command (see below). To paste data to a paste area:

1. Select the paste area by clicking on the first cell in it.
2. Click on Edit in the menu bar to open to Edit menu.
3. Click on Paste. The data is pasted to the paste area.

SHORT CUT

You can press the Enter key after step 1 instead of choosing the Paste command to complete the paste procedure.

Let's use PLAY.XLS to practice moving and copying the contents of cells within a worksheet.

1. Select a cell or a range.
2. Click on Edit in the menu bar.
3. Click on Cut.
4. Select a paste area.
5. Click on Edit in the menu bar to open the Edit menu.
6. Click on Paste. The contents of the cell or range are moved to the paste area.
7. To copy a cell or a range, use steps 1 through 6, except that in step 3 select Copy instead of Cut.

Inserting New Cells into the Paste Area

When you use the Paste command you replace the contents of the cells in the paste area with the contents of the cells in the Windows Clipboard. The Insert Paste command allows you to insert cells between existing cells in the paste area so that the contents of the paste area are not replaced. To use the Insert Paste command:

1. Click on the first cell in the paste area.
2. Click on Edit in the menu bar to open the Edit menu.

3. Click on Insert Paste. If you did not cut or copy the contents of an entire row or column, the Insert Paste dialog box, shown in Figure 4.13, is displayed.

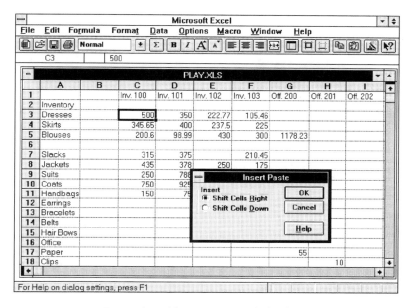

Figure 4.13. The Insert Paste dialog box.

4. In the Insert Paste dialog box select either the Shift Cells Right option or the Shift Cells Down option to shift the cells in the paste area right or down.

5. Choose OK.

If you cut or copy the contents of a row or column, Insert Paste will automatically insert a new row or column between the existing rows or columns in the paste area.

N O T E

Pasting Multiple Copies of the Same Data in a Single Operation

When you cut or copy the contents of a cell or a range, they are placed in the Windows Clipboard. You can then paste this data to many areas of a worksheet in one operation. To paste multiple copies of the same data:

1. Cut or copy the contents of the cell or range.

2. Select multiple nonadjacent paste areas.

3. Click on Edit in the menu bar to open the Edit menu.

4. Click on Paste. The contents of the Clipboard are pasted into each paste area.

You cannot paste multiple copies of the same data in one paste operation using the Insert Paste command.

N O T E

Moving or Copying Cell Contents Using the Formula Bar

You can use the formula bar to copy or move the contents of a cell. Copying data in the formula bar is useful if you need to move or copy repeated characters to different locations in the same cell or to other cells. Moving data in the formula bar allows you to rearrange the order of the data in the cell or to move it to other cells.

To move or copy data in the formula bar:

1. Select the cell that contains the characters you want to move or copy.
2. Click on the formula bar and select the characters you want to move or copy.
3. Click on Edit in the menu bar to open the Edit menu.
4. Click on either Cut or Copy.
5. To move or copy the characters to another cell, select the cell and press Enter.
6. To insert the cut or copied characters in the formula bar, position your insertion point where you want to paste the characters.
7. Click on Edit in the menu bar.
8. Click on Paste.

Undoing a Command or Action

If you execute a command in your worksheet and then realize you made a mistake, you can reverse the command by using the Undo feature. For example, suppose you moved an entire block of data and then realized that you moved the wrong block. Undo can immediately reverse the command and return your worksheet to the same condition it was in before you moved the block. To undo a command:

1. Click on Edit in the menu bar to open the Edit menu.
2. Click on Undo. The Undo command in the menu reflects the last command or action taken. In the example above, the Undo command would say Undo Paste, as shown in Figure 4.14.

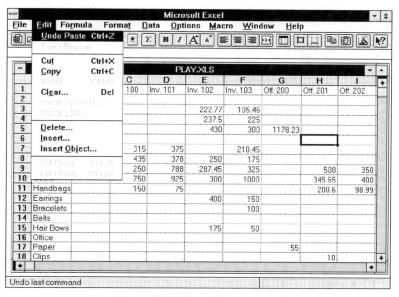

Figure 4.14. The Undo command.

If, after you undo a command, you change your mind again, you can chose the Redo command and the command you undid will be executed.

You can only undo or redo the last command you chose or the last cell entry you typed or edited. If you make a mistake, you must undo or redo immediately. Undo will not reverse the effects of the File Delete, Data Delete, or Data Extract commands.

N O T E

Repeating a Command

You can repeat the last command you executed using the Repeat feature. For example, if you copied and pasted data and then realized that you wanted to copy to two paste areas in your worksheet, you could repeat the command and paste the data to a second location. To repeat a command:

1. Click in the cell or area where you want to repeat the command.
2. Click on Edit in the menu bar to open the Edit menu.
3. Click on Repeat. The Repeat command reflects the most recent command you executed. In the example above, the Repeat command would say *Repeat Paste*.

Finding Cells and Data

The Find feature lets you search through a worksheet to find cells that contain specific data or formulas. For example, you might want to find all cells that contain the data *500*. Instead of scrolling through the entire worksheet, you can use Find to locate each cell that contains this data. To find data in a worksheet:

1. You can search forward or backward from the active cell. If you want to search forward through the entire worksheet, select a single cell at the beginning of the worksheet. To search only part of the worksheet, select the range you want to search.

2. Click on Formula in the menu bar to open the Formula menu.

3. Click on Find. The Find dialog box is displayed, as shown in Figure 4.15.

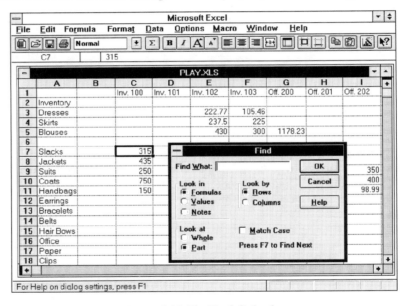

Figure 4.15. The Find dialog box.

4. In the Find What text box type in the characters you are searching for. These characters can include any letter, number, punctuation, or DOS wildcard (DOS wildcards are covered in Chapter 10). Unless you enable Match Case, the search function is not case-sensitive. If you search for a character that is also used as a DOS wildcard (? or *), you must precede the character with a tilde (~).

5. In the Look In option box indicate whether you want to search for cell formulas, cell values, or cell notes. You can search for only one option at a time. If you want to search for more than one option (for example, values and notes) you must repeat the search for each option.

6. In the Look At option box select either Whole, to search for a complete and exact match of the characters you entered in the Find What text box, or Part, to locate all cells that contain the characters as all or part of a word. For example, if you entered *Pen* in the Find What text box and selected Whole, Find would locate only those cells containing *Pen*. The cell could not contain anything else. If you selected Part, Find would locate all of the cells that contained those characters anywhere in the cell, such as *Red Pen* and *Pens*.

7. In the Look By option box, select either Rows to search across rows, or Columns to search up and down columns.

8. If you enable Match Case, Find will locate only cells whose contents exactly match the uppercase and lowercase entries in the Find What text box.

9. To search forward from the active cell, click on OK. To search backward through the worksheet from the active cell, hold down the Shift key and click on OK.

10. Find will stop at the first matching cell. To find the next matching cell, press F7.

Finding and Replacing Data in Cells

You can use the Replace command to search for the contents of a cell and replace them with different contents. The Replace feature searches only the actual contents of a cell. It does not search for notes or for values produced by formulas. For example, if you search for *500*, Replace will locate only those cells in which you typed *500*. If you have a cell that contains a formula whose result is 500, Replace will not locate that cell. To find and replace the contents of a cell:

1. You can search forward or backward from the active cell. If you want to search forward through the entire worksheet, select a single cell at the beginning of the worksheet. To search and replace only part of the worksheet, select the range you want to search.

2. Click on Formula in the menu bar to open the Formula menu.

3. Click on Replace. The Replace dialog box is displayed, as shown in Figure 4.16.

4. In the Find What text box, type the characters you are searching for. These characters can include any letter, number, punctuation, or DOS wildcard (DOS wildcards are covered in Chapter 10). Unless you enable the option, the search function is not case-sensitive. If you search for a character that is also used as a DOS wildcard (? or *), you must precede the character with a tilde (~).

5. In the Look At option box, select either Whole, to search for a complete and exact match of the characters you entered in the Find What text box, or Part, to locate all occurrences of the characters within the cells.

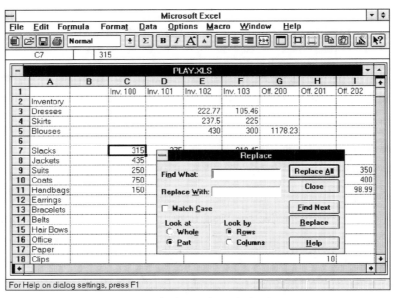

Figure 4.16. The Replace dialog box.

6. In the Look By option box, select Rows to search across rows, or Columns to search up and down columns.

7. If you enable Match Case, Replace will locate only cells where the contents exactly match the uppercase and lowercase entries in the Find What text box.

8. If you want to replace the data in the active cell, choose Replace. Excel replaces the data in the active cell and finds the next occurrence of the characters you are replacing. To search backward from the active cell, press Shift and click on Replace.

9. If you want to skip the active cell without replacing the data and go on to find the next occurrence of the data, chose the Find Next button. To search backward from the active cell, press Shift and click on Find Next.

10. If you are sure that you want to replace every occurrence of the data in the worksheet or range (without viewing them first), you can use the Replace All. This is much faster, but it gives you no control over individual replacements. You will not see the replacements occurring, but the changes will be made. Replace All can be risky. Be certain you want to change *all* occurrences of the data. Often it is best to do the first several occurrences one at a time, just to be sure.

11. When you are finished, choose Close to return to the worksheet.

Review Exercises for Chapter 4

- ◆ Practice selecting cells and ranges in PLAY.XLS.
- ◆ Practice moving from one area of the worksheet to another using the mouse and mouse/keyboard movement and selection keys.
- ◆ Use the GoTo command to select a range.
- ◆ Use the SUM function to total row 3 in PLAY.XLS.
- ◆ Copy the formula to the rest of the rows in PLAY.XLS using your mouse or mouse/keyboard to select the range to which you will copy.
- ◆ Clear all of the formulas in the worksheet.
- ◆ Use the Undo command to cancel the last action.
- ◆ Practice inserting and deleting rows and columns.
- ◆ Practice moving and copying cells and ranges.

Before You Go On...

Before you continue on to the next chapter, you should be able to move around a worksheet easily and quickly using the mouse and mouse/keyboard movement and selection keys. You should know how to select ranges as well as multiple nonadjacent ranges. You should understand the difference between relative and absolute references. You should be able to move or copy data within a worksheet. You should know how to edit cells and how to delete data in cells and ranges. You should be able to use the Find and Replace features.

Chapter 5

FORMATTING YOUR WORKSHEET

What You Will Learn in This Chapter

- How to use printer fonts and display fonts
- How to use built-in and custom number formats
- How to align data in cells
- How to change column width
- How to change row height
- How to hide and unhide columns and rows
- How to apply borders and shading to cells and ranges
- How to use patterns in a worksheet
- How to use Autoformat
- How to change your worksheet display

Previous chapters focused on some important basics. Though it is necessary to master these features, they produce rather dull results. In this chapter, you are going to learn to use Excel to produce worksheets that allow you to express your imagination and personality.

The worksheets you have produced so far use Excel's default settings. The programmers at Microsoft made certain decisions regarding the generic formatting of worksheets. These decisions determine the appearance of your worksheet when it is printed. You will be happy to learn that you are not forced to use these settings; you can change some or all of them at any point in a worksheet. By changing margins, column widths, row heights, cell borders, and other formatting features, you can change the entire appearance of a worksheet. Simple enhancements, such as boldface or underlining, can also change the impact of your data. By applying these formatting features you will be able to create polished and attractive worksheets.

Using Fonts to Enhance Your Worksheet

The ability to recognize fonts is a powerful feature of Excel. Fonts allow you to enhance your data by changing the size and appearance of your type. For example, you might select a very large font, or an italic typeface. Using a variety of typefaces in your worksheets will add aesthetic appeal and sophistication to your work.

Excel differentiates between **printer fonts**, which are fonts that your printer recognizes and will print, and **screen display fonts**, which will appear on the screen but will not always print.

Printer Fonts

Printer fonts are fonts that are recognized by your printer. Your printer comes with its own, internal set of fonts. Most laser printers also allow you to add fonts using either **soft fonts** or **print cartridges**. In order to use soft fonts and cartridges with Excel, they must be properly installed, and your Microsoft Windows printer driver must be configured to recognize them. (See Chapter 9 for information on how fonts work with your printer, and Appendix A for information on how to configure Windows to recognize them).

If you are using Windows 3.1, you also have **Truetype fonts**, which are installed with the program. These are scalable fonts that allow you to change the point size of the font when you select it.

Screen Display Fonts

Screen display fonts are installed with Windows. They determine how your worksheet will appear in the document window. If your printer driver does not recognize the display font you select, your worksheet will be displayed on the screen with the font, but it will print with the default print font. Display fonts are useful if you are doing a presentation on a large monitor, or if you wish to create on-screen slide show presentations.

Your screen display may be limited by your monitor or video card.

N O T E

Selecting Fonts

To select a font:

1. Select the cell, range, or worksheet you want to format.
2. Click on Format in the menu bar.
3. Click on Font. The Font dialog box is displayed, as shown in Figure 5.1.

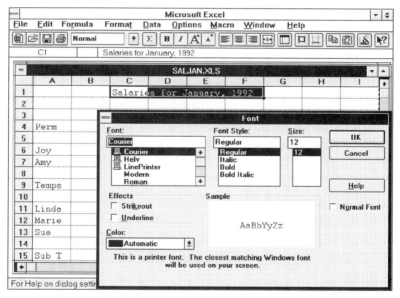

Figure 5.1. The Font dialog box.

4. Select a font. The font list box contains a list of all of the fonts available. Printer fonts are identified by a printer graphic next to the font name, and Truetype fonts are identified by a Truetype logo next to the font name. If a font does not have either a printer graphic or a Truetype logo next to it, it is a screen display font, and will not print. When you select either a printer font or a Truetype font, you will see a prompt in the bottom of the Font dialog box that says `This is a printer font. The closest matching Windows font will be used on your screen`. Most laser printers can print up to 300 **dpi** (dots per inch). Your screen does not have this

capability, so Windows will try to match the resolution of your selected font as closely as possible.

5. Choose OK.

Font Style and Size

You can use font attributes to change the appearance or size of a font you have selected. For example, suppose you are using a particular font and you want the data you have selected to be in italics. You can tell Excel to change your data to italics by selecting the Italic font style in the Font dialog box. To change a font style or size:

1. Select the cell, range, or worksheet you want to format.
2. Click on Format in the menu bar.
3. Click on Font to display the Font dialog box.
4. Select the style or size you want. If you choose a style or size that is not available on your printer, another style or size will be substituted when you print your worksheet.
5. Click on OK.

Font Color

You can also change the color of the contents of the cell, range, or worksheet. This attribute depends entirely upon your hardware. If you do not have a color monitor, you cannot change color. If you do not have a color printer, the changed color will appear on your screen display but will not print. To change a color attribute:

1. Select the cell, range, or worksheet you want to format.
2. Click on Format in the menu bar.
3. Click on Font to display the Font dialog box.
4. Click on Color to open the Color drop-down list. Select a color.
5. Click on OK.

Underline and Strikeout

Underline can be used to underline a cell, range, or worksheet. Strikeout is used to indicate a particular cell or range of data by drawing a line through the data, as shown in Figure 5.2.

Underline and strikeout can be selected separately, or they can both be selected for the cell or range you have chosen. To select underline or strikeout:

1. Select the cell or range you want to format.
2. Click on Format in the menu bar.
3. Click on Font to display the Font dialog box.

4. In the Effects box, select Underline, Strikeout, or both.

5. Click on OK.

Figure 5.2. Example of Strikeout in a worksheet.

Returning to the Default Display Font

Excel automatically defaults to a particular screen display font, which is used to display the worksheet in your document window. If you are using Windows 3.0, the default screen display font in Excel is Helvetica (Helv) 10. If you are using Windows 3.1, the default is sans serif 10. When you return to the default display font, any font or font attributes previously used in the cell or range you select will no longer be in effect. To return to the default font:

1. Select the cell or range you want to format.

2. Click on Format in the menu bar.

3. Click on Font to display the Font dialog box.

4. Enable Normal font.

5. Click on OK.

When you select a font or font attribute, the Sample box in the Font dialog box displays a sample showing how that font or font attribute will look in your worksheet.

N O T E

Understanding Number Formats

Number formats determine how your numbers will appear in a worksheet. Excel contains many types of number formats, and you can also create your own custom formats.

To understand how number formats work in Excel, you must understand what constitutes a number, and how number values are identified by Excel.

Understanding Number Values

As you learned in Chapter 2, two basic types of data can be entered into a worksheet: constant values and formulas. Constant values are information you type into a cell. They can be changed only if you edit the information. Formulas are instructions entered into a cell that calculate new values from the existing values. The results of a formula will change if you change the existing values used in its calculation.

The syntax you use when typing constant values into cells tells Excel what type of constant value you are using. There are two types of data you can input when using constant values: numbers and text. Text is identified as a text value. Numbers have three types of values: date, time, and numeric. Even though a formula value is not constant, the result of a formula is a number, and its appearance can be affected by applying built-in formats. Numeric values are made up of the following types of data: scientific, fractions, percentages, and whole and negative numbers.

Each type of value has its own syntax, as discussed below. The syntax determines what kind of value you are using—not solely whether your characters are alpha or numeric. For example, the number sequence 12345 is recognized as a text value as long as it is preceded by a single quotation mark ('). You will also note that while the a date value is considered a number, it can include text. For example, the format mmm-yy could be typed in as Mar-92.

Text Values

Text values can contain any alpha character or any combination of alpha and numeric or punctuation characters. Numeric values can be changed to text values if the characters in the data string are preceded by a single quotation mark ('). A cell can contain up to 255 text characters.

Syntax	Appears as
ABCD	ABCD
abcd	abcd
TC2v4	TC2v4
R&R	R&R
'12345	12345

Numeric Values

Numeric values can contain numeric characters and the following specific special characters:
+ - ( ) , / $ % . E e

Syntax	Appears as
67.22E+12	67.22E+12
-450	-450
$123.45	$123.45
12,345	12,345
(450)	(450)
1 1/2	1 1/2
8.5%	8.5%

Date Values

Date values are identified as numbers in Excel and usually follow one of the listed built-in formats. You can type either upper or lowercase letters in dates.

Syntax	Appears as
m/d/yy	03/31/92
d-mmm-yy	31-Mar-92
d-mmm	31-Mar
mmm-yy	Mar-92
m/d/yy h:mm	3/31/92 15:52

Time Values

Time values are identified as numbers in Excel and follow one of the listed formats. If you do not specify AM or PM, Excel will display the time using the 24-hour clock (Navy Time). Time formats are not case-sensitive—you can use either upper or lowercase AM or PM.

Syntax	Appears as
h:mm AM/PM	5:23 PM
h:mm:ss AM/PM	5:23:35 PM
h:mm	17:23
h:mm:ss	17:23:35
m/d/yy h:mm	3/31/92 17:23

Using Built-In Number Formats

Built-in number formats change the appearance of numbers. All cells in Excel start with the default general number format. So far, all of our worksheets have used only the general number format. In addition to the general number format, Excel comes with a number of built-in formats. These can be applied to numbers to change the way they appear in the worksheet. (The original syntax you used to type in the number will not change.) When you type a number into a cell formatted as general, Excel may assign a built-in number format depending upon what characters you type into the number. For example, if you type a dollar sign ($) when you are entering a number, Excel will assign that cell a currency format. If you type a percent sign (%) when you are entering a number, Excel will assign that cell a percentage format. (Remember, however, as explained above, a number is recognized as a number in Excel only if its syntax identifies it as a numeric, time, or date value.)

Although you can assign a built-in number format to each cell, it is faster to enter all of your numbers, then select a range and change the formatting for the range. If you select a cell(s) that contains text, it will not be affected by changing the number format. Selected blank cells *will* have their formatting changed, however; if you enter numbers at a later date they will appear with the format you have chosen. The built-in number formats (called **categories**) and their format codes are listed in Table 5.1. You can use any of these formats or create your own custom number formats.

Built-in number formats are divided into eight categories. Except for the General category, all of the format codes are made up of symbols that represent how the number will look when it is formatted. When the format code in a category has two sections separated by a semicolon (;), the first section determines how positive numbers will appear and the second section determines how negative numbers will appear. If the second section has [RED] in it, negative numbers will be displayed in red if you have a color monitor.

A few notes about the following table: The All category contains the General format code and all of the format codes in all of the categories that follow.

Category	Format Code	Pos. Value	Neg. Value	Fraction
All	General	5	-5	0.5
Number	0	5	-5	1**
	0.00	5.00	-5.00	0.5
	#,##0	5	-5	1**
	#,##0.00	5.00	-5.00	0.5
	#,##0_);(#,##0)	5	(5)	1**
	#,##0_);[RED](#,##0)	5	(5)*	1**
	#,##0.00_);(#,##0.00)	5.00	(5.00)	0.5
	#,##0.00_);[RED](#,##0.00)	5.00	(5.00)*	0.5
Currency	$#,##0_);($#,##0)	$5	($5)	$1**
	$#,##0_);[RED]($#,##0)	$5	($5)*	$1**
	$#,##0.00_0;($#,##0.00)	$5.00	($5.00)	$0.50
	$#,##0.00_);[RED]($#,##0.00)	$5.00	($5.00)*	$0.50
Percentage	0%	500%	-500%	50%
	0.00%	500.00%	-500.00%	50.00%
Fraction	# ?/?	5	-5	1/2
	# ??/??	5	-5	1/2
Scientific	0.00E+00	5.00E+00	-5.00E.00	5.00E+00

Category	Format Code	Looks Like
Date	m/d/yy	4/28/92
	d-mmm-yy	28-Apr-92
	d-mmm	28-Apr
	mmm-yy	Apr-92
	m/d/yy h:mm	4/28/92 9:40
Time	h:mmm AM/PM	9:40 AM
	h:mm:ss AM/PM	9:40:50 AM
	h:mm	9:40
	h:mm:ss	9:40:50
	m/d/yy h:mm	4/28/92 9:40

* If you have a color monitor, this number will be displayed in red.

** If a number has more digits to the right of the decimal point than the format code, the number is rounded to as many decimal places as there are zeros to the right of the decimal point in the format code. If there are no zeros to the right of the decimal point in the format code, the number is rounded to the nearest whole number. For example, the format code 0 contains no decimal places, therefore, .4 would be rounded to 0, and .5 would be rounded to 1. If the format code contained one decimal place (0.0) and the number was .44, the number would be rounded to .4; if the number was .45, the number would be rounded to .5.

Table 5.1. Built-in Number Formats.

Let's use the currency format to add dollar signs and two decimal places to all of the numbers in the first row of figures in EXPJAN.XLS.

1. Open the EXPJAN.XLS worksheet.
2. Select row 7.
3. Click on Format in the menu bar.
4. Click on Number to display the Number Format dialog box, as shown in Figure 5.3.

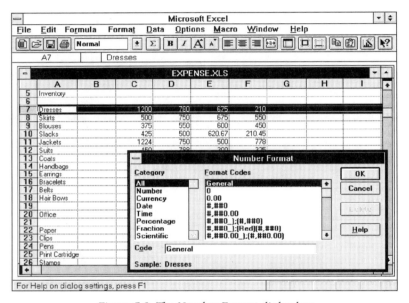

Figure 5.3. The Number Format dialog box.

5. Click on Currency in the Category list box. All of the built-in formats available for currency appear in the Format Codes list box. Select the option that will format your numbers with a dollar sign ($) and two decimal places. The selection appears in the Code text box, as shown in Figure 5.4.

   If your active cell contains a number (in this case it contains text), the Sample line at the bottom of the dialog box will show you how the number will appear in this format. If your active cell contains text, the text will appear in the Sample line. It will not be affected by the number format.

6. Click on OK.

Notice that even though you selected the entire row, only the cells that contain numbers are affected by the number format.

Let's format the rest of the numbers in the EXPJAN.XLS worksheet (except the totals). To add two decimal places but no dollar sign:

1. Select the range C8 through R34.

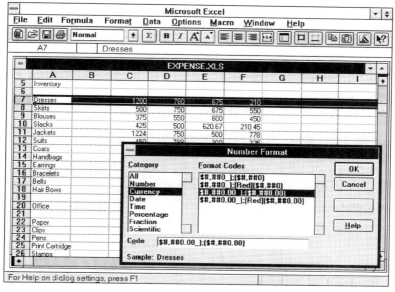

Figure 5.4. The Code text box showing the dollar sign selection.

2. Click on Format in the menu bar.

3. Click on Number to display the Number Format dialog box.

4. Click on Number in the Category list box. All of the built-in format codes available for the numbers category appear in the Format Codes list box. Select the option for formatting the numbers with two decimal places, as shown in the Sample line in the bottom of the Number Format dialog box and in Figure 5.5.

5. Click on OK.

Finally, let's format the totals in EXPJAN.XLS, using the currency format to add dollar signs and two decimal places to all of the totals in row 36.

1. Select row 36.

2. Click on Format in the menu bar.

3. Click on Number to display the Number Format dialog box.

4. Click on Currency in the Category list box. All of the built-in format codes available for currency appear in the Format Codes list box. Select the option for formatting the numbers with dollar signs and two decimal places, as shown in Figure 5.4.

5. Click on OK. Save your worksheet.

Your worksheet now looks like the one shown in Figure 5.6. Some of the numbers in row 36 have been replaced by number signs (#). Do not worry about this. It indicates that the cell is not wide enough to contain the formatted number. We will fix this later in the chapter. All of the numbers in the first row are formatted with dollar signs, commas separating the thousands, and two decimal places. All of the numbers in cells C8 through R34 have commas separating thousands and have two decimal places. You cannot see all of the numbers in row 36, but they have been formatted with dollar signs, commas separating the thousands, and two decimal places.

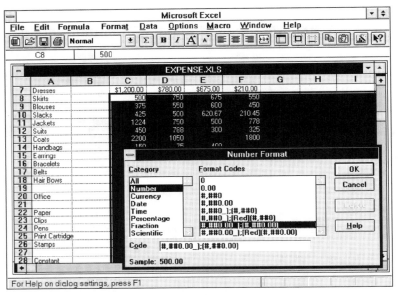

Figure 5.5. The option for formatting the numbers with two decimal places.

Using Date Formats

Finally, let's add a date to our worksheet. Type today's date in cell A1 of EXPJAN.XLS, following this format: 4/21/92 (month/day/year). To change the format of the date in this cell:

1. Select cell A1.
2. Click on Format in the menu bar.
3. Click on Number to display the Number Format dialog box.
4. Click on Date in the Category list box. All of the built-in format codes for dates appear in the Format Codes list box. Select the code that will format your date as 21-Apr-92.
5. Click on OK.

Your date format has now been changed to reflect your choice. Built-in date and time formats are shown in Table 5.1.

	A	B	C	D	E	F	G	H	I	J	K	L	M	N	O	P	Q	R	S
1																			
2																			
3																			
4			Inv. 100	Inv. 101	Inv. 102	Inv. 103	Off. 200	Off. 201	Off. 202	Rent	Phone	Electric	Salaries	Tax FIC	Tax Fed	Tax State	Tax City	Tax Dis	Totals
5	Inventory																		
6																			
7	Dresses		$1,200.00	$780.00	$675.00	$210.00													$2,865.00
8	Skirts		500.00	750.00	875.00	550.00													2,475.00
9	Blouses		375.00	550.00	800.00	450.00													1,975.00
10	Slacks		425.00	500.00	620.67	210.45													1,756.12
11	Jackets		1,224.00	750.00	500.00	778.00													3,252.00
12	Suits		450.00	788.00	300.00	325.00													1,863.00
13	Coats		2,200.00	1,050.00		1,800.00													5,050.00
14	Handbags		150.00	75.00	400.00														625.00
15	Earrings				500.00	150.00													650.00
16	Bracelets					100.00													100.00
17	Belts				175.00														175.00
18	Hair Bows					50.00													50.00
19																			
20	Office																		0.00
21																			
22	Paper						55.00												55.00
23	Clips							10.00											10.00
24	Pens							25.00											25.00
25	Print Cartridge							100.00											100.00
26	Stamps								50.00										50.00
27																			
28	Constant																		0.00
29																			
30	Rent									2,500.00									2,500.00
31	Phone										375.23								375.23
32	Electric											305.78							305.78
33	Salaries												5,980.00						5,980.00
34	Taxes													598.00	700.00	400.00	150.00	75.00	1,923.00
35																			
36	Totals		$6,524.00	#####	#####	#####	$55.00	#####	$50.00	#####	####	####	#####	####	$700.00	$400.00	$150.00	$75.00	######

Figure 5.6. EXPJAN worksheet with built-in number formats.

Creating a New Number Format

In addition to the built-in number formats included with Excel, you can create custom number formats and add them to the Format Codes in the appropriate category. Appendix F lists all of the symbols that can be used in creating a custom number format.

To add a custom number format:

1. Select the cell or range to which you want to apply the custom number format. (If you select a blank cell, you will still be able to add a number format, but the cell will be formatted with the new format. If you later forget that you have formatted this cell and enter a number in it, the number will reflect the custom format.)
2. Click on Format in the menu bar.
3. Click on Number to display the Number Format dialog box.
4. Click on the Category in which you wish to add a custom format.
5. In the Code text box use the Backspace key to erase the existing built-in number format, and type the new number format you wish to add. The existing format will be replaced by the new custom number format.
6. Click on OK. The custom number format has been added to the Format Codes list box, and the cell or range you selected has been formatted with it.

Let's add a custom number format in the Date Category:

1. Click on cell A1.
2. Click on Format in the menu bar.
3. Click on Number to display the Number Format dialog box.
4. Click on Date. A list of date format codes appears in the Format Codes list box.
5. In the Code text box, use the backspace key to erase the existing built-in number format, and type *d/mmm/yyyy*.
6. Click on OK. The new custom number format has been added to the Format Codes list box, and the contents of the cell you selected appear in the worksheet with the new custom number format, as shown in Figure 5.7.

Deleting a Number Format

When you delete a custom number format, any cell or range in the worksheet containing this format will default to the general number format. To delete a custom number format:

1. Click on Format in the menu bar.
2. Click on Number to display the Number Format dialog box.
3. Click on the Category in which you wish to delete a format.
4. In the Format Codes list box, select the custom format you wish to delete.
5. Click on Delete.

6. Click on OK. The custom number format has been deleted from the Format Codes list box. The custom number format has also been deleted from any cells or ranges containing the format and they have been changed to a general number format.

N O T E

You can only delete custom number formats. Built-in number formats cannot be deleted.

Figure 5.7. Cell A1 reflects the new custom number format.

Aligning Data in Cells and Ranges

Aligning data in cells determines the location of the data in the cells. Excel allows you to align data to the left, right, top, bottom, of a cell, or to center it vertically or horizontally. You can repeat characters across an entire cell, rotate the text in a cell, center text across a selected group of columns, align text vertically in the top, center, or bottom of a cell, wrap long entries in a cell, and justify wrapped text in a cell. Figure 5.8 shows a worksheet with different types of aligned data. The default align setting in Excel is the General Alignment Option Data, entered using the General alignment option automatically places text to the left of a cell, numbers to the right, and errors values in the center. When you select a range, the data in each cell of the range is aligned.

Horizontal Alignment

Horizontal alignment aligns data horizontally within a cell. You can use Left, Center, Right, Fill, Justify, and Center Across Selection.

Cells A4 through A9 in Figure 5.8 show left-aligned text. The text is aligned at the left border of the cells. You can left-align any type of data in a cell.

Cells D4 through D9 in Figure 5.8 show the result of using center alignment. The text in each of the selected cells is centered between the left and right borders of each cell. You can center-align any type of data in a cell.

Cells B4 through B9 in Figure 5.8 are an example of right-aligned text. The text in each cell is aligned at the right border of the cell. You can right-align any type of data in a cell.

	A	B	C	D	E	F	G	H	I
1				*Fun with Formatting*					
2	This worksheet shows samples of alignment		This is a sample of text which has been justified			C a t s			
3	Cats	Age		Coat					
4	Tabby	8.00		Gray & White					
5	Cleo	7.50		Black & White		********************************			
6	Sheba	7.00		Black		*Household Pets*			
7	Soph	6.00		Tabby		********************************			
8	Sally	5.00		Tabby					
9	Lila	4.50		Tabby					

Figure 5.8. Worksheet showing different types of aligned text.

The Fill option repeats the contents of a selected cell until the cell is filled. If blank cells to the right of the active cell have been selected and the Fill option is enabled, the blank cells are also filled with the contents of the active cell. Cell F5 originally contained one asterisk (*). When cells F5 through H5 were selected and the Fill option was used, the asterisk repeated to fill all of the cells in the range. You can use the Fill option to repeat any kind of data in a cell or range.

Justify aligns text at both the right and left borders of a cell. The justify command can be used only with cells that contain text. If you select cells that contain numbers or formulas, a prompt appears informing you that nontext cells are in the selection. Cell C1 in Figure 5.8 is an example of wrapped text that has been justified.

Cell B1 in Figure 5.8 is an example of how data looks when it has been centered across a selection of columns. The data is typed in one cell and then centered across selected columns. You can use the Center Across Selection alignment option with any kind of data.

Wrap Text

Wrap Text is used when data does not fit between the left and right borders of the cell. The text wraps to a new line at the cell's right border, and the row height adjusts to accommodate it. Cell A1 in Figure 5.8 is an example of wrapped text.

You can insert returns (using Enter) and tabs into data that has been wrapped. Wrap Text can be used with any type of data in a cell.

Vertical Alignment

Vertical alignment aligns text vertically within a cell. You can use Top, Center, and Bottom vertical alignment.

Cell A3 in Figure 5.8 contains text that has been vertically aligned at the top of the cell. Top align can be used with any type of data in a cell.

Cell B3 in Figure 5.8 contains text that has been vertically aligned in the center of the cell. Center align can be with used with any type of data in a cell.

Cell C3 in Figure 5.8 contains text that has been vertically aligned at the bottom of the cell. Bottom align can be used with any type of data in a cell.

Orientation

The Orientation feature rotates the data in a cell. The row height automatically adjusts to accommodate the rotated data. There are four orientation choices. The selections under Orientation in your Alignment dialog box show the direction the data will be rotated for each selection. Cell F2 in Figure 5.8 shows how text appears when it has been rotated. You can rotate any type of data in a cell.

Aligning Data

To apply the preceding alignment options:

1. Select the cell or range you want to format.
2. Click on Format in the menu bar.
3. Click on Alignment. The Alignment dialog box is displayed, as shown in Figure 5.9. Figure 5.9.
4. Select the alignment options you want.
5. Click on OK.

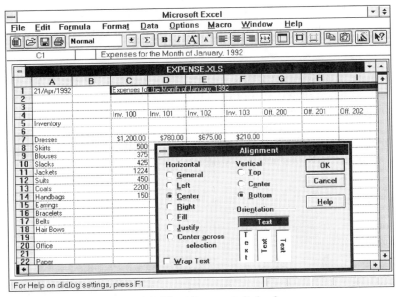

Figure 5.9. The Alignment dialog box.

Let's add a title to our EXPJAN.XLS worksheet and then center it across a selection.

1. In cell C1, type *Expenses for the Month of January, 1992.*
2. Select cells C1 through R1.
3. Click on Format in the menu bar.
4. Click on Alignment to display the Alignment dialog box.
5. Select Center across selection in the Horizontal options box.
6. Click on OK.

Your title is now centered between columns C and R.

Adding Returns or Tabs to Wrapped Text

You can enter returns and tabs in cells with wrapped text.

1. Select the cell or range in which you have wrapped text.
2. To insert a return, click on the location in the formula bar where you want the return to take effect, and press Alt+Enter. To insert a tab, click on the location in the formula bar where you want the tab to take effect and press Ctrl+Tab.

Changing Column Width

When we formatted the numbers in the EXPJAN.XLS worksheet, in some of the cells the numbers were replaced with number signs (#). This happens when you enter more numbers than can fit between the borders of a cell. If you enter more text than can fit between cell borders and the Wrap Text feature has not been selected, one of two things will happen. If there are any blank cells to the right of the active cell, the text will extend across columns into the blank cells. If there are no blank cells or not enough blank cells to the right of the active cell for the text to fit, the text will appear in the formula bar, but only the text that can fit in the active and blank cells will be displayed in the worksheet and printed. You can remedy this situation by changing the widths of the affected columns. When you change the width of one cell in a column, the entire column changes to accommodate the new width.

There is more than one way to change the width of a column:

1. Position your pointer (the shape will change to a horizontal double-headed arrow bisected by a vertical line) on the right border of the column heading whose width you want to change.
2. Drag the column to the width you want.

Or,

1. Select a cell in a column, in a range, or in multiple nonadjacent ranges.
2. Click on Format in the menu bar.
3. Click on Column Width to display the Column Width dialog box, as shown in Figure 5.10, on the next page.
4. The Column Width text box contains the default column width. The number represents the number of characters that will fit in the cells in the column according to the font type and size. If you have too many characters for your font or size, your data will not fit into the cell. Type in the width you want for the column.
5. Click on OK.

Or,

1. Select the cell in the column that contains the longest data string. You may also select ranges or multiple nonadjacent ranges.
2. Click on Format in the menu bar.
3. Click on Column Width to display the Column Width dialog box.
4. Click on Best Fit.

Excel automatically determines the best width for your column and adjusts it accordingly. When you use the Best Fit option, Excel adjusts the column width to accommodate the length of the data in the cell you have selected.

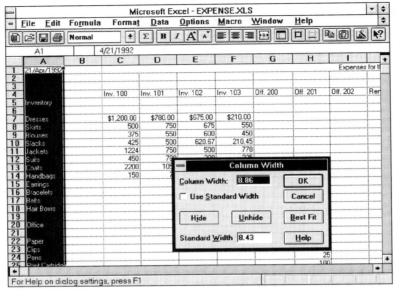

Figure 5.10. The Column Width dialog box.

Let's adjust the column widths in EXPJAN.XLS. The cells that contain too much data are located in rows 25 and 36. We are going to use Best Fit to adjust the column widths.

1. Select cells C36 through S36.
2. Click on Format in the menu bar.
3. Click on Column Width to display the Column Width dialog box.
4. Click on Best Fit.

The number signs have been replaced by the formatted totals in row 36. EXPJAN.XLS is almost done. The words *Print Cartridge* in cell A25 do not fit in the standard column width.

1. Click on cell A25.
2. Click on Format in the menu bar.
3. Click on Column Width to display the Column Width dialog box.
4. Click on Best Fit.

Save your worksheet, which now looks like the one shown in Figure 5.11.

Changing Row Height

Row height will change to accommodate font and size changes. It will not change if you rotate text in a cell and then change your mind, or if you have wrapped text in a cell and then deleted some of the text in the cell. When this happens, you will need to change the row height manually.

Expenses for the Month of January, 1992

	A	C	D	E	F	G	H	I	J	K	L	M	N	O	P	Q	R	S
1	21/Apr/1992																	
4		Inv. 100	Inv. 101	Inv. 102	Inv. 103	Off. 200	Off. 201	Off. 202	Rent	Phone	Electric	Salaries	Tax FICA	Tax Fed	Tax State	Tax City	Tax Dis	Totals
5	Inventory																	
7	Dresses	$1,200.00	$780.00	$675.00	$210.00													$2,885.00
8	Skirts	500.00	750.00	675.00	550.00													2,475.00
9	Blouses	375.00	550.00	600.00	450.00													1,975.00
10	Slacks	425.00	500.00	620.67	210.45													1,756.12
11	Jackets	1,224.00	750.00	500.00	778.00													3,252.00
12	Suits	450.00	788.00	300.00	325.00													1,863.00
13	Coats	2,200.00	1,050.00		1,800.00													5,050.00
14	Handbags	150.00	75.00	400.00														625.00
15	Earrings			500.00	150.00													650.00
16	Bracelets				100.00													100.00
17	Belts			175.00														175.00
18	Hair Bows				50.00													50.00
19																		
20	Office																	0.00
22	Paper					55.00												55.00
23	Clips						10.00											10.00
24	Pens						25.00											25.00
25	Print Cartridge						100.00											100.00
26	Stamps							50.00										50.00
28	Constant																	0.00
30	Rent								2,500.00									2,500.00
31	Phone									375.23								375.23
32	Electric										305.78							305.78
33	Salaries											5,980.00						5,980.00
34	Taxes												598.00	700.00	400.00	150.00	75.00	1,923.00
36	Totals	$6,524.00	$5,243.00	$4,445.87	$4,623.45	$55.00	$135.00	$50.00	$2,500.00	$375.23	$305.78	$5,980.00	$598.00	$700.00	$400.00	$150.00	$75.00	$32,160.13

Figure 5.11. The worksheet with column widths changed.

When you change the height of one cell in a row, the entire row adjusts to accommodate the new cell height. To change the height of several adjacent rows, select a range. If you want to change the height of cells in nonadjacent rows, select a multiple nonadjacent range. To change row height:

1. In the row header, position your pointer on the bottom or top border of the row whose height you want to change.
2. Drag the row up or down to the height you want.

Or,

1. Select a cell in a row or range, or select multiple nonadjacent ranges.
2. Click on Format in the menu bar.
3. Click on Row Height to display the Row Height dialog box, as shown in Figure 5.12.

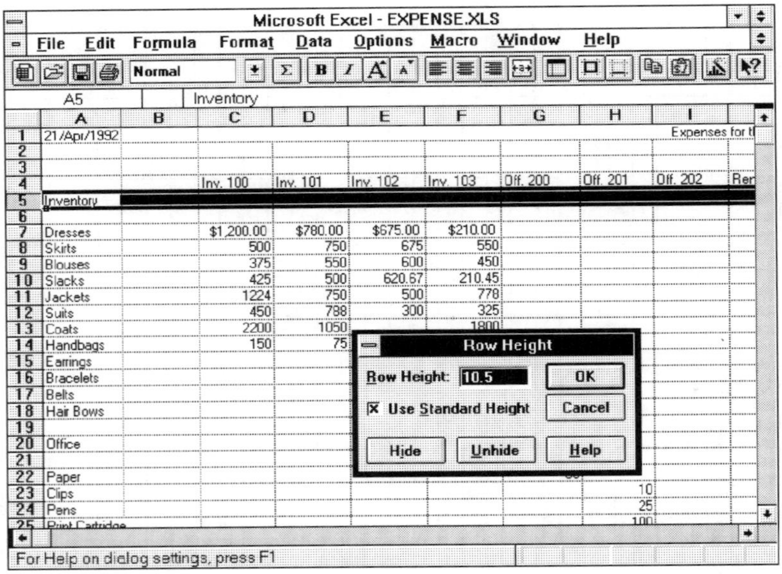

Figure 5.12. The Row Height dialog box.

4. The Row Height text box contains the current row height. Type in the height you want for the row.
5. Click on OK.

Or,

1. Select a cell in a row or range, or multiple nonadjacent ranges whose height you wish to change.
2. Click on Format in the menu bar.

3. Click on Row Height to display the Row Height dialog box.

4. Select Use Standard Height. Excel will calculate the best height for the row.

Hiding Columns and Rows

When you hide a column or a row, the data is not seen on the screen and it is not printed out. This is useful if you have a worksheet that contains some sensitive data that you do not want others to see. You can hide the columns or rows that contain the sensitive data and print out the worksheet showing the rest of the data. You can hide single columns or rows, ranges, or multiple nonadjacent ranges. Let's practice hiding columns and rows using the PLAY.XLS worksheet.

1. Open the PLAY.XLS worksheet.

2. Select columns C and D.

3. Click on Format in the menu bar.

4. Click on Column Width to display the Column Width dialog box.

5. Click on Hide. Columns C and D are now hidden. Notice that the column headings now read A, B, E, F, and so on, and that the border between columns B and E is much heavier. This indicates that there are hidden columns.

Now let's hide a row:

1. Select row A12.

2. Click on Format in the menu bar.

3. Click on Row Height. The Row Height dialog box is displayed, as shown in Figure 5.12.

4. Click on Hide. Row 12 is now hidden. Notice that the row headings now read 10, 11, 13, 14, and so on, and that the border between rows 11 and 13 is much heavier. This indicates that there is hidden row. Your worksheet now looks like the one shown in Figure 5.13.

N O T E

When you hide a column or row that contains numeric values that are used in a formula somewhere in the worksheet, the result of the formula does not change. The data in the cells in the hidden columns or rows still exists—it just doesn't show.

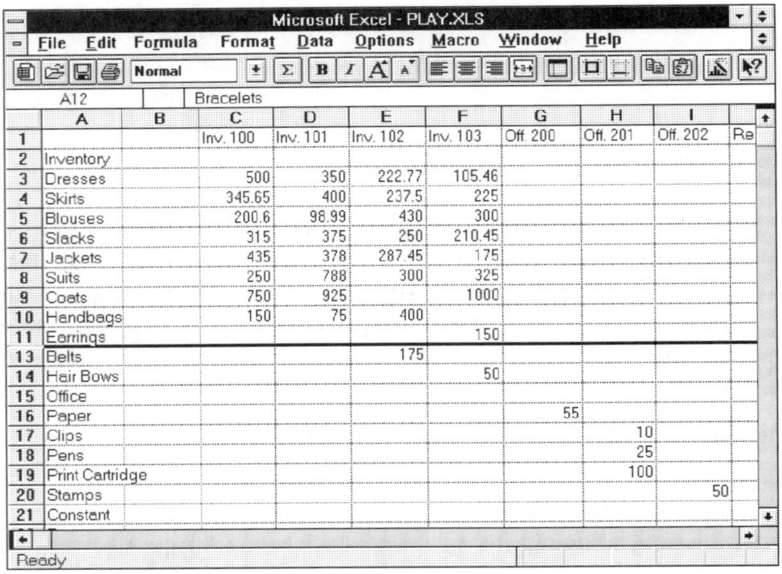

	A	B	C	D	E	F	G	H	I	
1			Inv. 100	Inv. 101	Inv. 102	Inv. 103	Off. 200	Off. 201	Off. 202	Re
2	Inventory									
3	Dresses		500	350	222.77	105.46				
4	Skirts		345.65	400	237.5	225				
5	Blouses		200.6	98.99	430	300				
6	Slacks		315	375	250	210.45				
7	Jackets		435	378	287.45	175				
8	Suits		250	788	300	325				
9	Coats		750	925		1000				
10	Handbags		150	75	400					
11	Earrings					150				
13	Belts				175					
14	Hair Bows					50				
15	Office									
16	Paper						55			
17	Clips							10		
18	Pens							25		
19	Print Cartridge							100		
20	Stamps								50	
21	Constant									

Figure 5.13. Worksheet with hidden rows.

Unhiding Columns or Rows

Let's unhide the columns and rows in PLAY.XLS. Since hiding a row was the last command you executed, use Undo to reverse the Hide command:

1. Click on Edit in the menu bar.
2. Click on Undo Row Height.

Row 12 is unhidden. To unhide a row if Undo is not available:

1. Select the row headings adjacent to the hidden row(s). In PLAY.XLS, select row headings A11 and A13.
2. Click on Format in the menu bar.
3. Click on Row Height to display the Row Height dialog box.
4. Click on Unhide.

Row 12 is unhidden. An alternative method is to:

1. Position your pointer (the shape will change to a vertical double-headed arrow bisected by a horizontal line) below the row heading of the hidden row.
2. Drag down.

To unhide a hidden column:

1. Select the column headings adjacent to the hidden column(s). In PLAY.XLS, select column headings B and E.
2. Click on Format in the menu bar.
3. Click on Column Width to display the Column Width dialog box.
4. Click on Unhide. Columns C and D are exposed.

Or,

1. Position your pointer to the right of the hidden column's column heading.
2. Drag to the right.

Borders and Shading

Borders and shading are a great way to add interest to your worksheets. You can select a range of cells and change the outside border of the range or the borders of every cell within the range. You can select individual cells and change their top, bottom, left, and right borders, using one or any combination of border choices. Excel provides you with eight border styles from which to choose.

Figure 5.8 shows some of the border styles. The range A1:I1 has been selected and the outline of the range is a heavy line. Range E3:I9 has been outlined with a double line. Range A2:I2 has double lines on the left and right borders of the cells in the range. Cells A3, B3, and C3 have a double line on the top, bottom, left, and right borders of the cells.

To apply border styles and shading to your worksheet:

1. Select the cell, range, or multiple nonadjacent ranges you want to format.
2. Click on Format in the menu bar.
3. Click on Border. The Border dialog box is displayed, as shown in Figure 5.14.
   a. To change the outline of a cell or range, select the style you want in the Style box and select Outline in the Border box.
   b. To change the left or right border of a cell or each cell in a range, select the style you want and select Left or Right.
   c. To change the top or bottom border of a cell or each cell in a range, select the style you want and select either Top or Bottom.
   d. To change all of the borders of each of the cells within a range, select the style you want and select Left, Right, Top, and Bottom. If you want to change only the left and right borders of the each of the cells within a range, as shown in Figure 5.8, select the style you want and select Left and Right.
4. To apply shading to a cell or range or to multiple nonadjacent ranges, make your selection and select Shade.

5. If you have a color monitor, you can use the Color drop-down list to choose a color for the borders. If you have a color printer, you will be able to print your worksheet with these colors.

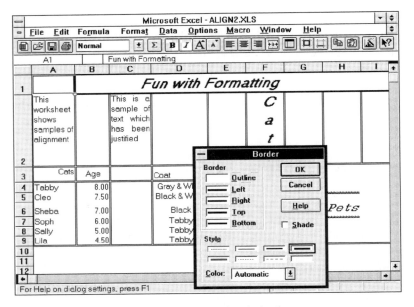

Figure 5.14. The Border dialog box.

If border styles of two cells overlap, only one style can be used. Excel determines which border style will be used in this order: no line, dotted line, small-dash line, long-dash line, light line, medium line, heavy line, and double line.

N O T E

Using Patterns in Worksheets

You can carry the concept of shading even further by using patterns instead of shading in your cells and ranges.

If you have a color monitor, you can change the foreground and/or background colors of a selected cell or range. If you have a color printer, you can print your worksheet showing the new foreground and/or background colors. You can change both the pattern and the color in your selected cell or range, change just the pattern and leave the color setting at the default, or change the background color setting and leave the pattern setting at none. To use patterns and/or colors in a cell or range:

1. Select the cell, range, or multiple nonadjacent ranges you want to format.
2. Click on Format in the menu bar.
3. Click on Patterns. The Patterns dialog box is displayed, as shown in Figure 5.15.
4. Select the choices you want in the Pattern, Foreground, and Background drop-down list boxes. The Sample box will show what the new format will look like.
5. After changing the pattern, foreground color, and background color, you may change your mind and decide not to use all of the options. If you decide you do not want to have a pattern, select None in the Pattern drop-down list box. If you decide you want to use the default color in either foreground or background, select Automatic in either the Foreground or Background drop-down list boxes.
6. Click on OK.

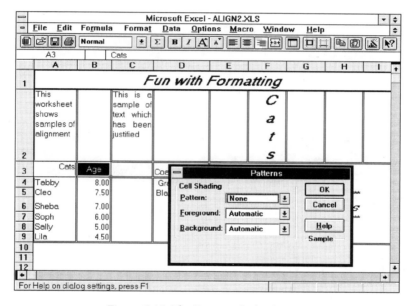

Figure 5.15. The Patterns dialog box.

Using Autoformat

Excel has provided fourteen built-in formats, called **table formats**, that you can apply to any selected range or to an entire worksheet. These table formats include a variety of fonts, text and number formats, borders, patterns, and colors. For example, the financial formats add a dollar sign to the first numeric entry in each column, and add borders and dollar signs to totals rows.

You can apply an entire built-in format, or exclude unnessary or unappealing aspects of the format. For example, in the Financial 1 format, you could choose to exclude the pattern.

The rest of the format would remain the same. You can exclude any combination of formatting options in any of the built-in formats.

Using a built-in format is a quick and easy way to give your worksheets a polished and professional appearance. To take advantage of these built-in formats for presentation purposes, you will need a color monitor. If your printer will accommodate the formatting options, you can print your worksheets with all of the options intact. To format a range or entire worksheet using Autoformat:

1. Select the range or the worksheet. If you select a cell, Autoformat will apply the format to the entire block that contains it.

2. Click on Format in the menu bar.

3. Click on Autoformat. The Autoformat dialog box is displayed, as shown in Figure 5.16.

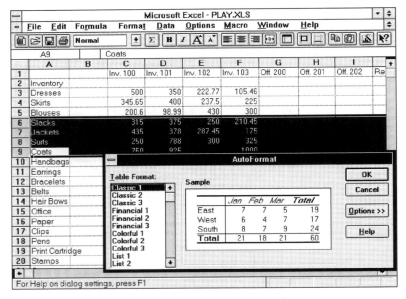

Figure 5.16. The Autoformat dialog box.

4. Select the format you want from the Table Format list box. The Sample box will display each format you highlight in the Autoformat dialog box.

5. Click on OK.

You cannot apply the formats to a single cell. If you select a single cell, the Autoformat feature will format the entire block that contains it. You cannot format multiple nonadjacent ranges. You must select and format each range individually.

N O T E

Modifying Table Formats

Autoformat allows you to determine which formatting options will be used. For example, you may choose to use all of a format's options except its font. To select the formatting options you want to use:

1. Select the range you want to format, or select the entire worksheet.
2. Click on Format in the menu bar.
3. Click on Autoformat to display the Autoformat dialog box.
4. Click on Options. You will see a list of the formatting options that will be applied to your selection, as shown in Figure 5.17.
5. Disable any options you do not want to affect your selection (to disable an option, click on the check box to clear the x).
6. Click on OK.

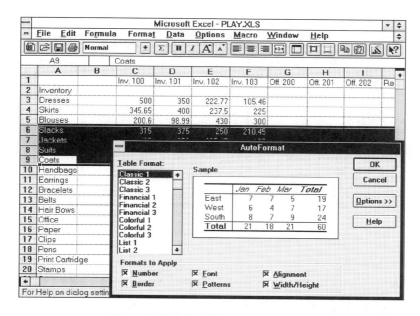

Figure 5.17. A list of formatting options.

If you change your mind and choose not to use the Autoformat format feature after you have applied it to a selection, you can immediately use the Undo feature.

N O T E

Changing Your Worksheet Display

You can change the way some items are displayed on the screen in your worksheet. You can also change the color of gridlines and column and row headings. To change your worksheet display:

1. Click on Options in the menu bar.
2. Click on Display. The Display Options dialog box is displayed, as shown in Figure 5.18.

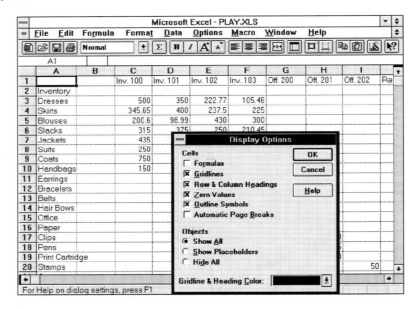

Figure 5.18. The Display Options dialog box.

3. Select from the options listed below.
4. Click on OK.

The following options are available in the Display Options dialog box.

Cells

The following items will affect the way the cells and/or their contents are displayed in a worksheet:

♦ **Formulas**. Selecting this option displays the formula rather than the results in a cell that has a formula entered into it. This option also left-aligns the contents of every cell in a worksheet, and doubles the width of all columns in the worksheet.

◆ **Gridlines**. Selecting this option displays the gridlines in your worksheet. If you disable this option, the gridlines will not be displayed. This option will not affect the way gridlines will print. See Chapter 9 for information on printing gridlines.

◆ **Row & Column Headings**. Selecting this option displays the row and column headings in your worksheet. If you disable this option the row and column headings will not be displayed. This option will not affect whether or not row and column headings will print. See Chapter 9 for information on printing row and column headings.

◆ **Zero Values**. If you select this option, zero values will be displayed (for example, in a formula where the result is 0). If you disable this option, zero values will be displayed as blank cells (in the above example, the result of 0 will be displayed as a blank cell). Cells that have been specifically formatted to display zeros will not be affected by this option.

◆ **Outline Symbols**. If you select this option, outlining symbols will be displayed if you have created an outline in the worksheet. Outlines will be covered in Chapter 6. If you disable this option, the outlining symbols will not be displayed.

◆ **Automatic Page Breaks**. If you select this option, soft page breaks (page breaks that are automatically inserted by Excel) will be displayed. If you disable this option, soft page breaks will not be displayed. Hard page breaks (page breaks that you insert manually with the Set Page Break command in the Options menu) are always displayed.

Objects

The following items affect the way objects appear in a worksheet.

◆ **Show All**. If you select this option all graphic objects will be displayed, including toolbars, notes, drawn objects, embedded charts, and pictures. If you disable this option, graphic objects will not be displayed in the worksheet.

◆ **Show Placeholders**. If you select this option, pictures and embedded charts will be displayed as gray rectangles in order to speed worksheet scrolling. If you disable this option, pictures and embedded charts will be displayed normally. Graphic objects other than pictures and embedded charts are not affected by this option.

◆ **Hide All**. If you select this option, no graphic objects will be displayed in a worksheet. If you disable this option, graphic items will be displayed normally.

Gridline and Heading Color

You can change the color of gridlines and row and column headings in the Gridline and Heading Color drop-down list box. Select a color and click on OK. Both the gridlines and the headings have been changed to the new color. You cannot change the gridline and heading colors in a range; the entire worksheet will automatically be changed to the new color. In addition, you cannot set the gridlines to one color and the headings to another color; they must both be the same color.

Review Exercises for Chapter 5

◆ Select different display fonts and font sizes for one of your worksheets, then return to the default display font.

◆ Open PLAY.XLS. Experiment with the built-in number formats.

◆ Create a new custom number format.

◆ Practice aligning data in cells in your PLAY.XLS worksheet.

◆ Change the column widths to accommodate text and numbers that do not fit properly into a column.

◆ Change the height of a row and then return it to Standard Height.

◆ Hide a column or a row and then unhide it.

◆ Add more interest to your worksheet by changing the cell borders.

◆ Add a pattern or two to blank cells in your worksheet.

◆ Familiarize yourself with AutoFormat. Apply several of the formats to different sections of the worksheet.

◆ Change your worksheet display to eliminate all gridlines.

◆ Unless you are enamored of your changes, close the worksheet without saving them.

Before You Go On...

Before you go on you should be familiar with basic formatting features available to you in Excel. You should understand the difference between printer fonts and display fonts. You should understand number values and number formats. You should be able to apply built-in number formats. You should be familiar with the alignment feature and know how to change the alignment in your worksheets if necessary. You should know how to adjust column width and row height.

Chapter 6

ADVANCED EDITING FEATURES

What You Will Learn in This Chapter

- ◆ How to use Fill and the fill handle
- ◆ How to use Autofill
- ◆ How to open multiple windows in a document
- ◆ How to split windows into multiple panes
- ◆ How to freeze titles
- ◆ How to hide windows
- ◆ How to spellcheck your document
- ◆ How to use the View and Zoom commands
- ◆ How to name selected areas of a worksheet
- ◆ How to outline a worksheet
- ◆ How to use text notes, sound, and text boxes in a worksheet
- ◆ How to customize your worksheet settings with the Workspace feature
- ◆ How to use Help

Now that you are comfortable with Excel's basic editing and formatting features, you are ready to advance to more sophisticated methods of managing worksheets. Although you have created worksheets in previous chapters, the methods you used were fairly simple. In this chapter, you are going to learn how to refine your editing techniques and maximize Excel's advanced editing features to produce and edit worksheets with even greater efficiency and speed. You are not going to create a worksheet in this chapter; open a worksheet so that you can try out the features we are going to cover.

Copying Data Using the Fill Command or by Dragging

In Chapter 4 you learned how to cut, copy, and paste data within a worksheet. Occasionally you will want to copy data from one cell of a column or row to the rest of the cells in the column or row. For example, in EXPENSE.XLS, you entered a formula into the first cell of both the Totals row and the Totals column, then copied and pasted the formula into all of the following cells in the column and row. There is an easier way to do this, using the Fill command. You can copy data to cells that are up or down from, or left or right of, the active cell.

You can use Fill to copy data to adjacent or nonadjacent cells and ranges. If you are copying data to adjacent cells or ranges, an even faster way to accomplish the task is to use the **fill handle** to drag and simultaneously copy the data.

Fill Right, Fill Left, Fill Down, and Fill Up

1. Select the cells or ranges that you want to fill (that is, to which you want to copy the data). The cells or ranges may be adjacent or nonadjacent to the active cell.

2. To access Fill Right and Fill Down, click on Edit in the menu bar. To access Fill Left and Fill Up, hold down Shift and click on Edit in the menu bar.

3. Click on the command you would like to activate.

   a. If you have selected a cell to the right of the active cell, Fill Down will be dimmed; if you have selected a cell down from the active cell, Fill Right will be dimmed.

   b. If you have selected a cell to the left of the active cell, Fill Up will be dimmed; if you have selected a cell up from the active cell, Fill Left will be dimmed.

   c. If you have selected nonadjacent ranges, neither of the two commands showing will be dimmed, but you can still copy in only one direction.

4. The data is copied from the active cell to the cell(s) or range(s) you selected.

Let's practice using the Fill command to copy data to a range.

1. On your practice worksheet, type *250* into cell A1, as shown in Figure 6.1.

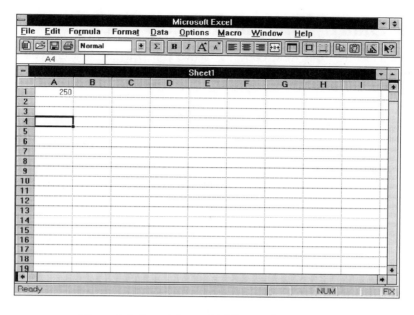

Figure 6.1. A worksheet with 250 typed into cell A1.

2. Select cells A1 through A7.
3. Click on Edit in the menu bar.
4. Click on Fill Down to repeat the data in the selected range, as shown in Figure 6.2.

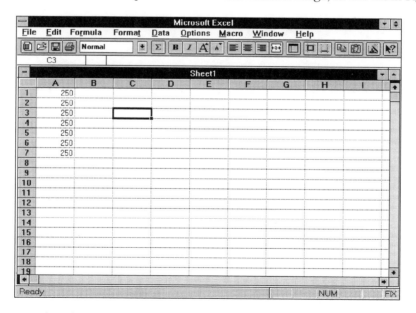

Figure 6.2. The same worksheet after Fill Down was applied to the selected range.

Copying Data by Dragging the Fill Handle

You can simultaneously drag and copy the active cell(s) to an adjacent cell or range by dragging the fill handle. The fill handle is the small solid square in the lower-right corner of the last cell in the selection, as shown in Figure 6.3.

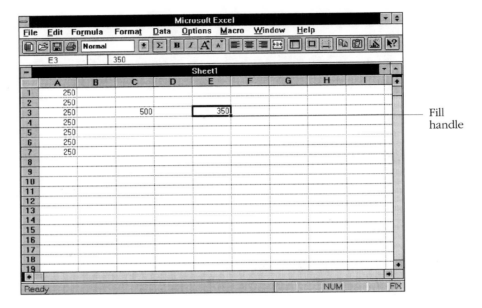

Fill
handle

Figure 6.3. The fill handle.

Let's experiment with copying a range down two columns by dragging the fill handle.

1. On your practice worksheet, type *500* into cell C3, and *350* into cell E3.

2. Select cells C3 through E3. Bring the mouse pointer (the shape will change to a solid cross) to the fill handle in the last cell in the selected range (cell E3) and drag down to row 10. As you drag, a dotted border appears around the range you are selecting, as shown in Figure 6.4.

3. Release the mouse button. Cells C3 through C10 are filled in with the figure 500. Cells E3 through E10 are filled in with the figure 350.

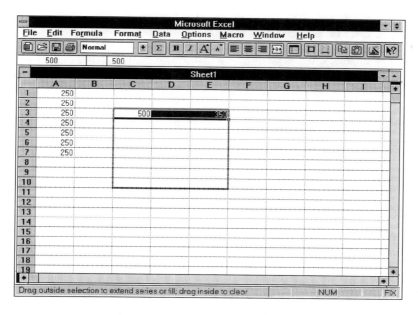

Figure 6.4. A dotted border around a selected range.

Creating a Series Using Autofill or by Dragging

Excel can create a series by extending different types of data in a sequence. It does this by recognizing a pattern or **step value** (for example, the numbers 1, 3, and 5 have a step value of 2) in the data and then incrementing the data according to the step value across a row or down a column. For example, if you type the word *January* into a cell, Excel will recognize the word as an incremental data type (data capable of being incremented by Excel) with a step value of 1 (it will increment one month at a time), and will continue the pattern by filling the selected cells with February, March, and so on. If you select the sequence *Figure 1, Figure 3,* Excel will recognize the step value as 2, and continue the sequence in the selected cells with *Figure 5, Figure 7,* and so on. If you leave a blank cell in between the selected sequence, Excel will repeat the blank cell in the extended sequence or series.

In its simplest form, an Excel series extends a sequence incrementally. The methods we are going to work with in this chapter do just that. You can also plot linear growth trends using the Autofill command. If you want to use the Autofill command to plot growth and trends, you should purchase an advanced user's manual, as these features are beyond the scope of this book.

Creating a Series Using Autofill

Autofill extends a series by repeating the step value and extending sequentially the incremental data that it recognizes. If the cell contains data that can be incremented, it will be incremented; data that is not recognized as incremental will be repeated. For example, if you have the data *Figure 1, Figure 2* in selected cells, Autofill will repeat the word *Figure* and increment the numbers in the target range. The result will be *Figure 3, Figure 4,* and so on. Other types of text are recognized as incremental data types. For example, if your selected cell contains the data *Quarter 4,* Autofill will continue the sequence with *Quarter 1, Quarter 2,* and so on. Since the word *Quarter* is recognized as an incremental data type, and there can only be four quarters in a whole, Autofill correctly extends the sequence to *Quarter 1*. The following table contains the types of incremental data which can be used with Autofill:

Data Type	Extended Series
[Text]1	[Text]2, [Text]3, [Text]4
Quarter 3	Quarter 4, Quarter 1
Qtr3	Qtr4, Qtr1, Qtr2
Q3	Q4, Q1, Q2
1st [Text]	2nd [Text], 3rd [Text]
1, 3, 5	7, 9, 11
January	February, March
Jan	Feb, Mar
30-Dec-92	31-Dec-92, 1-Jan-93
Feb-92, Apr-92	Jun-92, Aug-92
1992, 1993	1994, 1995
30-Dec	31-Dec, 1-Jan
Saturday	Sunday, Monday
Sat	Sun, Mon
11:00 PM	12:00 AM, 1:00 AM
11:15 PM, 11:30 PM	11:45 PM, 12:00 AM
13:00 Hours	14:00 Hours, 15:00 Hours
95, 90, 85	80, 75, 70
1, 3, 4	5.66, 7.16, 8.66

To create a series using Autofill:

1. Type the starting series value(s).
2. Select the starting series value and extend the selection in the row or column in which you want to extend the series.

3. Click on Data in the menu bar.

4. Click on Series. The Series dialog box is displayed, as shown in Figure 6.5.

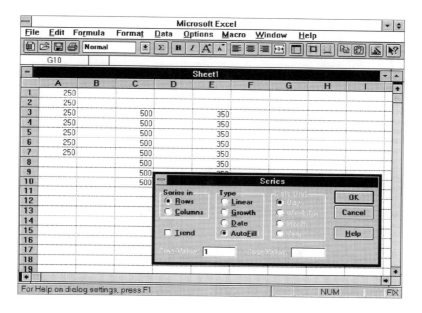

Figure 6.5. The Series dialog box.

5. Select the Row or Column option.

6. Select Autofill.

7. Click on OK.

Let's use our practice worksheet to create a series.

1. In cell A13, type *January.*

2. In cell C13, type *February.*

3. Block cells A13 through C13. Then, while holding down the Ctrl key, block cells E13 through G13 to select nonadjacent ranges.

4. Click on Data in the menu bar.

5. Click on Series to display the Series dialog box.

6. Select Rows in the Series In option box.

7. Select Autofill in the Type option box.

8. Click on OK. *January, February, March,* and *April* are written across row 13 with a blank cell between each month.

When you select cells to extend a series, you can include in the selection cells that contain text that is not recognized as an incremental data type. Excel will continue the series and repeat the text, as shown, for example, in Figure 6.6.

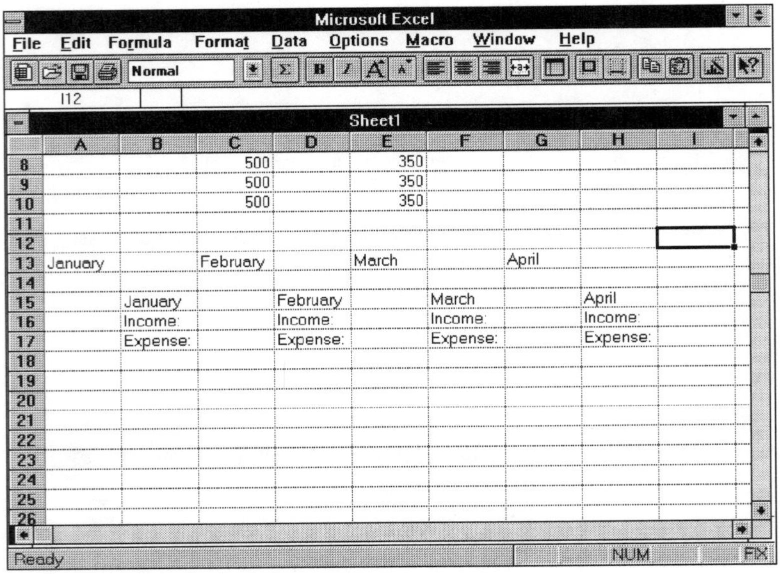

Figure 6.6. Repeated text in a series.

Cell B15 contains the incremental data type *January*. Cell B16 contains the text *Income:*, and cell B17 contains the text *Expense:*. Although Excel automatically recognizes *January* as an incremental data type with a step value of 1, we have typed in the next sequence in the series because we want a blank cell between each group. We then extended the series to include March and April, and to fill the text that Autofill did not recognize as an incremental data type. To reproduce this series:

1. In cell B15, type *January*.
2. In cell B16, type *Income:*
3. In cell B17, type *Expense:*
4. In cell D15, type *February*.
5. In cell D16, type *Income:*
6. In cell D17, type *Expense:*
7. Select the nonadjacent ranges B15:D17 and F15:H17.
8. Click on Data in the menu bar.
9. Click on Series to display the Series dialog box.
10. Select Rows in the Series In option box.
11. Select Autofill in the Type option box.
12. Click on OK. The series is extended to include March and April, and the text *Income:* and *Expense:* has been included with the rest of the series.

Creating a Series by Dragging

You can create a series using the fill handle by simultaneously dragging and extending the starting value(s) to an adjacent cell or range. Let's create a series by dragging the fill handle.

1. On your practice worksheet, type the incremental data type *Monday* in cell A20.
2. Select cell A20. Bring the mouse pointer to the fill handle in cell A20, and drag with the mouse across the row to cell G20. As you drag, a dotted border appears around the range you selecting.
3. Release the mouse button. Cells A20 through G20 are filled in with the names of the days of the week.

Opening Multiple Windows Into a Worksheet

Multiple windows are useful for working with large worksheets. By opening multiple windows into a worksheet, you can view different parts of the worksheet in each window. You can scroll through the active window to access different parts of the worksheet without affecting the display in the other windows.

When you open a new window into a worksheet, each window is normal size. You can view several windows simultaneously by sizing and moving them. You can open as many windows as you like into a worksheet.

It is important to remember that by opening windows you change only the display; the worksheet is still only one document. Any changes you make to the worksheet in one window will take effect in all other windows for that worksheet. If you scroll through the worksheet in another window, you will see the changes you have made, even if they were made in a different window.

While you cannot make changes in the worksheet in one window without affecting the entire worksheet, you can set a different display for each window. For example, in Window 1 you can view the values in a cell, while in Window 2 you can view its formula. Figure 6.7 shows EXPJAN.XLS displayed in two windows. In EXPJAN.XLS:1, the values in Column S are displayed. In EXPJAN.XLS:2, the formulas for the same column are displayed.

When you close a document that has been displayed in multiple windows, the windows will be closed with the document. When you open the document again, the multiple windows will be displayed. To permanently close the multiple windows, close all of the windows except one, restore that window to normal size, then save the window before you close it.

N O T E

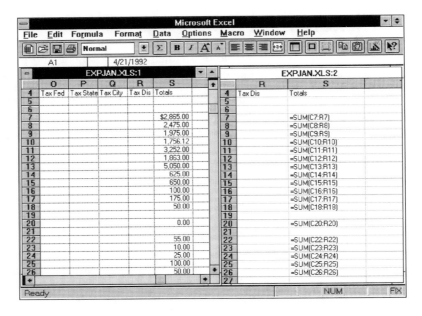

Figure 6.7. EXPJAN.XLS displayed in two windows.

To open a new window into a worksheet:

1. Open the worksheet you want to display in multiple windows. If the worksheet is already open, switch to it.
2. Click on Window in the menu bar.
3. Click on New Window. The worksheet is now displayed in two normal-sized windows. The windows are identified in the title bar by a colon (:) and a number following the worksheet name (for example, EXPJAN.XLS:1).
4. To switch windows, click on Window in the menu bar. A list of all open windows will be displayed at the bottom of the menu.
5. Click on the window you want to view.

Sizing and Moving Windows

If you want to view more than one window, you will have to size or move the windows. For example, in Figure 6.7 you will notice that the windows have been sized so that both windows fit on the screen at the same time.

Sizing Windows

There are many ways you can size windows. Figure 6.8 labels the elements of your screen that allow you to resize the window.

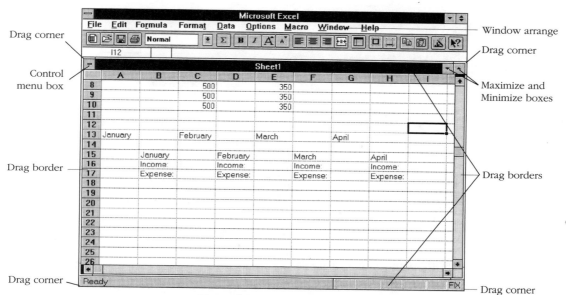

Figure 6.8. Resizing elements.

To size a window:

1. You can bring the mouse pointer (a double arrow) to any corner or border on the window and drag the border to change the window size.

2. You can use the keyboard with the Size command to resize the window. Click on the Size command in the document control menu box. The pointer will change to a four-headed pointer. Use the arrow movement keys to move the pointer to the border you want to size, then use the arrow keys to move the border to size the window. When you are finished, press Enter.

3. Drag the Size box or any of the window edges to change the size of the window incrementally.

To arrange the windows, use the Arrange command:

1. Click on Window in the menu bar.

2. Click on Arrange. The Arrange dialog box is displayed, as shown in Figure 6.9.

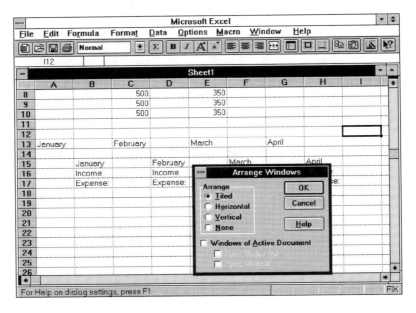

Figure 6.9. The Arrange dialog box.

The following options are available:

◆ **Tiled**. Arranges all open windows in squares or rectangles on the screen.

◆ **Horizontal**. Arranges all open windows so that they are spaced horizontally and evenly on the screen.

◆ **Vertical**. Arranges all open windows so that the are spaced vertically and evenly on the screen.

◆ **None**. Allows you to change the horizontal or vertical synchronization of the active window without arranging the windows, if Windows of Active Document is enabled.

◆ **Windows of Active Document**. If this option is selected, only the existing windows of the currently active document will be arranged. If this option is cleared, all open, unhidden windows will be arranged.

◆ **Sync Horizontal**. This option can be selected only if the Windows of Active Document box is checked. However, once this option is selected, you can clear the Windows of Active Document box and the Sync Horizontal option will still be enabled. This option enables synchronized (or simultaneous) horizontal scrolling in all of the windows of the active document. If this option is not enabled, each window will scroll independently of the other windows.

◆ **Sync Vertical**. This option can be selected only if the Windows of Active Document box is checked. However, once this option is selected, you can clear the Windows of Active Document box and the Sync Vertical option will still be enabled. This option enables synchronized (or simultaneous) vertical scrolling in all of the windows of the active document. If this option is not enable, each window will scroll independently of the other windows.

N O T E

You can also use the minimize, maximize, and reset buttons to change windows into icons and resize them. These features are explained in Chapters 1 and 2.

Moving Windows

When working with more than one window, you might find it useful to be able to move a window to a different location on the screen. To do this, click anywhere in the title bar and, while holding down the left mouse button, drag the window to its new location.

You can also use the keyboard with the Move command to move a window. Click on the Move command in the document control menu box. The pointer will change to a four-headed pointer. Use the arrow movement keys to move the window to a new location. When you are finished, press Enter.

Splitting Windows into Panes

Splitting your worksheet window into multiple panes is another way to display different sections of your worksheet in one screen. This is different from opening multiple windows in a document, because you are not actually creating or opening new windows; you are merely splitting one window into two or four **panes**, or sections. When you split a window into four panes, it splits above and to the left of the active cell.

Your scroll options when working in a split window are not the same as they are when you are working in multiple windows. If the window is split into two horizontal panes, the panes scroll together horizontally, and scroll independently vertically. If the window is split into two vertical panes, the panes scroll together vertically, and scroll independently horizontally. If your window is split into four panes, when you use the horizontal scroll arrows on the left side of the screen, the top and bottom panes on the left side scroll together. If you use the horizontal scroll arrows on the right side of the screen, the top and bottom panes on the right side scroll together. If you use the vertical scroll arrows on the top, the left and right top panes scroll together, and if you use the vertical scroll arrows on the bottom, the left and right bottom panes scroll together. Figure 6.10 shows a window split into four panes.

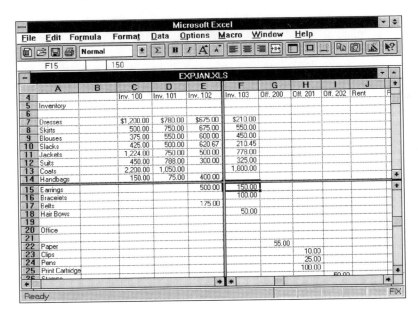

Figure 6.10. A window split into four panes.

As with multiple windows, if you make a change in the worksheet in one pane, the change is reflected in the other panes.

To split a window into two panes, use the vertical or horizontal split box. Position your mouse pointer on the horizontal or vertical split box. Now start to drag. The split box becomes a horizontal or vertical line that drags with the mouse. When the split box or line is in the position you want, release the mouse button.

To split a window into four panes using the mouse, click on the cell where you want the vertical and horizontal intersection of the split window to be. Then select the Split command in the Window menu.

To split the window into four panes with the keyboard, select the Split command in the document control menu box. Your pointer will change to a four-headed pointer. Use the arrow movement keys to move the vertical and horizontal split lines to the position you want. When you are finished, press Enter.

Removing Splits

To remove the split and return the window to normal:

1. Select Remove Split in the Window menu; or
2. Move the split box lines back to their normal positions.

Freezing Titles

When you are working with very large worksheets, it can be difficult to keep track of which rows and columns you want to enter your data into. Typing data into the wrong cells can be a real nuisance to straighten out. Excel has a very useful feature to help you avoid this problem. You can create row or column titles in your worksheet and then freeze them so that as your worksheet scrolls in the window, the titles remain on the screen. For purposes of illustration, in this section we will be using the EXPJAN.XLS worksheet, as shown in Figure 6.11.

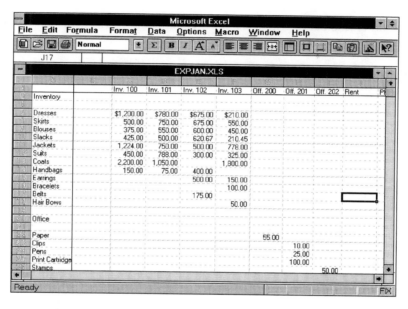

Figure 6.11. Worksheet EXPJAN.XLS with titles frozen in rows and columns.

To freeze titles in a row:

1. Click on the row header for the row directly below the row containing the titles you want to freeze, or drag the split box to the bottom of the row containing the titles you want to freeze. For example, in the EXPJAN.XLS worksheet, you would select row 5 (the row directly below the one with the titles) and click on the row heading. The entire row is selected.
2. Click on Window in the menu bar.
3. Click on Freeze Panes. The titles in the row are frozen.

To freeze titles in a column:

1. Click on the column heading of the column to the right of the one containing the titles you want to freeze, or drag the split box to the right of the column containing

the titles you want to freeze. For example, in the EXPJAN.XLS worksheet, you would select column B (the column directly to the right of the column with the titles) and click on the column heading. The entire column is selected.

2. Click on Window in the menu bar.
3. Click on Freeze Panes. The titles in the column are frozen.

To freeze titles in both columns and rows:

1. Select the cell one row below and one column to the right of the titles you want to freeze. In the EXPJAN.XLS worksheet, this would be cell B5.
2. Click on Window in the menu bar.
3. Click on Freeze Panes. The titles in the column and row are frozen.

Unfreezing Titles

To unfreeze titles:

1. Click on Window in the menu bar.
2. Click on Unfreeze Panes.

N O T E

If you have opened multiple windows into a worksheet, you can freeze different titles in each window.

Hiding Windows

You can use the Hide command to hide windows in Excel. This reduces the number of open windows on your screen, which avoids clutter if you are working with multiple documents and want to use the Arrange command to view them in several windows at a time. When you use the Hide command, the window remains open, but is not visible until you "unhide" it. If you are linking documents (see Chapter 7), using the Hide command will not affect the link. To hide a window:

1. Switch to the window you want to hide.
2. Click on Windows in the menu bar.
3. Click on Hide. The window is still open, but it is hidden.

Unhiding Windows

You can unhide a window if you want to view it or make changes to it. To unhide a window:

1. Click on Windows in the menu bar.
2. Click on Unhide. The Unhide dialog box is displayed, as shown in Figure 6.12.
3. Select the window you want to unhide and click on OK, or double-click on the window you want to unhide. The window is unhidden.

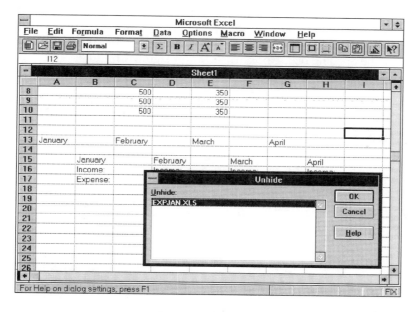

Figure 6.12. The Unhide dialog box.

Spell Checking Your Document

Once you have typed a document in Excel, you should use the Speller to check for misspelled words and some types of capitalization errors. You can check a whole document or parts of a document. If the Speller cannot find a word in its dictionary, it will assume the word is misspelled and suggest alternative spellings based upon the pattern of the letters you have typed. The Speller will check the spelling of text in worksheets, macro sheets, graphic objects, or the formula bar. Unless you select a range, Excel will check the entire document, starting with the active cell. When it has finished checking from the active cell to the end of the document, a dialog box will be displayed asking if you want the Speller to continue checking from the beginning of the sheet. If no misspelled words are found in the document, a dialog box will appear informing you that the Speller has finished spellchecking the entire document. If misspelled words are found in the document, the Spelling dialog box is displayed with various options. To spellcheck a document:

1. Open the document or, if it is open, switch to it. You can select a range to spellcheck. If you do not select a range, the entire document will be checked.
2. Click on Options in the menu bar.
3. Click on Spelling. The Speller will check the range, or, if no range is selected, Speller will check the whole document from the active cell to the end. A dialog box will then appear asking if you want the Speller to check the document from the beginning of the sheet. If there are no misspelled words, a dialog box will be displayed informing you that the Speller has finished checking the document. If there are misspelled words, the Speller will move to the first misspelled word and display the Spelling dialog box, as shown in Figure 6.13.

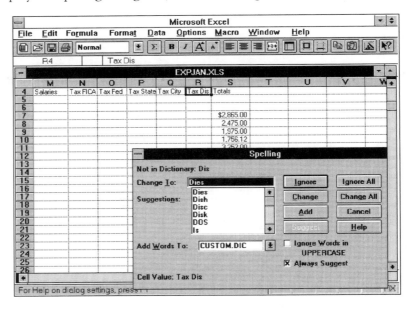

Figure 6.13. The Spelling dialog box.

The following choices are available:

♦ **Suggestions**. If the word is not found in the dictionary, the Speller assumes that it is misspelled. Based on the pattern of the letters, various alternatives are displayed in the Suggestions list box. If not all of the suggestions fit in the list box, you can use the scroll arrows to scroll the list. If you find the correct spelling of the word in the Suggestions list, select it and click on the Change button. The selected word is displayed in the Change To text box, and the misspelled word is replaced by the selected word. The Speller will continue to check the rest of the document.

◆ **Change To**. If the correct spelling of the word is not found in the Suggestions list, you can manually edit the word in the Change To text box. When you are finished typing in the correct spelling, click on Change. The misspelled word will be replaced by the word typed in the Change To text box.

◆ **Ignore**. If the word is not found in the dictionary, the Speller assumes it is misspelled. Abbreviations, technical terms, and names are assumed to be misspelled words when they are correctly spelled simply because they are not in the dictionary. If you click on the Ignore button, the Speller will skip the word and continue to check the rest of the document.

◆ **Ignore All**. The Ignore button skips the selected word only once; if the Speller finds the word again in the document, it will stop again. Selecting Ignore All instructs the Speller to skip the word every time it is encountered in the current spellcheck process.

◆ **Change**. Clicking on the Change button replaces the misspelled word with the word in the Change To text box.

◆ **Change All**. Selecting Change All replaces the misspelled word with the word in the Change To text box throughout the entire document.

◆ **Add**. As mentioned above, certain words may not be found in the dictionary even though they are correctly spelled. You can add words that you use frequently to the custom dictionary. When the Speller selects the word during the spellcheck process, click on Add. The word will be added to the Custom dictionary. The next time you spellcheck a document with the word, it will be recognized by the dictionary.

◆ **Cancel/Close**. Each of these choices closes the dialog box and ends the spellcheck process. If you have not made any changes during the spellcheck process, the button is a Cancel button. If you replace a word or add a word to the dictionary, the button becomes a Close button.

◆ **Help**. Displays the Help window for the Speller. Help is covered later in this chapter.

◆ **Suggest**. By default, Excel displays a list of alternative words in the Suggestions list box. By disabling the Always Suggest box, you can selectively display suggested words by clicking on the Suggest button. If the Always Suggest box is selected, the Suggest button is dimmed.

◆ **Always Suggest**. If this box is selected, the Speller will display a list of suggested words every time it finds a misspelled word. If this box is disabled, you can display a list of suggested words on a word-by-word basis by clicking on the Suggest button.

◆ **Ignore Words in UPPERCASE**. If this box is selected, the Speller will skip words that contain only uppercase letters. This feature is convenient for spellchecking documents filled with acronymns. If it is disabled, the Speller will find misspelled words regardless of case.

When you replace a misspelled word with a word from the Suggestions list, the replacement word always assumes the case of the word it is replacing. For example, *Werk* would be replaced with *Week*, and *werk* with *week*.

N O T E

◆ **Add Words To**. This drop-down list contains the names of all supplemental dictionaries used by the Speller. The custom dictionary (CUSTOM.DIC) comes with the program; you can add additional dictionaries. When you add a word to a supplemental dictionary with the Add button, the word is added to the dictionary selected in the Add Words To list.

The Speller will also check headers, footers, notes, and objects. The Speller will not check formulas or words that contain numbers (Such as *Werk1*). To access Spelling while a chart window is active, choose Spelling from the Chart menu.

N O T E

Let's spellcheck the worksheet SALJAN.XLS.

1. Open the worksheet, as shown in Figure 6.14.

	A	B	C	D	E	F	G	H	I
1			Salaries for January, 1992						
2									
3			Week1	Week2	Week3	Week4	Tital		
4	Perm								
5									
6	Joy		500	500	500	500	2000		
7	Amy		550	550	550	550	2200		
8									
9	Temps								
10									
11	Linda		300		250		550		
12	Marie		175	275		400	850		
13	Sue			230	150		380		
14									
15	Sub T								
16									
17	Perm		1050	1050	1050	1050	4200		
18	Temps		475	505	400	400	1780		
19									
20	Total		1525	1555	1450	1450	5980		
21									
22									

Figure 6.14. The SALJAN.XLS worksheet.

2. Change cell G3 to read *Tital.*

3. Select cell A1 to start checking at the beginning of the document.

4. Click on Options in the menu bar.

5. Click on Spelling. The Spelling dialog box is displayed, and the misspelled word is selected. Click on the correct spelling *(Total)* in the Suggestions list and click on the Change button. The word is replaced with the selected word.

6. The Speller continues, finding the "misspelled" word *Perm.* Since this is an abbreviation and is not misspelled, click on Ignore All. The word will be skipped throughout the rest of the worksheet.

7. The Speller continues, finding *Amy.* Again, this is spelled correctly. Click on Ignore All.

8. The Speller continues, finding the word *Temps.* Click on Ignore All.

9. There are no more misspelled words in the worksheet. A dialog box is displayed with the message that Excel has finished spellchecking the entire sheet.

10. Click on OK. The spellcheck is completed.

The View Command

Excel's View command allows you to change a worksheet's display options and print settings, and to save the changed version as a view without having to save a separate version of the worksheet. You can save several views and have the option of displaying or printing the worksheet with a variety of settings. You can change the following settings and save them with View: print settings, display settings, row heights and column widths, hidden rows and columns, window size, window position, panes, frozen titles, and selected cells.

Creating Views

To create a view:

1. Make the changes to any of the allowed settings.

2. Click on Window in the menu bar.

3. Click on View to display the View dialog box.

4. Choose Add. The Add View dialog box is displayed, as shown in Figure 6.15.

5. Type a name for the view in the Name text box.

6. You can choose to include new print settings and hidden rows and columns, as well as the other changes made in the allowed settings.

7. Click on OK. The view is saved as part of the worksheet.

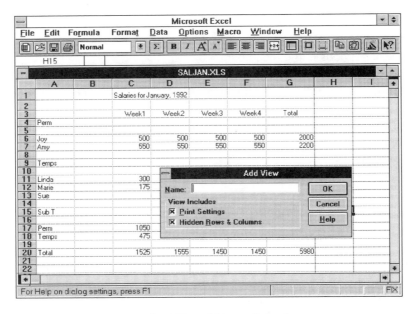

Figure 6.15. The Add View dialog box.

Displaying or Printing Views

Once you have created and saved a view, you can display it whenever you want.

1. Open the worksheet containing the view.
2. Click on Window in the menu bar.
3. Click on View to display the View dialog box.
4. In the Views list box, select the view you want to display or print.
5. Click on Show.

Once the view is displayed, you can print it like you would any other worksheet.

Deleting Views

If you want to delete a view from a worksheet:

1. Open the worksheet containing the view you want to delete.
2. Click on Window in the menu bar.
3. Click on View to display the View dialog box.
4. In the Views list box, select the view you want to delete.
5. Click on Delete.
6. Click on Close.

The Zoom Command

You can use the Zoom command to change the size of the worksheet on your screen. The Zoom command is for display purposes only. It will have no effect on the size of the worksheet when it is printed. To to change the size of your worksheet using Zoom:

1. Click on Window in the menu bar.
2. Click on Zoom to display the Zoom dialog box.
3. Select one of the following options:

   ◆ **200%**. Click on 200% to see the worksheet at twice its normal display size.

   ◆ **100%**. Click on 100% to return the worksheet to normal display size.

   ◆ **75%**. Click on 75% to shrink the size of the displayed worksheet to 75% of its normal display size.

   ◆ **50%**. Click on 50% to shrink the size of the displayed worksheet to half of its normal display size.

   ◆ **25%**. Click on 25% to shrink the size of the displayed worksheet to a quarter of its normal display size.

   ◆ **Fit Selection**. Clicking on Fit Selection instructs Excel to calculate a zoom factor to enable all of the currently selected cells to fit in the current window.

   ◆ **Custom**. Custom allows you to enter a more specific zoom factor for displaying the worksheet. You can enter a zoom factor anywhere between 10% and 400%.

4. Click on OK.

To return your worksheet to normal display size, click on 100% in the Zoom dialog box.

Names

Throughout this book you have been using cells, ranges, and nonadjacent ranges to select areas of text. You are now going to take this one step further and assign names to these selections. Excel allows you to name cells, ranges, formulas, and values. Naming specific areas, values, or formulas in a worksheet makes it easier for you to locate them and/or to copy them to other areas of the worksheet. For example, if you want to quickly find a row of subtotals in a very large worksheet and you have named the range of subtotals *Subtotals,* you can use your Goto command to locate the range by using its name.

Using names also makes it easier to read and remember formulas. For example, you might have a formula that subtracts expenses from income on a worksheet. You could enter the formula as =G12–G22 on your worksheet and try to remember where it is located, or you could name the formula =Income–Expenses, which is easy to remember, and you can quickly locate it using the Goto command.

You can give a formula or constant value a name and use that name throughout the worksheet. Then, when you want to change either the formula or the value, you simply have to change it once and all of the other named formulas or values will automatically be updated throughout the worksheet. For example, suppose you are creating a sales worksheet and you must incorporate New York City's 8.25% sales tax. If you give the value 8.25% the name *Tax* and use that name in all formulas using the New York City sales tax, then when the tax is changed to 8.5% you need only change the value in the name *Tax*. All of the formulas using the name *Tax* in the worksheet will be automatically updated.

Defining Names for Cells and Ranges

If you define a name for a cell or a range, the name applies only to that cell or range. You can then use that name to locate the cell or range, copy the cell, or replace a cell reference in a formula with the name.

In order to replace a cell reference in a formula with a name you must first apply the name. Applying names is covered later in this chapter.

To define a name for a cell, range, or nonadjacent range:

1. Select the cell, range, or nonadjacent range.
2. Click on Formula in the menu bar.
3. Click on Define Name to display the Define Name dialog box, shown in Figure 6.16.

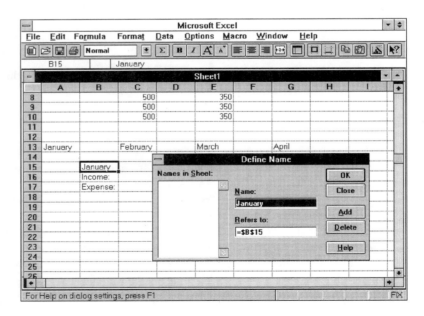

Figure 6.16. The Define Name dialog box.

4. The Names in Sheet list box lists all of the existing defined names for the worksheet.

5. In the Name text box, type the name you want to give the cell, range, or nonadjacent range. If the active cell, or a cell immediately above or to the left of the active cell, contains text, Excel proposes that text as the name. You do not have to accept the proposed name.

6. In the Refers To text box, Excel gives the cell reference of the selected cell or range. You can either accept the cell reference or type in a new one. If you type in a new cell reference, the reference must begin with an equal sign (=).

7. If you want to define more names and you know the cell references for those names, choose Add and repeat steps 5 and 6.

8. Choose OK.

Defining Names for Constant Values and Formulas

To define a name for a constant value or formula:

1. Click on Formula in the menu bar.

2. Click on Define Name to display the Define Name dialog box.

3. In the Name text box, type the name you want to give the value or formula.

4. In the Refers To text box, type the value or formula. For example, if you want to use the defined name *Tax* to represent New York City's 8.25% sales tax, you would have typed *Tax* in the Name text box, and you would type *8.25%* in the Refers To box.

5. If you want to define more names, choose Add and repeat steps 3 and 4.

6. Choose OK.

Now, if New York City's sales tax goes up to 8.5%, you only have to change the value in the Refers To text box in the Define Name dialog box; the value of each occurrence of the name Tax throughout the worksheet will automatically change.

N O T E

The first character in a defined name must be a letter or an underlined character. This character can be followed by letters, numbers, periods, or underlines. You cannot have spaces between characters in a defined name. Use an underline or a period. A defined name can be 255 characters long and is not case-sensitive.

Creating Names for Columns and Rows

Define Name assigns a name to an entire range. The columns and rows in that range do not have individual names.

When you use Create Name instead of assigning a name to the entire range, each column and row in the selected range is assigned the same name as the name in the first column and row. Then, when you apply the names, the cell references in the formulas in the range will be replaced with the names. This makes it easier to identify the action the formula is performing and easier to type in new formulas. For example, it is easier to identify what is being calculated in the formula =Week1+Week2+Week3+Week4 in a formula cell than it is to identify what is being calculated in the formula =C6+D6+E6+F6.

Let's create names for the column and rows in the SALJAN.XLS worksheet.

1. Open the worksheet.
2. Select the range A3:G20.
3. Click on Formula in the menu bar.
4. Click on Create Names to display the Create Names dialog box, as shown in Figure 6.17.
5. Select the Top Row and Left Column options. Click on OK.

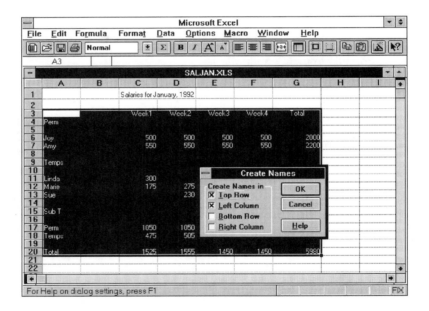

Figure 6.17. The Create Names dialog box.

You have now created and defined names for all of the columns and rows in your worksheet. These names were taken from the titles in row 3 (Week1, Week2, Week3, and Week4) and the titles in column A. Each of the titles in row 3 refers to all of the cells in the column beneath the title within the selected area. Each of the titles in column A refers to all of the cells in the row to the right of the title within the selected area.

If you had selected Top Row, the names created would have been Week1, Week2, Week3, Week4, and Total. Week1 would include all of the cells selected in the Week1 column, Week2 would include all of the cells selected in the Week2 column, and so forth.

For example, Week1 is located in cell C3. The defined name Week1 refers to cells C4 through C20.

If you had selected Left Column, Excel would have created a name for each of the titles in Column A. Each of those names would include all of the cells in every row that had been selected to the right of the title column. For example, *Amy* is located in cell A7, and refers to cells B7 through G7.

If you had chosen Right Column, Excel would have created a name for each of the titles in the last column, and each name would include all of the cells in the row to the left of the title.

If you had selected Bottom Row, Exel would have created a name for each of the titles in the bottom row of the range, and each name would include all of the cells in the column above the title.

Pasting Names Containing Formulas or Values

You can quickly and easily paste a defined name containing a formula or constant value into a cell or formula bar. This allows you to add values or formulas to existing values or formulas, or to insert formulas into blank cells. For example, if cell G7 contained *100* and you wanted to calculate the New York City sales tax for that amount in cell G8, you would select cell G8, type *=G7** and position your pointer in the formula bar after the asterisk. If you had defined the constant value *8.25* as *Tax*, you could then paste the name *Tax* into the formula bar. The formula in the cell would calculate the result of 100 * 8.25%, or 8.25. To paste a name:

1. Select the cell or or click on the location in the formula bar where you want to paste the name.
2. Click on Formula in the menu bar.
3. Click on Paste Name. The Paste Name dialog box is displayed, as shown in Figure 6.18.
4. In the Paste Name list box, select the name you want to paste.
5. Click on OK.

Using Goto to Locate Names

You can use the Goto command to locate a named area quickly.

1. Click on Formula in the menu bar.
2. Click on Goto to display the Goto dialog box.
3. In the Goto list box, select the named area you want to locate.
4. Choose OK. Excel will find and highlight the named area you selected.

You can press F5 to open the Goto dialog box.

SHORT CUT

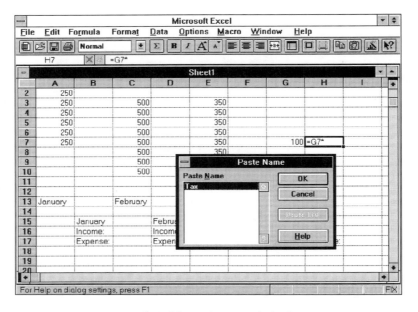

Figure 6.18. The Paste Name dialog box.

Listing Defined Names in a Worksheet or Macro Sheet

If you select Paste List in the Paste Name dialog box, all of the names defined on your worksheet or macro sheet will be pasted into your document, starting at the active cell. This makes it easy to identify all of the defined names at a glance. On a worksheet the list of names takes up two columns. The left column lists the names and the right column lists the cell references to which the names refer. On a macro sheet, the list of names takes up five columns. The columns include a name column, a reference column, a column for the type of macro you have named, a column for the macros's assigned shortcut keys, and a column for the category. To list all of your names in SALJAN.XLS:

1. Select a cell several rows below the last cell containing data in the worksheet.
2. Click on Formula in the menu bar.
3. Click on Paste Name to display the Paste Name dialog box.
4. Click on Paste List.

All of the names you defined in SALJAN.XLS are listed in the first column, and all of the cell references for those names are listed in the second column.

Editing Values or Formulas in Names

To edit a value or a formula in a name:

1. Click on Formula in the menu bar.
2. Click on Define Name to display the Define Name dialog box.
3. In the Refers To text box, edit the value or formula. For example, if you wanted to change the value in the name *Tax* from 8.25% to 8.5%, you would edit the value in the Refers To text box to read *8.5%*.
4. Click on OK.

Applying Names

When you apply names, Excel searches for all of the formulas in the selected cells and replaces references or values with the names defined for them. For example, if you defined the cell C1 as *June* and the cell D1 as *July,* and your formula is =C1+D1, Excel would replace the formula with =June+July each time it was encountered. To apply names to formulas:

1. To apply names to all of the formulas in the worksheet, select a single cell. To apply names to some of the formulas, select a range.
2. Click on Formula in the menu bar.
3. Click on Apply Names to display the Apply Names dialog box, shown in Figure 6.19.

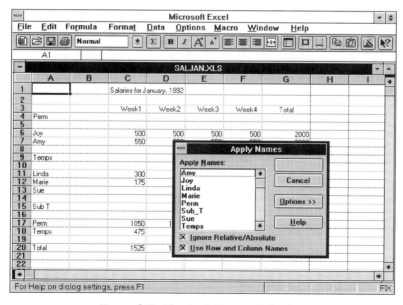

Figure 6.19. The Apply Names dialog box.

The following choices are available:

◆ **Apply Names**. The Apply Names list box contains a list of all the defined names in the worksheet. Select the name or names you want to use to replace references. For example, if you have ten names listed, but you only want to replace *C1+D1,* you would select only *June* and *July.* To select more than one name, hold down Ctrl+Up Arrow key or Ctrl+Down Arrow key, and press the Spacebar to add the name to the selection.

◆ **Ignore Relative/Absolute**. When you created or defined names, you probably noticed that all of the cell references in the Create Names and Define Name dialog box were absolute. If Ignore Relative/Absolute is checked, Excel will replace all references regardless of reference type. If this option is cleared, absolute references will be replaced only by defined names with absolute cell references, relative references will be replaced only by defined names with relative cell references, and mixed references will be replaced only by defined names with matching mixed cell references. Since cell references in defined names default to absolute, it is a good idea to leave this option checked.

◆ **Use Row and Column Names**. If this option is checked, row and column titles will be used to replace references contained in the named row or column if names for the cell references cannot be found. For example, if you have named cell C1 *June,* and cell D1 *July,* and your formula is =C1+D1+E1, it will be changed to read *=June+July+E1.* However, if you have created the column name *August* for Column E, then the formula will be changed to *=June+July+August.* See the items under "Option Buttons," below, for information further qualifying this choice.

◆ **Options Button**. When you click on the Options button, you display the following options:

  ◆ **Omit Column Name if Same Column**. Select this option if you want to omit the column name when the cell referenced in the formula is in the same column as the formula. This will work only if the referenced cell is also included in a named row. For example, in SALJAN.XLS we have named all of the columns and rows. Column C is named *Week1,* row 17 is named *Perm,* and row 18 is named *Temps.* The formula in cell C20 calculates the values in cells C17+C18; however, when the names are applied, the cell references in the formula will be replaced with the row names Perm and Temp. The column name for column C (Week1) will be omitted.

  ◆ **Omit Row Name if Same Row**. Select this option if you want to omit the row name when the referenced cell in the formula is in the same row as the formula. This will work only if the referenced cell is also included in a named column.

  ◆ **Name Order**. This option determines which named range appears first when a reference is replaced by both a named row and a named column.

4. Click on OK.

Let's apply names to the SALJAN.XLS worksheet:

1. Select a single cell.
2. Click on Formula in the menu bar.
3. Click on Apply Names to display the Apply Names dialog box. We are going to leave all of the options exactly as they are.
4. Click on OK.

Each of the formula references has been replaced by a defined name. If you click on cell G6, you will see in the formula bar that the formula *=C6+D6+E6+F6* has changed to *=Week1+Week2+Week3+Week4*. Because the referenced cells (C6, D6, E6, F6) are in the same defined row as the formula, the row name *(Joy)* is omitted and the column names *(Week1, Week2, Week3, and Week4)* are used in the formula.

Deleting Names

There will be times when you will have defined names in your worksheet that you no longer wish to use. To delete these names:

1. Click on Formula in the menu bar.
2. Click on Define Name to display the Define Name dialog box.
3. In the Names in Sheet list box, select the name you want to delete.
4. Click on Delete. The name is deleted and the dialog box remains open.
5. If you want to delete more names, repeat steps 3 and 4.
6. Choose Close to close the dialog box.

WARNING

Once you delete a defined name, it cannot be undeleted. If any of the formulas in your worksheet contain a name you have deleted, the formula will display an error value. You will have to edit the formulas containing the deleted name. Be very careful when deleting defined names. If you are not sure whether the name is contained in any formulas, use the Name Changer add-in macro to delete names.

Deleting Names with the Name Changer Add-in Macro

When you use the Name Changer add-in macro to delete names on the worksheet, you will be warned if the name you want to delete is being used in the worksheet. To use the Name Change add-in macro to delete a name:

1. Open the CHANGER.XLA macro file. You will not see a document on your screen.
2. Click on Formula in the menu bar.
3. Click on Change Name to display the Rename a Name dialog box, as shown in Figure 6.20.

4. In the From list box select the name you want to delete.

5. Click on Delete. If the name you want to delete is being used in the worksheet, you will receive a message and be asked to confirm the deletion. If you want to delete the name anyway, click on OK.

6. Click on Close to close the dialog box.

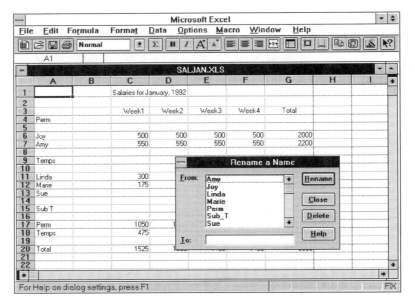

Figure 6.20. The Rename a Name dialog box.

Changing Names

The Name Changer add-in macro also allows you to change a defined name on your worksheet. When you change a defined name using the Name Changer add-in macro, it will replace all of the old names on the worksheet with the new name. To change a name:

1. Open the CHANGER.XLA macro file. You will not see a document on your screen.

2. Click on Formula in the menu bar.

3. Click on Change Name to display the Rename a Name dialog box.

4. In the From list box, select the name you want to change.

5. In the To text box, type the new name.

6. Click on Rename. The macro changes the defined name and replaces the old name with the new one throughout the entire worksheet.

7. Click on Close to close the dialog box.

Outlining a Worksheet

An outline sets forth the main points of a subject first. It is then filled in with different levels of subordinate information. Because of the format of an outline, it is easy to determine the different levels of information. When you outline data in a worksheet, you can include up to eight levels of information. Once you have outlined your worksheet, you can hide subordinate levels of data by collapsing them, enabling you to move quickly through large amounts of data, format, copy, and paste just the visible cells, and create charts using the visible data. You can determine which levels of subordinate information to display and which to hide. You can display all levels, hide all but the top level, or choose the number of levels you want to display. You can even control the formatting of the outline levels.

Before we create an outline, either use the various editing and formatting features available to revise the SALJAN.XLS worksheet to look like Figure 6.21, or create a new worksheet like the one shown in Figure 6.21. When you have finished editing or creating your worksheet, use the Save As command to save it. Name it SALOUT.XLS to represent salary outline.

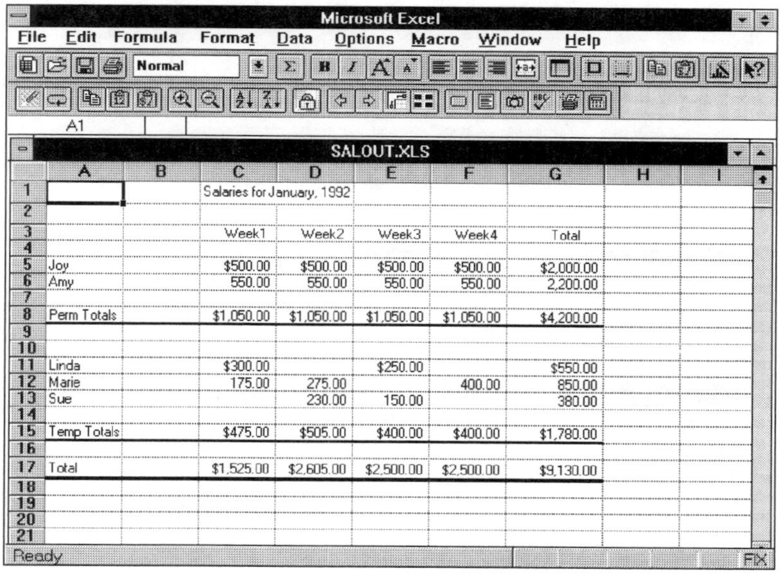

Figure 6.21. The SALOUT.XLS worksheet.

You can create an automatic outline using the Outline command. You have to display the Utility toolbar on the screen in order to create a manual outline or to manipulate outline levels and data. To display the Utility toolbar:

1. Click on Options in the menu bar.
2. Click on Toolbar to display the Toolbars dialog box, as shown in Figure 6.22.

3. In the Show Toolbars list box, select Utility.

4. Click on Show. The Utility toolbar is displayed, as shown in Figure 6.23. The tools you will be using to creat the outline are labeled.

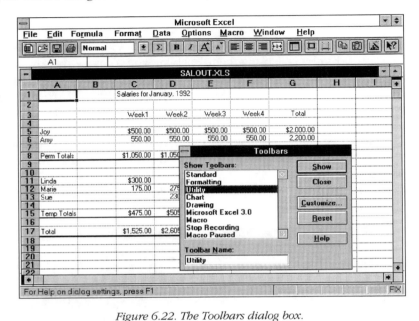

Figure 6.22. The Toolbars dialog box.

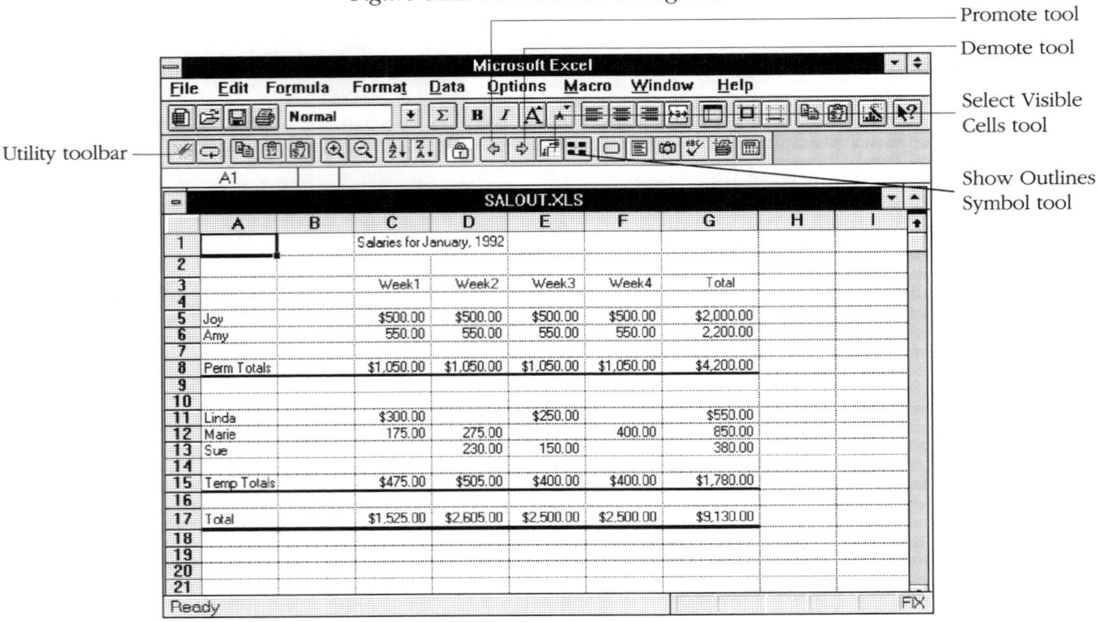

Figure 6.23. The Utility toolbar.

If you are not satisfied with the location on the window of the Utility toolbar, refer to Chapter 12 for information on how to move and use toolbars.

N O T E

You can create an outline by using the Outline command, or by using the outlining tool or the Utility toolbar. Once an outline is created, you need to use the outlining tools to work with the data. When you use the Outline command, Excel determines row and column levels and automatically creates an outline. You can also automatically create an outline usine the Utility toolbar.

The options in the Outline dialog box affect all of the outlines you create, automatic or manual, using the Outline command or the Utility toolbar. If you are using the Utility toolbar to create your outline, check the settings in the Outline dialog box before you begin.

N O T E

Creating Automatic Outlines

To create an outline using the Outline command:

1. Select the range you want to outline. If you want to outline the entire worksheet, select a single cell.
2. Click on Formula in the menu bar.
3. Click on Outline to display the Outline dialog box.
4. You can choose among the following options:

   ◆ **Summary Rows Below Detail**. This option represents the most usual design for a worksheet, with the summary (or total) row following the detailed information, as in the worksheet shown in Figure 6.21. If your summary information precedes your detailed information, clear this option.

   ◆ **Summary Columns to Right of Detail**. When this option is checked, the information in the summary columns is to the right of the detailed information in the columns. If the summary information precedes the detailed information in columns, clear this option.

   ◆ **Automatic Styles**. When this option is enabled, Excel automatically applies built-in styles to the summary rows and columns in an outline.

   ◆ **Create**. This option automatically assigns outline levels to your worksheet. If you have checked Automatic Styles, the built-in styles are applied to the summary rows and columns in the outline.

   ◆ **Apply Styles**. This option applies row and column level styles to an outline or part of an outline that does not currently have them.

5. When you have made your choices, click on Create. Your outline will automatically be created.

To create an outline using the Utility toolbar:

1. Click on Formula in the menu bar.
2. Click on Outline to display the Outline dialog box.
3. Make sure the settings in the Outline dialog box are correct.
4. Click on OK.
5. Click on the Show Outline Symbols tool. You will receive a prompt asking if you want an outline created.
6. Click on OK to create your outline using the settings in the Outline dialog box.

Let's create an outline in SALOUT.XLS.

1. Click on Formula in the menu bar.
2. Click on Outline to display the Outline dialog box.
3. Leave the default settings as they are.
4. Click on Create.

Your worksheet is now outlined. Figure 6.24 shows the outlined worksheet and identifies the parts of the outline detailed below.

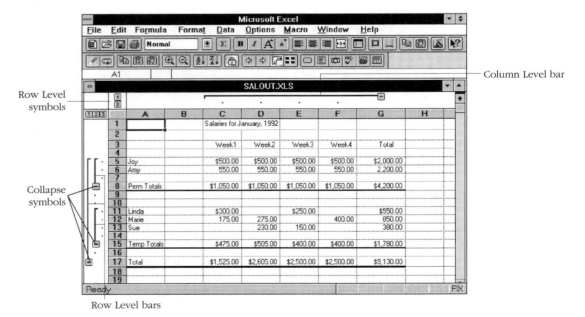

Figure 6.24. Outlined SALOUT.XLS worksheet.

- ◆ **Row and Column Level Symbols**. These columns display the corresponding number (or level) of data in an outline. If you click on the level 1 symbol, only the highest summary level will be displayed; if you click on the level 2 symbol, the information for levels 1 and 2 will be displayed, and so on.
- ◆ **Row and Column Level Bars**. When you click on these bars, you hide the rows or columns marked (or indicated) by the row or column level bar. Row and column level bars work independently of each other. Each hides only the row or column it marks.
- ◆ **Collapse Symbol**. Click on the collapse symbols to hide the rows or columns marked by the row or column level bar.
- ◆ **Expand Symbol**. This symbol indicates that a row or column has subordinate levels that have been collapsed. Click on the expand symbols to display collapsed levels.

Creating Manual Outlines

Remember, the settings in the Outline dialog box will affect an outline that you create manually. To manually create an outline:

1. Select all rows or columns subordinate to the highest level.
2. Click on the Demote tool.
3. Continue selecting each subordinate level of rows or columns, and click on Demote until you have created all outline levels.

Hiding Outline Symbols

When you hide the outline symbols, you do not affect the outline. It just doesn't show. To hide outline symbols, click the Show Outline Symbols tool.

Displaying Outline Symbols

To display hidden outline symbols, click the Show Outline Symbols tool.

Clearing an Outline

When you clear an outline from a worksheet, only the data that is not hidden will remain. If you want to clear your worksheet outline but retain all of its hidden data, first expand any levels you have collapsed. To clear an outline:

1. Select all of the rows included in the outline.
2. Click on the Promote tool until all subordinate levels are gone.
3. Select all of the columns included in the outline.
4. Click on the Promote tool until all subordinate levels are gone.

Demoting Rows or Columns

To demote a row or column one or more levels:

1. Select the row or column you want to demote.
2. Click on the Demote tool once for each level you want to demote the row or column.

If you have selected automatic styling, the styling will change to reflect the change in the row or column levels.

Promoting Rows or Columns

To promote a row or column one or more levels:

1. Select the row or column you want to promote.
2. Click on the Promote tool once for each level you want to promote the row or column.

If you have selected automatic styling, the styling will change to reflect the change in the row or column levels.

Collapsing Levels

To collapse a level, click on the level bar or the collapse symbol that indicates the data you want to hide.

Expanding Levels

When a row or column is marked with an expand symbol, click on the expand symbol to display collapsed data.

Displaying Specific Levels

Use the row and column level symbols to display or hide rows or columns according to their level. Click the level symbol to determine how many levels will be visible. The level 1 symbol not only indicates the highest level, it also means that if you click on it, only one level of data will be visible. If you click on level 2, the data for levels 1 and 2 will be displayed.

N O T E

If you want to hide or display individual rows or columns inside a level, select the row or column and choose either the Row Height or Column Width commands in the Format menu. Select Hide or Unhide.

Selecting Outline Sections

When you want to select a summary row or column plus all of its subordinate rows or columns in an outline, hold down Shift and click the level bar or the collapse or expand symbol for the row or column.

Selecting Visible Cells

You may at times want to copy visible cells or create a chart from the visible cells in an outline. When the selection in your outline includes hidden rows or columns and you want only the visible cells to be selected:

1. Select the cells in the outline that you want to use.
2. Click the Select Visible Cells tool, **or** click on Formula in the menu bar.
3. Click on Select Special to display the Select Special dialog box, as shown in Figure 6.25.
4. Click on Visible Cells Only.
5. Now you can copy or chart the visible cells.

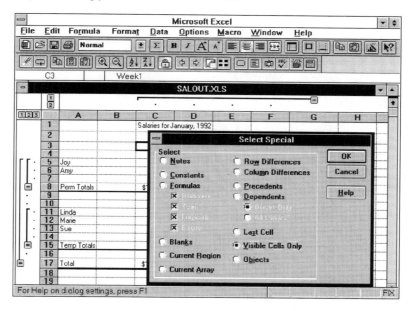

Figure 6.25. The Select Special dialog box.

Applying Styles to Outlines

Excel has built-in styles that you can apply to the levels of an outline.

1. Select the outline or the range to which you want to apply the styles.
2. Click on Formula in the menu bar.
3. Click on Outline to display the Outline dialog box.
4. Click on Apply Styles.

The built-in styles are applied to your outline.

Notes and Text Boxes

You can write helpful messages and insert them into your worksheet or attach them to a cell. This is a useful way to include reminders to yourself or to provide information to anyone else who is working with your worksheet.

You can insert a text box anywhere in the worksheet and, using the line tool, you can draw an arrow or arrows to the cell(s) referred to in the text box. Text boxes will appear on the printed worksheets.

Notes are attached to specific cells and are moved or copied when the cell is moved or copied. Cells that have notes display a note marker, so you know that the cell contains a note. The notes are not displayed in the worksheet, but can be viewed by opening the Cell Note dialog box. Printing notes is optional.

You can also attach sound notes to your cells and then play back the sound. This feature can really enhance slide presentations. To use sound notes with worksheets, you must either be running Microsoft Windows 3.0 with Multimedia Extensions 1.0 or higher, or you must be running Microsoft Windows 3.1.

Text Boxes

Text boxes are a great way to display comments on a worksheet. They become a part of the worksheet and can be formatted to enhance the appearance of your work. Text boxes appear on the printed worksheet.

Creating Text Boxes

In order to create a text box, you must use the Drawing toolbar. To display the drawing toolbar:

1. Click on Options in the menu bar.
2. Click on Toolbars to display the Toolbars dialog box, as shown in Figure 6.22.
3. Click on Drawing, then click on Show. The Drawing toolbar in displayed, as shown in Figure 6.26. The tools we will be using to create the text box are labeled.

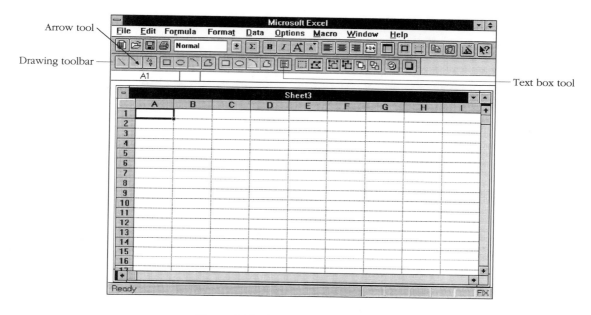

Figure 6.26. The Drawing toolbar labeled.

Now that the Drawing toolbar is displayed, you can create a text box.

1. Click on the Text Box tool on the Drawing toolbar.
2. Position the pointer (the shape becomes a cross hair) in the worksheet where you want any corner of the text box to be located.
3. Drag until the text box is the size and shape you want.
4. Click in the text box and type the text you want to appear in the box. The text will wrap to fit in the box; you can press Enter to start a new line anywhere in the box.
5. When you are finished, click outside the text box or press the Esc key.

SHORT CUT

You can create more than one text box without having to reselect the Text Box tool for each one, by simply double-clicking the first time you select the Text Box tool. You cannot enter text into the text boxes until all of the text boxes have been created. If you do, you will have to reselect the Text Box tool.

Editing Text Boxes

You can edit text in a text box.

1. Select the text box by clicking inside or on the border of the box.
2. Position the insertion point on the text you want to edit and edit the text the same way you would edit cell text in a formula bar.

N O T E

As with text in a formula bar, if you start typing without first positioning your insertion point, all of the text in the text box is replaced.

Formatting Text Boxes

You can use text, font, and pattern formats in text boxes. You can also change the text and box orientation. For information on how the various formatting features work, see Chapter 5.

To apply formats to text boxes:

1. Select the text box by clicking inside or on the border of the box.
2. To change the patterns and borders of the text box, double-click on the border of the text box, or select Patterns from the Format menu or the shortcut menu.
3. To change font or text formats in a selected text box, choose font or text from the Format menu.
4. When you are finished, choose OK.

Moving and Sizing Text Boxes

You can resize or move a text box after it has been created. Select the text box by clicking inside or on the border of the box. The border changes appearance. To move the box, point to the *border* (not the handles) and drag the box to a new location. To resize the text box, point to one of the *handles* and drag the box to a new size. When you are finished moving or resizing, click outside of the box.

Copying Text into Text Boxes

You can copy text into a text box from other sections of a worksheet. To copy text into a box.

1. Select the cell containing the text you want to copy.
2. The contents of the cell will be displayed in the formula bar. Select the text you want to copy.
3. Click on Edit in the menu bar.
4. Click on Copy.
5. Bring the insertion point to where you want to copy the text in the text box and click. The insertion point should be flashing in the text box.
6. Click on Edit in the menu bar.
7. Click on Paste. The text is pasted into the text box.

SHORT CUT

You can use the shortcut key Ctrl+V to paste text.

Drawing Arrows from Text Boxes to Cells

You can draw arrows from the text box to any location in the worksheet. This allows you to immediately reference the text box to a corresponding cell. To draw arrows, you must have the Drawing toolbar displayed.

1. Click on the Arrow tool on the Drawing toolbar.
2. Position the cross hair pointer at the location in the worksheet where you want to begin your arrow.
3. Drag to where you want the arrowhead to point.
4. You can format the appearance of the arrow:
   a. Double-click on the arrowhead to display the Patterns dialog box, as shown in Figure 6.27.
   b. Select the line and arrowhead options you want to format the appearance of your arrow.
5. When you are finished, select OK in the Patterns dialog box.

Deleting Text Boxes or Arrows

To delete a text box or an arrow:

1. Select the text box or arrow.
2. Click on Edit in the menu bar.
3. Click on Clear to delete the selected text box or arrow.

N O T E

If text is selected in a text box, only that text is deleted when you choose the Clear command.

Let's create and format a text box and arrow in our PETFOOD.XLS worksheet, as shown in Figure 6.28.

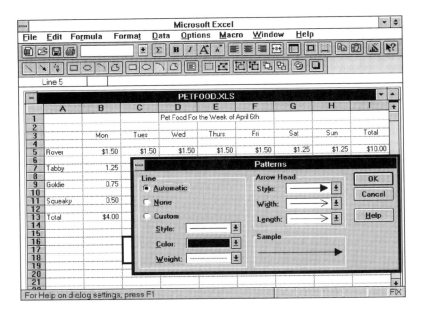

Figure 6.27. The Patterns dialog box.

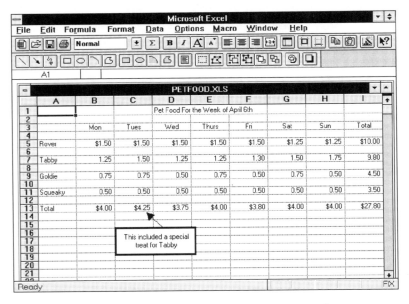

Figure 6.28. PETFOOD.XLS worksheet with text box and arrow.

It may take you a while to get the hang of dragging tools, but keep at it. If you make a mistake and can't correct it, clear the box or arrow and start again.

1. Open the PETFOOD.XLS worksheet.

2. Click on the Text Box tool in the Drawing toolbar.

3. Bring the cross hair pointer to the approximate location where you want to begin creating the text box shown in Figure 6.28. (You might want to start around cell C16.)

4. Pressing down on the mouse button, drag the box until it occupies approximately six cells, as shown in Figure 6.28.

5. Release the mouse button and click outside of the text box. To move or resize the box, click in the box to select it, then click on the border or handle, respectively, and drag.

6. Select the text box by clicking in it. Bring the insertion point to the upper-left corner of the inside of the box and click. The insertion point should be flashing in the box.

7. Type *This included a special treat for Tabby,* as shown in Figure 6.28.

8. Click outside the box.

9. Select the box again and choose Font in the Format menu. Select Helv 8 or an equivalent font. The text now fits more comfortably in the box.

10. While the box is still selected, choose Text in the Format menu. Set the Horizontal and Vertical Alignment for Center.

11. Finally, while the box is still selected, choose Patterns in the Format menu. Select a heavier border weight.

12. Click outside of the box. The text box should appear similar to the one in Figure 6.28.

13. To draw the arrow, click on the Arrow tool in the Drawing toolbar.

14. Bring the cross hair pointer to the beginning of the arrow (on the box border) and drag up to *$4.25.*

15. Release the mouse and click outside the arrow. Move the arrow if necessary to position it properly. When you have finished moving it, click outside the arrow.

16. Format the arrow by double-clicking on the arrowhead to display the Patterns dialog box.

17. Change the weight of the line to make it slightly heavier.

18. Click outside of the arrow. Congratulations! You have completed a text box and arrow.

Text Notes

As stated earlier, text boxes appear when the worksheet is printed. If you do not want your comments to display on the worksheet or to appear on the worksheet when it is printed, you should use text notes to record your comments. Text notes do not display on the worksheet and, if you decide to print them, they are printed on a separate sheet of paper. Text notes are attached to specific cells. If you move or copy the cell, the text note moves or copies with the cell. You can display note indicators in cells with text notes so that you can identify them quickly. The note indicators do not print when you print the worksheet. You can also view text notes in the Info Window (covered later in this chapter).

Creating Text Notes

To create a text note:

1. Select the cell to which you want to attach a text note.
2. Click on Formula in the menu bar.
3. Click on Note to display the Cell Note dialog box, as shown in Figure 6.29.

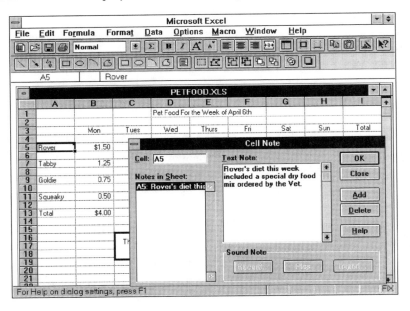

Figure 6.29. The Cell Note dialog box.

4. The Cell text box indicates the cell to which the note will be attached. If you want to attach the note to a different cell, type the correct cell reference in the Cell text box.

5. Bring the insertion point to the Text Note box, if it is not already there, and type the information you want in the text note. The text will wrap automatically. Do not press Enter; if you want to start a new line, press Ctrl+Enter to insert a line break.

6. Click on OK to attach the note to the cell. Unless you have chosen not to display a note indicator (see the "Workspace" section later in this chapter), a note indicator will appear in the upper-right corner of the cell to which you attached the note.

Editing Text Notes

You edit a text note in the Cell Note dialog box the same way you would edit cell information in a formula bar.

1. Click on Formula in the menu bar.

2. Click on Note to display the Cell Note dialog box.

3. The cell reference and the first few words of all of the notes in the worksheet are displayed in the Notes in Sheet list box. Click on the note you want to edit. The text of the note will appear in the Text Note box.

4. Bring the insertion point to the Text Note box and edit the note.

5. When you are finished, choose OK.

Copying Text Notes

You can copy a text note into another cell. To copy a text note:

1. Select the cell containing the note you want to copy.

2. Click on Edit in the menu bar.

3. Click on Copy.

4. Select the cell to which you want to copy the note.

5. Click on Edit in the menu bar.

6. Click on Paste Special.

7. Select the Notes option button.

8. Choose OK to copy the note to the selected cell.

WARNING

If you copy a note into a cell that already contains a note, the copied note will overwrite the existing one.

Adding Text Notes to Multiple Cells

You can add the same note to multiple cells or you can add different notes to multiple cells all at one time. You can also use this method to copy notes to other cells.

1. Select the first cell to which you want to attach a text note.
2. Click on Formula in the menu bar.
3. Click on Note to display the Cell Note dialog box.
4. In the Text Note box, type the text you want to appear in the note.
5. Click on Add. The note is attached to the selected cell and the cell reference and the first few words of the note are displayed in the Notes In Sheet box.
6. With the insertion point in the Cell text box, select the next cell to which you want to add a note, or type the cell reference in the Cell text box. (You can move the dialog box to select a cell behind it. To do this, click in the title bar and drag the box to a new location.)
7. The text of the last note you typed is in the Text Note box. To type a new note, delete the text and type in a new note.

    To copy text from another text note into the selected cell, select the note you want to copy in the Notes In Sheet box. The text of the note will appear in the Text Note box.
8. Click on Add.
9. Repeat steps 6 to 8 for each new note you want to add or copy.
10. When you are finished, choose OK.

Viewing Text Notes

After you have attached text notes to cells, you will want to be able to view them quickly. To view a text note:

1. Double-click on the cell to which the note is attached, or choose Note from the Formula menu to display the Cell Note dialog box.
2. Select the note you want to view in the Notes In Sheet box. The text of the selected note will appear in the Text Note box.
3. When you are finished, click on Close.

Searching for Text in Notes

You can search a worksheet to find notes that contain a specific character string.

1. Click on Formula in the menu bar.
2. Click on Find to display the Find dialog box, as shown in Figure 6.30.

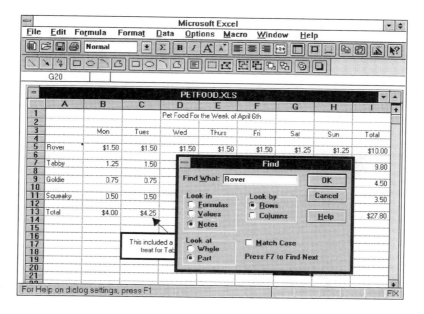

Figure 6.30. The Find dialog box.

3. In the Find What text box, type in the text or string you want to search for.

4. In the Look In options box, select Notes.

5. If you want to find note text that matches the uppercase and lowercase letters in the Find What text box, select Match Case.

6. Select OK.

Printing Text Notes

In order to print text notes you must select the correct options in the Page Setup and Print dialog boxes. You can choose to have the worksheet and the notes print separately or together. If you choose to have them print together, the worksheet will print first, followed by the notes. If you have specified a print area (see Chapter 9 for additional information about printing and print areas), only the notes attached to cells in the print area will print. To print text notes:

1. Click on File in the menu bar.

2. Click on Page Setup to display the Page Setup dialog box, as shown in Figure 6.31.

3. If you want to print the cell references with the text notes, enable Row & Column Headings. If you clear Row & Column Headings, the notes will print without cell references.

4. Click on the Print command button to display the Print dialog box, as shown in Figure 6.32.

5. To print just the notes, choose the Notes option in the Print option box. To print the notes and the worksheet, choose Both. To print just the worksheet, choose Sheet.

6. Choose OK.

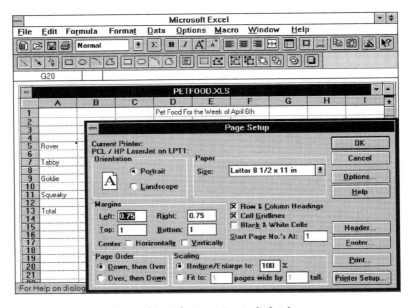

Figure 6.31. The Page Setup dialog box.

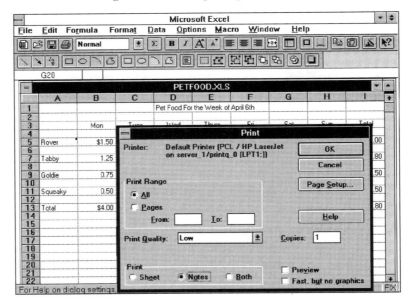

Figure 6.32. The Print dialog box.

N O T E

If you enable Row & Column Headings and print both the worksheet and the notes, the worksheet will print with row and column headings. If you want to print the worksheet without row and column headings and print the notes with cell references, you must print the worksheet and notes separately. Print the worksheet with Row & Column Headings disabled, and print the notes with Row & Column Headings enabled. Page Setup is explained in detail in Chapter 9.

Deleting Text Notes

To delete a text note:

1. Double-click on the cell to which the note is attached or choose Note from the Formula menu to display the Cell Note dialog box.
2. In the Notes In Sheet box, select the note you want to delete.
3. Click on Delete.
4. A dialog box is displayed warning you that the note will be permanently deleted. To delete the note, click on OK. To cancel the deletion, click on Cancel.
5. Click on Close to close the dialog box.

WARNING

If you delete a note, it is permanently deleted. You cannot restore it using the Undo command.

Deleting All Notes

You can delete all of the notes in a worksheet in one operation.

1. Click on Formula in the menu bar.
2. Click on Select Special to display the Select Special dialog box.
3. In the Select box, select the Notes option.
4. Choose OK.
5. Click on Edit in the menu bar.
6. Click on Clear to display the Clear dialog box.
7. In the Clear options box, select Notes.
8. Choose OK. All of the notes in the worksheet have been deleted.

Using Sound Notes

You can add sound notes to a cell and then play them back. This is a great way to add interest to presentations. To use sound notes, you must be running Windows 3.1, or Windows 3.0 with Multimedia Extensions 1.0 or higher.

Importing Sound Notes

1. Select the cell to which you want to attach a sound note.
2. Click on Formula in the menu bar.
3. Click on Note to display the Cell Note dialog box.
4. Click on the Import button in the Sound Note box.
5. Select a Sound File from the list.
6. Click on OK. You are returned to the Cell Note dialog box.
7. Click on Add. The sound note is added to the cell.

Playing Sound Notes

To play a sound note, select the cell containing the sound and double-click on the cell. The sound note will play. You can also play sound notes from the Cell Note dialog box:

1. Click on Formula in the menu bar.
2. Click on Note to display the Note dialog box.
3. Cells with attached sound notes are listed in the Notes In Sheet box with an asterisk (*).
4. Select the sound note you want to play.
5. Click on the Play button in the Sound Note box to play the sound note.

Recording Sound Notes

If you have recording hardware installed in your computer, you can record your own sound notes. To record a sound note:

1. Select the cell for which you want to record a sound note.
2. Click on Formula in the menu bar.
3. Click on Note to display the Note dialog box.
4. In the Sound Note box, choose the Record button to display the dialog box for recording sounds.
5. Choose the Record button.

6. When you are finished recording, choose the Stop button.

7. If you want to play the sound, choose the Play button.

8. Click on OK. You are back in the Cell Note dialog box.

9. Click on Add to attach the sound note to the selected cell.

Copying Sound Notes

You copy a sound note the same way you copy a text note. See "Copying Text Notes" above.

Erasing Sound Notes

You can attach only one sound note to a cell. If you want to attach another sound note to a cell that already contains one, you must first erase the existing sound note. To erase a sound note:

1. Select the cell whose sound note you want to erase.

2. Click on Formula in the menu bar.

3. Click on Note to display the Cell Note dialog box.

4. In the Sound Note box, choose the Erase button. The sound note is erased, the Erase button becomes a Record button, and the Import button becomes available again. Now you can record or import another sound note in the selected cell.

Workspace

The Workspace command allows you to customize some of your worksheet settings. You can decide whether you want the status bar, formula bar, or scroll bar to be displayed; set up keys to navigate the worksheet; change the key you press to access the Excel menu bar or the Lotus 1-2-3 Help feature; change the reference style of row and column headings and cell references; and control certain editing features. The Workspace command also allows you to access the Info window. To use the Workspace command:

1. Click on Options in the menu bar.

2. Click on Workspace to display the Workspace Options dialog box, as shown in Figure 6.33.

3. Select from any of the available choices.

4. Click OK when you are finished.

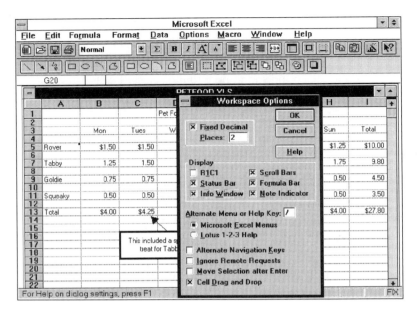

Figure 6.33. The Workspace Options dialog box.

The following options are available when you display the Workspace dialog box.

Fixed Decimal

This option tells Excel where to place the decimal point in the numbers you enter in a worksheet. The fixed decimal is defaulted to two places. This means that if you type *10034* without entering a decimal point, Excel will automatically place the decimal point two places to the left of the last number entered and the number will be formatted as *100.34*. If you change the number of fixed decimal places to three instead of two, the number would be formatted as *10.034*. If you clear this option or change the fixed decimal to zero, you must enter the decimal point manually. You can override this option when entering a number by typing a decimal point when you enter the number.

R1C1

The default display settings in worksheets is to label each column with a letter and each row with a number. Thus, the location of the first cell in column A, row 1 is referred to as the cell reference A1. You can change the format of cell references to the R1C1 reference method by selecting the R1C1 box. When you use the R1C1 reference, each row is identified by number, but each column is also identified by number (column A becomes column 1). This makes the cell reference of the first cell in the first column and first row of the worksheet R1C1, where R stands for row and C stands for column. R1C1 means the cell located in row 1, column 1. If you use the R1C1 reference, cell E3 would be referenced as R3C5, indicating that it is located in row 3, column 5.

Status Bar

When this option is selected the status bar is displayed in the Excel window. If this option is cleared, the status bar is not displayed.

Info Window

When this option is selected the Info window is displayed for the active worksheet or macro sheet, as shown in Figure 6.34.

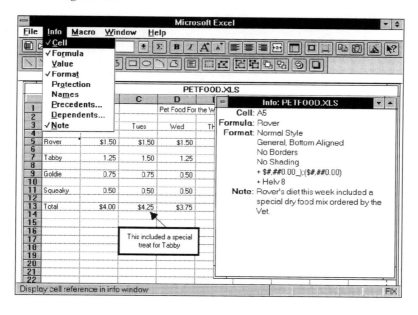

Figure 6.34. The Info window for the active worksheet.

You can determine the types of information the Info window will display for the active cell in your worksheet by clicking on Info in the menu bar to open the Info menu. You can choose from among the following options:

- ◆ **Cell**. Displays the cell reference of the active cell.
- ◆ **Formula**. Displays the contents of the active cell as they appear in the formula bar.
- ◆ **Value**. Displays the text, number constant, formula, function, or value produced in the active cell.
- ◆ **Format**. Lists all of the format settings for the active cell, including the alignment, number, font, border, and shading formats.
- ◆ **Protection**. Displays the protection status of the active cell.
- ◆ **Names**. Displays the names of any named areas included in the active cell.

- **Precedents**. Displays any cells that are referred to by a formula in the active cell. For example, if the active cell is C36 and it contains the formula *=SUM(C7:C34),* the direct precedents displayed will be C7:C34. If the active cell does not contain a formula, Precedents will be blank.

- **Dependents**. Displays any cells with formulas that depend on or refer to the active cell. For example, if cell C34 is the active cell, and cell C36 contains the formula *=SUM(C7:C34),* then cell C36 is listed as a dependent of cell C34.

- **Note**. Displays a note if one is attached to the active cell.

Arranging Windows

You can change the way your windows are displayed when the Info window is active by choosing Window in the menu bar and then choosing Arrange. The Arrange dialog box allows you the following options: Tiled, Horizontal, and None. Once you have selected your option, click on OK.

Moving Between Windows

There are two ways to move between the Info window and the worksheet. If either the Info window or the worksheet is not visible:

1. To switch to the worksheet window from the Info window, click on Window in the menu bar and click on the document name.

2. To switch to the Info window from the document window, click on Window in the menu bar and click on Info.

If both the document window and the Info window are visible, click on the window you want to switch to.

Printing the Info Window

To print the information contained in the Info window:

1. Select the cell or cells for which you want to print the Info window information. If you select more than one cell, the information for each cell selected will print in consecutive order.

2. Switch to the Info window.

3. Click on File in the menu bar.

4. Click on Print to display the Print dialog box.

5. Click on OK.

N O T E

You can also choose Print Preview or Page Setup in the Info window File menu.

Scroll Bars

When selected, this option displays the scroll bars in the document window. When the option is cleared, the scroll bars are not displayed.

Formula Bar

When selected, this option displays the formula bar, showing the contents of the active cell. When this option is cleared, the formula bar is not displayed.

Note Indicator

When selected, this option displays a small dot in the upper-right corner of any cell that has an attached note.

Alternate Menu or Help Key

This option allows you to change the key you press to access either the Excel menu bar or Help for Lotus 1-2-3 Users. The default key is a slash (/). You can either accept the default or select a new key. You can choose to have the key activate either the Excel menu bar or Help for Lotus 1-2-3 Users, depending on the option you select.

Alternate Navigation Keys

When selected, this option substitutes an alternate set of keyboard movement keys. The following table shows the alternate movement keys.

Navigation Keys

Ctrl+Left Arrow	Moves left one screen
Ctrl+Right Arrow	Moves right one screen
Ctrl+PgUp	In a workbook, next worksheet
Ctrl+PgDn	In a workbook, previous worksheet
Tab	Move right one screen
Shift+Tab	Move left one screen
Home	Moves to the upper-left corner of the screen

Function Keys

F5	Positions the entered cell or range in the upper-left corner of the window
F6	Next window of the same document
Shift+F6	Previous pane of the same window

In Data Find Mode (used in Databases)

Left Arrow	Moves to the previous field of the current record
Right Arrow	Moves to the next field of the current record
Home	Moves to the first record
End	Moves to the last record

Text Alignment Prefix Characters

' (single quote)	Aligns data to the left
" (double quote)	Aligns data to the right
^ (caret)	Centers data
\ (backslash)	Repeats characters across the cell

Ignore Remote Requests

When this option is selected, Excel does not respond to remote requests made by other applications.

Move Selection After Enter

When selected, this option automatically moves the active cell down one row after you press Enter to enter a value or formula in a cell.

Cell Drag and Drop

When selected, this option allows you to move and copy cells and data by dragging with the mouse.

Help

The Help feature is the last item on your menu bar. When you click on Help in the menu bar, you have immediate, on-screen access to the answers to your Excel questions. This means that you can be working in a document, hit a snag, and access the Help feature without having to leave your document. The Help menu lists all of the Help commands, as shown in Figure 6.35.

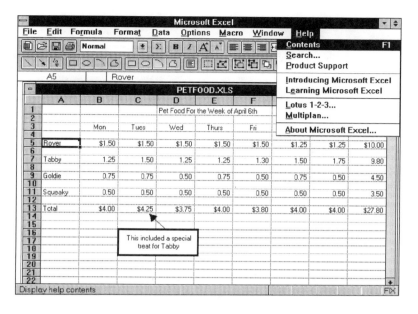

Figure 6.35. The Help menu.

You can press the F1 key from anywhere in Excel to access the Help feature.

SHORT CUT

You can specify the feature you want help with before you even open the Help menu.

1. Press Shift+F1. The mouse pointer changes to a question mark.
2. Select the command or feature about which you want help. The help topic for the command or feature will be displayed.

You can also access context-sensitive information (specific to what you are doing at a given moment) by clicking on the Help command button found in most dialog boxes.

To exit Help from any window, click on Exit in the File menu or select Close in the Control menu box.

Contents

Contents displays the categories of topics covered in the Help feature. To view more information about an item on the list click on the item.

Search

The Search command allows you to search through Help to find the topics that interest you. To use the Search feature:

1. Select the Search command in the Help menu to display the Search dialog box.
2. Type the feature you want to access in the Text box, or select the feature from the list.
3. Select Show Topics.
4. A list of related topics appears in a list box in the bottom half of the dialog box. Select the topic you want.
5. Select Go To. The topic you selected is now in the Help window.

Product Support

The Product Support command contains general support information about Excel, including commonly asked questions and information about how to get technical support.

Introducing Microsoft Excel

This command contains a tutorial that covers the basic features of Excel 4.0, explains its new features, and provides information for Lotus 1-2-3 users about adapting to Excel 4.0.

Learning Microsoft Excel

This command contains a tutorial with an introduction and sections covering basic information about worksheets, charts, databases, macros, and toolbars.

Lotus 1-2-3

This command explains how to perform Lotus 1-2-3 tasks in Excel 4.0. When you select a Lotus 1-2-3 command from the list, the Help feature explains the equivalent Excel 4.0 command.

Multiplan

This command tells users how to perform Microsoft Multiplan tasks in Excel 4.0. If there is no exact equivalent, a topic is displayed showing which Excel 4.0 commands accomplish a similar task.

About Microsoft Excel

This command provides information about the version of Excel you are using, who it is licensed to, the serial number, available memory on your terminal, and whether or not there is a math co-processor on your terminal.

The Help Window Menu Bar

All of the Help commands except for Introducing Microsoft Excel, Learning Microsoft Excel, and About Microsoft Excel bring up a window with a menu bar containing the following commands: File, Edit, Bookmark, and Help.

File

The File menu allows you to:

1. Choose Open to open any Help file from any directory.
2. Print the current Help topic by choosing Print Topic.
3. Choose Printer Setup to select and configure the printer you want to use in Help.
4. Choose Exit to exit the Help feature.

Edit

The Edit menu has two choices:

1. Choose Copy to copy the current Help topic to the Windows Clipboard. You can then retrieve the topic into a document or document window by choosing Paste in the Edit menu in your document window.
2. Choose Annotate to add comments of your own to any topic displayed in the Help window. When you choose Annotate, the Help Annotate dialog box is displayed. Type in your comments and choose OK. The next time you choose this topic in Help, a paper clip will be displayed next to the topic title. To see your annotation, click on the paper clip.

Bookmark

The Bookmark command allows you to create a list of topics that can be quickly accessed from the menu. To use the Bookmark command:

1. Go to the Help topic you want to add to the Bookmark list.
2. Select Bookmark.
3. Select Define. The Bookmark Define dialog box is displayed, as shown in Figure 6.36.

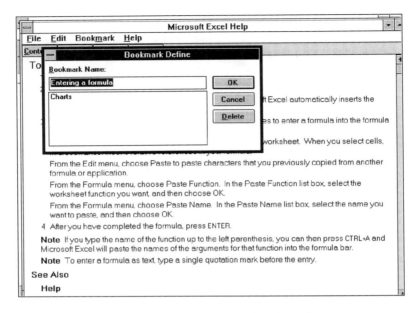

Figure 6.36. The Bookmark Define dialog box.

4. The name of the current topic is displayed in the Bookmark Name text box. You can accept the name or type in a name of your choosing.

5. Choose OK.

6. Return to the Help Contents list by clicking on the Contents command button.

7. Select Bookmark. The topic you entered is displayed in the menu.

8. Select that topic. You are in the Help window for that topic.

Help

The Help command provides information on how to use the Help feature.

Command Buttons

The Command buttons Contents, Search, Back, and History are found in the Help window. These buttons provide ways to access topics while in the Help feature.

Contents

The Contents command button displays the categories of topics covered in Help. To view more information about an item on the list and click on the item.

Search

The Search command button allows you to search through Help to find the topics that interest you. To use the Search feature:

1. Click on the Search command button.
2. Type the feature you want to access in the Text box, or select the feature from the list.
3. Select Show Topics.
4. A list of related topics appears in a list box in the bottom half of the dialog box. Select the topic you want.
5. Select Go To. The topic you selected is now in the Help window.

Back

The Back command button takes you back one topic at a time through all of the topics you have viewed in Help during the current session.

History

The History command button displays the last forty Help topics you viewed, with the most recent one first. To redisplay a topic, double-click on it.

Jump Terms

Jump terms are phrases that appear in the Help window with a solid underline. These are other Help topics related to the topic in the window. You can find out more about the current topic by selecting a jump term, which brings up an additional help topic. Jump terms are really a cross-referencing feature. Bring the mouse pointer to the jump term and click. To return to the original topic, click on the Back command button.

Defined Terms

Terms in a Help window with a dotted underline are defined in the Help feature. To access the definition of a defined term, bring the mouse pointer to the defined term and hold down the left mouse button. A small box with the definition of the term will be displayed. When you release the mouse button the definition will be removed.

Review Exercises for Chapter 6

◆ Open a new worksheet. Enter the title *Monday* in cell B1. Use Autofill to extend the series across row 1 to include every day through Friday. Enter the title *Total* in cell G1.

◆ In column A, enter the following titles, starting with cell A3. You should have a blank cell between each title: *Transportation, Lunch, Entertainment, Clothing, Miscellaneous,* and *Total.* Adjust the column widths so that the titles fit in the column.

◆ Enter *5.00* into cell B3. Use Fill to repeat the figure across the row for every day of the week.

◆ Fill in the rest of the worksheet using amounts of your own choice.

◆ Enter a formula in cell G3 to calculate the total for transportation.

◆ Select the nonadjacent cells G3, G5, G7, G9, and G11.

◆ Use Fill to copy the formula into these cells.

◆ Enter a formula into cell B13 to calculate the total for Monday.

◆ Select cells B13:G13. Use Fill to copy the formula into these cells.

◆ Name the file *Exercise.* Open a second window into the worksheet.

◆ Either drag the windows or use the Tile option in the Arrange command to display the windows side by side.

◆ Scroll both windows to display column G. In one of the windows, change the display to show formulas. (Click on Display in the Options menu. In the Display Options dialog box, select Formulas.)

◆ Close one of the windows. Either drag the remaining window or use the Tile option to return the window to normal size. Save the worksheet.

◆ Create names for each title row and column. Apply the names. Click in the formula cells and note the difference in the formulas.

◆ List all of your defined names starting in row 15.

◆ Create a text box for a cell. Type in appropriate text and format the text box any way you want. Draw an arrow from the text box to the cell it refers to.

◆ Create a text note for a cell. Use the Info Window to view the note.

Before You Go On...

Before you go on you should be comfortable with all of the advanced editing features in Excel. You should be able to create a series, open multiple windows into a document, split a window into panes, freeze titles, hide windows, use View and

Zoom, define and apply names, create outlines, create notes and text boxes, customize the workspace, and use the Help feature. At this point you should be comfortable with all of the elements involved in creating, editing, and formatting worksheets, and you should be able to work with simple formulas.

Chapter 7

WORKING WITH MULTIPLE DOCUMENTS

What You Will Learn in This Chapter

- How to copy information between documents
- How to link cells and ranges between documents
- How to consolidate data from multiple documents
- How to edit documents as a group
- How to use workbooks

Until now we have worked with only one worksheet at a time. However, one worksheet is frequently just part of a system that comprises many documents. A common application is to create summary worksheets from several source worksheets. For example, an accounting system might contain individual worksheets for income and expense, which could then be fused into an income and expense worksheet.

In this chapter, we are going go learn how to work with multiple documents. We will create an income worksheet for Frills and Thrills, and then combine the income and expense worksheets we have created into an income and expense worksheet. We will then learn how to link the spreadsheets, so that any changes we make in the income or expense worksheets will automatically be reflected in the income and expense worksheet.

As you will discover, the ability to link worksheets in Excel is a powerful feature that will save you hours of time and facilitate the process of creating a cohesive whole from individual parts.

Copying Information Between Documents

You can copy information or data from one document into another. The procedure is the same as copying information in a single document, except that you must switch documents or windows. Both documents should be open and unhidden. It is easier if you have both document windows displayed on the screen at the same time. If you have any other documents open, hide them, so that only the two documents you are working on are visible. (To hide a document, switch to the document and select Hide in the Window menu.) Use the Tile option in the Windows Arrange command to view both document windows on the screen at the same time. To copy information between documents:

1. Switch to the document from which you are copying data. Select the data you want to copy.
2. Click on Edit in the menu bar.
3. Click on Copy.
4. Switch to the document to which you want to copy the data.
5. Select the cell or the upper-left corner of the range to which you want to copy the data.
6. Click on Edit in the menu bar.
7. Click on Paste. The data has been copied from one document to another.

You can take this procedure one step further by creating links between the cells or ranges in the documents you are combining.

You can also cut and paste, rather than copy and paste, data from one document to another.

N O T E

Linking Cells and Ranges Between Documents

When you link cells and ranges between documents, you copy the data from the **source document** and paste link it into the new document (the **dependent document**). When you link data between documents, you create a **reference** in the dependent document. The reference refers to the cell address(es) in the source document for the linked data. For example, if you copy the contents of cell B3 from the source document and then paste link them into the new document, what is pasted is not actually the data itself but the reference for the data. The reference tells Excel that the data is linked, and where to find the data itself. When both the source document and the dependent document are open and you change the data in a linked cell in the source document, Excel immediately notices the change of data in the referenced address and updates the data in the dependent document.

Let's create a link between two cells. Open a new worksheet and type *700* into cell B3, as shown in Figure 7.1.

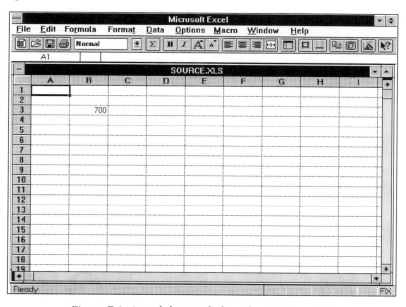

Figure 7.1. A worksheet with the value 700 in cell B3.

Name the document SOURCE. Then create another new worksheet. While it is still empty, name it DEPEND. If you have any other documents open, hide them, so that only these two documents are visible. (To hide a document, switch to the document and select Hide in the Window menu.) Use the Tile option in the Arrange command in the Window menu to view both windows on the screen at the same time, as shown in Figure 7.2.

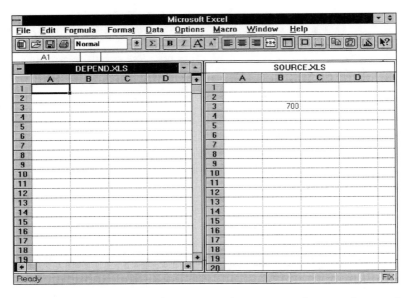

Figure 7.2 The Tile option used to view two document windows simultaneously.

To create a link:

1. Select cell B3 in SOURCE.XLS.
2. Click on Edit in the menu bar.
3. Click on Copy.
4. Select cell B3 in DEPEND.XLS.
5. Click on Edit in the menu bar.
6. Click on Paste Link. A reference has been created linking cell B3 in the source and dependent documents.

To understand how the reference works, click on cell B3 in the source document. Notice that the value contained in the cell is displayed in the formula bar, as shown in Figure 7.3. Now click on cell B3 in the dependent document. Notice that the reference (=SOURCE.XLS!$B$3), not the value, is displayed in the formula bar, as shown in Figure 7.4. Excel has pasted the document name and the cell address of the source document (*not* the cell value) in the dependent document. Because the link references the cell address and not the cell value, changes made in the referenced cell address are automatically updated in the dependent document.

You can link cells or ranges between worksheets or between worksheets and charts.

You can link one cell or range to more than one worksheet. You do not have to link a cell or range in one worksheet to the same cell or range in another worksheet. You can also link nonadjacent ranges. If you link named cells or ranges, the reference is the name, not the address, of the referenced cell or range.

N O T E

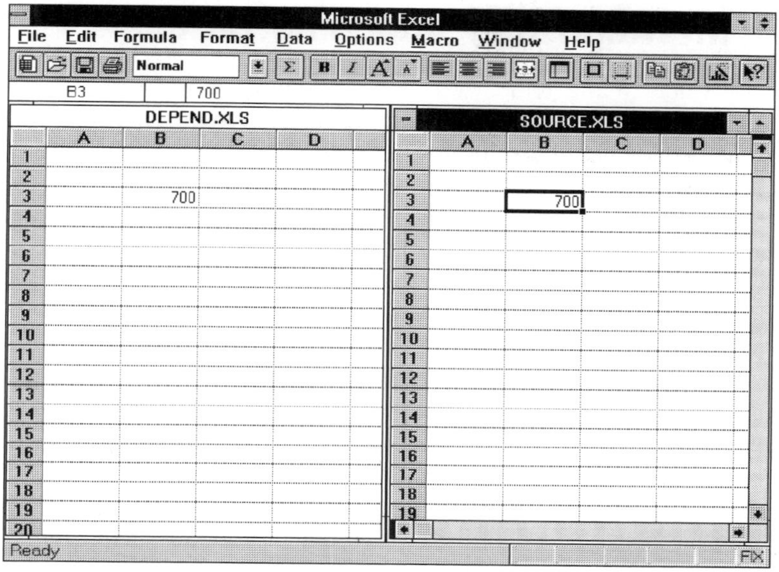

Figure 7.3. Value in cell B3 in SOURCE.XLS shows in the formula bar.

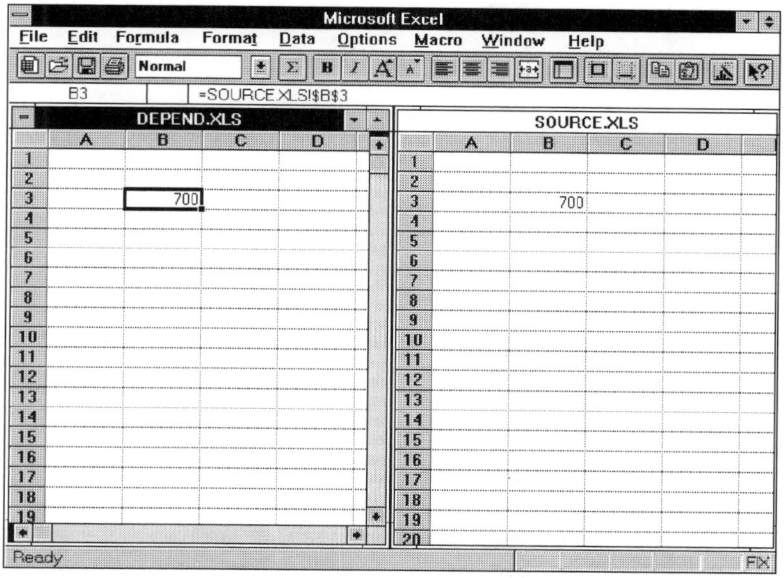

Figure 7.4. Reference in cell B3 in DEPEND.XLS shows in the formula bar.

Changing the Value in the Referenced Cell

Let's change the value of the referenced cell and see what happens in the dependent document. Click on cell B3 in SOURCE.XLS and change the value from 700 to 500. Now click outside of cell B3. Notice that the value in cell B3 in DEPEND.XLS has been automatically updated to reflect the change in the referenced cell. If you click on cell B3 in DEPEND.XLS, you will see that the reference in the formula bar is unchanged. The value in the cell has changed because you changed the value in the referenced cell.

Linking with External References

In the above example, we created a link with the source document and the dependent document opened. This enabled you to copy from the source document and paste link to the dependent document. You can also create a link with only the dependent document open. To do this, you must enter an **external reference** in the dependent document. The external reference creates the same reference that would be created using paste link. To do this you must know the addresses or names of the cells or ranges you are referencing in the source document. To create an external reference:

1. In the dependent document, select the cell or upper-left corner of the range you want to link.

2. Type in the address or name of the cell or range you want to reference. The following rules apply:

   a. All external references must begin with an equal sign (=).

   b. The address must include the name of the source document followed by an exclamation point (!), followed by an absolute cell or range reference; for example, =SOURCE.XLS!$B$3:$E$8. The dollar signs ($) indicate that the cell reference is absolute (see Chapter 4 for an explanation of relative and absolute cell references).

   c. If the source document is in another directory, you must enter the entire path with the name of the document. The name should be surrounded by single quotes and then followed by an exclamation point (!) and the cell or range address; for example, ='C:\ACCOUNT\SOURCE.XLS'!$B$3.

   d. If you are referencing a named cell or range, you must enter the name of the document, followed by an exclamation point (!), followed by the cell or range name; for example, =SOURCE.XLS!TOTALS.

Saving Linked Documents

You save linked documents the same way you save any document. It is advisable to save the source document first, and then save the dependent document.

Moving or Renaming Source Documents

If you move or rename a source document while the dependent document is closed, you must manually edit the dependent document to redirect the link.

1. Open the dependent document.
2. Click on File in the menu bar.
3. Click on Links to display the Links dialog box, as shown in Figure 7.5.

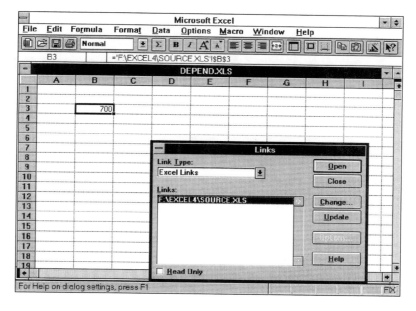

Figure 7.5. The Links dialog box.

4. Select or type Excel Links in the Link Type text box.
5. Select the moved or renamed source document(s).
6. Click on the Change command button to display the Change Links dialog box, as shown in Figure 7.6, on the next page.
7. From the file list select the moved or renamed document.
8. Choose OK. The link has been redirected in the dependent document and you are returned to the Links dialog box.
9. If you have selected more than one source document in step 5, repeat steps 7 and 8 for each selected source document.
10. Click on Close to close the Links dialog box.

If you move or rename a source document while the dependent document is open, the dependent document is automatically updated to reflect the redirected links.

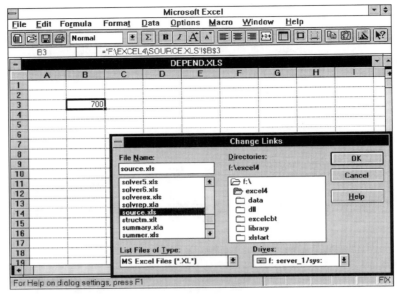

Figure 7.6. The Change Links dialog box.

Updating Links

If you make a change in the referenced cell in a source document and the dependent document is not open, the change is not automatically reflected in the dependent document. If you open the changed source document and then, while the source document is open, you open the dependent document, the link will automatically update. If, however, you open the dependent document while the source document is closed, you will receive a message asking if you want to update the link. If you choose Yes, all changes in the referenced cells in the source document will be updated in the dependent document. If you choose No, the changes in the referenced cells will not be updated in the dependent document. If you choose No then change your mind, you can update the changes to the dependent document manually:

1. Click on File in the menu bar.
2. Click on Links to display the Link Type dialog box.
3. Select or type Excel Links in the Link Type text box.
4. Select the source document(s) containing information that has been changed and not updated in the link.
5. Click on the Update command button.
6. Click on Close to close the Links dialog box.

Viewing a List of Source Documents

If you have opened a dependent document and have not opened the source document(s), you can see a list of all of the source documents referenced in the dependent document:

1. Click on File in the menu bar.
2. Click on Links to display the Links dialog box.
3. Select or type Excel Links in the Link Type text box.
4. All of the source documents referenced in the dependent document are listed in the Links list box.
5. Click on Close to close the Links dialog box.

Opening a Source Document

If you have opened a dependent document and have not opened the source document(s), you can list and open the source documents that are referenced in the dependent document.

1. Click on File in the menu bar.
2. Click on Links to display the Links dialog box.
3. Select or type Excel Links in the Link Type text box.
4. All of the source documents referenced in the dependent document are listed in the Links list box.
5. Select the source document(s) you want to open.
6. Click on Open to open the source document(s).

SHORT CUT

If you double-click on a cell containing a reference in the dependent document, the source document containing the referenced cell is opened and the active cell is the referenced cell.

Removing Links from Single Cells

To remove a link from a dependent document when only single cells are linked, simply clear the contents of the cell, or replace the reference in the linked cell in the dependent document with a new value, or copy the value from the source document and use Paste rather than Paste Link to paste the value in the dependent document.

Removing Links from Ranges

When you link ranges between documents, you create an **array** in the dependent document. Excel treats all of the cells in the linked range or array as a single unit. (Arrays will be covered in greater detail in Chapter 8.) You cannot change part of the array. You must remove the link by clearing the entire array or by replacing all of the data in the entire array with the values in the source document. To clear the array, select the entire array in the dependent document and choose Clear in the Edit menu. To replace the array with the values in the range in the source document:

1. Select the entire array (or range) in the source document.
2. Click on Edit in the menu bar.
3. Click on Copy to copy the values in the source document.
4. Select the array in the dependent document.
5. Click on Edit in the menu bar.
6. Click on Paste Special to display the Paste Special dialog box, as shown in Figure 7.7.
7. Select Values and click on OK.

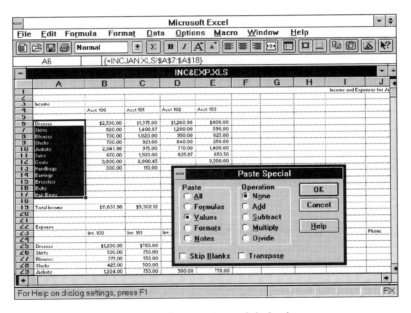

Figure 7.7. The Paste Special dialog box.

All of the references in the array in the dependent document have been replaced with the values in the source document and the link has been removed. Once the link is removed, the array no longer exists and you can now edit the values in these cells individually.

SHORT CUT

Click on any cell in the array and press Ctrl+/ (slash) to select the entire array.

N O T E

If you have tried to change part of an array, a dialog box will appear informing you that you cannot change part of an array. Choose OK in the dialog box and press the Esc key to cancel the action.

Linking Two Worksheets to a New Worksheet

In Chapter 4 you created an expense worksheet for Frills and Thrills. We are now going to create an income worksheet for January 1992, which, along with the expense worksheet, will be combined and linked into an income and expense worksheet. Open a new worksheet and create the income worksheet shown in Figure 7.8.

		Salaries for January, 1992				
		Week1	Week2	Week3	Week4	Total
Perm						
Joy		500	500	500	500	2000
Amy		550	550	550	550	2200
Temps						
Linda		300		250		550
Marie		175	275		400	850
Sue		230		150		380
Sub T						
Perm		1050	1050	1050	1050	4200
Temps		705	275	400	400	1780
Total		1755	1325	1450	1450	5980

Figure 7.8. The INCJAN.XLS worksheet.

After you have typed the worksheet, apply whatever formatting is necessary for an attractive and polished appearance. Save the worksheet and call it INCJAN.XLS.

You are now going to copy and link data from the income worksheet to the income and expense worksheet.

1. If the INCJAN.XLS worksheet is not open, open it.

2. Open a new worksheet and save it as INC&EXP.XLS. (It is not necessary to save the worksheet until it is completed; we are saving it now to make the following instructions clearer.)

3. Hide all other open documents.

4. Use the Tile option in the Window Arrange command to view both document windows simultaneously.

5. Switch to the INCJAN.XLS document window.

6. Select the range C4:F4.

7. Click on Edit in the menu bar.

8. Click on Copy.

9. Switch to the INC&EXP.XLS document window.

10. Select cell B4, which will become the upper-left corner of the dependent range.

11. Click on Edit in the menu bar.

12. Click on Paste Link. The range in the dependent document (INC&EXP.XLS) has been linked to the range in the source document (INCJAN.XLS).

13. Following steps 5 through 12, link the following ranges:

From INCJAN.XLS	**To INC&EXP.XLS**
A7:A18	A6
C7:F18	B6

Your INC&EXP.XLS document should now look like the one shown in Figure 7.9.

Remember, you must select the entire range in the source document when you copy it. When you paste-link it in the dependent document, you need only select the cell in the upper-left corner of the range it is being pasted to.

N O T E

14. Close the INCJAN.XLS worksheet and open the EXPJAN.XLS worksheet. Retile the document windows so that you can view both document windows simultaneously.

15. Link the following nonadjacent ranges:

From EXPJAN.XLS	To INC&EXP.XLS
C4:R4	B23
A7:A18; A22:A26; A30:A34*	A25
C7:F18; G22:I26; J30:R34*	B25

*These are nonadjacent ranges that are being pasted as one range into the dependent document.

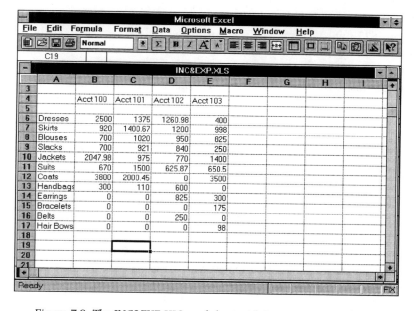

Figure 7.9. The INC&EXP.XLS worksheet with January income linked.

16. Close the EXPJAN.XLS worksheet. All of your links have been created. You are now ready to complete the INC&EXP.XLS worksheet.

17. Return the INC&EXP.XLS document window to normal size. Save the worksheet; if you make a mistake, you do not want to have to recreate your links.

18. Type in all additional titles, as shown in Figure 7.10, on the next page. Just type in the titles—we are going to use formulas to fill in the figures.

19. Enter a formula in cell R6 to calculate the total of row 6 (Dresses). Copy the formula to cells R7:R19 to calculate the totals of rows 7 through 19. Cell R19 will have a zero value because the formula for Total Income in row 19 has not yet been entered. We'll do that next.

20. In cell B19, enter a formula to calculate the total of cells B6:B17 (the total of all income for Acct 100). Copy the formula to cells C19:E19 to total the income for Accts 101, 102, and 103. Cell R19 now reflects the sum of cells B19:E19.

21. Enter a formula in cell R25 to calculate the total of cells B25:Q25 (row 25). Copy the formula to cells R26:R48 to calculate the totals of rows 26 through 48. Cell R48 will have a zero value because the formula for Total Expenses in row 48 has not yet been entered. We'll do that next.

22. In cell B48 enter a formula to calculate the total of cells B25 through B46 (the total of all expenses for Inv. 100). Copy the formula to cells C48:Q48 to total the income for all of the accounts in each of the columns C through Q. Cell R48 now reflects the sum of the values in cells B48:Q48.

23. In cell S25 enter a formula to calculate the difference between the income from Dresses (cell R6) and the expense for Dresses (cell R25). We are using a subtraction operator for this formula, which should read =R6-R25.

    Copy this formula to cells S26:S36 to calculate the difference between the income and expense for each corresponding item (Skirts, Blouses, etc.). Office and constant expenses (such as rent) do not reflect any income. They are strictly expense items. Therefore, in cell S37, enter a formula to show the difference between the income for Paper (0, because there is no income for Paper) and the expense for Paper (R37). Your formula should look like this: =0-R37.

    Copy this formula to cells S38:S46 to reflect the difference between the income (which will always be zero) and the expense for each corresponding item (Clips, Pens, etc.).

24. In cell B50 enter a formula to show the difference between the Total Income in column B and the Total Expense in column B. The formula should read =B19-B48.

    Copy this formula to cells C50:R50. The values in cells C50 through Q50 will show the difference between the Total Income and Total Expense for each of the accounts in the column. The value in cell R50 will show the difference between the Total Income for all items and the Total Expense for all items for the month of January 1992. The value, $4,698.32, reflects the net income for Frills and Thrills for the month.

25. Format your worksheet. Select the entire worksheet, using the Select All button. Format the entire worksheet with a number format to add a decimal point and two decimal zeros. Then select rows 6, 19, 25, 48, and 50, and apply a currency format to add dollar signs ($) and two decimal zeros. Center the title for the worksheet and align all columns to fit the data. To get rid of all zero values:

    a. Click on Options in the menu bar.
    b. Click on Display to display the Display Options dialog box.
    c. Clear the Zero Values check box.
    d. Choose OK.

26. Save your worksheet, which should now look like the one shown in Figure 7.10.

Income and Expenses for January, 1992

Income

Income	Acct 100	Acct 101	Acct 102	Acct 103	Totals
Dresses	$2,500.00	$1,375.00	$1,260.98	$400.00	$5,535.98
Skirts	920.00	1,400.67	1,200.00	998.00	4,518.67
Blouses	700.00	1,020.00	950.00	825.00	3,495.00
Slacks	700.00	921.00	840.00	250.00	2,711.00
Jackets	2,047.98	975.00	770.00	1,400.00	5,192.98
Suits	670.00	1,500.00	625.87	650.50	3,446.37
Coats	3,800.00	2,000.45		3,500.00	9,300.45
Handbags	300.00	110.00	600.00		1,010.00
Earrings			825.00	300.00	1,125.00
Bracelets				175.00	175.00
Belts			250.00		250.00
Hair Bows				98.00	98.00
Total Income	$11,637.98	$9,302.12	$7,321.85	$8,596.50	$36,858.45

Expense

Expense	Inv. 100	Inv. 101	Inv. 102	Inv. 103	Off. 200	Off. 201	Off. 202	Rent	Phone	Electric	Salaries	Tax FICA	Tax Fed	Tax State	Tax City	Tax Dis	Totals
Dresses	$1,200.00	$780.00	$675.00	$210.00													$2,865.00
Skirts	500.00	750.00	675.00	550.00													2,475.00
Blouses	375.00	550.00	600.00	450.00													1,975.00
Slacks	425.00	500.00	620.67	210.45													1,756.12
Jackets	1,224.00	750.00	500.00	778.00													3,252.00
Suits	450.00	788.00	300.00	325.00													1,863.00
Coats	2,200.00	1,050.00		1,800.00													5,050.00
Handbags	150.00	75.00	400.00	150.00													625.00
Earrings			500.00	150.00													650.00
Bracelets				100.00													100.00
Belts			175.00														175.00
Hair Bows				50.00													50.00
Paper					55.00												55.00
Clips						10.00											10.00
Pens						25.00											25.00
Print Cartridge						100.00											100.00
Stamps							50.00										50.00
Rent								2,500.00									2,500.00
Phone									375.23								375.23
Electric										305.78							305.78
Salaries											5,980.00						5,980.00
Taxes												598.00	700.00	400.00	150.00	75.00	1,923.00
Total Expense	$6,524.00	$5,243.00	$4,445.67	$4,623.45	$55.00	$135.00	$50.00	$2,500.00	$375.23	$305.78	$5,980.00	$598.00	$700.00	$400.00	$150.00	$75.00	$32,160.13
Net Income or Loss	$5,113.98	$4,059.12	$2,876.18	$3,973.05	($55.00)	($135.00)	($50.00)	($2,500.00)	($375.23)	($305.78)	($5,980.00)	($598.00)	($700.00)	($400.00)	($150.00)	($75.00)	$4,698.32

Figure 7.10. The INC&EXP.XLS worksheet.

Consolidating Data from Multiple Worksheets

You can **consolidate** similar types of data from several source worksheets and link them as one entry in a dependent worksheet. For example, you could consolidate the total income for dresses entered into three worksheets (one for January, one for February, and one for March) into one consolidated total in the dependent worksheet to reflect the total income for dresses for the first quarter of 1992. If the values in any of the source worksheets change, the change will be reflected in the dependent worksheet.

   You can consolidate data by category or by position. You can use cell addresses or cell or range names to consolidate data.

   When you link consolidated data, Excel creates an outline in your dependent worksheet. This outline works the same way as an outline you create using the Outline command. For information on how outlines are used in Excel, refer to Chapter 6. If you want to undo a consolidation (see below), you must delete the outline.

Consolidating Data by Category

When you consolidate data by **category**, you are telling Excel to consolidate the data from source areas containing similar data in different locations. For example, if the total income for dresses was located in cell D5 in the worksheet for January, and in cell F7 in the worksheet for February, and in cell H23 in the worksheet for March, Excel would consolidate the values from these three cells into the dependent worksheet. Excel uses the **labels** (or titles) for each source area to determine category names. You must select a label for each source when you consolidate data by category. For example, if the title Total Dresses appears in column D in the worksheet for January, in column F in the worksheet for February, and in column H in the worksheet for March, and you select each of these titles as part of the source, Excel will label the consolidated data Total Dresses. To consolidate data from several sources by category:

1. Select the destination area for the consolidated data in the dependent worksheet.
2. Click on Data in the menu bar.
3. Click on Consolidate to display the Consolidate dialog box, as shown in Figure 7.11.
4. When you use the Consolidation feature, you must use functions instead of operators in formulas. Select the function you want to use in the Function text box. (The default function is SUM.) You can use eleven worksheet functions when you consolidate data: SUM, AVERAGE, COUNT, COUNTA, MAX, MIN, PRODUCT, STDEV, STDEVP, VAR, and VARP. Some of the most commonly used functions are covered in Chapter 8. For information on how to use all of the functions available in Excel, refer to your Excel manual or purchase an advanced user's manual.
5. Move your insertion point to the Reference text box. If your source worksheet is open, select the source area on the worksheet, including the category labels you want to use. If the source worksheet is not open, click on Browse and select the

worksheet that contains the source from the list in the Browse dialog box, then click on OK. Excel will enter the filename in the Reference text box and you need only type in the cell reference or name. **Or,** type the complete path and filename for the worksheet that contains the source data. Follow the filename with an exclamation point (!), and type in the cell reference or name.

6. Click on Add. The cell reference or name appears in the All References list box.

7. Repeat steps 5 and 6 for all of the source areas you want to include in the link.

8. Check Top Row in Use Labels In if the labels (or titles) for the source areas are located in the top row of the source area. If the labels are located in the left column of the source areas, check Left Column.

9. If you want to create links to the source areas when consolidating data from multiple documents, check the Create Links To Source Data check box. If you do not check the box, you will consolidate your data, but it will not be linked.

10. Click on OK.

The data from all of the source worksheets is consolidated into one entry in the dependent worksheet, containing the source label and values.

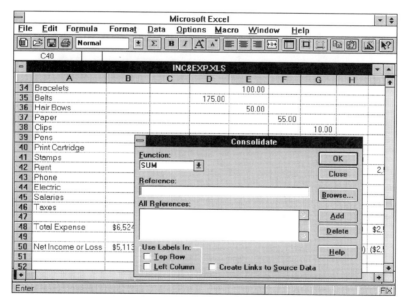

Figure 7.11. The Consolidate dialog box.

Consolidating Data by Position

When you consolidate data by **position**, you are telling Excel to consolidate similar data from several source worksheets when the data is located in the same address in each source worksheet. When you consolidate data by position, you do not identify source labels and they are not copied into the dependent worksheet. If you want to label the data in your dependent worksheet, you must type the labels in. To consolidate by position:

1. Select the destination area for the consolidated data in the dependent worksheet.
2. Click on Data in the menu bar.
3. Click on Consolidate to display the Consolidate dialog box.
4. Select the function you want to use in the Function text box. (The default function is SUM.)
5. Move your insertion point to the Reference text box. If your source worksheet is open, select the source area on the worksheet. If the source worksheet is not open, click on Browse and select the worksheet that contains the source from the list in the Browse dialog box, then click on OK. Excel will enter the filename in the Reference text box and you need only type in the cell reference or name. **Or,** type the complete path and filename for the worksheet that contains the source data. Follow the filename with an exclamation point (!), and type in the cell reference or name.
6. Click on Add. The cell reference or name appears in the All References list box.
7. Repeat steps 5 and 6 for all of the source areas you want to include in the link.
8. If you want to create links to the source data, check the Create Links To Source Data check box. If you do not check the box, you will consolidate your data, but it will not be linked.
9. Click on OK.

N O T E

You can undo consolidation by choosing the Undo command from the Edit menu immediately after you consolidate, or by deleting the data. If you have linked the data, you must also remove the outline.

Changing the Location of Consolidation Source Areas

You can change the location of consolidated source areas only if you have not created links to the source area. If you have created links to the source areas, the references in the dependent worksheet will not update to reflect the new locations of the source areas, and the links will no longer be valid. You must delete the data and the outline before you can adjust the consolidation. To change the reference to a source area:

1. Select the destination area in the dependent worksheet you want to change.
2. Click on Data in the menu bar.
3. Click on the source area you want to change in the All References list box to display the source area in the Reference text box.

4. Edit the source area in the Reference text box.
5. Choose Add.
6. Select the old reference in the All References list box.
7. Click on Delete.
8. Choose OK to reconsolidate your data.

Adding Source Areas to an Existing Consolidation

You can add a source area to consolidated data only if you have not created links to the source areas. If you have created links to the source areas, you must delete the data and the outline before you can adjust the consolidation. To add a source area to an existing consolidation:

1. Select the destination area in the dependent worksheet where you want to add a new source area.
2. Click on Data in the menu bar.
3. Enter the new source area in the Reference text box.
4. Choose Add.
5. Choose OK to reconsolidate your data.

Deleting References to a Source Area in Consolidated Data

You can delete a reference to a source area in consolidated data only if you have not created links to the source areas. If you have created links to the source areas, you must delete the data and the outline before you can adjust the consolidation. To delete a reference to a source area from consolidated data:

1. Select the destination area in the dependent worksheet from which you want to remove a reference to a source area.
2. Click on Data in the menu bar.
3. Select the source area you want to delete in the All References list box.
4. Click on Delete.
5. Choose OK to reconsolidate your data.

Editing Documents as a Group

If you edit documents as a **group**, you can edit cells and ranges in one document and have the same cells and ranges in several other documents reflect the changes. You can format a range in one document in a group and the same format will be applied to the same range in every document in the group. You can add data to cells and copy and cut cells and ranges in one document in the group, and these changes will be duplicated in each document in the group. You can print all of the documents in a group with a single click of the Print command. Macro sheets can also be edited as groups.

Creating Groups

To create a group:

1. Open the worksheets and macro sheets you want to edit as a group. You can have other documents open at the same time, even if you don't want to include them as part of the group.

2. Switch to the document window in which you want to make changes. This is the sheet that contains the active cell and that will be the active document. Once you select a group, any changes you make to this document will be duplicated in all of the other documents in the group.

3. Click on Options in the menu bar.

4. Click on Group Edit to display the Group Edit dialog box listing all of the current open sheets, as shown in Figure 7.12. If you have not created a group edit during this Excel session, all of the open sheets will be selected. If you have created a group during this Excel session, all of the open sheets will be listed, but only the sheets included in the previous group will be selected.

5. Select the sheets you want to include in the current group.

6. Click on OK. Excel will add the word Group in the title bar to all of the sheets you have selected. The sheet containing the active cell will be on top.

N O T E

Groups are *temporary* collections of documents. If you switch to another document window while you are in Group Edit, you will end the group editing session and the group will disappear. You must remain in the active document. Permanent groups, called workbooks, will be discussed later in this chapter.

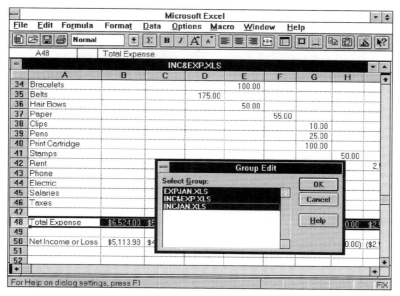

Figure 7.12. The Group Edit dialog box.

Viewing All of the Sheets in a Group

If you want to view all of the sheets in a group simultaneously:

1. Click on Window in the menu bar.
2. Click on Arrange to display the Arrange Windows dialog box.
3. Select the Tiled, Horizontal, or Vertical option button.
4. Select the Documents of Active Group check box.
5. All of the documents in the group are displayed. If you have opened any other documents and they are not part of the group, they are not displayed.

Adding or Deleting Group Documents

You can add documents to or delete documents from an existing group. While you are in the active document:

1. Click on Options in the menu bar.
2. Click on Group Edit to display the Group Edit dialog box.
3. Add the documents to or delete them from the selection in the list.
4. Click on OK.

Entering Data in a Group

To enter data in a group:

1. Create a group.
2. In the active document, select a cell in which you want to enter data.
3. Type the data and either click on another cell or press Enter.

The data you entered in the active cell will be duplicated in the same location in every document in the group.

Copying Data, Formulas, and Formats in a Group

You can copy the contents, formulas, and formatting for a single cell, a range, or the entire active document to every other document in a group.

1. Create a group.
2. In the active sheet select the cells, the range, or the entire worksheet.
3. Click on Edit in the menu bar.
4. Click on Fill Group to display the Fill Group dialog box, as shown in Figure 7.13. Select the All option if you want to copy the contents, formulas, and formatting for the selected cells. Select the Formulas option if you only want to copy the formulas for the selected cells. Select the Formats option if you only want to copy the formatting for the selected cells.
5. Click on OK. The selected cells have been copied to the same location in all of the documents in the group.

Using Workbooks

Creating a group is a useful way to temporarily connect documents for editing purposes during a work session. However, the group is temporary; once you switch to a document other than the active document or close the session, the group no longer exists. **Workbooks** permanently group or bind documents into a single workbook document or file. This is an excellent way to keep related worksheets together.

Workbooks can contain bound or unbound documents. Bound documents can only be bound into one workbook. Unbound documents will appear in the workbook contents, but the document is not included in the workbook file and can be used with more than one workbook. As you will see, there are advantages to using both bound and unbound documents in workbooks.

Workbooks are saved the same way any document is saved—by using the Save or Save As command. Excel automatically assigns an .XLW extension to a workbook. To open a workbook, use the Open command in the File menu and select the workbook document in the file list. When you open or close the workbook, all of the worksheets bound in the workbook file are automatically opened or closed. You can quickly switch among the contents of the workbook by selecting a document from the Workbook Contents menu. If you choose to display the documents in several windows, the workbook will keep track of each window's position on the screen.

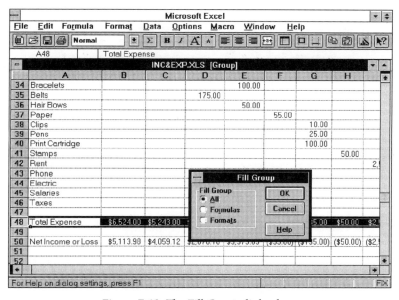

Figure 7.13. The Fill Group dialog box.

Workbooks are an excellent way to organize sensitive files. Instead of applying passwords to each file, you can bind the files in a workbook and assign a password to the workbook file.

Creating Workbooks

When you create a workbook, you bind documents into a workbook file. To create a workbook:

1. Click on File in the menu bar.
2. Click on New to display the New dialog box.
3. Select Workbook.
4. Click on OK: Excel displays an empty Workbook Contents window, as shown in Figure 7.14, on the next page.

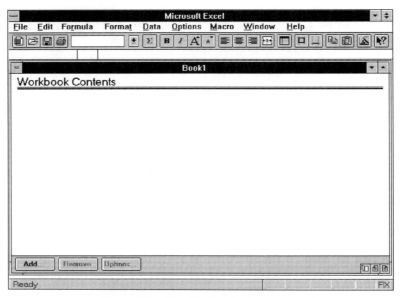

Figure 7.14. The Workbook Contents window.

Once the workbook is created, you can add existing documents to it, or you can create new documents to add to it. To add and open an existing file to a workbook:

1. In the Workbook Contents window, click on the Add command button to display the Add To Workbook dialog box, as shown in Figure 7.15.

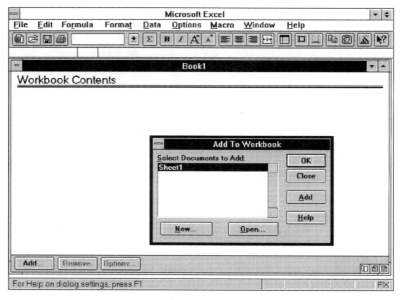

Figure 7. 15. The Add To Workbook dialog box.

2. Click on Open.

3. Select the document you want to add to the workbook.

4. Choose OK. The document is opened and added to the workbook as a bound document.

5. Close the Add To Workbook dialog box by selecting Close.

To add an open file to a workbook:

1. In the Workbook Contents window, click on the Add command button to display the Add To Workbook dialog box listing all of the open files that are not in the workbook.

2. Select the document you want to add to the workbook. To select more than one open document, hold down the Shift key while you select the documents. If the documents are not in sequence, hold down the Ctrl key while you select them.

3. Choose OK. The documents are added to the workbook as bound documents.

4. Close the Add To Workbook dialog box by selecting Close.

To add a new document to a workbook:

1. In the Workbook Contents window, click on the Add command button to display the Add To Workbook dialog box.

2. Click on New to display the New dialog box.

3. Select the type of document you want to create and add to the workbook.

4. Choose OK. The document is created and added to the workbook as a bound document.

5. Close the Add To Workbook dialog box by selecting Close.

Binding and Unbinding Workbook Documents

When you bind a document into a workbook, it cannot be accessed outside of the workbook. You should bind documents when you want to keep them together in a group for easier management or for security reasons. For example, you can bind sensitive financial records into a workbook and assign a password to the workbook file. Only persons with the password will be able to access any of the workbook documents.

You can also assign extended names of up to thirty-one characters to bound documents. These names, however, are for display purposes only. The file will be displayed in the Workbook Contents window with the extended name, but if you unbind the file, you will be using the unbound document with its old name.

When you display a bound worksheet, the workbook name is displayed along with the document name in the title bar. You can link bound worksheets or edit them as a group just as you would any other worksheet. When you link bound worksheets, the reference will also include the workbook name.

You should unbind files if you want to be able to use them with more than one workbook or when you want to be able to use them outside of workbooks. Unbound files will be displayed in the Workbook Contents window, but will not be included in the workbook document file.

You can bind or unbind the same workbook documents at will. When you add a document to a workbook, it is automatically bound. To unbind the document:

1. Open the workbook as you would open any file.
2. In the Workbook Contents window, select the document you want to unbind.
3. Click on the Options command button to display the Document Options dialog box, as shown in Figure 7.16.
4. In the Store Document In option box, select Separate File (Unbound).
5. Click on OK. The file will still be listed in the Workbook Contents window, but it will be an unbound document.

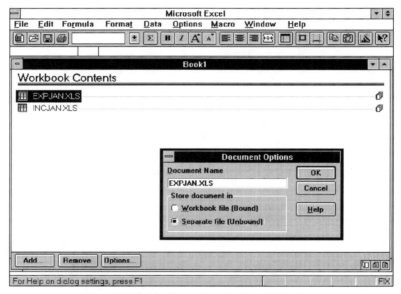

Figure 7.16. The Document Options dialog box.

When you add a document to a workbook it is automatically bound. If you have unbound a file, you can bind it again. To bind a file:

1. Open the workbook as you would open any file.
2. In the Workbook Contents window, select the document you want to bind.
3. Click on the Options command button. The Document Options dialog box is displayed.
4. In the Store Document In option box, select Workbook File (Bound).
5. Click on OK. The file is bound into the workbook.

SHORT CUT

When you add a file to a workbook, it is listed with a bound icon. You can bind or unbind a document by clicking on the icon. Figure 7.17 shows an example of bound and unbound document icons.

Giving Bound Documents Extended Names

Bound documents can be given names of up to thirty-one characters. This makes it easier to identify files in the Workbook Contents window. To give a document an extended name:

1. Open the workbook as you would open any file.
2. In the Workbook Contents window, select the bound document you want to give an extended name.
3. Click on the Options command button to display the Document Options dialog box.
4. In the Document Name text box, type in a document name of up to thirty-one characters. You can use any combination of characters, including spaces.
5. Click on OK. The document will be listed in the Workbook Contents window with the extended name.

Moving Between Workbook Documents

Once you open a workbook, you can switch easily between the documents in the workbook by clicking on the Left and Right Paging and Contents icons found in the lower-right corner of all workbook document windows as well as the Workbook Contents window. Figure 7.17, on the next page, labels these buttons. If you click on the Contents button, you can switch documents from the Workbook Contents window.

1. Click on the Contents button in the lower-right corner of any workbook document window. The Workbook Contents window is displayed.
2. Double-click on the document to which you want to move.

You can also move between workbook documents in the order in which they are listed in the Workbook Contents window.

1. Switch to any document in the workbook.
2. To move to the next document as listed in the Workbook Contents window, click on the Right Paging button in the lower-right corner of the document window.
3. To move to the previous document as listed in the Workbook Contents window, click on the Left Paging button in the lower-right corner of the document window.

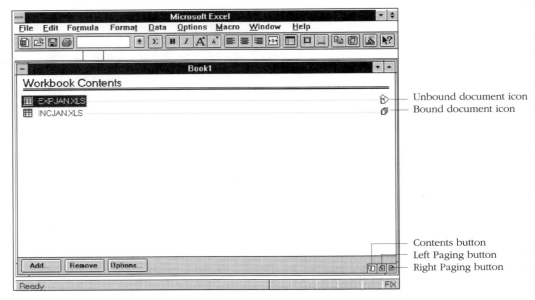

Figure 7.17. Elements of the Workbook Contents window.

Reordering the Workbook Contents Window

You can rearrange the order of documents in the Workbook Contents window.

1. In the Workbook Contents window, select the document you want to move.
2. Click on Edit in the menu bar.
3. Click on Cut.
4. Select the document in the location into which you want to insert the cut document.
5. Click on Edit in the menu bar.
6. Click on Paste. The document is inserted into its new location.

You can also reorder documents in the Workbook Contents window by dragging them to a new location.

Removing Workbook Documents

To remove a document from a workbook:

1. In the Workbook Contents window, select the document you want to remove from the workbook.
2. Click on Remove.

You can also remove a document from the workbook by dragging the document out of the Workbook Contents window to any place in the Excel workspace.

Review Exercises for Chapter 7

- ◆ Open two worksheets. Copy information from one worksheet to another.
- ◆ Link the data from SALJAN.XLS to a new worksheet you create. Link some of the data as single cells and some of the data as ranges.
- ◆ Practice updating the links in your new document.
- ◆ Remove a link from a single cell.
- ◆ Remove a link from a range.
- ◆ Consolidate and link the Totals data in INCJAN.XLS and EXPJAN.XLS to a new worksheet. Note how the outline works.
- ◆ Open three new worksheets. Create a group consisting of the three new worksheets.
- ◆ Enter data into the active worksheet and format it. Then switch to another document to end the group.
- ◆ Switch back to the former active worksheet, enter new data, and format it.
- ◆ Recreate the group and use Fill Group to copy the data to all of the other documents in the group.

Before You Go On...

Before you go on you should be able to copy data from one document to another. You should be familiar with both using paste link and entering external references to create links between documents. You should know how to redirect links in a dependent document. You should know how to delete links from single cells and from ranges in a dependent document. You should be able to consolidate data from multiple worksheets into a dependent worksheet. You should be comfortable working with group edit and with workbooks.

Chapter 8

WORKING WITH CALCULATIONS

What You Will Learn in This Chapter

- ◆ How to use parenthetical expressions in formulas
- ◆ Understanding text, comparison, and reference operators
- ◆ Using basic functions
- ◆ Using arrays
- ◆ Using arrays in functions

You have already learned how to use arithmetic operators and to construct simple formulas. You have used the SUM function to add a range of cells. This chapter will discuss the rest of the operators available, and will show you how to use more advanced formulas. You will learn how to use functions and arrays to enter formulas more quickly and efficiently.

Using Parenthetical Expressions to Build More Complex Formulas

Throughout this book we have been using simple formulas to calculate addition, subtraction, multiplication, and division. The result of each formula was calculated by following and performing, in order, the instruction of each operator encountered. For example, the formula =50-10+30 produces a result of 70 by subtracting 10 from 50, then adding 30. If we used the formula =10+5*2, the result would be 30: 10 added to 5 (15) multiplied by 2 (30). Such a formula performs each operation in the order in which it is encountered. If we wanted the result to be 20—that is, 10 added to the result of 5 multiplied by 2—this formula would not work. We would have to use the parenthetical expression =10+(5*2). to indicate to Excel the order in which the calculations are to be done.

In Excel formulas, parenthetical expressions are calculated first, then the rest of the formula is calculated based on the result of the values enclosed in the parenthetical expression. Parenthetical expressions can be used anywhere in a formula, and you can use as many parenthetical expressions in a formula as you wish. More than one parenthetical expression must be used if you want more than one operation in your formula calculated in a specific order. The use of parenthetical expressions (or the lack of them) will affect the results of your formulas.

Each of the following formulas uses the same values, but the first uses no parenthetical expression, the second uses one parenthetical expression, and the third uses two parenthetical expressions. Therefore, each produces a different result:

```
=10+10*2-5-3 equals 32
=10+(10*2)-5-3 equals 22
=10+(10*20)-(5-3) equals 28
```

Each of these formulas contains the same values—it is the use and placement of parenthetical expressions that determines the result. If your formula does not produce the value you expected, check to see if you need to use a parenthetical expression; or, if you have used parenthetical expressions, that they are placed correctly in the formula.

Understanding Operators

Operators, you will recall, are the parts of the formula that specify or identify the type of operation you are performing on a value. There are four types of operators that can be used in Excel: arithmetic, text, comparison, and reference. In Chapter 2 you learned about arithmetic operators; here we will discuss the remaining operators in greater detail. Table 8.1 contains a list of all operators and how they are used.

Type	Operator	Description	Example
Arithmetic. Performs basic mathematical operations; uses numeric values to produce numeric results.	+	Addition	=100/2*10% divides 100 by 2 and then multiplies the result by .10 for a final result of 5
	–	Subtraction (negative number if used with only one operand)	
	/	Division	
	*	Multiplication	
	%	Percentage (one operand only)	
	∧	Exponentiation	
Tex. Joins two or more text values or a text value and a numeric value into a single combined text value.	&	The **ampersand** connects two text values to produce one text result. If an operand refers to a cell that contains a formula, the operator combines the value of the formula and the text value as one single text value.	=Call me&A1 combines text operator *Call me* with value in cell A1. If value in cell A1 is *George,* the result of this operator is *Call me George.* If cell A1 contains the formula =100/2*10%, the result of this operator is *Call me 5.*
Comparison. Compares two values to produce a logical value of True or False.	=	Equal	=100/2*10% > 45 will produce a logical value of False, since the result of 100 ÷ 2 x .10 is not greater than 45.
	>	Greater than	
	<	Less than	
	≥	Greater than or equal to	
	≤	Less than or equal to	
	<>	Not equal to	

Table 8.1. Types of Operators

continued ...

...from previous page

Type	Operator	Description	Example
Reference: Combines two cell references into a single cell reference.	:	*Range:* Combines a group of cells into one reference known as a range.	=SUM(A1:A5) is the same as typing =A1+A2+A3+A4+A5. The colon (:) represents a range; A1:A5 refers to cells A1 through A5. The SUM function is generally used to add values enclosed in the parentheses that follow it.
	space	*Intersection:* Produces one reference for the cells that the two references have in common. If the two references have no cells in common, the result will be a #NULL error value.	If the range B3:D3 is named *Cat,* and C3:C7 is named *Dog,* then reference for the intersection cell C3 (the cell address both ranges have in common) is *Cat Dog.*
	.	*Union:* Combines two references (or ranges) into one reference.	=SUM(A1:A5.C4:D6) is the same as typing the formula =A1+A2+A3+A4+A5+C4+C5+C6.

Table 8.1. Types of Operators

The Text Operator

The text operator, the ampersand, allows you to enter a formula that will connect text to text values in a cell and produce one text value, or to join text values with number values to produce a new value. For example, if cell A1 contained the text value *"January,"* you could combine the words *"Totals for"* with the text contents in cell A1 to produce the result *"Totals for January."* If cell A1 contained the formula *"=100/5,"* you could combine the words *"January Average is"* with the value in cell A1 to produce the result *"January Average is 20."* There are some rules you must follow when you use the Text operator.

◆ You must always begin the formula with an equal sign (=) and the text you want to add to the value in the cell. For example, you can enter the formula =*"Totals for"* &A1 to produce the result *"Totals for January."* You **cannot** enter a formula that reads =&A1 *"Totals."*

In the first example, the text that is being added to the value in cell A1 immediately follows the equal sign (=), and the formula is correct. In the second example, the cell address immediately follows the equal sign (=), and you will receive an error message telling you that this is not a valid formula.

◆ The text you want to add to the value in a cell must be enclosed by quotation marks (" ") in the formula. If you want a space between the text you are adding and the value in the cell to which you are adding it, you must include the space inside the quotation mark. If you do not enclose the text in quotations marks, you will receive an error value in the cell. The error value informs you that Excel cannot calculate the formula. Error values always begin with a number sign (#).

◆ The cell address that contains the value you are connecting to text must be preceded by an ampersand (&). For example, in the formula =*"Totals for "&A1*, the text *Totals for* is enclosed in quotation marks. One space is included after the word *for* to produce a space between the words *Totals for* and the value in the cell. The cell address (A1) is preceded by an ampersand (&).

◆ You cannot use the text operator to connect the values in two cells. For example, if cell A1 contained the value *"Total,"* and cell B1 contained the value *"50,"* you could not use the text operator to combine the values in these two cells to produce the result *"Total 50."*

Comparison Operators

Comparison operators are used in formulas to compare two values. If the two values match, the formula produces a result of TRUE. If the two values do not match, the formula produces a result of FALSE. For example, the formula =100/2 > 25 will produce a value of TRUE, since the first value, 50 (produced by dividing 100 by 2), is greater than the second value. The formula =100/5 = 45 is FALSE, since the first value, 50, is not equal to the second value, which is 45. You must begin this formula with an equal sign (=).

Reference Operators

Reference operators combine two cell references in a formula into a single cell reference. You have already used one type of reference operator, the colon (:), to combine two cell references into a single range. For example, the formula =*SUM(A1:A5)* combines the references to cells A1 and A5 in a single range. The colon instructs Excel to include the values of cells A1 and A5, as well as all of the cells in between. Therefore, the formula =SUM(A1:A5) instructs Excel to calculate the sum of the values of cells A1, A2, A3, A4, and A5.

There are two more kinds of reference operators available:

◆ **Intersection**. The intersection operator compares two named ranges and searches for any cells in common. If there are any cells in common in the two ranges, Excel produces one reference for all the cells the two ranges have in common. For example, if the range A1:A5 is named *Sue's,* and the range C5:C8 is named *Cats,* then the reference for the intersection cell C5 (the cell address both ranges have in common) is *Sue's Cats.*

◆ **Union**. The union operator combines two ranges into one reference. For example, =SUM(A1:A4.D1:D3) is the same as =A1+A2+A3+A4+A5+D1+D2+D3. Excel combines the cells in the first range and the cells in the second range to calculate the function SUM.

N O T E

You cannot use the union operator with named ranges. If you do, you will receive in error value.

Using Functions to Simplify Formulas

A function consists of a built-in **function name** (or formula) and a value (or group of values) that performs the specified calculation ordered by the function name and produces a result. The values you insert into a function are called **arguments**; the values that the calculation produces are called **results**. You have already used the SUM function to simplify a formula such as =A1+A2+A3+A4, by typing =SUM(A1:A4). Excel has many more functions; we will cover some basic ones here.

The AVERAGE Function

Frills and Thrills has a worksheet called INCJAN.XLS, which includes the income for each item in the store by account number and then totals the income for all of the items. Clarisse would like to know the average income for each item and the average income for each account. To figure this out, we could add the income for each item in each account and then divide the result by the number of accounts. For example, to calculate the average income for all dresses sold for Acct. 100, Acct. 101, Acct. 102, and Acct. 103 we could enter the formula *=C7+D7+E7+F7/4,* or *=SUM(C7:F7)/4.*

Either of these formulas will total the income for dresses for each account, then divide the result by 4 (the number of accounts) to produce an average. But there is an easier way. We could simplify the process by using the AVERAGE function. When we use the AVERAGE function, we need to know the only range of cells whose values are to be included in the average. We needn't count the cells; Excel will do this for us. To use the AVERAGE function:

1. Open the INCJAN.XLS worksheet.
2. Select cell H7.
3. Click on Formula in the menu bar to open the Formula menu.
4. Click on Paste Function. The Paste Function dialog box is displayed, as shown in Figure 8.1.

     The Paste Category list box shows you a list of all of the functions available in Excel. Explaining each one goes beyond the scope of this book; if you need to know about all of the functions, we suggest you either look them up in the Function Reference manual that came with the program, or buy an advanced user book.

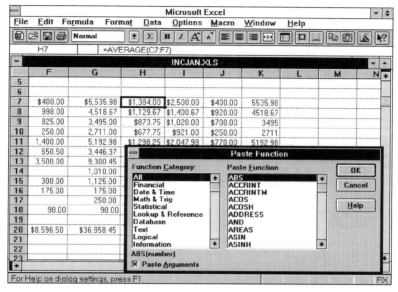

Figure 8.1. The Paste Function dialog box.

The Paste Function list box shows you all of the functions available in the function category you selected. The default function category is All, and all of the functions available in Excel are listed in the Paste Function list box when that category is selected.

5. Select AVERAGE in the Paste Function list box.
6. Click on OK.
7. The correct syntax for the AVERAGE function appears in the formula bar, and looks like this:

```
=AVERAGE(number1,number2...)
```

The formula begins with an equal sign (=), and is followed by the built-in formula (or function) AVERAGE, which is followed by a parenthetical expression that contains the syntax for the values or arguments you are going to use in the formula. You must replace the arguments with the values or the cell addresses that contain the values you want to use in the formula. These values can be numbers, individual cells, or ranges. If you clear the Paste Arguments check box, your formula will not include the syntax for the arguments, and will look like this:

```
=AVERAGE()
```

8. Edit the formula in the formula bar to reflect the range of cells you want to include in the average for dresses. The cells that contain the income for row 7 (dresses) are contained in the range C7:F7. Therefore, change the formula to look like this:

   =AVERAGE(C7:F7)

   This formula tells Excel to add the values of the cells in the range C7:F7 and then divide the result by the number of cells you added to produce the average income for dresses for all accounts. Excel will automatically calculate the number of cells included in the argument (enclosed in the parenthetical expression) that have been added, and divide the sum by that number to produce an average. Excel not only averages the values of the cells contained in the argument, it copies the formatting of the first cell in the range. Therefore, the resulting value is $1,384.

9. Copy the formula to cells H8:H18; the formula adjusts to reflect the new row address.

When you copy a function, the formatting in the function you are copying is also copied. For example, the value in cells H8 through H18 is formatted with dollar signs ($) even though the values in the corresponding rows for that formula are not.

N O T E

You now have the average income for each item sold in January. Now we need to calculate the average income for each account. To do this:

1. If the INCJAN.XLS worksheet is not open, open it.
2. Select cell C22.
3. Click on Formula in the menu bar to open the Formula menu.
4. Click on Paste Function to display the Paste Function dialog box.
5. Select AVERAGE in the Paste Function list box.
6. Click on OK.
7. The AVERAGE function (including the syntax for the arguments) appears in the formula bar. You must replace the arguments with the values or the cell addresses that contain the values you want to use in the formula. The arguments can be replaced with numbers, individual cells, or ranges.
8. Edit the formula in the formula bar to reflect the range of cells you want to include in the average for Acct. 100. The range C7:C18 contains the income for Acct. 100. Therefore, change the arguments in the formula to look like this:

   =AVERAGE(C7:C18)

This formula tells Excel to add the values of the cells in the range C7:C18, then divide the result by the number of cells you added to produce the average income for all items for Acct. 100. Excel will automatically calculate the number of cells included in the argument (enclosed in the parenthetical expression) that have been added, and divide the sum by that number to produce an average.

9. Copy this formula to cells D22:F22. Notice that the formula adjusts to reflect the new address.

The MAX and MIN Functions

If your worksheet is large and contains many rows and columns of number values, you can use the MAX and MIN functions to quickly determine the largest and smallest value in a column or row.

Using the MAX Function

To determine which account in the INCJAN.XLS worksheet brought in the greatest income for each item:

1. Open the INCJAN.XLS worksheet.
2. Select cell I7.
3. Click on Formula in the menu bar to open the Formula menu.
4. Click on Paste Function to display the Paste Function dialog box.
5. Select MAX in the Paste Function list box.
6. Click on OK.
7. The MAX function (including the syntax for the arguments enclosed in the parenthetical expression) is displayed in the formula bar, and looks like this:

    ```
    =MAX(number1,number2...)
    ```

    You must replace the arguments with the values or the cell addresses that contain the values you want to use in the formula. The arguments can be replaced with numbers, individual cells, or ranges.

8. Edit the formula to reflect the cells for which you want to find the largest value. Since we want the largest amount of income for the item in row 7 (dresses), change the formula to look like this:

    ```
    =MAX(C7:F7)
    ```

    This formula instructs Excel to locate the largest number (or value) contained in the range C7:F7. The result ($2,500) will appear in cell I7. This is the largest amount of income for dresses in any account in the worksheet.

Using the MIN Function

To determine which account in the INCJAN.XLS worksheet brought in the smallest amount of income for each item:

1. Open the INCJAN.XLS worksheet.
2. Select cell J7.
3. Click on Formula in the menu bar to open the Formula menu.
4. Click on Paste Function to display the Paste Function dialog box.
5. Select MIN in the Paste Function list box.
6. Click on OK.
7. The MIN function (including the syntax for the arguments enclosed in the parenthetical expression) is displayed in the formula bar, and looks like this:

   `=MIN(number1,number2...)`

   You must replace the arguments with the values or the cell addresses that contain the values you want to use in the formula. The arguments can be replaced with numbers, individual cells, or ranges.

8. Edit the formula to reflect the cells for which you want to find the smallest value. Since we want the smallest amount of income for the item in row 7 (dresses), change the formula to look like this:

   `=MIN(C7:F7)`

   This formula instructs Excel to locate the smallest number (or value) contained in the range C7:F7. The result ($400) will appear in cell I7. This is the smallest amount of income for dresses in any account in the worksheet.

When you paste any Excel function, you will always see the syntax for that function in the formula bar. All functions look like this:

`=FUNCTION(argument)`

The first entry is an equal sign (=), which indicates that a formula is to follow. The second entry is the name of the function you have pasted. The third entry, enclosed in parentheses, is the syntax of the argument. You must replace the third entry (the argument) with the values you want to use in your formula using the syntax indicated in the function.

Using Arrays

Arrays can simplify formula entry in your worksheet. A single array can replace several formulas to produce the same result. For example, suppose you wanted to compute the square root of all of the values in cells A1:A7 and see the results in cells B1:B7. You could enter the formula in each cell to calculate the square root in cells B1, B2, B3, B4, B5, B6, and

B7, or you could enter the formula in B1 and then copy it to cells B2:B7. An even quicker way to calculate the square root of the values in cells A1:A7 would be to use an array. When you use an array, you can replace the formulas in all seven cells B1:B7 with one formula and achieve the same results.

Entering an Array Formula into a Range of Cells

We are going to see how to enter an array formula in our INCJAN.XLS worksheet to produce the same result with one formula that was produced by entering a formula into each of the cells G7:G18 (the Totals column).

1. Open the INCJAN.XLS worksheet.
2. Click on cell K7 (or the first available blank column in row 7).
3. Select the range of cells in which you want the results of your formula to appear. We want to total the accounts for each item in the worksheet, so we will select cells K7:K18. Rows 7 through 18 contain all of the items for which Frills and Thrills received income in January.
4. Enter the following formula:

    =C7:C18+D7:D18+E7:E18+F7:F18

    This formula has four ranges, each separated by the plus operator (+). When the array is created, Excel will use the values of the first cell address in each range, and will perform the action indicated by the operator (+). Cell K7 will contain the sum of the values of C7, D7, E7, and F7. Excel will then go on to the next cell address in the range and produce the sum of the values of C8, D8, E8, and F8. Next, Excel will add the values of cells C9, D9, E9, and F9, and will continue to add the values of the corresponding cell addresses until it reaches the end of the range, C18, D18, E18, and F18. This single formula will produce twelve values, one for each row in the range. If you click on cells K7:K18, you will see that each cell contains the original formula that you entered into cell K7.

5. To create the array, press Ctrl+Shft+Enter. Excel will automatically surround your formula with curved brackets ({ }) and copy the formula to each cell in the range. The totals for all accounts in each item will appear in your selected cells (K7:K18). If you compare these values with the values in the Totals column (column G), you will see that they are the same.

Excel views an array range as a single entity, and does not allow you to edit sections of it. You cannot clear or delete individual cells or ranges that are only a portion of the array range. You cannot insert cells into an array range. If you try to do any of these things you will receive an error message. To return to the worksheet, click on OK in the error message, and press Esc. You must convert the formulas in the range to constant values if you want to perform editing features in the array range.

You can format cells in an array range independently. You can also copy a cell or range of cells in an array to another part of the worksheet. When you copy a cell or range of cells from an array range to another part of a worksheet, Excel will change the cell addresses in the formula to reflect the new address, just as it does with any formula that is based on relative references.

Clearing an Array Range

You cannot clear an individual cell or ranges of cells within an array range. You can, however, clear the entire array range. To clear the range:

1. Select the array range.
2. Click on Edit in the menu bar to open the Edit menu.
3. Click on Clear.
4. Choose OK.

Deleting an Array Range

You cannot delete individual cells or ranges of cells within an array range. You can, however, delete the entire range:

1. Select the array range.
2. Click on Edit in the menu bar to open the Edit menu.
3. Click on Delete.
4. Choose OK.

Converting the Formulas in an Array Range to Constant Values

When you convert the formulas in an array range to constant values, the formula in each cell takes on the value that is reflected in that cell. For example, if cell A1 shows a value of 10 and cell A2 shows a value of 15, when you convert the formulas in these cells to a constant value, the formula in cell A1 will be replaced by the value 10, and the formula in cell A2 will be replaced by the value 15. Once you have converted the array range into a range that contains constant values, the array is no longer in effect and each cell can be edited individually. You can delete and/or clear individual cells or ranges of cells, and you can insert cells into the rows or columns that formerly contained the array. To convert the formulas in an array range to constant values:

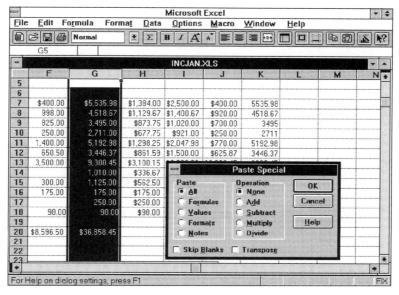

Figure 8.2. The Paste Special dialog box

1. Select the array range.
2. Click on Edit in the menu bar to open the Edit menu.
3. Click on Copy.
4. Click on Edit in the menu bar to open the Edit menu.
5. Click on Paste Special. The Paste Special dialog box is displayed, as shown in Figure 8.2.
6. Under Paste, select the Values option.
7. Click on OK.

Using Array Constants

You have just created an array using cell references. Excel used the values in those referenced cells to produce the results of the array formula. You can also enter an array formula using values instead of cell addresses, or using a combination of the two. When you enter values instead of cell references in an array formula, these values are referred to as **array constants**. When you enter an array constant in an array formula, you must surround the values in the array constant with curved brackets ({ }) and separate each value with a comma (,). For example, suppose you wanted to calculate the state and city taxes that Frills and Thrills paid on the total of each item sold in the month of January. The state tax is 5% and the city tax is 3%. You could enter a single formula that would calculate each tax for each total. The formula would look like this:

```
=G7:G18*{.05,.03}
```

Each cell in the range G7:G18 contains a value that reflects the total for each item sold. This is followed by an operator informing Excel that the value contained in each cell in the range is going to be multiplied. The curved brackets that enclose the values .05 and .03 indicate that these are array constants (constant values instead of cell references). To see the results of this array formula:

1. Open the INCJAN.XLS worksheet.
2. Select the range L7:M18.
3. Enter the formula =G7:G18*{.05,.03} in cell L7.
4. Press Ctrl+Shft+Enter.

You have created an array range in which columns L and M contain the results of the formula and show you the state and city tax for the total amount in sales of each item.

Using an Array Constant in a Function to Project a Trend

You can also include array constants in functions. This is very useful in projections. For example, Clarisse would like to calculate the projected total sales for Frills and Thrills for the next three months. Two months have gone by since we created the income worksheet for January, and we now know the total sales for January, February, and March. We will use an array constant in a function to calculate the projected total sales for the next three months based on the total sales for the previous three months. To predict the sales for Frills and Thrills for the months of April, May, and June:

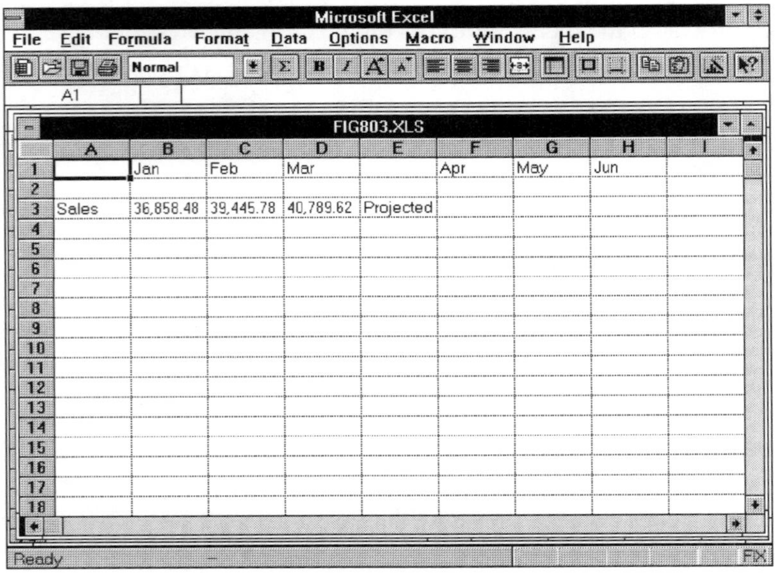

Figure 8.3. The titles and total sales for January, February, and March

1. Open a blank worksheet.
2. Enter the titles and amount of total sales for January, February, and March, as shown in Figure 8.3.
3. Select cells F3:H3.
4. Click on Formula in the menu bar to open the Formula menu.
5. Click on Paste Function to display the Paste Function dialog box.
6. Select TREND in the Paste Function list box.
7. Click on OK.
8. The TREND function is displayed in the formula bar. Notice that the syntax for the argument (enclosed in parentheses) contains three possible types of arguments separated by commas. We are going to add a fourth argument—an array constant—but we will not use the second and third arguments. Excel identifies each type of argument by the comma that separates it. So, we need to tell Excel that the second and third argument types are blank, and that the array constant is the fourth argument. If we do not, Excel will try to calculate the formula using the array constant as the second argument type, and an error will result. To tell Excel to calculate the values of argument types one and four, edit the formula to read as follows:

```
=TREND(B3:D3,,{4,5,6}
```

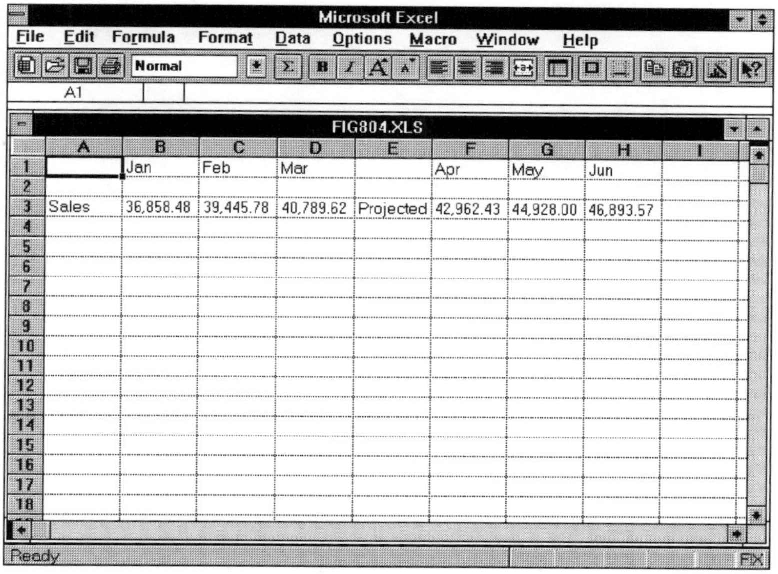

Figure 8.4. Projected sales for the next three months

This formula tells Excel that it is going to calculate a trend using the values in argument one (the values contained in the cells in B3:D3), skip argument types two and three (they are blank, the commas are used instead of an argument), and calculate the fourth, fifth, and sixth values (the values 4,5,6 contained in the array constant) for the trend.

9. Press Ctrl+Shft+Enter to create the formula. Your worksheet now looks like the one shown in Figure 8.4. The values in cells B3, C3 and D3 (sales for January, February, and March) have been used to project the values in cells F3, G3, and H3 (projected sales for April, May, and June).

Review Exercises for Chapter 8

◆ Practice creating parenthetical expressions in formulas. Notice the difference parentheses can make to the resulting value.

◆ Use the text operator to combine text with the value of the contents in a cell in a formula.

◆ Use a comparison operator to compare two values in a formula.

◆ Use the reference union operator to calculate the sum of two or more ranges in a formula.

◆ Use the AVERAGE function to calculate the average expense for all items in the INC&EXP.XLS worksheet.

◆ Replace one or more formulas in a worksheet with an array formula. Convert the array formulas to constant values. Do not save the worksheet, unless you want all of the cells that contained array formulas to contain constant values.

Before You Go On...

Before you go on to the next chapter, you should know how to use parenthetical expressions in your formulas. You should be familiar with all of the types of operators you can use in Excel. You should understand functions and arrays, and be able to use them to simplify entering formulas and to create more sophisticated formulas, such as projections.

USING PRINT ENHANCEMENTS WITH YOUR WORKSHEETS

What You Will Learn in This Chapter

- ◆ How to change page orientation
- ◆ How to center your documents on a page
- ◆ How to use Page Numbering
- ◆ How to reduce or enlarge your printed worksheet
- ◆ How to use headers and footers
- ◆ How to use Print Preview
- ◆ How to set and remove a print area
- ◆ How to set and remove print titles
- ◆ How to set and remove manual page breaks
- ◆ How to use the Windows Print Manager
- ◆ How to use Printer Setup
- ◆ How to troubleshoot common printing problems

In Chapter 3 you learned how Excel works with Microsoft Windows to print your documents, and how to print a worksheet using the Print dialog box. In this chapter, you are going to learn how to use Microsoft Excel's many features to enhance the appearance of your printed worksheets. You will also learn how to use the Print Preview feature, and how to troubleshoot some of the things that can go wrong when printing a document.

Page Setup

Most of the features you will use to control and enhance the appearance of your printed worksheet are found in Page Setup. We will use this command to change page margins, define headers and footers, determine whether gridlines and column and row headings will print, and set page size and orientation. The options available in Page Setup vary depending upon the type of document you are working with. In this chapter, you will learn how to use Page Setup with a worksheet. Printing documents other than worksheets will be detailed in the chapters covering those documents. To use Page Setup:

1. Click on File in the menu bar.
2. Click on Page Setup. The Page Setup dialog box is displayed, as shown in Figure 9.1.

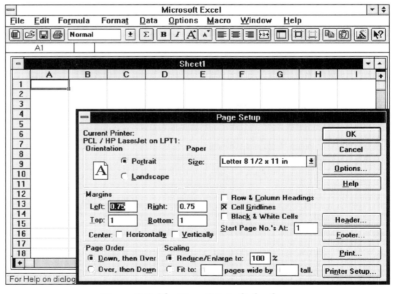

Figure 9.1. The Page Setup dialog box.

3. Select the options you want to use to control the appearance of your printed worksheet.
4. Click on OK. The options you have selected will be saved with the worksheet.

Changing Paper Size

You use the Paper Size command to specify what size paper you are going to print the worksheet on. Your paper size choices depend upon the printer you are using. Change the paper size in the Paper Size drop-down list box.

Changing Orientation

Orientation refers to whether the data is printed straight up and down on a page with the data parallel to the short edge of the paper (portrait), or sideways on a page with the data parallel to the long edge of the paper (landscape). You can select only one orientation for a worksheet. If you want to have some pages print out in landscape and others in portrait, you will have to print one set of pages first, then change the orientation and print the other set of pages. Some printers can support only portrait orientation. To set page orientation, select either Portrait or Landscape. A sample page appears to the left of the options displaying a page in the appearance of your choice.

Margins

Margins determine the distance in inches between the edges of the page and the edges of the printed document. The size of your margins may be limited by your printer. If you are using headers and footers, be sure the margins are large enough so that the data does not overlap with the top or bottom margin when printed. If all of the columns and rows on a page cannot fit within the specified margins, Excel prints the page on two sheets of paper, with the overflow on the second page. Or you can use the Fit To option (see below) to fit the worksheet on one printed page. Excel's left and right margins default to .75 inch, the top and bottom margins to 1 inch. To change the margins, change the settings in the appropriate text boxes in the Margins box.

Center Horizontally or Vertically

You can center the document horizontally or vertically on a page by selecting either or both options in the Margins box.

Row and Column Headings

If you select this option, your worksheet will print row and column headings, and cell references when printing notes.

Cell Gridlines

If this option is selected, your worksheet will print the cell gridlines. If you disable the option, your worksheet will print without gridlines.

Black and White Cells

In Excel, color formats in cells and text boxes are printed as patterns. Selecting Black and White Cells removes the patterns, and the cells and text boxes will print in black and white.

Start Page No.'s At

This option allows you to tell Excel what page number you want headers and footers in your worksheet to begin numbering with. The default page number is 1.

Page Order

You can use this command to change the page sequence on your worksheet. The default is for worksheets to print down and then over. By selecting the Over, then Down option, you can change this sequence. For example, you might have a document that includes tables of data and charts on the worksheet. If the charts are placed to the right of each table, you may want to print each chart immediately after its table. If you choose the Over, then Down option, the charts will print immediately after their associated tables.

Scaling

The scaling options allow you to reduce or enlarge your printed worksheet.

Reduce/Enlarge to

The Reduce/Enlarge to option allows you to specify the percentage of reduction or enlargement for a document. For example, reducing to 50 percent will cause the worksheet to print at one-half of its normal print size; enlarging the worksheet to 150 percent will cause it to print 50 percent larger than its normal print size. The default setting for the Reduce/Enlarge option is 100 percent. The Reduce/Enlarge feature must be supported by your printer to work.

Fit to

Fit to reduces the worksheet when it prints so that it can fit on one page. For example, if you have a worksheet that prints on two pages, you can reduce it to fit on one page by entering *1* in the Fit to text boxes. Or, if you have a worksheet that fits only on 8.5-by-14-inch paper and you want to print it on 8.5-by-11-inch paper, you can use the Fit to option to reduce it when it prints so that it will fit on the smaller paper size.

Headers and Footers

Headers are text and/or numbers that print at the top of every page. Footers are text and/or numbers that print at the bottom of every page. All documents contain a default header that prints the document name, and a default footer with the word *Page* and the page number. These default headers and footers can be edited or deleted (see below, "Editing or Deleting a Header or Footer"). Headers always print .5 inch from the top of the page and, if not centered, .75 inch from the left or right edge of the page. Footers always print .5 inch from the bottom of the page and, if not centered, .75 inch from the left or right edge of the page. If you set margins, be sure that there is enough room for the header and footer, or the data in your worksheet may overlap with the header or footer.

Creating a Header or Footer

Headers and footers are created the same way. The only difference is that when you create a header you use the Header dialog box, and when you create a footer you use the Footer dialog box. To create a header or footer:

1. Click on File in the menu bar.
2. Click on Page Setup. The Page Setup dialog box is displayed.
3. Click on either the Header or Footer command button. The Header or Footer dialog box is opened, as shown in Figure 9.2.
4. Enter text using the parameters set forth below.

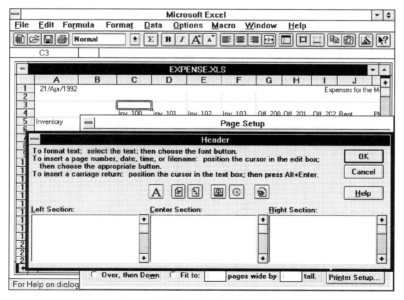

Figure 9.2. The Header dialog box.

5. Choose OK to return to the Page Setup dialog box.

6. Choose OK. The Page Setup dialog box is closed.

Left, Center, and Right Sections

There are three sections available for entering data in a header or footer. Data entered in the Left Section box will be left-aligned and will print .75 inch from the left edge of the page. Data entered in the Center Section box will be centered on the page. Data entered in the Right Section box will be right-aligned and will print .75 inch from the right edge of the page.

Codes Used in Headers and Footers

There are several codes that you can use to enter specific types of data in a header or a footer. Click on the appropriate tool and the following code will be inserted:

Tool	Tool name	Code	Action
A	Font	—	Displays the Font dialog box.
#	Page Number tool	&p	Inserts the page number
	Total Pages tool	&n	Inserts the total number of pages
	Date tool	&d	Inserts the current date.
	Time tool	&t	Inserts the current time.
	Filename tool	&f	Inserts the filename of the active document.

In addition to the tools displayed above, there are codes that do not have tools but can be typed to insert specific types of data in headers and footers:

Code	Action
&B	Print the characters that follow in bold.
&I	Print the characters that follow in italic.
&U	Underline the characters that follow.
&S	Strikethrough the characters that follow.
&P+number	Print the page number plus the code number.
&P-number	Print the page number minus the code number.
&&	Print a single ampersand.
Alt+Enter	Insert a return (Enter).

Using Fonts in Headers and Footers

Clicking on the Font tool will open the Font dialog box. This dialog box works in the same way as the Font dialog box discussed in Chapter 5. Apply any of the available fonts or font attributes you want to the data in your header or footer. Font changes made in your header or footer will not affect data in the body of the worksheet.

Editing or Deleting a Header or Footer

When you open a new worksheet, it already has a default header or footer. You might want to edit or delete the default header or footer, or you might want to edit or delete a header or footer you created yourself.

To edit or delete a header or footer:

1. Click on File in the menu bar.
2. Click on Page Setup. The Page Setup dialog box is displayed.
3. Click on either the Header or Footer command button. The Header or Footer dialog box is opened.
4. Edit or delete the data in the sections of the header or footer.
5. Choose OK. The header or footer is altered or deleted and you are returned to the Page Setup dialog box.
6. Click OK to close the Page Setup dialog box.

If you change your mind when editing or deleting a header or footer, you can click on the Cancel button to restore the previous header or footer.

N O T E

Print Preview

The print preview feature allows you to view a document on your screen exactly as it will be printed. You will be able to see margins, page breaks, headers and footers, and font and size changes. To use Print Preview:

1. Click on File in the menu bar.
2. Click on Print Preview to open the Print Preview window, as shown in Figure 9.3. To move around in the Print Preview window, use your arrow keys or the scroll bar to move to different sections of the page. The PgUp and PgDn keys will move you up or down the page a screen at a time. The status bar shows you the page you are currently previewing. You can enlarge the size of your document on the screen while you are in Print Preview. You can change your page setup, change your margins, and even print your document from Print Preview.

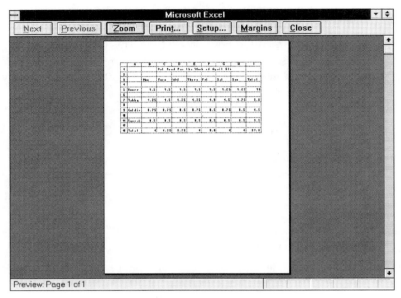

Figure 9.3. The Print Preview window.

3. Click on Close when you have finished viewing your worksheet to return to the document window.

Moving Between Pages

Click on Next to go to the next page, and on Previous to go to the previous page.

Worksheets are sometimes wider than they are long. If your worksheet is too wide to fit on one page, the Next and Previous buttons will move you across the width and length of the worksheet. If the last page is being displayed, the Next button is dimmed. If the first page is being displayed, the Previous button is dimmed.

Using Zoom

When you click on Zoom you enlarge your worksheet to its actual size in the preview window. You will be able to view only portions of the worksheet, and will have to scroll through the worksheet to see it all.

If you know the area of the worksheet you want to see enlarged, position your mouse pointer (shaped like a magnifying glass) in that location and click. The entire worksheet will be enlarged, but the area you wish to see will be displayed on the screen.

Click on Zoom to return your worksheet to normal preview size.

Using Print

The Print button returns you to the document window and opens the Print dialog box, which is covered in Chapter 3. If you wish to print the worksheet, click on OK. If you do not want to print the worksheet, click on Cancel. Either way, you will not be returned to the preview window, but will remain in the document window.

Using Setup

The Setup button allows you to open the Page Setup dialog box from within the preview window to determine whether gridlines will print, and to change headers, footers, orientation, page margins, and page size. These options are discussed earlier in this chapter. When you have selected your options, choose OK.

Using Margins

When you select the Margins button, the margin settings for the left, right, top, and bottom of your worksheet appear on the preview window as dotted lines with handles at the ends, as shown in Figure 9.4. You can increase or decrease the margins by dragging the margin handles. As you are dragging, the status bar will display the changes in the size of the margin.

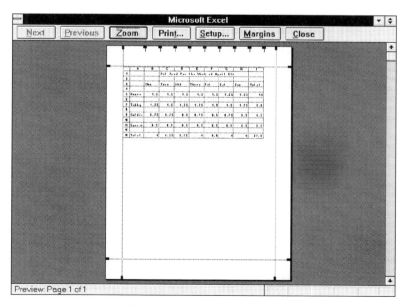

Figure 9.4. The Margin settings.

The Margins feature in Print Preview also allows you to change your worksheet's column widths from within the preview window. You can change the width of a column by dragging the column handle located across the top of the page.

Excel will not allow you to decrease your margin size beyond the paper size set for the worksheet. If you try to decrease your margins beyond this point, Excel will not make the change. You cannot drag a column handle beyond the left or right margin of the worksheet. You can, however, increase the column width as much as you want. If the columns extend

N O T E beyond the page, Excel will repaginate the worksheet. All of the margin and column width changes you make in the preview window will be in effect when you return to the document window.

Setting a Print Area

The Set Print Area feature enables you to print out selected sections of a worksheet, instead of the entire document. You can print a range or multiple nonadjacent ranges by defining the range(s) as the print area. When you send the worksheet to print, only the area(s) you defined will print. If you select multiple nonadjacent ranges, each range is printed on a separate page, in the order in which it was selected. To print a range:

1. Select the range or multiple nonadjacent ranges.
2. Click on Options in the menu bar.
3. Click on Set Print Area. The selected range or multiple nonadjacent ranges is defined as the Print_Area.
4. Click on File in the menu bar.
5. Click on Print. The Print dialog box is displayed.
6. Select the options you want for this print job.
7. Choose OK.

If you select the Notes option in the Print dialog box, only the text notes from the print area will print.

N O T E

Removing a Print Area

You can remove a print area only from an entire worksheet. A print area cannot be removed from a range or from multiple nonadjacent ranges. If your currently selected print area is a range or multiple nonadjacent ranges, you must do the following to remove it:

1. Select the entire worksheet.
2. Click on Options in the menu bar.
3. Click on Remove Print Area.

Setting Print Titles

The Set Print Titles feature allows you to pick a row or column title that will print on every page of the worksheet. Column titles are printed at the top of each page, and row titles are printed at the left side of each page. To set a print title:

1. Select the entire row, column (click on the row or column heading), or multiple adjacent range that contains the information you want to print on every page.
2. Click on Options in the menu bar.
3. Click on Set Print Titles. The Set Print Titles dialog box is displayed. Unless you have already chosen other ranges for print titles, the range you have selected appears in either the Titles for Rows text box or the Titles for Columns text box.
4. You can change the range you have selected by editing the text in the Titles for Rows or Titles for Columns text boxes, or you can select a new range while the Set Print Titles dialog box is open.
5. Choose OK. Excel automatically defines the name of this range as Print_Title.

The titles will first print in the range in which they appear. Subsequently, they will print at the top or left side of every page.

N O T E

Removing Print Titles

There are three ways to delete the print titles in your worksheet:

1. Click on Options in the menu bar.
2. Click on Set Print Titles. The Set Print Titles dialog box is displayed.
3. Delete the text in the Titles for Rows or Titles for Columns text boxes.
4. Choose OK.

Or,

1. Click on Formula in the menu bar.
2. Click on Define Name. The Define Name dialog box is displayed.

3. Select Print_Titles and click on Delete.

4. Choose OK.

Or,

1. Select the entire worksheet.

2. Click on Options in the menu bar.

3. Click on Remove Print Titles.

Setting Manual Page Breaks

Excel sets automatic page breaks when a document is too long to fit on one page. You may not want a page break where Excel has set it. To set your own page break:

1. If you want to break the page horizontally, select the cell in the left column directly below the gridline where you want the page break to occur.

2. If you want to break the page horizontally and vertically, select the cell below and to the right of the gridlines where you want the page break to occur.

3. Click on Options in the menu bar.

4. Click on Set Page Break. Manual page breaks are easy to spot: they are darker than automatic page breaks. You cannot control whether or not they will appear on the screen—they always appear.

When you set a manual page break, the automatic page breaks in the rest of the worksheet adjust to reflect the new pagination.

N O T E

Removing Manual Page Breaks

If you have edited your worksheet and added or removed data or rows or columns, you may want to remove your manual page break to accommodate the changes. To remove a manual page break:

1. Select a cell directly below or to the right of the manual page break.

2. Click on Options in the menu bar.

3. Click on Remove Page Break.

To remove all of the manual page breaks in a worksheet:

1. Select the entire worksheet.
2. Click on Options in the menu bar.
3. Click on Remove Page Break.

Using the Windows Print Manager

As you learned in Chapter 3, when you print a job in Excel, it is first transmitted to the Microsoft Windows Print Manager. If there is a problem, a Print Manager dialog box will appear stating the nature of the problem. You should switch programs and delete the job from the Print Manager, then correct the problem and send the job again. To cancel a job in the Print Manager:

1. Press Ctrl+Esc to access the Windows Program Manager Task List (see Chapter 20 for information about switching programs).
2. Double-click on Print Manager to access the Windows Print Manager.
3. Select the job and choose Delete (refer to your Windows manual for information about the Windows Print Manager).
4. The job is deleted from the Print Manager.
5. To return to Excel, bring up the Task List again and double-click on Microsoft Excel.

You can also cancel a print job from the Now Printing dialog box by choosing Cancel. This will cancel whatever portion of the job has not yet been sent to the Windows Print Manager. However, once the Now Printing dialog box disappears from the window, the job has already been sent to the Windows Print Manager and can no longer be cancelled from Excel. To cancel a job in the Windows Print Manager:

1. Press Ctrl+Esc to access the Task List.
2. If the Print Manager is still on the list, it means that at least part of the job is still being held in that facility. Double-click on Print Manager to access the Windows Print Manager.
3. Select the job and choose Delete (refer to your Windows manual for information about the Windows Print Manager).
4. The job is deleted from the Print Manager. However, some of the job may already be in the printer's memory buffer and will continue to print. Either let it finish printing or turn the printer off and then back on. This will delete anything that is being held in the printer's memory buffer.
5. To return to Excel, bring up the Task List again and double-click on Microsoft Excel.

Using Printer Setup

You can use Printer Setup to make changes to your printer setup, including selecting font cartridges and changing printers, the paper source (print bins), printer resolution, number of copies to print, and page orientation. Remember, fonts and font cartridges must be properly installed and your Microsoft Windows Print Driver must be properly installed and configured (see Appendix A) before changes can be made in Printer Setup. To use Printer Setup:

1. Click on File in the menu bar.
2. Click on Page Setup. The Page Setup dialog box is displayed.
3. Click on the Printer Setup command button. The Printer Setup dialog box is opened, as shown in Figure 9.5. A list of all of your installed printers is displayed.

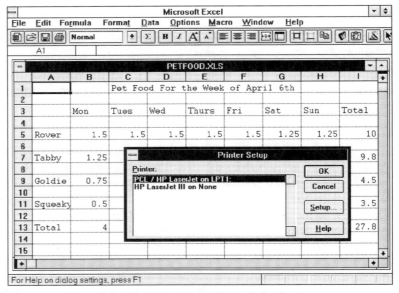

Figure 9.5. The Printer Setup dialog box.

4. Highlight the printer you want to use and click on Setup. The selected printer's dialog box is displayed. Figure 9.6 shows the dialog box for the Hewlett-Packard LaserJet Series II.
5. Make any changes you want in Printer Setup.
6. Choose OK three times to close three dialog boxes and return to the main menu.

NOTE

If you are changing a font cartridge in Printer Setup, it must be done before a document is formatted with the new cartridge.

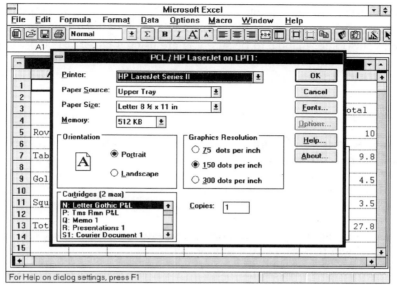

Figure 9.6. The dialog box for the Hewlett-Packard LaserJet Series II.

Common Print Problems

Listed below are some of the most common printing problems and their possible solutions. Your printer manual is also an excellent reference for troubleshooting.

You sent the job to the printer but it did not print

Check the following items:

1. Is the printer plugged in and turned on?
2. Is the printer on-line?
3. Are you using the correct cable, and is it securely plugged in at both ends?
4. Is the correct printer selected? Is it set for the correct port?
5. Is there paper in the printer?
6. Check for a manual feed message in the Current Print Job dialog box.

Your paper keeps jamming in the printer

Check the following:

1. If you are using a printer with a tractor feed, do the tractor wheels line up? The pin feeds should be exactly even or the paper will not line up properly. Is the paper securely locked in? Is it properly loaded? Check your printer manual.

2. If you are using a laser printer, make sure there is no paper trapped inside the printer. Take the paper out of the tray, fan it, and put it back. Reinsert the tray.

3. Check your printer manual to be sure you are using a paper size and weight that is acceptable to your printer.

4. If the problem persists, place a service call.

You get a *Not Enough Memory* message code on your printer

You are trying to send fonts or graphics that are too large to fit in your printer's memory buffer. Increase the memory in your printer or send smaller fonts and graphics.

The print is uneven, too light, or there are vertical fade-outs on the page

Make sure that your printer ribbon or cartridge is properly installed and does not need to be replaced. If the problem persists, place a service call.

Review Exercises for Chapter 9

- ◆ Open a worksheet. Using Page Setup, change your orientation and center your worksheet horizontally on the page.
- ◆ Set your worksheet to print without row and column headings.
- ◆ If your worksheet does not fit exactly on the page, scale it to size.
- ◆ Create a new header or footer.
- ◆ Use Print Preview to see how your worksheet looks.
- ◆ Make changes to the worksheet from within Print Preview.
- ◆ Set a print area for your worksheet.
- ◆ Set a print title in a row or column.
- ◆ Preview your worksheet again in Print Preview and print it.

Before You Go On...

Before you go on to the next chapter, you should be familiar with the options available to you in Page Setup. You should be able to change the page size and orientation of your worksheet. You should know how to scale (enlarge or reduce) the size of your worksheets to print them. You should know how to determine whether or not gridlines and row and column headings will show when you print. You should be able to create and edit headers and footers. You should be comfortable previewing your documents in Print Preview. You should be able to set print areas and print titles and insert manual page breaks. You should know how to use the Windows Print Manager in case of a printer problem.

Chapter 10

SYSTEM AND DOCUMENT MANAGEMENT

What You Will Learn in This Chapter

- How to change directories
- How to list files using DOS wildcards
- How to open a document from a floppy disk
- How to save to a floppy disk
- How to delete a document
- How to set passwords

253

This chapter is concerned with system and document management. By **system management**, we mean organizing your hard drive. Consider a file cabinet. If you take all of your files and dump them into a drawer without subdividing them, the next time you need a file from that drawer you are going to have to sift through the entire mess. Your hard drive is the equivalent of that file cabinet. Directories are the equivalent of the divisions in your file cabinet. Excel carries the analogy a little further by characterizing directories as **folders**.

You already have several directories on your hard drive. If you followed the automatic installation of Excel for Windows, you have a directory called EXCEL, which is located in the root directory of the hard drive. Think of the root directory as the entire file cabinet and Excel as a drawer in the file cabinet. On most computers, the root directory of the hard drive is called C:\. Excel for Windows is located in C:\EXCEL. The C: represents the hard drive, the slash mark represents the root directory, and EXCEL is a directory located within the root directory.

Your Excel program files are located in the EXCEL directory. The **path** indicates the location of a directory on your hard drive; in this case, the path is C:\EXCEL. Assuming you followed the automatic installation of Excel you also have a directory with the path C:\EXCEL\LIBRARY. What this path designation means is that Excel's library files are located in a subdirectory called LIBRARY, which is a subdivision of the directory EXCEL. Even though LIBRARY is a subdirectory of EXCEL, it is acceptable to call it a directory when it is referred to alone. For example, you would say "the EXCEL subdirectory LIBRARY" but "the LIBRARY directory". This convention will be followed in this chapter.

System and document management within Excel is limited to creating a new document, opening an existing document, saving a document, deleting a document, and setting passwords. If you wish to do more complex system and document management, such as creating new directories; copying, moving, or renaming documents; or deleting several documents at once, you will have to use the File Manager in the Windows Main program group. Appendix D provides comprehensive information on the File Manager.

Changing Directories

When you open Excel you will always start out in the same (default) directory. Sometimes you will want to change that directory. To change your directory:

1. Click on File.
2. Click on Open to display the Open dialog box.
3. In the Directories list box double-click on the directory you want. Notice that Excel represents directories as file folders.

You have changed your directory. You now see a list of Excel documents contained in the changed directory. You can open and edit any of these documents; when you save them, they will be saved in the changed directory.

Listing Files by Type

Excel's Open feature automatically defaults to a file list box containing all Excel files with an .xl* extension. This list contains worksheets, macros, charts, workbooks, templates, and add-ins. You can instruct the file list box to contain only the type of document you specify, or to list all of the files in the directory. To list only one type of document:

1. Click on File in the menu bar.
2. Click on Open to display the Open dialog box.
3. Click on the List Files of Type drop-down menu, shown in Figure 10.1. To see only worksheets in the file list box, click on Worksheets (*.XLS).

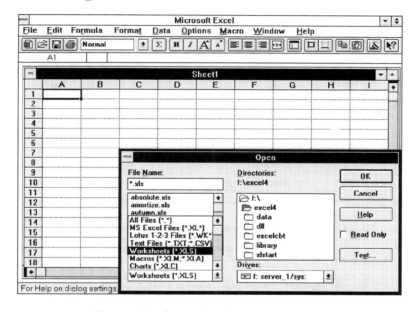

Figure 10.1. The List Files of Type drop-down menu in the Open dialog box.

The file list box now contains only worksheets, as shown in Figure 10.2 on the next page.

You can list a select group of the files in a directory by using DOS wildcards. When you type an asterisk (*) instead of a name or an extension, you are using the DOS wildcard that represents *all*. That is, when you selected Worksheets (*.XLS) in the file list box, you used the DOS wildcard * to print all of the documents in the directory with an .XLS extension.

The file list box default *.XL* uses two DOS wildcards. The first asterisk tells Excel to list all of the files, the second asterisk tells Excel to list all of the files in the directory with the extension .XL or .XL and any third letter (remember, you are limited to a three-letter extension). This default gives you a list of all worksheets (*.XLS), macros (*.XLM, *.XLA), charts (*.XLC), workbooks (*.XLW), templates (*.XLT), add-ins (*.XLL), and toolbars (*.XLB).

To list all of the files in the directory:

1. Click on File in the menu bar.
2. Click on Open to display the Open dialog box.
3. Click on the List Files of Type drop-down box. Click on All Files (*.*). All of the files in the current directory are listed.

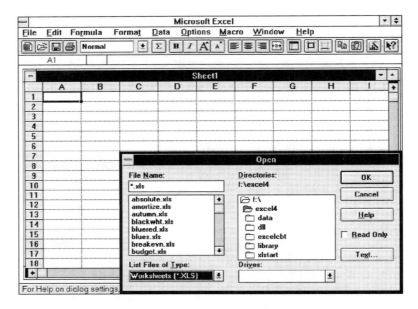

Figure 10.2. The File list box containing only worksheets.

Opening Documents on a Floppy Disk

Chapter 3 covered opening a document in your current directory. Sometimes you will want to open a document stored on a floppy disk.

To open a document on a floppy disk:

1. Insert the disk in the floppy drive.
2. Click on File in the menu bar.
3. Click on Open to display the Open dialog box.
4. Select the floppy's drive letter (A or B) in the Drives drop-down menu, as shown in Figure 10.3.
5. Select the document you want from the file list box.
6. Choose OK.

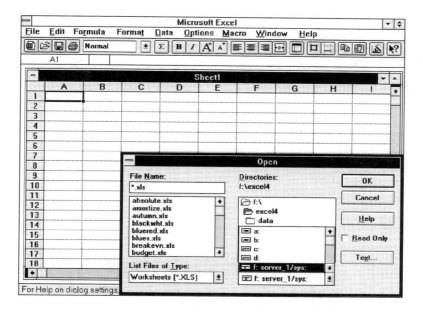

Figure 10.3. The Drives pull-down menu.

Saving to Floppy Disks

Chapter 3 explains the Save and Save As features in detail. There will be times when you want to save a document to a floppy disk. To save a document on a floppy disk:

1. Insert the disk in the floppy drive.
2. Click on File in the menu bar.
3. Click on Save As to display the Save As dialog box.
4. Type A:[filename] or B:[filename]—for example, A:GEORGE.XLS—in the Save As text box.
5. Choose OK.

N O T E

You can copy your documents using the Save As feature. You can open a document in the C:\EXCEL directory and then save the document to another directory by typing a new path in the Save As text box. For example, if you type *C:\EXCEL\LIBRARY\GEORGE.XLS,* Excel will save your document, which is now in the C:\EXCEL directory, to the C:\EXCEL\LIBRARY directory as well.

When you save a document, you do not have to worry about whether or not you use uppercase or lowercase characters to type in the name and/or path.

N O T E

Deleting a Document

To delete a document:

1. Click on File in the menu bar.
2. Click on Delete. The Delete Document dialog box is displayed, as shown in Figure 10.4.

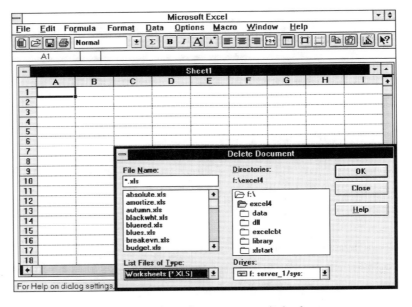

Figure 10.4. The Delete Document dialog box.

3. Select the file you wish to delete and click on OK.
4. You will be asked to confirm the deletion. Chose Yes to delete the file and No to cancel the action.

If you wish to delete several files simultaneously, you must use the File Manager in Windows. (See Appendix D.)

Setting Document Passwords

Excel allows you to set several types of passwords for your documents. Using a **protection password** prevents unauthorized persons from opening a document. If you want others to be able to open a document but do not want them to be able to save changes to it, you can use a **write reservation password**. Only those who know the password will be able to save changes to the document. Passwords can also prevent anyone from changing selected cells, graphic objects, and/or window position or size. Passwords can contain any combination of letters, symbols, and numbers, and can be up to fifteen characters long. They are case-sensitive.

Setting Protection Passwords

A protection password must be entered before the document can be opened and before linked data can be accessed from it. To set a password for a document:

1. Open the document.
2. Click on File in the menu bar.
3. Click on Save As to display the Save As dialog box.
4. Click on Options to display the Save Options dialog box.
5. In the Protection Password text box, type the password you have chosen. As you type, you will see an asterisk appear for each character you type, as shown in Figure 10.5. The password you have chosen will never appear on the screen.

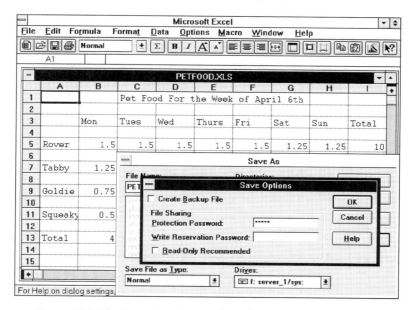

Figure 10.5. The Protection Password text box with password entered.

6. Click on OK.

7. The Confirm Password dialog box appears on the screen, as shown in Figure 10.6, asking you to retype the password. Do so.

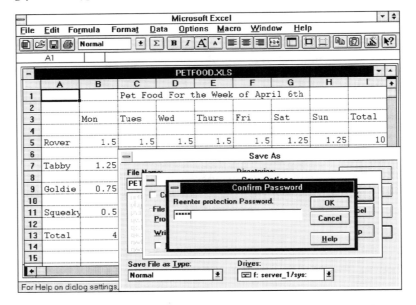

Figure 10.6. The Confirm Password dialog box with password entered.

8. Choose OK. You have returned to the Save As dialog box.

9. Choose OK.

If this document has already been saved, a prompt will ask whether you wish to replace the existing document. If you chose Yes, the only version of the document will be password protected. If you wish to have two copies of the document—one with a password and one without—chose No and give the document a new name. The newly saved document (the one with the new name) will be password protected. The old document will not.

WARNING

Once you have set a password, it can be removed only from within the document. If you forget your password, you are out of luck. Be careful

Setting Write Reservation Passwords

Setting a write reservation password allows anyone to open the document, but only those who know the password can save changes to it. When you open a document that is protected with a write reservation password, Excel asks for the password. If you do not know the password, you must open the document as read-only (you cannot save any changes to it). You can, however, save the document with a different name. The new document will not be password protected. To set a write reservation password:

1. Open the document.
2. Click on File in the menu bar.
3. Click on Save As to display the Save As dialog box.
4. Click on Options.
5. In the Write Reservation Password text box, type in the password you have chosen. An asterisk will appear for each character you type.
6. Click on OK.
7. The Confirm Password dialog box appears. You will be asked to retype the password. Do so.
8. Click on OK to return to the Save As dialog box.
9. Choose OK.

If this document has already been saved, a prompt will be displayed asking whether you wish to replace the existing document. If you chose Yes, the only version of the document will be write reservation password protected. If you wish to have two copies of the document—one with a password and one without—chose No and give the document a new name. The newly saved document (the one with the new name) will be write reservation password protected. The old document will not.

Once you have set a password, it can be removed only from within the document. If you forget your password, you are out of luck. Be careful.

WARNING
Sometimes you do not want to actually protect a document, but you would like to remind yourself or others not to make any unnecessary changes. You can do this by using the Read-Only Recommended feature. When you have enabled Read-Only Recommended, you will receive a message every time you open the file reminding you that the file is preferably read-only, and that no unnecessary changes should be made. You will then be able to choose to open the file with read-only enabled. If you choose Yes, you will not be able to save any changes to the document. If you choose No, you have disabled read-only and all changes can be saved. If you choose Cancel, the document will not be opened and you will be returned to the document already on your screen. To enable Read-Only Recommended:

1. Open the document.
2. Click on File in the menu bar.
3. Click on Save As to display the Save As dialog box.

4. Click on Options and select the Read-Only Recommended check box.

5. Click on OK.

6. You are returned to the Save As dialog box. Click on OK.

Remember, the Read-Only Recommended feature is just a reminder not to make any unnecessary changes to the document. It does not ask for a password, and anyone who opens the document can disable Read-Only Recommended.

Deleting a Password

To delete a password from your document:

1. Open the document.

2. Click on File in the menu bar.

3. Click on Save As to display the Save As dialog box.

4. Click on Options.

5. In either the Protection Password or the Write Reservation Password text box, delete the asterisks representing the password.

6. Click on OK to return to the Save As dialog box.

7. Click on OK. A prompt will be displayed asking if you want to replace the existing document. Click on Yes.

Disabling Read-Only Recommended

To stop the Read-Only Recommended prompt from appearing when you open a document:

1. Open the document. When the Read-Only prompt appears, say No.

2. Click on File in the menu bar.

3. Click on Save As to display the Save As dialog box.

4. Click on Options.

5. Disable the Read-Only Recommended check box.

6. Click on OK to return to the Save As dialog box.

7. Click on OK. Say Yes to replace the existing document.

Even if you do not wish to protect the entire document, there may be times when you wish to protect specific cells or graphic objects within a document. You may, for example, wish to protect the cells containing formulas in a worksheet.

Excel has two ways to protect cells—locking and hiding. When you lock a cell, you prevent the contents of that cell from being changed by anyone who does not have the password. When you hide a cell, you prevent anyone from seeing the formula in that cell; only the formula result is shown. You can also lock graphic objects so they cannot be selected, resized, moved, or reformatted.

Protecting Worksheet Cells

1. Select the cell or group of cells you wish to protect.
2. Click on Format in the menu bar.
3. Click on Cell Protection. The Cell Protection dialog box is displayed, as shown in Figure 10.7.

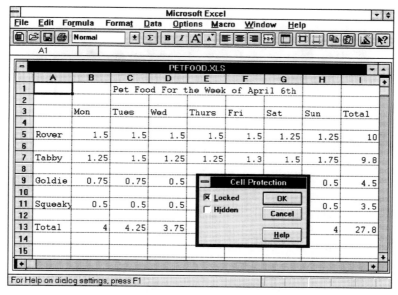

Figure 10.7. The Cell Protection dialog box.

   a. All cells are initially set as locked cells. Locked cells cannot be edited if the document is protected. If the document is not protected, a locked cell can be edited.

   b. Hidden cells will display values, but not formulas.

4. Select the Lock or Hidden check box.
5. Choose OK.
6. Click on Options in the menu bar.
7. Click on Protect Document. The Protect Document dialog box is displayed, as shown in Figure 10.8.

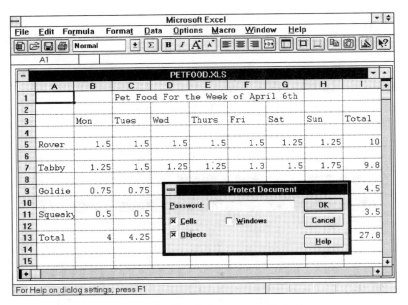

Figure 10.8. The Protect Document dialog box.

8. Select the items you wish to protect. You can protect cells, objects, windows, or any combination of the three.

9. In the Password text box, type in the password you have chosen. An asterisk will appear for each character you type.

10. Select OK.

11. In the Confirm Password dialog box, retype the password.

12. Choose OK.

Protecting Graphic Objects

1. Select the graphic objects you wish to protect. Charts created with a worksheet can be selected as graphic objects.

2. Click on Format in the menu bar.

3. Click on Object Protection.

4. Select the protection criteria you wish to use.

5. Choose OK.

6. Click on Options in the menu bar if the active document is a worksheet or workbook. Click on Chart in the menu bar if the active document is a chart.

7. Click on Protect Document to display the Protect Document dialog box.
8. Select the items you wish to protect.
9. In the Password text box, type in the password you have chosen. An asterisk will appear for each character you type.
10. Select OK.
11. In the Confirm Password dialog box, retype the password.
12. Choose OK.

Protecting a Document Window

When you protect a document window, you prevent anyone from resizing, moving, opening, or closing windows within the document. Before you protect a document window, be sure you have all of the windows within the document sized and positioned exactly as you want them. Then:

1. Click on Options in the menu bar
2. Click on Protect Document to display the Protect Document dialog box.
3. Select Windows.
4. Type a password in the Password text box.
5. Click on OK.
6. In the Confirm Password dialog box retype the password.
7. Click on OK.

When you open a protected document window, the control box, the maximize button, and the borders are not seen.

Removing Cell, Graphic Object, and Document Protection

1. Open the document.
2. If the document is a worksheet or workbook, click on Options in the menu bar. If the document is a chart, click on Chart in the menu bar.
3. Click on Unprotect Document. The Password box is displayed.
4. Type the password in the Password text box.
5. Click on OK.

Review Exercises for Chapter 10

- ◆ Change your directory in Excel and then change back to the default directory.
- ◆ List only worksheets in the Open feature.
- ◆ Save a document to a floppy disk.
- ◆ Retrieve the document from the floppy disk.
- ◆ Delete a document that you no longer need.
- ◆ Choose a password and set it for your current document.
- ◆ Remove the password.
- ◆ Enable and disable Read-Only for a document.
- ◆ Set password protection for a cell or graphic image, and then delete the password protection.

Before You Go On...

Before you continue on to the next chapter, you should understand how your hard disk can be divided into directories and subdirectories. You should know how to change directories in Excel. You should be able to save a document to or open a document from a floppy disk. You should be familiar with the DOS wildcard *, and know how to list specific types of documents in the Open feature. You should be familiar with the types of passwords that can be used in Excel and how to use them.

Chapter **11**

CUSTOMIZING MICROSOFT EXCEL

What You Will Learn in This Chapter

- ◆ How to create and use document templates
- ◆ How to create and use styles
- ◆ How to use and edit built-in toolbars
- ◆ How to create custom tools and toolbars
- ◆ How to record and run a command macro
- ◆ How to use macro sheets

267

As you have seen, Excel is the most sophisticated and complete package there is for organizing, manipulating, analyzing, and presenting data. Though this makes it an exciting and fun package to use, some of the more advanced features require multiple commands, which can slow you down. You will be happy to learn that Excel has several features that allow you to customize the program to provide shortcuts for accomplishing even the most intricate tasks. In addition, you can create patterns and formatting styles that allow you to avoid retyping and reformatting documents that you use often.

Document Templates

A template is a document that is used as a pattern for other, similar documents. For example, the accountant for Thrills and Frills must create an income worksheet and an expense worksheet for every month, based on the ones we created for January. Instead of retyping these worksheets each month, the accountant can create templates for them and then fill in only the data that changes from month to month. In addition to saving you typing time, templates also maintain document consistency, since the same template can be shared by several users. Templates can be created for worksheets, charts, and macro sheets.

Creating Templates

You can create a template from an existing worksheet, chart, or macro sheet, or you can create a new document and save it as a template. To create a template:

1. Open the document you want to use as a template, or type a new document to use.
2. Click on File in the menu bar.
3. Click on Save As to display the Save As dialog box.
4. In the File Name text box, type the name for the template. If you do not add an extension, Excel will assign the extension .XLT to the name.
5. In the Save File As Type drop-down list, select Template.
6. Click on OK. The document has been saved as a template.

 When you create a chart from a chart template, the data used to create the template is not used for the new chart. Instead, the data in the active worksheet is used. Only the formatting characteristics of the template are used in the new chart.

N O T E

Let's use our EXPJAN.XLS worksheet to create a template for expense worksheets.

1. Open the EXPJAN.XLS worksheet.
2. Click on cell C1 and, in the formula bar, delete the word *January* under the heading "Expenses for the Month of January, 1992".

3. We are now going to clear the figures that will be replaced each month, leaving the column and row headings, the Totals formulas, and the currency format intact. Select cells C7 through R35.

4. Click on Edit in the menu bar.

5. Click on Clear to display the Clear dialog box.

6. Select Formulas. This will allow us to clear the figures, but leave the currency format intact.

7. Click on OK. The data in cells C7 through R35 has been deleted, but the currency format for those cells remains intact. In addition, the formulas in the Totals column and row remain intact, since we did not clear the data in row 36 or column S.

8. In the Save As dialog box, save this template with the name *EXPENSE*. Excel will add the .XLT extension.

Since we did not clear the currency format or formulas when we cleared the figures, these will be included in every document we create with the template. When you add figures to the new worksheet, they will automatically be formatted with the currency format, and the totals will automatically be calculated. All you have to do is insert the correct month in Cell C1 and type in the figures for each account.

Using Templates

Once you have created a template, you can use it over and over to create new documents. When you open a template, Excel creates an unsaved copy of the template for you to use, and assigns it a suggested filename based on the name of the template. For example, if you open the template EXPENSE.XLT, Excel will copy it and give it the suggested or temporary name *EXPENSE1*. When you save the new document, you can accept the temporary name or replace it with a name of your choice. Any changes you make will be saved with the new document, and will not affect the template. To use a template:

1. Click on File in the menu bar.

2. Click on Open to display the Open dialog box.

3. In the file list box, double-click on the template you want to open. A copy of the template is opened, and Excel has assigned it a temporary filename.

4. Edit the document as you would any document.

5. Save the document using the Save As dialog box. You can save the document with the suggested name, or you can give it another name.

SHORT CUT

Documents saved in the startup directory are also listed in the New dialog box, giving you quicker access to the templates. Just choose the New command in the File menu, and select the template in the New dialog box.

Editing the Original Template Document

You might want to make a change in the original template. To do this, you will have to open the template itself, not a copy of it. To open and edit an original template document:

1. Click on File in the menu bar.
2. Click on Open to display the Open dialog box.
3. Highlight the template you want to edit.
4. Hold down the Shift key and click on the OK command button. The original template document is opened.
5. Edit the template.
6. Save the template. The template is saved with your changes.

Formatting Worksheets with Styles

Styles are a quick way to format cells and ranges. Each style contains a combination of formats. When you apply a style to a cell or range, all of the formats in the style are automatically assigned to the cell or range. If you change or redefine a style, all of the cells containing that style will change to reflect the change.

There are six types of formats that you can apply to a cell: Number, Font, Alignment, Border, Pattern, and Protection. You can include any or all of these formats in a style.

Excel comes with several styles already defined. You can redefine these, or create custom styles. The default style is Normal.

Applying Styles

When you apply a style to a cell or range, the formats in the style will override any formats previously contained in the cell or range. For example, if you have formatted a cell with the Helvetica 10 point type, and then apply to that cell a style in Helvetica 12, the font format of the cell changes to Helvetica 12. However, if you apply a style to a cell or range first, then manually change the format in the cell or range, the new format overrides the style format.

There are two ways to apply a format—using the Style box in the Standard or Formatting toolbar, or using the Style command in the Format menu.

Using the Style Box

1. Select the cells to which you want to apply a style.
2. In the toolbar, click the arrow next to the Style box to display the available styles, as shown in Figure 12.1. Click on the style you want to apply.

Another way to apply styles with the Style box is to click on the Style box in the toolbar, type in the name of the style you want to apply, and then press Enter.

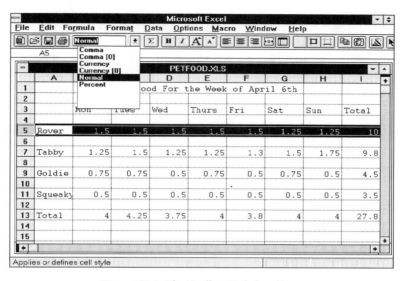

Figure 12.1. The Toolbar Style box list.

Using the Style Command

1. Select the cell or range to which you want to apply a style.
2. Click on Format in the menu bar.
3. Click on Style. The Style dialog box is displayed, as shown in Figure 12.2.

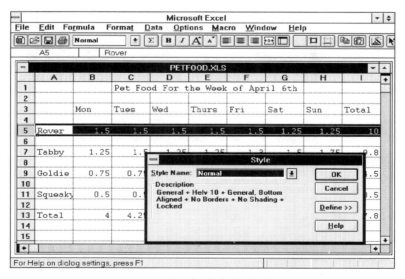

Figure 12.2. The Style dialog box.

4. In the Style Name drop-down list, select the style you want to apply. Click on OK. The style is applied to the selected cell or range.

Alternatively, you may simply type the name of the style you want to apply into the Style Name box, and click on OK.

Let's use styles to format the SALJAN.XLS worksheet.

1. Open the SALJAN.XLS worksheet.

2. Select row 6 by clicking on its row heading, then select the nonadjacent row 20 by holding down the Ctrl key and clicking the row heading 20.

3. Open the Style dialog box.

4. Select Currency(0) in the Style Name drop-down list. The description will appear in the Description box, as shown in Figure 12.3.

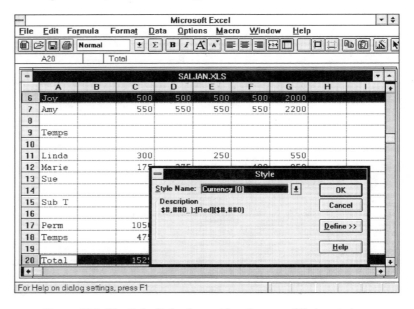

Figure 12.3. The Style dialog box with a Currency(0) description.

5. Click on OK. Rows 6 and 20 are formatted with the Currency(0) style.

In the next section we will create a style to format the rest of the cells with a currency format that does not have dollar signs ($).

Creating Styles

In addition to the styles that come with Excel, you can create your own, custom styles. When you create a style, you assign a name to a combination of formats. There are three ways to create a format: by example, by definition, or by copying a style from one document to another.

Creating Styles by Example

When you format a style by example, you select a cell that already contains the combination of formats you want, and assign it a style name.

To create a style by example with the toolbar Style box:

1. Select a cell that contains the combination of formats you want in the style.
2. Click the current style name in the Style box in the toolbar.
3. Type in a new name for the style.
4. Press Enter. The formats contained in the selected cell are saved with the new style name.

To create a style by example with the Style command:

1. Select a cell that contains the combination of formats you want in the style.
2. Click on Format in the menu bar.
3. Click on Style to display the Style dialog box is displayed.
4. In the Style Name box, type in a name for the style.
5. Click on OK. The formats contained in the selected cell are saved with the new style name.

Creating Styles by Definition

When you create a style by definition, you build a style by specifying the combination of formats you want in the Style dialog box. To create a style by definition:

1. Select a cell with as many formats as possible that you want to include in the new style, or click on a cell with the Normal style.
2. Click on Format in the menu bar.
3. Click on Style to display the Style dialog box is displayed.
4. Click on the Define command button. The Style dialog box expands, as shown in Figure 12.4. All of the options available for formatting a style are listed.
5. In the Style Name box, type a name for the new style.
6. In the Style Includes box, select only the formats you want to include in the new style. Disable the formats you do not want to include (if a format is already selected, click on the box to disable the selection).
7. The command buttons for the selected formats are in the Change box. Disabled items will be dimmed. To change a format, click on the corresponding command button. The dialog box for the format is displayed. For example, if you click on Number, the Number Format dialog box is displayed, as shown in Figure 12.5.

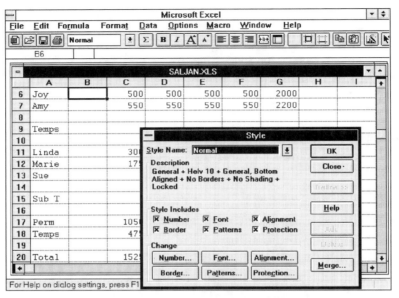

Figure 12.4. An expanded Style dialog box.

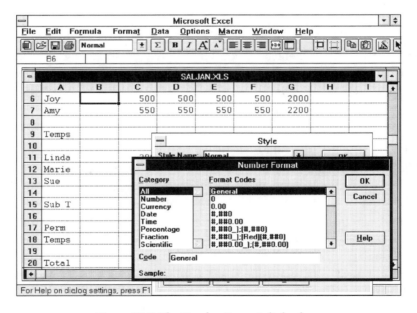

Figure 12.5. The Number Format dialog box.

8. Select the format(s) you want from the dialog box.

9. Click on OK. The Style dialog box reappears.

10. Repeat steps 7 through 9 for each format you want to change.

11. Click on OK to define the style, apply the style to the selected cell(s), and close the dialog box all in one step. **Or,** click on the Add command button to define the style and keep the Style dialog box open so you can create other styles. **Or,** click on the Close command button to close the dialog box without applying the style to the selected cell(s).

Copying Styles from Other Worksheets

When you create a style, it is attached to the active worksheet. To use the styles of one worksheet in another worksheet, you must copy the styles using the Merge command. You cannot copy just one style with the Merge command; all of the styles in the worksheet are copied. To copy styles from another worksheet:

1. Open both the worksheet that contains the styles you want to copy, and the worksheet you want to copy the styles to.
2. Switch to the worksheet you want to copy the styles to.
3. Click on Format in the menu bar.
4. Click on Style to display the Style dialog box is displayed.
5. Click on the Define command button. The Style dialog box is expanded, as shown in Figure 12.4.
6. Click on the Merge command button. Excel displays a list of all of the worksheets that are open in the workspace.
7. Select the name of the worksheet that contains the files you want to copy.
8. Click on OK. All of the styles will be copied from the worksheet you selected in step 7 to the active worksheet.
9. Click on the Close command button to close the Style dialog box.

SHORT CUT

When you copy styles from one worksheet to another, the style names are also copied. If the active worksheet contains any styles with the same name as the styles you are copying, Excel will ask if you want to replace the existing styles with the new ones. You will receive this warning only once, regardless of the number of conflicting style names. If you choose to continue, all of the styles with conflicting names will be replaced.

Copying One Style from Another Worksheet

When you use the Merge command, all of the styles in a worksheet are copied to the active worksheet. You may wish to copy only one style. For example, suppose you created a new style in the source worksheet, and also made changes to the Normal style. You might want to copy the new custom file to the target worksheet, but not the changes made in the Normal style. If you use the Merge command, the Normal style in the source worksheet will overwrite the Normal style in the target worksheet.

To copy one style from another worksheet:

1. Open both the worksheet that contains the style you want to copy, and the worksheet that you want to copy the style to.
2. Select the worksheet you want to copy the style from (the **source** worksheet).
3. Select a cell containing the style you want to copy, and select Copy in the Edit menu.
4. Switch to the worksheet you want to copy the style to (the **target** worksheet).
5. Paste the cell into the target worksheet. The style is pasted into the target worksheet with the cell.

Redefining Styles

Once you have created a style, you can redefine it. Any of the cells in the worksheet that contain the style will reflect the new formats. However, if you have applied any individual formatting to a cell that contains the style, the formatting of that cell will not automatically reflect the redefined style. You must reapply the style. For example, let's suppose that you applied to a cell a style named Totals containing 12 point Helvetica, and then reformatted the cell for 10 point Helvetica. If you redefine the Totals style to contain a Times Roman 11 point font, the cell containing the Totals style will not be updated automatically. You must select the cell and reapply the Totals style.

You can also redefine the built-in styles that come with Excel. There are two ways to redefine a format: by example, using the Style box in the Standard or Formatting toolbar; or by definition, using the Style command in the Format menu.

Redefining Styles by Example

To redefine a cell by example:

1. Select a cell that has been assigned the style you want to change.
2. Format the cell with the new formatting you want the style to have.
3. Reapply the style name to the cell using either the Style box on the toolbar or the Style command in the Format menu.
4. An Excel dialog box is displayed asking if you want to redefine the style based on the selected cell.
5. To redefine the existing style, select Yes. All of the cells containing the style will be updated to reflect the changes in the style.

Redefining Styles by Definition

To redefine a style by definition:

1. Click on Format in the menu bar.
2. Click on Style to display the Style dialog box.

3. Click on the Define command button. The Style dialog box expands, as shown in Figure 12.4.

4. In the Style Name box, select or type the name of the style you want to redefine. Whether you select or type the style name, the formats of the currently selected style are displayed in the Description box, and serve as the starting point for redefining the style.

5. In the Style Includes box, select only the formats you want to include in the redefined style. Disable the formats you do not want to include (if a format is already selected, click on the box to disable the selection).

6. The command buttons for the selected formats are in the Change box. Disabled items will be dimmed. To change a format, click on the corresponding command button. The dialog box for the format is displayed.

7. Select the format(s) you want from the dialog box.

8. Click on OK. The Style dialog box reappears.

9. Repeat steps 7 through 9 for each format you want to change.

10. Click OK to accept the changes, apply the redefined style to the selected cell(s), and close the dialog box all in one step. **Or,** click on the Add command button to accept the changes and keep the Style dialog box open so that you can create or redefine other styles. **Or,** click on the Close command button to close the dialog box without applying the style to the selected cell(s).

All cells that were formatted with the style that has been redefined will be updated to reflect the changes in the style. All cells that have not been formatted individually or with a style are automatically assigned the Normal style. If you redefined the Normal style, any entry you make in these cells will reflect the redefined Normal style.

Normal Style

When you start a new worksheet, all of the cells default to the Normal style. The normal style in Excel has the following formats: the font is sans serif 10 if you are using Windows 3.1, and Helvetica 10 if you are using Windows 3.0; the number format is General; the alignment is General; there are no borders; there is no shading; and protection is locked.

Sometimes the Normal style formats are unsuitable for the worksheet you are creating. If you redefine the Normal style before you enter data, all of the data will reflect the redefined style. In addition, if you apply another built-in style or create a new style, the changes in the redefined Normal style will also be reflected in the built-in or new custom style.

When you redefine the Normal style for a worksheet, the redefined style applies only to that worksheet. If you start a new worksheet, the Normal style returns to the original default formats listed above. You can make permanent changes to the Normal style by editing the EXEL4.INI file.

Deleting Styles

If you have a style you no longer wish to use, you can delete it. When you delete a style, any cells formatted with that style return to the Normal style. Any formats you added to the cell after you applied the style remain in the cell. The style is deleted in the active worksheet only. If the same style is in another worksheet, it will not be deleted.

To delete a style:

1. Click on Format in the menu bar.
2. Click on Style to display the Style dialog box.
3. In the Style Name box, select or type the style name you want to delete.
4. Click on the Define command button. The Style dialog box is expanded, as shown in Figure 12.4.
5. Click on the Delete command button. The style is deleted. The Style dialog box remains open so that you can delete other styles.
6. Click on Close to close the Style dialog box.

Using Toolbars

Toolbars are great shortcuts you can use to execute commands and macros. When you click on an icon in a toolbar, the corresponding command is executed. Toolbars can make Excel so user-friendly that almost anyone can begin to use the program immediately, since the tools have icons, or pictures, that describe their functions.

You can use the built-in toolbars or create custom toolbars. There is no limit to the number of toolbars you can create.

Displaying and Hiding Toolbars

Excel comes with several built-in toolbars. The default is the Standard toolbar. When you execute Excel, this toolbar is automatically displayed across the top of the screen, as shown in Figure 12.6.

You can display several toolbars at a time, and you can position toolbars anywhere on the screen. You can also change the shape and orientation of toolbars. When you change the shape or position of a toolbar, it remains that way until you change it again, even if you exit Excel.

There are two ways to display or hide toolbars: with the toolbar shortcut menu; or with the Toolbars command in the Options menu.

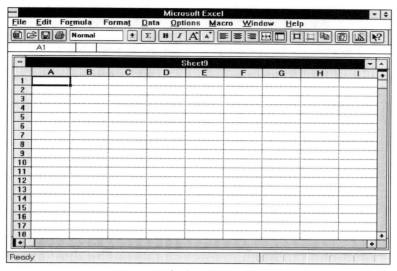

Figure 12.6. The Standard toolbar.

Displaying or Hiding Toolbars Using the Toolbar Shortcut Menu

To display or hide a toolbar using the toolbar shortcut menu:

1. Position the mouse pointer anywhere in an open toolbar.
2. Click the right mouse pointer. The toolbar shortcut menu is displayed, as shown in Figure 12.7.

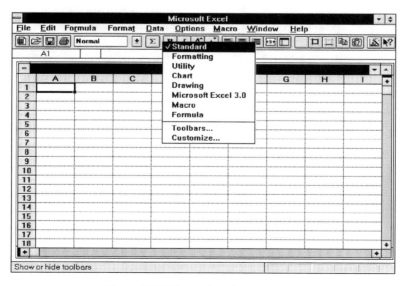

Figure 12.7. The toolbar shortcut menu.

3. To open a toolbar, click on it. A check mark will appear in the toolbar shortcut menu next to the name of all displayed toolbars.

4. To hide a toolbar, click on the name of the toolbar you want to hide. The check mark will disappear and the toolbar will be hidden.

Displaying or Hiding Toolbars Using the Toolbars Command

To display or hide toolbars with the Toolbars command:

1. Click on Options in the menu bar.

2. Click on Toolbars. The Toolbars dialog box is displayed, as shown in Figure 12.8.

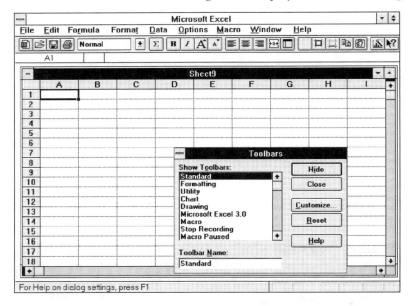

Figure 12.8. The Toolbars dialog box.

3. In the Show Toolbars box, select the toolbar you want to display or hide.

4. If the toolbar is displayed, the Hide command button will appear. If the toolbar is hidden, the Show command button will appear. Simply click on one of these buttons to perform the command.

N O T E

If you create too many toolbars to fit in the toolbar shortcut menu, click on More Toolbars in the toolbar shortcut menu. The Toolbars dialog box will be displayed, and will allow you to scroll down the list of toolbars.

Changing the Position and Shape of a Toolbar

You can position a toolbar anywhere in the Excel application window. If you drag the toolbar near the edge of the application window or above the formula bar, Excel places the toolbar in an area called a **toolbar dock**. The border of the toolbar changes from thick to thin when the toolbar is dragged to a toolbar dock position.

A toolbar placed in an area other than a toolbar dock (usually in the document window) is called a **floating toolbar**. A floating toolbar has its own title bar displaying the name of the toolbar. You can change the shape of a floating toolbar. Figure 12.9 shows a window with a floating toolbar and four toolbars in toolbar docks.

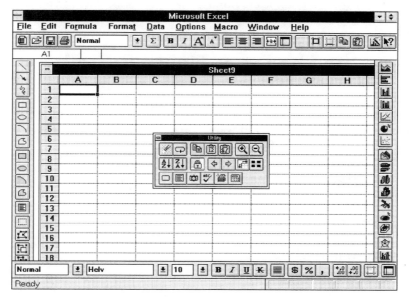

Figure 12.9. The Excel window with a floating toolbar and four toolbars in toolbar dock.

Moving Toolbars to Toolbar Docks

If you have more than one toolbar displayed, you might want to move one of them to another toolbar dock. To move the toolbar to a toolbar dock:

1. Position the mouse pointer in a blank area in the toolbar that you want to move to a different toolbar dock.

2. Drag the toolbar to the location of the toolbar dock. As you drag the toolbar, the shape becomes a large rectangle with a thick border. When the toolbar is in the correct location to position in a toolbar dock, the thick border changes to a dotted border that is the same shape as the toolbar.

Moving Toolbars to Floating Toolbar Positions

A toolbar that is not in a toolbar dock is a floating toolbar. To move a toolbar to a floating toolbar position:

1. Position the mouse pointer in a blank area in the toolbar.
2. Drag the toolbar to a new location in the application window.

SHORT CUT

You can quickly move toolbars on and off the toolbar dock. If you double-click the title bar in a floating toolbar, Excel returns the toolbar to its last toolbar dock. If you double-click a toolbar in a toolbar dock, Excel moves the toolbar to its last floating position.

Changing the Shapes of Floating Toolbars

You can change the shape of a floating toolbar the same way you change the shape of a document window. Position the mouse pointer (a double-sided arrow) on the border of the floating toolbar and drag to the size you want. If you change the height, Excel automatically adjusts the width so that the tools fit, and vice versa.

Editing Toolbars

You can add, delete, move, and copy tools in a toolbar.

Adding Tools to a Toolbar

1. In the toolbar shortcut menu, choose Customize, or, in the Toolbars dialog box, click on the Customize command button. The Customize dialog box is displayed, as shown in Figure 12.10.
2. In the Categories box, select the category from which you want to add a tool. Excel displays the tools for that category in the Tools box. If you click on a tool in the Tools box, a description of the tool is displayed.
3. Drag the tool from the Tools box to the place on the displayed toolbar where you want to add the tool. Excel resizes the toolbar to accommodate the added tool.
4. Click on the Close command button to close the Customize dialog box.

Deleting Tools from a Toolbar

1. In the toolbar shortcut menu, choose Customize; or click on the Customize command button in the Toolbars dialog box. The Customize dialog box is displayed.

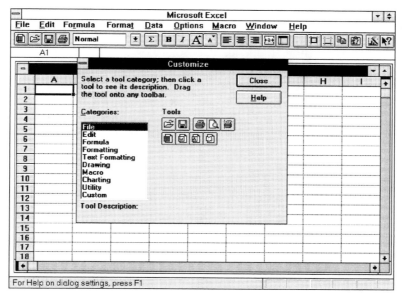

Figure 12.10. The Customize dialog box.

2. Drag the tool off the toolbar and place it anywhere in the window where there is no toolbar. The tool is deleted from the toolbar.

3. Click on the Close command button to close the Customize dialog box.

WARNING

If you have created a custom tool (see below) and deleted it from the toolbar, it is permanently deleted. It is a good idea to create a storage toolbar to move custom tools to when you want to remove them from a toolbar. You can then move the custom tool from the storage toolbar back to the toolbar (or another toolbar) when you want to use it again. Tools that come with the Excel program are not permanently deleted when you delete them from a toolbar; they are still available in the Customize dialog box.

Moving Tools

1. In the toolbar shortcut menu, choose Customize, or click on the Customize command button in the Toolbars dialog box, to display the Customize dialog box.

2. Drag the tool to a new location on the same toolbar, or to a location on another displayed toolbar. Excel will adjust the toolbars to accommodate the change.

3. Click on the Close command button to close the dialog box.

Copying Tools

1. In the toolbar shortcut menu, choose Customize, or click on the Customize command button in the Toolbars dialog box, to display the Customize dialog box.
2. While holding down the Ctrl key, drag the tool to a new location on the same toolbar or to a location on another displayed toolbar. Excel will adjust the toolbars to accommodate the change.
3. Click on the Close command button to close the dialog box.

Resetting Edited Toolbars

If you have edited a built-in toolbar, you can restore it to its original configuration.

1. In the toolbar shortcut menu, choose Toolbars, or click on Toolbars in the Options menu, to display the Toolbars dialog box.
2. In the Show Toolbars box, select the toolbar you want to restore.
3. Click on the Reset command button. The toolbar is restored to its original configuration.
4. Click on the Close command button to close the dialog box.

If the Reset button has changed to a Delete button, you have selected a custom toolbar and not a built-in toolbar. You cannot reset a custom toolbar.

N O T E

Creating Custom Toolbars

In addition to the built-in toolbars that come with Excel, you can create custom toolbars. When you create a new toolbar, you start with a blank bar and add tools to it.

Let's create a Formula toolbar containing tools we can use to build formulas.

1. From the Options menu or the toolbar shortcut menu, choose Toolbars to display the Toolbars dialog box.
2. In the Toolbar Name text box, type *Formula*.
3. Choose the Add or Customize command button. Excel displays a new blank toolbar in its own toolbar window, as shown in Figure 12.11, and displays the Customize dialog box so you can add tools to the new toolbar.
4. In the Categories box, select Formula to display the tools used in building formulas.
5. Drag each of the formula tools to the new Formula toolbar. Excel will resize the tool bar as you add new tools.

6. Click on the Close command button to close the dialog box. You have created a new toolbar called Formula.

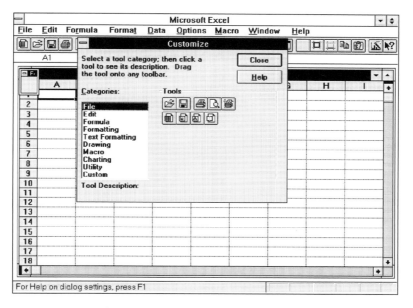

Figure 12.11. The Blank Formula toolbar.

You can now display or hide the Formula toolbar, move it in or out of a toolbar dock, and edit it.

You can also drag tools from another displayed toolbar to the new toolbar as you create it by holding down the Ctrl key and dragging the tool to the new toolbar. If you change your mind while creating the toolbar, you can remove a tool by dragging it off the toolbar and placing it anywhere where there is no toolbar.

N O T E

Deleting Custom Toolbars

You can delete custom toolbars, but not built-in toolbars. To delete a custom toolbar:

1. From the Options menu or the toolbar shortcut menu, choose Toolbars.
2. In the Show Toolbars box, highlight the toolbar you want to delete.
3. Click on the Delete command button. The toolbar is deleted.
4. Click on the Close command button to close the dialog box.

Toolbar Keyboard Shortcuts

Most tools can be accessed only with a mouse. The exceptions are the following toolbar and tool keyboard shortcuts:

Tool name	Keyboard shortcut
Show or hide Standard toolbar	Ctrl+7
Demote	Alt+Shift+Right Arrow
Promote	Alt+Shift+Left Arrow
Style box	Ctrl+S
AutoSum	Alt+=
Select visible cells	Alt+;
Show outline symbols	Ctrl+8
Font Name box	Ctrl+P
Font Size box	Ctrl+F

Customizing Tools

You can use the built-in tools that come with Excel to create custom tools, then use these custom tools to execute macros. You can also copy a **tool face**, or icon, to another tool.

Copying Tool Faces to Other Tools

You can use this feature to copy a built-in tool face to another tool in a displayed toolbar. Only the picture on the tool changes; the action remains the same. To copy a tool face:

1. From the toolbar shortcut menu, choose Customize or Toolbars; or choose Toolbars from the Options menu.

2. While the Customize or Toolbars dialog box is open, point to the tool you want to copy and click the right mouse button. The tool shortcut menu is displayed, as shown in Figure 12.12. (Either the Toolbars or Customize dialog box must be open to use the tool shortcut menu.)

3. Choose Copy Tool Face in the tool shortcut menu.

4. If the tool you want to copy is not displayed in a toolbar, click the tool you want to copy in the Customize dialog box, and choose Copy Tool Face in the Edit menu.

5. Click on the toolbar tool to which you want to copy the face. You can copy a face only to a tool in a displayed toolbar.

6. From the Edit menu or the tool shortcut menu, choose Paste Tool Face.

You can restore a tool to its original face by clicking on the tool you want to reset and choosing Reset Tool Face from the tool shortcut menu.

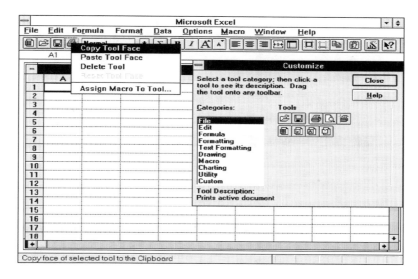

Figure 12.12. The tool shortcut menu showing the Copy Tool Face drop-down list.

Creating Custom Tools and Assigning Macros to Them

You can create custom tools and assign existing macros to them.

1. In the toolbar shortcut menu, choose Customize, or click on the Customize command button in the Toolbars dialog box, to display the Customize dialog box.

2. In the Categories box, select Custom to display the Custom tools, as shown in Figure 12.13. None of the custom tools in the box has a macro or an action assigned to it.

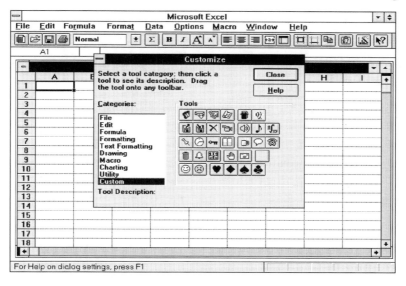

Figure 12.13. The Customize dialog box displaying custom tools.

3. Drag the tool you want from the Tools box to the position on the toolbar where you want to add the tool. The Assign To Tool dialog box is displayed, as shown in Figure 12.14.

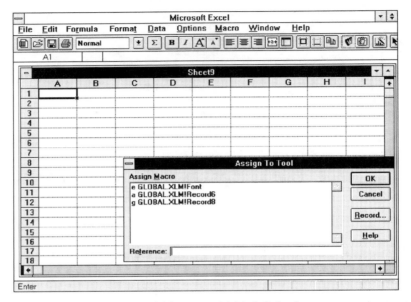

Figure 12.14. The Assign To Tool dialog box.

4. In the Assign Macro box, select the name of the command macro you want to assign to the tool, or type a macro name or cell reference in the Reference text box (macros will be covered later in this chapter).

5. Click on OK. The macro has been assigned to the custom tool.

Creating a Custom Tool and Recording a New Macro for It

1. In the toolbar shortcut menu, choose Customize, or click on the Customize command button in the Toolbars dialog box, to display the Customize dialog box.

2. In the Categories box, select Custom to display the Custom dialog box. None of the tools in the Custom dialog box has a macro or an action assigned to it.

3. Drag the tool you want from the Tools box to the position on the toolbar where you want to add the tool. The Assign To Tool dialog box is displayed.

4. Click on the Record command button in the Assign To Tool dialog box to display the Record Macro dialog box. See the section on macros later in this chapter to learn how to use the Record Macro dialog box.

5. When you are finished, choose Stop Recorder from the Macro menu.

What Are Macros?

A **macro** is a mini-program that customizes Excel by adding commands and functions (**add-in macros**) or speeding up tasks by recording keystrokes and mouse actions and then playing them back on command (**command macros**). A macro can consist of simple commands (building a simple formula, for instance) or very complex features. Use macros to record tasks that you perform frequently.

We'll cover simple command macros in this book. For information on advanced macro features, look for *Power Shortcuts...Excel 4.0* (MIS:Press) at your local bookstore.

When you record a command macro, Excel creates an instruction for each action you complete. These instructions are called **macro functions**, and they are stored on a **macro sheet** you create or on a **global macro sheet**. If you do not open a macro sheet before recording a macro, Excel will automatically assign the macro to the last macro sheet you created, if it is open. If it is not open, Excel will create a new macro sheet. If you select a global macro sheet, Excel will automatically add the macro to the global macro sheet. Macro sheets are explained later in the chapter.

Recording Command Macros

To record a command macro:

1. Click on Macro in the menu bar.
2. Click on Record to display the Record Macro dialog box, as shown in Figure 12.15.

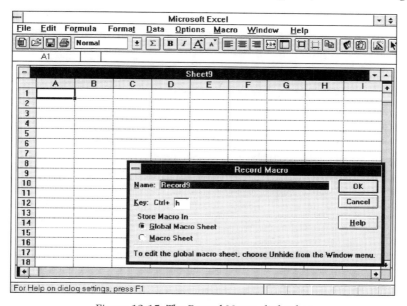

Figure 12.15. The Record Macro dialog box.

If no documents are open:

1. Click on File in the menu bar.
2. Click on Record Macro. The Record Macro dialog box is displayed, as shown in Figure 12.15. A suggested name for the macro is displayed in the Name text box, and a suggested shortcut key combination is displayed in the Key text box. The macro name or shortcut key is used to run the macro.
3. Make changes if you wish in the Name and Key text boxes. The shortcut key can be only one letter. Be sure the shortcut key you choose is not being used by another macro. If you use a capital letter, you must use the Shift key as well as the Ctrl key in combination with the letter to run the macro.
4. Select an option in the Store Macro In box.
5. Choose OK. Excel enters the macro name in the specified macro sheet, and starts recording. A Recording prompt appears in the status bar.
6. Perform the actions you want to record in the macro.
7. When you are finished, choose Stop Recorder in the Macro menu.

Pausing While Recording Command Macros

You can pause while recording a command macro. The recorder will ignore all actions until you start recording again. For example, you might want to check a command or see how a feature is going to work before you record it. To pause while recording a command macro:

1. Click on Macro in the menu bar.
2. Click on Stop Recorder.
3. To resume recording, click on Start Recorder in the Macro menu.

Recording to Global Macro Sheets

If you are creating macros that you want to use with several worksheets, you should record them to the global macro sheet. Since the global macro sheet is automatically opened when you start Excel, global macros can be run at any time while you are in the program. You don't have to remember to open, save, or name the macro sheet.

The global macro sheet is a hidden document. To display or edit it, you must expose it by choosing the Unhide command from the Window menu. When you are finished using it, remember to hide it again by switching to the global macro sheet and choosing Hide in the Window menu.

The global macro sheet is named GLOBAL.XLM, and is stored in the default directory (see Appendix A for information about the default directory).

To record to the global macro sheet:

1. Click on File in the menu bar.
2. Click on Record Macro to display the Record Macro dialog box.
3. Select Global Macro Sheet in the Store Macro In option box.
4. Supply the rest of the information required by the Record Macro dialog box.
5. Choose OK. Excel will record the macro to the global macro sheet.
6. Perform the actions you want to record in the macro.
7. When you are finished, choose Stop Recorder in the Macro menu.

Recording to Macro Sheets

When you record a macro to a macro sheet, you must remember to create a new macro sheet or open an existing one before you record the macro. If you do not create or open a macro sheet, Excel will create a new macro sheet and record to it. The next time you choose the Record command, the macro you record will be added to the new macro sheet Excel created.

To record to an existing macro sheet, open the sheet, select an empty cell, and then choose Set Recorder in the Macro menu. The macro is stored on the sheet, beginning at the empty cell.

In order to run a macro that has been recorded to a macro sheet, you must first open the sheet to which it was recorded. You must remember to save the sheet before exiting Excel.

To create a new macro sheet:

1. Click on File in the menu bar.
2. Click on New. The New dialog box is displayed.
3. Select Macro Sheet.
4. Choose OK.

To open an existing macro sheet:

1. Click on File in the menu bar.
2. Click on Open to display the Open dialog box.
3. Select the macro sheet you want to open.
4. Choose O.

Let's record a command macro that will change the font in a worksheet to 12 point Helvetica.

1. Click on Macro in the menu bar.
2. Click on Record to display the Record Macro dialog box.

If no documents are open:

1. Click on File in the menu bar.
2. Click on Record Macro to display the Record Macro dialog box.

3. Change the name to Font in the Name text box.

4. Leave the suggested shortcut key as is.

5. Select Global Macro Sheet in the Store Macro In option box.

6. Choose OK. A Recording prompt appears in the status bar.

7. Click on Format in the menu bar to open the Format menu.

8. Click on Font to display the Font dialog box.

9. Select Helvetica in the Font list; select Regular in the Font Style list; and select 12 in the Size list.

10. Click on OK to close the Font dialog box.

11. Choose Stop Recorder in the Macro menu. The command macro has been recorded to the global macro sheet.

Writing or Editing Command Macros

Instead of recording a command macro, you can manually enter formulas into a cell in a style sheet to create or edit a command macro. These formulas tell Excel how to perform each step of the macro. To write a command macro:

1. Create a new macro sheet or open an existing one.

2. Write the macro in the macro sheet using Excel functions and conditions.

3. When you have finished, name the macro.

   a. Select the first cell of the macro.

   b. Click on Formula in the menu bar.

   c. In the Name box, type a name for the macro.

   d. Choose OK.

4. **Debug** the macro (iron out any problems it might have).

To edit a command macro:

1. Open the macro sheet with the macro you want to edit.

2. Write the changes in the macro using Excel functions and conditions.

3. Save the macro.

To write or edit a command macro, you must understand worksheet and macro functions and their arguments, as well as the macro command language for using conditions. If you want to write or edit complex macros, you should refer to your Excel manual or look for *Power Shortcuts...Excel 4.0* (MIS:Press) at your local bookstore. Both the manual and the book contain detailed explanations about functions and their arguments, as well as macro command language.

Running Command Macros

Once a macro has been recorded, you can run it. If the macro has been recorded to a macro sheet, you must first open the sheet. If the macro has been recorded to the global macro sheet, it is automatically opened when you start Excel.

To run a command macro:

1. Click on Macro in the menu bar.

2. Click on Run. The Run dialog box is displayed, as shown in Figure 12.16. All of the macros contained in the open macro sheet are displayed, as are the ones in the global macro sheet. The list shows the shortcut key, the macro sheet, and the name of the macro.

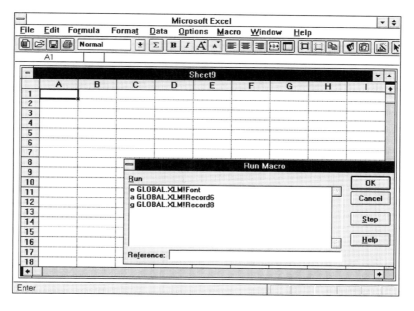

Figure 12.16. The Run dialog box.

3. Select the macro you want to run.

4. Click on OK. The macro you selected will run.

SHORT CUT

You can also run a macro by pressing the shortcut key defined for the macro or, if the macro has been assigned to a tool in a toolbar, by clicking on the tool.

Let's run our Font macro.

1. Open the PETFOOD.XLS worksheet.
2. Select the entire worksheet by clicking on the Select All button in the upper-left corner of the document window.
3. Click on Macro in the menu bar.
4. Click on Run to display the Run dialog box.
5. Select Font.
6. Click on OK. The Font macro will run and reformat the entire worksheet with the new font.

Review Exercises for Chapter 12

♦ Using the INCJAN.XLS worksheet, create a new template for income worksheets. Save the template with the name INCOME.XLT.

♦ Create a style using 12 point bold italic Helvetica. Name the style *Font1*.

♦ Copy the style to the PETFOOD.XLS worksheet.

♦ Select the entire PETFOOD.XLS worksheet and apply the Font1 style.

♦ Add a tool to the Standard toolbar. Reset the toolbar to restore it to its original configuration.

♦ Create a custom toolbar using tools of your choice.

♦ Practice positioning and sizing toolbars.

♦ Assign the macro named Font to a tool in your custom toolbar.

♦ Using your imagination, record a command macro to perform a simple task. Record it to the global macro sheet.

♦ Run the command macro you recorded in step 9.

Before You Go On...

Before you continue on to the next chapter you should be able to customize your documents using templates, styles, toolbars, and macros. You should know how to create, use, and edit a document template. You should be able to create, apply, copy, delete, and redefine a style. You should know how to position, size, and edit toolbars and how to create custom toolbars and tools. You should know how to record and run a command macro.

Chapter **12**

CREATING, EDITING, AND FORMATTING CHARTS

What You Will Learn in This Chapter

- Understanding the parts of a chart
- How to create and save an embedded chart
- How to save a chart as a separate document
- How to change chart types
- Mouse and keyboard movement keys within charts
- How to add, delete, or edit data series within charts
- How to change data values in charts
- How to delete charts
- How to use copy and paste special to create a chart
- How to format charts

Charts are a pictorial representation of worksheet data. For most people, it is easier to read a chart or graph than to read numbers in a worksheet. In addition, charts can represent the data in a worksheet in a number of ways. Charts are linked to worksheet data. When you upgrade the data in a worksheet, the chart is automatically upgraded.

A chart can be created as a graphic object included in the worksheet and saved with the worksheet. This is called an **embedded chart**. You can also create a **chart document**, which is a chart that is created as a separate document in its own window. A chart document is also linked to a worksheet. You can change your mind and save an embedded chart as a chart document, or save a chart document as an embedded chart.

Understanding the Parts of a Chart

Charts, like worksheets, are comprised of various parts. You should be familiar with the parts of a chart before you create one. The parts of a chart are labelled in Figure 12.1 and are used as follows:

- **Chart window**. The chart window is the same as the document window in a worksheet, except that it contains a chart instead of a worksheet and the menu bar changes to reflect a different type of document, as shown in Figure 12.1.
- **Chart**. The chart comprises the entire area inside the chart window, including labels, axes, and data markers.
- **Chart toolbar**. The Chart toolbar allows you to change chart types, format charts, and select the ChartWizard.
- **Plot area**. The plot area is the area in the chart window that Excel uses to plot your chart, including the axes and all data markers. The plot area does not include chart titles, unattached text, legends, and so forth.
- **Data marker**. A data marker is a bar, line, dot, or other symbol that represents one value in the chart. Each bar in Figure 12.1 is a data marker and represents one value. All of the data markers together comprise a chart data series.
- **Chart data series**. The chart data series is a group of related values, such as the figures in a row or column, that are being charted. For example, if you created a bar chart to show expenses for each day of the week, each bar would be a data marker, and all of the data markers together would be a chart data series, as shown in Figure 12.1. A chart can contain one or more data series. When you have more than one data series in a chart, the data markers for each series will contain the same color, pattern, or symbol.
- **Axis**. The axis is the line on which data in a chart is plotted. A chart contains two axes: the x-axis (the **category axis**), on which categories of data are plotted, and the y-axis (**value axis**), on which data values are plotted. In Figure 12.1, the x-axis contains the categories of data that are being charted ("Items"), and the y-axis lists the values along which the data is being charted ("Amounts"). Bar charts reverse the axes: the categories are plotted along the y-axis, the values along the x-axis.

◆ **Category names**. Category names appear along the x-axis and are the labels taken from the worksheet data used in the chart.

◆ **Chart data series name**. The data chart series name corresponds to the labels included in your worksheet data, which is plotted along the y-axis. If your worksheet data does not contain any labels (for example, if you selected a row or column of numbers only), the data chart series name defaults to the number of the series chosen; for example, Series 1, Series 2, and so on. You can replace the data chart series name with any name you choose.

◆ **Tick mark**. The tick mark is the small line that intersects the axes and marks off each category on the x-axis and each data value on the y-axis.

◆ **Tick mark label**. The tick mark label is the text attached to the tick mark.

◆ **Gridlines**. Gridlines in charts are the same as gridlines in worksheets, and are optional.

◆ **Chart text**. Chart text is the text in a chart that describes the data in the chart. Attached text is linked to a specific object in a chart (such as the chart title, the descriptions you add to the axes, or descriptions you add to describe series or data points), and cannot be moved unless the chart object is moved. Unattached text is independent of chart objects and can be moved anywhere you like in the chart window.

◆ **Legend**. The legend is an optional box that identifies the color or pattern of the data markers in a data series, and shows the name of each data series.

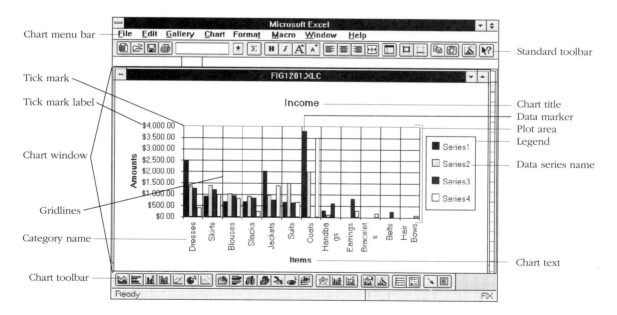

Figure 12.1. The parts of a chart.

Creating an Embedded Chart

The easiest way to create a chart in Excel is to use the ChartWizard tool on your toolbar. Using the ChartWizard tool, we are going to create a basic chart that contains the income for each account for the month of January, as shown in Figure 12.2, using our Income worksheet.

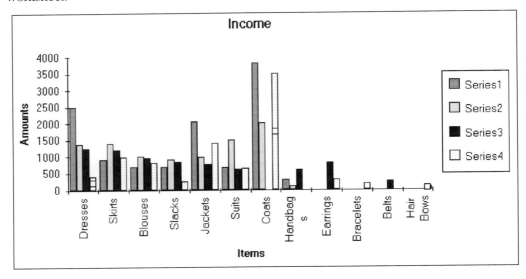

Figure 12.2. Chart showing January income from each item.

1. Open the INCJAN.XLS worksheet.
2. Select the nonadjacent ranges A7:A18 and C7:F18. We want the chart to contain the names of all of the items in the worksheet for which we received income. We also want the chart to contain the income for each account. We do not want the chart to contain any blank columns. Therefore, we need to select the nonadjacent ranges that contain all of this information.
3. Click on the ChartWizard in the toolbar. The shape of your mouse pointer has changed.
4. Move to the section of the worksheet where you want to position the chart and drag your pointer to create a rectangle of the size and shape you want.
5. The ChartWizard—Step 1 of 5 dialog box is displayed, as shown in Figure 12.3. Excel arbitrarily assigns the order in which your selected data will be plotted and displays your selection in this order in the Range text box. Excel takes the category names for the x-axis from the first first column or row if your selection contains one range. If you have multiple ranges containing columns that all start with the same row number, Excel will take the category names from the first column.

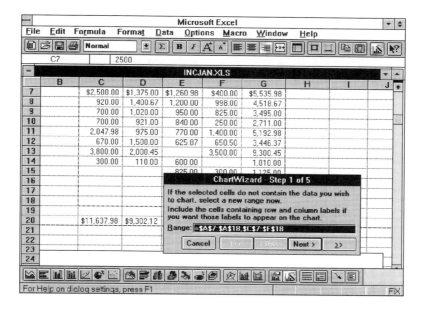

Figure 12.3. The ChartWizard—Step 1 of 5 dialog box.

6. Click on Next. The ChartWizard—Step 2 of 5 dialog box is displayed, as shown in Figure 12.4. You can choose one of fourteen chart types.

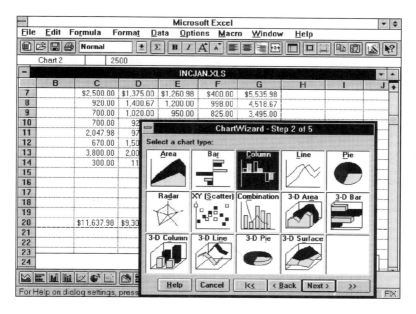

Figure 12.4. The ChartWizard—Step 2 of 5 dialog box.

7. Select Column and click on Next. The ChartWizard—Step 3 of 5 dialog box is displayed, showing ten styles of column charts.

8. Select the style numbered 1.

9. Click on Next. The ChartWizard—Step 4 of 5 dialog box is displayed, as shown in Figure 12.5.

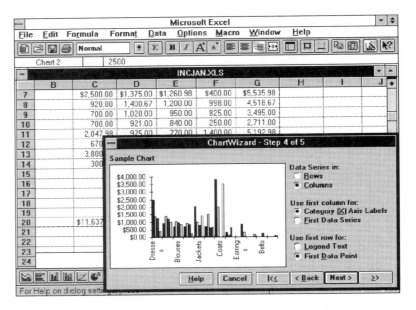

Figure 12.5. The ChartWizard—Step 4 of 5 dialog box.

You will see a sample of how your chart will appear, and you will be given three formatting choices. The Data Series In choice determines whether your data will be plotted in columns or rows. If you choose rows, each selected row of data will appear as a data series in the chart; if you choose columns, each selected column of data will appear as a data series in the chart. Since we want each column to be used as a data series, we will choose Columns.

The Use First Column For choice lets you choose whether the contents of the first row or column will appear along the x-axis as labels or as a data series. Since we want to use labels, select the Category [X] Axis Labels option.

The final choice, Use First Row For, lets you choose whether you want the values in the first row or column to appear as labels or values along the y-axis. If you choose Series (Y) Axis Labels, the y-axis will have labels; if you choose First Data Point, the y-axis will contain values. We want the y-axis to have values, and so we will choose First Data Point. The sample chart in the dialog box will change to reflect your choices.

9. Click on Next. The ChartWizard—Step 5 of 5 dialog box is displayed, as shown in Figure 12.6.

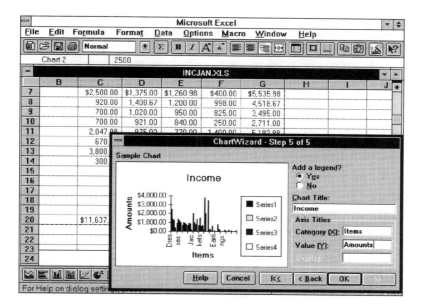

Figure 12.6. The CartWizard—Step 5 of 5 dialog box.

Choose Yes to add a legend to the chart, type in the title *Income* in the Chart Title text box, type *Items* in the Category [X] text box, and type *Amounts* in the Value [Y] text box to complete your chart. Notice how the sample chart in the dialog box changes to reflect each change.

10. Click on OK. Your embedded chart has been created.

11. If necessary, size your chart to accommodate the data it contains by dragging the handles in the center of the top, bottom, left, and right borders.

Before we continue, we will want to save our chart. To save the chart as part of the worksheet (embedded into the worksheet), simply save your worksheet. When you save a chart as an embedded document, the worksheet and the chart are located in the same document. When you open the worksheet, the chart is there as part of the document. When you make changes to worksheet data that is included in the chart, the chart will reflect these changes. To format or edit an embedded chart, you must double-click on the chart to open it. When you open an embedded chart, the menu bar choices change. To close the chart, click on File and then on Close.

Saving a Chart Document

You can also save your chart as a separate document. When you save a chart this way, you must open it as a separate document. This will not prevent any changes made in the worksheet data that is contained in the chart from taking effect in the chart. If your worksheet is particularly large, saving the chart as a separate document is usually a better choice: it is easier to locate the chart and you can format and edit it without taking up RAM with a large document. To save a chart as a separate document:

1. Double click on the chart to open it.
2. Click on File in the menu bar to open the File menu.
3. Click on Save As to display the Save As dialog box.
4. Name the chart. Excel automatically gives charts an XLC entension.

Save your chart using each of the above methods. If you look at the chart you will see that the legend contains four series; each series represents one of the four accounts. Each of the series is preceded by a box that contains the color or pattern for the columns corresponding to that series in the chart. Series 1 charts income for Acct. 100, series 2 charts income for Acct. 101, series 3 for Acct. 102, and series 4 for Acct. 103. Each income item is listed along the x-axis, and dollar amounts in thousands are plotted along the y-axis. When you look at the chart, you can quickly see the amounts of income for each account in proportion to the other accounts for that item, and the amount of income for each item in proportion to all of the other items.

Creating an Embedded 3-D Chart

We have just created a very simple, basic chart, using two ranges. Now let's take it one step further. Let's create a 3-D chart using three nonadjacent ranges to show the income and expense for each item for the month of January.

1. Open the INC&EXP.XLS worksheet.
2. Select the nonadjacent ranges A25:A46, R6:617, and R25:R46. Range A25:A46 contains the names of all of the income and expense items in the worksheet, and we want to use this range for our category names. Ranges R6:R17 and R25:R46 contain the totals for each item (dresses, shirts, etc.), and we want to use these for our data series.
3. Click on the ChartWizard in the toolbar; the shape of your mouse pointer will change.
4. Move to the section of the worksheet where you want to position the chart and drag your pointer to create a rectangle of the size and shape you want.
5. The ChartWizard—Step 1 of 5 dialog box is displayed. Excel arbitrarily assigns the

order in which your selected data will be plotted and displays your selection in this order in the Range text box. Excel takes the category names for the x-axis from the first column or row if your selection contains one range; if your selection contains nonadjacent ranges, Excel takes the category names for the x-axis from the first column or row of the first range, which is shown in the Range text box. We want our category names in the x-axis of our chart to reflect the labels in range A25:A46; thus we will have to edit the contents of the Range text box. In the Range text box, type *=$A$25:$A$46,$R$6:$R$17,$R$25:$R$46*. This will indicate to Excel that the labels in the range A25:A46 will be the category labels for the x-axis.

6. Click on Next. The ChartWizard—Step 2 of 5 dialog box is displayed. You can choose of fourteen chart types.

7. Select 3-D Column and click on Next. The ChartWizard—Step 3 of 5 dialog box is displayed, showing ten styles of column charts.

8. Select style 1.

9. Click on Next. The ChartWizard—Step 4 of 5 dialog box is displayed. You will see a sample of how your chart will appear, and you will be given three formatting choices.

The Data Series In choice determines whether your data will be plotted in columns or rows. If you choose rows, each selected row of data will appear as a data series in the chart; if you choose columns, each selected column of data will appear as a data series in the chart. Since we want each column to be used as a data series, we will choose Columns.

The Use First Column For choice lets you choose whether the contents of the first row or column will appear along the x-axis as labels or as a data series. Since we want to use labels, select the Category [X] Axis Labels option.

The final choice, Use First Row For, lets you choose whether you want the values in the first row or column to appear as labels or values along the y-axis. If you choose Series (Y) Axis Labels, the y-axis will have labels; if you choose First Data Point, the y-axis will contain values. We want the y-axis to have values, so we will choose First Data Point. The sample chart in the dialog box will change to reflect your choices.

10. Click on Next. The ChartWizard—Step 5 of 5 dialog box is displayed. Choose Yes to add a legend to the chart, type *Income and Expense* in the Chart Title text box, type *Items* in the Category [X] text box, and type *Amounts* in the Value [Y] text box to complete your chart. Notice how the sample chart in the dialog box changes to reflect each change.

11. Click on OK. Your embedded chart has been created.

12. If necessary, size your chart to accommodate the data it contains by dragging the handles in the center of the top, bottom, left, and right borders.

Your chart should look like the one shown in Figure 12.7.

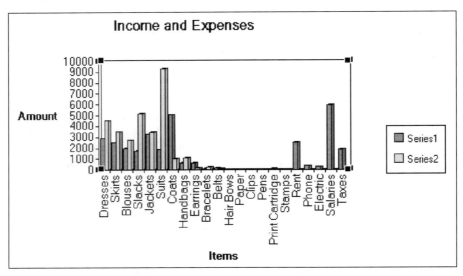

Figure 12.7. 3-D column chart created from INC&EXP.XLS.

Before we continue, save your chart as either an embedded chart or as a separate chart document.

Notice that the legend contains two different series—one series represents income, and the other represents expenses. Each of the series is preceded by a box that contains the color or pattern for the columns corresponding to that series in the chart. Series 1 charts expenses for the month of January, and Series 2 charts income. Each income and expense item is listed along the x-axis, and dollar amounts in thousands are plotted along the y-axis. When you look at the chart, you can quickly see the amounts of income and/or expense for each item, in proportion to each other and in proportion to the greatest amount of income and/or expense for the month.

Changing Types of Charts Using the Chart Toolbar

When you are using an embedded chart, there are two ways to edit a chart. If you have not opened the chart (to open an embedded chart, simply double-click on it), you can use the Chart toolbar to select the most popular types of charts.

1. Use GoTo or scroll through the worksheet until you have the chart on the screen.
2. Click on Options in the menu bar to open the Options menu.
3. Click on Toolbars to display the Toolbars dialog box.
4. Select Chart in the Show Toolbars list box.
5. Click on Show.

The Chart toolbar is now shown at the bottom of the Excel application window. The first seventeen buttons on the Chart toolbar contain the charts that correspond to the pictures on the button. Clicking on any of these buttons will change your chart to a different type. Click on a few to see the changes in your chart.

Changing Types of Charts Using the Chart Menu

If you have saved your chart as a separate chart document or if you have opened your embedded chart, you can change your chart type by using the chart menu.

1. If you have saved your chart as a separate document, open it now. If you have saved an embedded chart, open the worksheet, use GoTo or scroll through the worksheet to position the chart on the screen, and double-click on the chart to open it. The menu bar choices in the application window have changed to reflect a different kind of document.

2. Click on Gallery in the menu bar to open the Gallery menu.

3. The Gallery menu lists fourteen types of charts. When you select any of these types, you will open a dialog box that contains the various styles available to you for that type of chart. For example, if you select Area in the Gallery menu, the Chart Gallery dialog box will be displayed, as shown in Figure 12.8. The styles for area charts will be displayed.

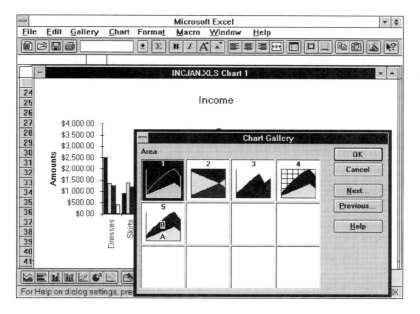

Figure 12.8. The Chart Gallery dialog box.

4. Select one of the styles and click on OK to change your chart type, or click on Cancel to exit the Chart Gallery without changing your chart type.

N O T E To view and select a style for a different type of chart, click on Next and Previous in the Chart Gallery dialog box. You will be shown samples of chart styles that correspond to the order in which the chart types are listed in the Gallery menu. For example, if you select Area in the Gallery menu and then click on Next, the Chart Gallery will display styles for Bar charts; if you click on Next again, the Chart Gallery will display styles for Column charts; if you then click on Previous, the Chart Gallery will display styles for Bar charts, again.

Setting a Default Type for All New Charts

At some point, you will probably decide that you prefer one type of chart for your data above all others. If this type is not the default chart type (which is the column chart), you will want to change the default.

1. Open a chart document or an embedded chart to display the chart menu.
2. Click on Gallery in the menu bar to open the Gallery menu.
3. If the chart that is displayed is not the type you want as your default, change it.
4. Select Set Preferred in the Gallery menu. The chart style that is being used for the currently displayed chart is now your default chart type.

To change any other chart to the default chart type, click on Gallery in the menu bar and click on Preferred in the Gallery menu.

N O T E

Mouse and Keyboard Movement Keys within Charts

Now that you have created two charts, you will want to format and edit them. Before you can format or edit an item in a chart, you must open the chart and select the chart item or text you want to edit. The following tables show the mouse and keyboard movement keys you can use to select items in a chart.

Selecting Chart Items with a Mouse

To	Do this
Select an item	Click the chart item you want to select.
Select a chart data series	Click any tick mark in the chart data series
Select a single data marker	Hold down the Ctrl key and click the data marker
Select gridlines	Click on a gridline
Select an axis	Click the axis or the area containing the axis tick mark labels
Select the entire plot area of a chart	Click on any area in the plot area that is not occupied by any other item, including gridlines
Select the entire chart	Click anywhere outside the plot area that is not occupied by any other item.

Selecting Chart Items with the Keyboard

When you select chart items using the keyboard, you can move from item to item or between the following categories of items:

Chart	Arrows
Plot area	Gridlines
3-D floor	First chart data series
3-D walls	Second chart data series, etc.
3-D corners	Drop lines
Legend	Hi-Lo lines
Axes	Up/Down bars
Text	Series lines

You can use the Up and Down Arrow keys to move between categories of items in the chart, and the Left and Right Arrow keys to select individual items within categories:

To	Press
Go to the first item in the next category	Up Arrow
Go to the last item in the previous category	Down Arrow
Go to the next item in the same category	Right Arrow
Go to the previous item in the same category	Left Arrow

Selecting Items Using Chart Menu Commands

You can use the chart menu commands to select either the entire chart or the plot area of a chart.

1. Click on Chart in the menu bar to open the Chart menu.
2. Click on either Select Chart or Select Plot Area.

You have selected either the entire chart or the plot area of the chart.

N O T E

When you select a chart item or text, it is marked with black or white selection squares. When a selected item or text is marked with black selection squares, it can be moved or sized with a mouse. Selected items or text marked with white selection squares cannot be moved or sized.

Cancelling a Selection

To cancel a selection for a chart item or text, click an area inside the chart window that is not occupied by any other chart item.

To cancel a selection for the entire chart, either click outside the chart window or press Esc.

Adding, Deleting, or Editing a Data Series Using the ChartWizard

The easiest way to add or delete a chart data series in an existing chart is to use the ChartWizard tool; you can also edit chart data series to change whether you plot the chart series by columns or rows.

1. Open the source document for the chart you want to changes.
2. Select the chart you want to change.
3. Click on the ChartWizard tool. The ChartWizard—Step 1 of 2 dialog box is displayed.
4. Either reselect the data in the worksheet you want to include in the chart or enter the range or nonadjacent ranges in the Range text box.
5. Click on Next. The ChartWizard—Step 2 of 2 dialog box is displayed.
6. Pick the options you want for the Data Series In, Use First Column For, and Use First Row For options in the dialog box.

Your chart now reflects the changes you made using ChartWizard.

Adding, Deleting, or Editing a Data Series Using the Edit Command

If you only want to add or delete data series in a chart, or change whether you are going to plot the chart by rows or columns, the ChartWizard is the easiest method to use. If, however, you want to do any of the above, and also want to change the name of a data series in your chart, you must use the Edit command. Let's change the names of the data series in the chart we created using the INCJAN.XLS worksheet.

1. Open the chart you want to change (if the chart is embedded, double-click on the chart; if the chart is a separate document, open it).
2. Click on Chart in the menu bar to open the Chart menu.
3. Click on Edit Series to display the Edit Series dialog box, as shown in Figure 12.9.

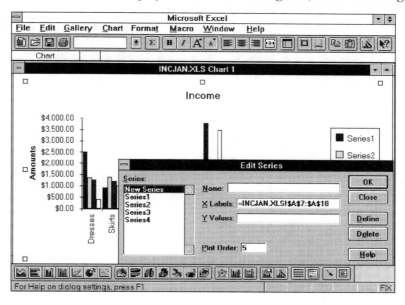

Figure 12.9. The Edit Series dialog box.

4. Select New Series if you want to add a new data series to the chart. Type in the range for the new data series using an external absolute reference. For example, if you wanted to add the totals from column G in the INCJAN.XLS worksheet to the chart, the reference would look like this:

   =INCJAN.XLS!$G$7:$G$18

   External references are discussed in Chapter 7.

5. If you want to give the data series a name of your own choosing, select the Name text box and type in the name.

6. We do not want to add a data series, but we do want to change the names of our data series. Click on Series 1 in the Edit Series dialog box. Select the Name text box and type Acct. 100. Click on Define.

7. Select Series 2 and then type Acct. 101 in the Name text box.

8. Repeat step 7 to rename Series 3 to Acct. 102 and to rename Series 4 to Acct 103.

N O T E

When you want to edit more than one chart data series, click on Define to make the change and leave the Edit Series dialog box open; when you want to edit only one chart data series, click on OK to make the change and close the Edit Series dialog box.

9. To delete a data series from your chart, select the data series in the Edit Series dialog box and click on Delete.

10. If you want to change the order in which your data is plotted in the chart, select the data series and change the number in the Plot Order text box.

11. Click on OK.

Your chart now looks like the one shown in Figure 12.10.

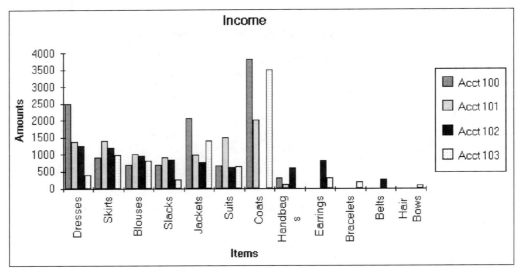

Figure 12.10. Chart with data series name in legend changed.

Changing Data Values in a Chart

When you change the values of the data in your source worksheet, the data automatically changes in the chart to reflect these changes. You can also change the data in some chart types and have the change reflected in the worksheet. The chart types that allow you to do this are: 2-D line charts, including xy (scatter) charts; bar charts; and column charts. You can increase or decrease the values shown by the data markers by dragging them. This allows you to quickly view a "what-if" scenario on your chart. When you drag data markers, the values they represent are also changed in the cells that contain that data in the source worksheet.

To change the data values:

1. Open the source worksheet.
2. Open the chart.
3. Hold down the Ctrl key and click on the data marker you want to change.
4. Drag the black selection square to change the value of the data marker. As you drag, the changing values will be reflected in the reference area and you will see a line along the y-axis also reflecting the change.

You cannot go beyond the values already established by the y-axis. For example, you cannot change the data marker in your chart to reflect a value of 4,000 if the values in the y-axis do not go beyond 3,500. The highest value you can adjust a data marker in that axis to reflect is 3,500.

N O T E

Deleting an Embedded Chart

Deleting an embedded chart is not the same as deleting a document in Excel. If you delete the entire document, your worksheet will also be deleted. If you only want to delete the chart and leave the worksheet and all other objects in the worksheet intact:

1. Open the worksheet that contains the embedded chart you want to delete.
2. Click once on the embedded chart.
3. Click on Edit in the menu bar to open the Edit menu.
4. Click on Clear.

The embedded chart has been removed from the worksheet.

If you change your mind you can click on Undo Clear in the Edit menu immediately after you clear the chart.

Deleting a Chart Document

You can delete a chart document the same way you delete any other document in Excel.

1. Be sure the chart document you want to delete is not open.
2. Click on File in the menu bar to open the File menu.
3. Click on Delete to display the Delete Document dialog box, as shown in Figure 12.11.
4. Select the chart you want to delete and click on OK.

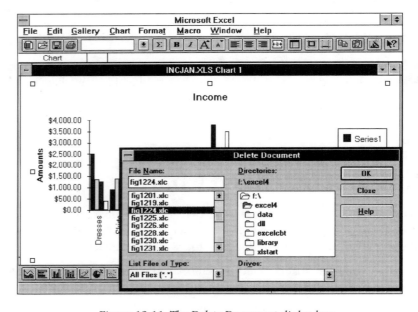

Figure 12.11. The Delete Document dialog box.

You cannot undo a Delete command. Be certain you want to delete the chart before you choose OK.

Clearing a Chart of Data or Formats

You can clear a chart of data, formats, or both. If you have formatted your chart and decide that you want to replace the data in the chart with different data, you can quickly clear all of the data and leave the formatting intact. If you decide that you do not like the formatting you have applied to your chart, you can quickly clear all formatting and leave the data intact. You can also clear everything in your chart and start from scratch. You can then create a new chart from a source worksheet using the Copy and Paste Special commands. To clear a chart:

1. Open the chart.
2. Select the entire chart.
3. Click on Edit in the menu bar to open the Edit menu.
4. Click on Clear. The Clear dialog box is displayed, as shown in Figure 12.12.

   a. To clear everything and leave a blank chart, select the All option.

   b. To clear the formatting and leave the data, select the Formats option.

   c. To clear the data and leave the formatting intact, select the Formulas option.

5. Click on OK.

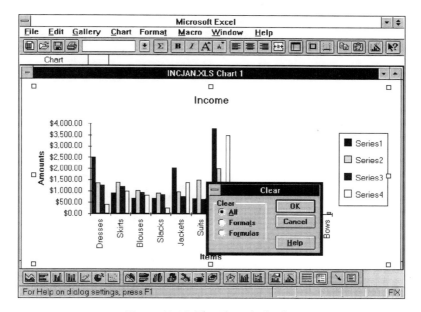

Figure 12.12. The Clear dialog box.

Copying Data to a Chart

To copy data from a source worksheet to a chart:

1. Open the source worksheet and the chart. It is easier to work with both document windows on the screen simultaneously. Click on Window in the menu bar to open the Window menu. Hide all documents except the ones you want to view. From within the Windows menu, click on Arrange and choose Tiled.

2. Make the worksheet the active document.

3. Select the data you want to include in your chart.

4. Click on Edit in the menu bar to open the Edit menu.

5. Click on Copy.

6. Switch to the chart window.

7. Click on Edit in the menu bar to open the Edit menu.

8. Click on Paste Special to open the Paste Special dialog box, shown in Figure 12.13.

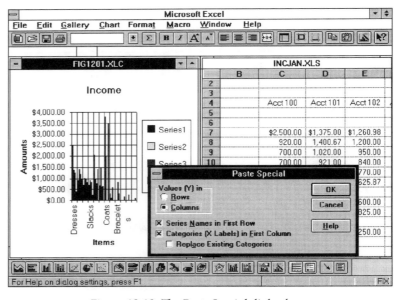

Figure 12.13. The Paste Special dialog box.

9. Select the options you want. The Replace Existing Categories option is applicable only when you are pasting data into an existing chart in which you have selected the Categories [X Labels] in First Column/Row. If you select Replace Existing Categories, the categories in the chart will be replaced with the categories you are pasting.

10. Select OK.

Adding Interest to Charts with Formatting

Using charts adds punch to your spreadsheet data. Charts allow for a fast, visual representation of data usually contained in rows and columns. You can enhance your charts with formatting features. You can add text to describe your data or to make a special point, add and delete gridlines, and even put arrows into your charts.

Adding Text to Charts

When you created the chart from the INCJAN.XLS worksheet in this chapter, you added some text during the creation process. You added a chart title, and a description of the data along the x and y axes. Later, you renamed the data series to reflect the accounts represented by the data markers. This change was reflected in the chart legend, making it easy to identify exactly which account each data marker represented. Now you are going to use text to further describe and enhance your chart.

Charts contain two types of text: **attached text** and **unattached text**. Attached text is attached to a chart object. For example, tick mark labels are attached to tick marks and describe the data along the corresponding axis. This text can be moved only if the chart object is moved. Unattached text can be inserted anywhere in a chart window. This text can be moved around at will. When you select attached text, it is surrounding by white selection squares. When you select unattached text, it is surrounded by black selection squares.

Adding or Editing a Chart Title or Axis Title

You can add or change a chart title or an axis title whenever you like. This is useful if your information has changed, or if you just want your text to be more descriptive. We are going to change the chart title and the axes titles in our income chart.

1. Open the chart that you created from the INCJAN.XLS worksheet.
2. Click on Chart in the menu bar to open the Chart menu.
3. Click on Attach Text. The Attach Text dialog box is displayed, as shown in Figure 12.14, on the next page.
4. Click on Chart Title.
5. Click on OK. The title area in the chart is surrounded by white selection sqares that contain the word *Title*. The word *Title* appears in the formula bar. You can edit this text just as you would edit any text in a worksheet cell. Type *Income for the Month of January* in the formula bar. To insert a line break to split your text into two lines, press Alt+Enter where you want to create a new line. Press Alt+Enter after the words *Income for the*.

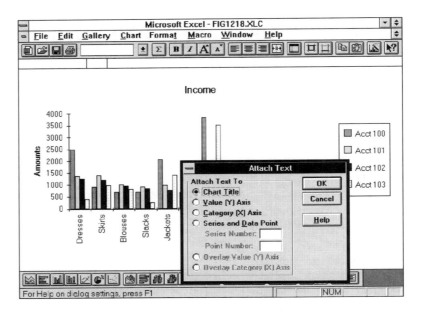

Figure 12.14. The Attach Text dialog box.

6. Press Enter. Your title has now been changed to look like this:

   ```
   Income for the
   Month of January
   ```

7. Select Value [Y] Axis.

8. Click on OK. The description area for the y-axis is surrounded by white selection squares that contain a Y Type *Dollar Amounts* in the formula bar. To enter a description that contains more than one line, use Alt+Enter to break the lines of text.

9. Press Enter.

10. Select Category [X] Axis.

11. Click on OK. The description area for the x-axis is surrounded by white selection squares that contain an X. Type *Items Listed for Income* in the formula bar. To enter text that is more than one line, use Alt+Enter to split the text and create a new line.

12. Press Enter. You worksheet now looks like the one shown in Figure 12.15.

If your chart already contains chart titles or axis titles and you just want to edit them, you can select the item, click on the existing text in the formula bar, and edit it.

SHORT CUT

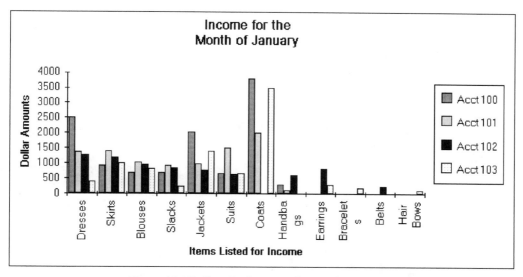

Figure 12.15. Chart with text and axis titles changed.

Adding a Label to a Data Marker

You can add labels to data markers in your charts to emphasize information. Labels added to data markers are attached to the data marker and are attached text. For example, we are going to add a label to the data marker in our income chart to pinpoint the item that brought in the most income in January.

1. Open the chart you created from the INCJAN.XLS worksheet.
2. Click on Chart in the menu bar to open the Chart Menu. Click on Attach Text to display the Attach Text dialog box.
3. Select Series and Data Point. Enter the number of the series and the data point to which you want to add a label. To add a label to the data marker that reflects the highest income for the month, enter 1 in Series Number and 7 in Point Number.

Or,

1. Select the data marker to which you want to add a label by holding down the Ctrl key and clicking on the data marker. In this case, select the data marker that reflects the highest income for the month. The data marker is surrounded by white and black selection squares.
2. Click on Chart in the menu bar to open the Chart menu.
3. Click on Attach Text to display the Attach Text dialog box. The Series and Data Point option has automatically been selected and the Series and Data numbers that correspond to the data marker you selected appear in the Series and Point Numbers

text boxes.

4. Click on OK.

5. Type *Highest Income* into the formula bar.

6. Press Enter. Your chart now looks like the one shown in Figure 12.16.

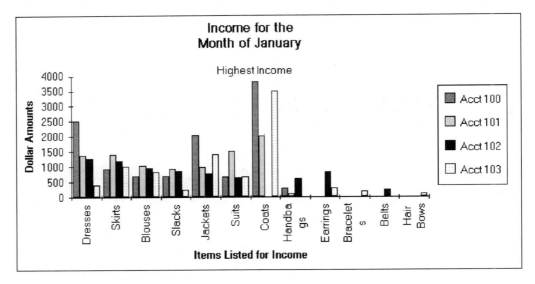

Figure 12.16. Chart with label added to data marker.

To unselect (remove) the selection squares from a chart item, click on any area in the chart that is not occupied by a chart area.

N O T E

Adding Unattached Text

You can add unattached text anywhere in the chart window. Unattached text is surrounded by black selection squares, and can be moved and resized at will. We are going to add unattached text to our income chart to identify the type of chart we created.

1. If it is not still open, open the chart that contains the data from the INCJAN.XLS worksheet.

2. While no other text is selected, and the formula bar is blank, type *This is a Column Chart*. If you want to add more than one line of unattached text, separate the lines of text by pressing Alt+Enter where you want the next line of text to begin.

3. Press Enter.

4. Excel has placed the text in the chart window and surrounded it with black selection squares.

5. Drag the text to the upper-left corner of the chart window. To see how it will look when it is printed, click on File and then on Print Preview in the File menu.

Editing Unattached Text

To edit unattached text in a chart:

1. Click on the text you want to edit.
2. Click on the formula bar to edit some of the text, or retype the text in its entirety.
3. Press Enter.

Deleting Text from Charts

To delete attached or unattached text from your charts:

1. Open the chart.
2. Click on the text to select it. It will be surrounded by either white or black selection squares.
3. Click on Edit in the menu bar to open the Edit menu.
4. Click on Clear.

The text has been deleted from the chart.

Changing the Fonts Used by Chart Text

You can change the font type and sizes of the text in your charts. (Remember, if your printer is not capable of printing the fonts you select, the fonts will show on the display, but will not print.) You can format all of the text in a chart using one font, or you can select different text and apply different fonts to each selection.

1. Open the chart that contains the text you want to change.

   a. To change the font for all of the text in the chart, click on Chart in the menu bar to open the Chart menu and choose Select Chart.
   b. To change the font for a single piece of attached or unattached text, click on the text to select it.
   c. To change the font of the tick mark labels in an axis, click the axis to select it.
   d. To change the font of the text in a legend, click the legend to select it.

2. Click on Format in the menu bar to open the Format menu.

3. Click on Font to display the Font dialog box (fonts are covered in detail in Chapter 5). Select the font you want.

4. If you want to add or change the border or pattern of the area you have selected, click on Patterns. Select the border and pattern you want from the options and drop-down boxes in the Pattern dialog box.

5. If you want to change the alignment or orientation of the text you have selected, click on Text. Select the options you want in the Text dialog box. The Text button is not available if you selected the entire chart or the legend.

6. Click on OK.

Changing the Border and Patterns in Selected Text Areas

You can add, delete, and change border and patterns styles in selected areas of attached and unattached text to add even more interest and/or emphasis to your charts.

1. Open the chart you want to format.

2. Select the text you want to format.

3. Click on Format in the menu bar to open the Format menu.

4. Click on Patterns to display the Patterns dialog box. Select the border style and pattern you want for the selected text. Borders and patterns are discussed in detail in Chapter 5.

5. If you want to delete a border or pattern, select the None option in the Border or Pattern option boxes. This is the default for charts.

6. Click on OK.

Changing Text Alignment and Orientation in Selected Text

You can change the alignment and orientation of selected text in your charts. The selected text will align between the area outlined by the selection squares. To change text alignment or orientation:

1. Open the chart you want to format.

2. Select the text you want to format.

3. Click on Format in the menu bar to open the Format menu.

4. Click on Text to display the Text dialog box.

5. Select the options you want. Text alignment and orientation are discussed in detail in Chapter 5.

6. To return attached text to the default alignment and orientation, select the Automatic Text option.
7. Click on OK.

Checking the Spelling of Text in Your Chart

You can check the spelling of all attached and unattached text in your chart.

1. Open the chart.
2. Click on Chart in the menu bar to open the Chart menu.
3. Click on Spelling. If Excel finds any misspelled words or words it cannot identify, you will be prompted.
4. You will be prompted when spelling check is complete. Choose OK.

Adding, Deleting, and Formatting a Chart Legend

The chart legend identifies each data series in your chart and shows you the color or pattern used for each data marker in the series. The text used in the legend is taken from the worksheet cells that contain the data series. If your data series does not contain any text that can be used as a data series label, Excel automatically names each data series in consecutive order, such as Series 1, Series 2, and so forth. You can change the name of the series in the legend by changing the text in the worksheet cells that contain the data series labels, or by using the Edit command in the menu bar. Changing the name of a series in a legend by using the Edit command is covered earlier in this chapter in the section titled "Adding, Deleting, or Editing a Data Series Using the Edit Command." When you create a legend, it is automatically positioned at the right edge of the chart. When you create a chart, you have the choice of adding a legend to your chart. If you do not select this option, you can still add a legend to your chart later. If you do select this option and then change your mind, you can delete the legend from the chart. You can also add, delete, or change borders and patterns for the legend, change the text size and type, and move the legend to another location on the chart.

Adding a Legend

1. Open the chart.
2. Click on Chart in the menu bar to open the Chart menu.
3. Click on Add Legend.

The legend has been inserted at the right border of the chart, and the chart has been resized to accommodate the legend.

Deleting a Legend

To delete a legend:

1. Open the chart.
2. Click on Chart in the menu bar to open the Chart menu.
3. Click on Delete Legend.

The legend has been deleted from your chart.

Formatting and Moving a Legend

You can move a legend to any location on your chart by dragging it with the mouse, or by using the Legend command on the Format menu. If you use the mouse to position the legend on sections of the chart that cannot be moved (such as data markers), the legend will overlap that section of the chart. If you move the legend to the edge of the chart window, Excel will adjust the size of the chart to accommodate the change. Excel will also automatically change the vertical or horizontal arrangement of the data series in the legend to accommodate the space available. For example, if you move the legend to the top of the chart, Excel will arrange the data series in the legend horizontally instead of vertically.

Moving a Legend with the Mouse

1. Open the chart that contains the legend you want to move.
2. Select the legend by clicking on it.
3. Drag the legend to where you want it in the chart.

Moving and Formatting a Legend Using the Legend Command

1. Open the chart that contains the legend you want to move or format. (If the chart is embedded, double-click on the chart to open it.)
2. Select the legend by clicking on it.
3. Click on Format in the menu bar to open the Format menu.
4. Click on Legend to display the Legend dialog box, as shown in Figure 12.17.
5. Select the option that will place the legend where you want it.
6. Click on Patterns in the Legend dialog box to display the Patterns dialog box.
7. Select the border and pattern styles you want to use for the legend. (Border and pattern styles are discussed in detail in Chapter 5.)
8. Click on Font in either the Legend dialog box or the Patterns dialog box. The Font dialog box is displayed. Select the options you want. (Fonts are discussed in detail in Chapter 5.)
9. Click on OK in whatever dialog box you are in. The dialog box will be closed and all of your changes will take effect.

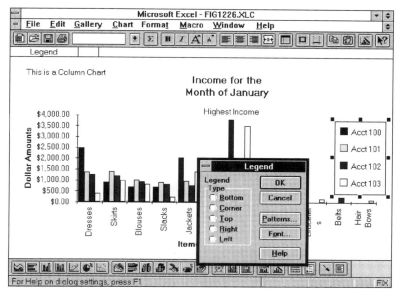

Figure 12.17. The Legend dialog box.

Adding, Deleting, and Formatting Axes

You have the choice of whether or not you want to display either, both, or none of the axes on your chart. You can delete one or both (the axes automatically show when you create a chart). You can also format each axis independently of the other. You can change the appearance of the axes, tick marks, and tick mark labels. For example, you can change the size and font of the text in the tick mark labels. When you create a chart, Excel automatically decides how many categories are displayed in the x-axis and how many values are displayed in the y-axis. You can change either of these defaults. For example, in the chart created from the INCJAN.XLS worksheet, the values along the y-axis (the **major units**) increment by 500. You can change this so that the major units increment by 250, as shown in Figure 12.18. You can change the increment values of the **minor units** along the axis. The minor units are the tick marks that mark off values within the major units. You can decide whether the x and y axis will intersect at the top or bottom of the chart. You can reverse the order of the values in the chart, placing the lowest value at the top of the y-axis and the highest value at the bottom. You can decide what the begining and ending values will be in the y-axis. You can also change the orientation of the tick mark labels and change the format of the axis itself.

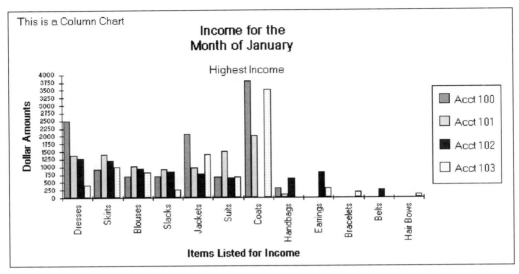

Figure 12.18. Major increments on the y-axis changed.

Adding or Deleting an Axis

You can determine whether or not the axes in your chart will be displayed. You can have both, one, or none shown in your chart.

1. Open the chart you want to change.
2. Click on Chart in the menu bar to open the Chart menu.
3. Click on Axes to display the Axes dialog box, as shown in Figure 12.19.
4. Select the check boxes for the axes you want to show on the chart. Clear the check boxes for the axes you do not want to be displayed on the chart.
5. Click on OK.

Formatting an Axis

When you format an axis, your formatting choices will change depending upon whether you are formatting an x-axis or a y-axis. When you format a y-axis you can control the beginning and ending values of the axis, the increments between the major units, the increments between the minor units, whether the axis starts with the highest or lowest value, and where the x and y axes will intersect. You can also change the format of the axis lines, the position of the tick marks and tick mark labels, and the font and orientation of the tick mark labels.

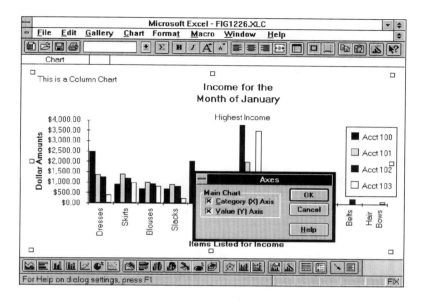

Figure 12.19. The Axes dialog box.

Formatting a Y-Axis

1. Open the chart you want to change.
2. Select the axis by clicking on the axis line or a tick mark label attached to it.
3. Click on Format in the menu bar to open the Format menu.
4. Click on Scale. The Axis Scale dialog box is displayed. Notice that the text in the upper-left corner of the dialog box identifies this as the Value [Y] Axis Scale.
5. Make the changes you want in the dialog box. You have the following choices:

   ♦ **Minimum**. This selection lets you decide the lowest value you want to appear on the axis. If the Auto check box is selected, the Minimum text box displays the lowest value found in all of the data series in the chart. To change the automatic value, type a new value into the text box.

   ♦ **Maximum**. This selection lets you decide the highest value you want to appear on the axis. If the Auto check box is selected, the Maximum text box displays the highest values found in all of the data series in the chart. To change the automatic value, type a new value into the text box.

   ♦ **Major Unit**. This selection lets you decide how much the values on the axis will increment between major tick marks. If the Auto check box is selected, Excel automatically calculates the increment. To change the increment, type a new value in the Major Unit text box.

◆ **Minor Unit**. Minor units are tick marks that indicate the values between the major units on the axis. For example, Figure 12.20 shows the minor units along the y-axis indicating each 100 value increment between the major units. To change this value type a new number in the Minor Unit text box.

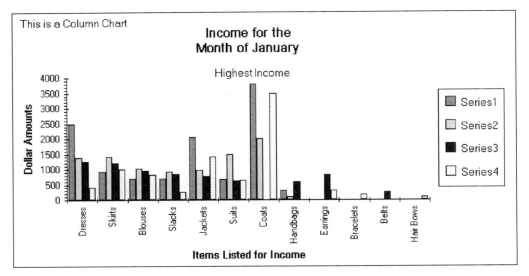

Figure 12.20. Minor units along the y-axis showing increments of 100.

If you want the minor units to be displayed along the y-axis, you must change the default options in the Patterns dialog box. To access the Patterns dialog box, click on Patterns in the Axis Scale dialog box.

N   O   T   E

◆ **Category (X) Axis Crosses At**. This choice lets you decide where you want the x and y axes to intersect. If the Auto check box is selected, Excel automatically intersects the x and y axes at the lowest value along the y axis. To change the location where the x and y axis intersect, type a new value in the Category (X) Axis Crosses At text box.

◆ **Logarithmic Scale**. This selection recalculates the Minimum, Maximum, Major Unit, and Minor Unit values as powers of 10. The values are based on the range of values in the data series in the chart. You cannot use a zero or a negative value to recalculate values on a logarithmic scale, and both the Major and Minor Units must contain a value of at least 10. If you have a value in the Minimum or Maximum text boxes that is not a power of 10, Excel will round the value up or down to the next power of 10.

◆ **Values in Reverse Order**. This selection reverses the values along the y-axis. Instead of displaying the lowest value at the bottom of the axis line, the lowest value is displayed at the top and the highest value is displayed at the bottom.

◆ **Category (X) Axis Crosses At Maximum Value**. When this selection is enabled, the x and y axis intersect at the point where the highest value is located along the y-axis. This selection overrides the Category (X) Axis Crosses At option.

6. To change the formatting of the axis line, tick marks, and tick mark labels, click on Patterns in the Axis Scale dialog box. The Patterns dialog box is displayed. Select the options you want.

7. To change font, color, size, and background of the tick mark labels, click on Fonts in the Axis Scale dialog box. Make the selections you within the Font dialog box. (Fonts are discussed in detail in Chapter 5.)

8. To change to orientation of the text along the axis, click on Text in the Axis Scale dialog box. The Text dialog box is displayed. Select the orientation you want for your text.

9. Click on OK to close the dialog box and have your changes take effect.

Formatting an X-Axis

1. Open the chart you want to change.
2. Select the axis by clicking on the axis line or a tick mark label attached to the axis line.
3. Click on Format in the menu bar to open the Format menu.
4. Click on Scale to display the Axis Scale dialog box is displayed. Notice that the text in the upper-left corner of the dialog box identifies this as the Value [X] Axis Scale.
5. Make the changes you want in the dialog box. You have the following choices:

◆ **Value (Y) Axis Crosses At Category Number**. This selection lets you specify the number of the category at which the x and y axes will intersect. Categories start with the number 1 and increment by one for each category. A category does not have to be labelled, and it does not necessarily have a tick mark. Each category does, however, contain the data markers for each data series. To change the value at which the x and y axes intersect, type a new value in the Value (Y) Axis Crosses At Category Number text box.

◆ **Number of Categories Between Tick Labels**. This selection lets you specify which categories will have tick mark labels. For example, if you type 1 in the Number of Categories Between Tick Labels text box, Excel will assign a tick mark label for every category, if you type 2 in the Number of Categories Between Tick Labels text box, Excel will assign a tick mark label for every other category along the axis; typing 3 in the text box would assign a tick mark label for every third category along the axis.

◆ **Number of Categories Between Tick Marks**. This selection lets you choose the number of categories along the axis that will be included between each set of tick marks. If you type 1 in the Number of Categories Between Tick Marks text box, each tick mark will have one category assigned to it, if you type 2 in the text box, two categories will be included between each set of tick marks, and so forth.

◆ **Category (Y) Axis Crosses At**. This choice lets you decide where you want the x and y axes to intersect. When this selection is checked, the x and y axes will intersect at the edge of the category indicated in the Value (Y) Axis Crosses At text box. If this selection is cleared, the y-axis intersects in the center of the first category.

◆ **Values in Reverse Order**. This selection reverses the values along the x-axis. The first value is shown last and the last value is shown first.

◆ **Category (Y) Axis Crosses At Maximum Value**. When this selection is enabled, the x and y axes intersect at the last category along the x-axis. This selection overrides the Category (Y) Axis Crosses At value.

6. To change the formatting of the axis lines, tick marks, and tick mark labels, click on Patterns in the Axis Scale dialog box. The Patterns dialog box is displayed. Select the options you want.

7. To change font, color, size, and background of the tick mark labels, click on Fonts in the Axis Scale dialog box. Make the selections you want from the Font dialog box. Fonts are discussed in detail in Chapter 5.

8. To change to orientation of the text along the axis, click on Text in the Axis Scale dialog box. The Text dialog box is displayed. Select the orientation you want.

9. Click on OK to close the dialog box and have your changes take effect.

Formatting Data Markers

You can change the pattern, color, spacing, and border styles of the data markers in your charts. You can change all or some of the data markers within a data series. To change the formatting of the data markers in your chart:

1. Open the chart you want to change.

2. To format all of the data markers in a data series, click on one of the data markers. To format one of the data markers in a data series, hold down the Ctrl key and click on the data marker you want to format.

3. Click on Format in the menu bar to open the Format menu.

4. Click on Patterns to display the Patterns dialog box.

5. Use the drop-down boxes under Border and Area to select the formatting you want to use for the data markers.

6. If you select the Apply To All check box, the options you have chosen will be applied to every data marker in every data series in the chart.

7. If you select the Invert If Negative check box, the foreground and background colors of the data markers that represent negative values will be reversed.

8. Click on OK.

Adding, Deleting, and Formatting Gridlines

You can add and delete major and minor gridlines in your charts to make it easier to locate and identify the values and categories on your charts, even if the chart style you originally selected does not include gridlines. Major gridlines intersect with the major units along the axes, and minor gridlines intersect with the minor units along the axes. You can change the color, style, and thickness of the gridlines in your charts.

Adding and Deleting Major Gridlines Using the Chart Toolbar

1. Open the chart you want to change.

2. Click the Horizontal Gridlines tool on the Chart toolbar. If the chart does not have gridlines, Excel will add them. If the chart has gridlines, Excel will delete them.

Adding and Deleting Major and Minor Gridlines Using the Gridlines Command

1. Open the chart you want to change.

2. Click on Chart in the menu bar to open the Chart menu.

3. Click on Gridlines to display the Gridlines dialog box, as shown in Figure 12.21, on the next page.

4. Select the check boxes to add any gridlines you want for your chart. Clear the check boxes to delete any gridlines you do not want in your chart.

5. Click on OK.

Formatting Gridlines

1. To format a major gridline, double click on one of the major gridlines. To format a minor gridline, double-click on one of the minor gridlines.

2. The Patterns dialog box is displayed.

3. Select the options you want to use for the gridlines.

4. Click on OK.

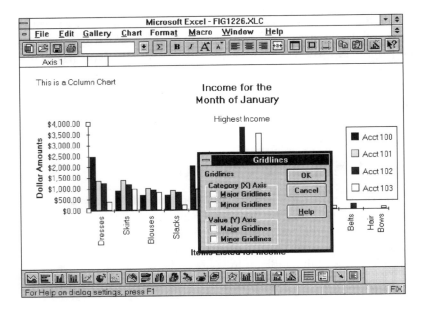

Figure 12.21. The Gridlines dialog box.

Adding, Deleting, and Formatting a Chart Arrow

You can add arrows to your charts to point to information you want to emphasize or to identify data or parts of a chart. Once you have added an arrow to your chart, you can change the style, color, and line weight of the arrow shaft, as well as the style, width, and length of the arrowhead. You can move and resize the arrow by dragging the handles at either end.

Adding One Arrow to a Chart Using the Chart Toolbar

You can add one arrow to your chart using the Arrow tool on the Chart toolbar. To add an arrow:

1. Open the chart you want to change.
2. Click on the Arrow tool (identified by its arrow icon) on the Chart toolbar.
3. Drag the handles at either end of the arrow to move and size it.

Adding One or Several Arrows to a Chart Using the Add Arrow Command

You can add more than one arrow to your chart using the Add Arrow command. To add one or several arrows to a chart:

1. Open the chart you want to change. (If the chart is embedded, double-click on the chart to open it.)
2. Click on Chart in the menu bar to open the Chart menu.
3. Click on Add Arrow. An arrow has been inserted in your chart.
4. Drag the handles at either end of the arrow to move and size it.

If the Delete Arrow command is displayed instead of the Add Arrow command, it means that you have selected an existing arrow. To add another arrow, select any item in the chart that is not an arrow and repeat steps 2, 3, and 4 above.

N   O   T   E

Deleting a Chart Arrow

You can select and delete any arrow on a chart. To delete an arrow:

1. Open the chart you want to change.
2. Select the arrow you want to delete.
3. Click on Chart in the menu bar to open the Chart menu.
4. Click on Delete Arrow.

The arrow has been deleted from the chart.

Formatting the Arrow Shaft and Arrowhead

To change the format of the arrow:

1. Double-click on the arrow to display the Patterns dialog box.
2. Under Line, select the options you want for the arrow shaft.
3. Under Arrow Head, select the options you want for the arrowhead.
4. Click on OK.

Review Exercises for Chapter 12

- ◆ Create a chart from an existing worksheet.
- ◆ Give the chart description and axes titles. Format the titles.
- ◆ If you do not have a legend on your chart, add one. Change the series names in the legend.
- ◆ Add comments to your chart with unattached text.
- ◆ Use chart arrows to point out areas of interest in your chart.
- ◆ Use the chart formatting features to change the patterns in your data markers and to add borders to text that contains special information.
- ◆ Add gridlines to your chart to make it easier to pinpoint data values.

Before You Go On...

Before you go on to the next chapter, you should be able to create a basic chart. You should understand and be able to identify the parts of a chart. You should know how to save the chart as either an embedded document or as a separate document. You should know how to add, delete, and change the series data for a chart. You should know how to copy data from a worksheet and use paste special to insert data into a chart. You should be familiar with the formatting features available to add interest to your charts.

CREATING AND EDITING A DATABASE

What You Will Learn in This Chapter

- ◆ The parts of a database
- ◆ How to create and use a database
- ◆ How to add and delete database records and fields
- ◆ The parts of a data form
- ◆ How to add, delete, and edit records using a data form
- ◆ How to define criteria in a data form
- ◆ How to use Find Next and Find Prev
- ◆ How to move around a data form
- ◆ How to sort a database
- ◆ How to set up and define comparison and computed criteria ranges
- ◆ How to find records using specified criteria
- ◆ How to extract and delete records using specified criteria

What Is a Database?

A **database** in Excel is a feature that allows you to organize, retrieve, and analyze all or some of the data in your worksheets. It allows you to take an entire worksheet or ranges of a worksheet, and reorder the data alphabetically and/or numerically by rows or columns. You can use the data in an existing worksheet, or you can create a worksheet for the express purpose of using the data in it as a database. You can search a database to find specific data, extract portions of a database, perform statistical calculations on all or part of the data in a database, and print a database.

Frills and Thrills is planning a series of fashion shows and special sales for some of its customers. The company keeps records of the names and addresses of all customers who have purchased more than $100 worth of merchandise in one visit. In this chapter you are going to create a sample database containing a portion of these names and addresses, the date and amount of each sale, and the tax collected for each sale. The database will eventually be used to provide Clarisse with a list of customers to invite to each fashion show.

The Parts of a Database

Before you can use a database in Excel, you must select the data you wish to use and inform Excel that this data is going to be used as a database. Once you have identified the area of your worksheet that is going to be used as a database, Excel identifies columns, rows, and data in the database as the parts of the database that make up the whole. These parts are used for organizing and retrieving data from your database. Figure 13.1 shows you the parts of a database. Following is a brief definition of each part of a database.

Database Range

A **database range** contains the area of the worksheet that is defined as a database. The first row of a database contains the field names.

Database Record

A **database record** contains all of the data in a row of a database. Every record contains data for the same fields as every other record. All of the records in Figure 13.1 contain the data for the fields Name, Street, City, State, Zip, Date of Sale, Amount of Sale, and Total.

Database Field

Every column in a database is identified as a separate **field**. Every cell within the column is also identified as a field. You can enter numbers, text, dates, or formulas into your fields. You can also leave fields blank if there is no data for that particular field. The database shown in

Figure 13.1 contains eight fields: Name, Street, City, State, Zip, Date of Sale, Amount of Sale, and Total.

Field   Field name   Record   Computed field

	A	B	C	D	E	F	G	H
1	Name	Street	City	State	Zip	Date of Sale	Amount of Sale	Total
2	Ms. Jane Smith	23 Main Street	New York	NY	100000	11/1/91	153.98	166.68
3	Ms. Mary Johnson	10 Park Ave.	Ft. Lee	NJ	118000	11/2/91	278.00	300.94
4	Ms. Elise Jones	23 Summit Drive	New York	NY	102000	11/2/91	350.99	379.95
5	Ms. Priscilla Smith	23 Elm Street	Greenwich	CT	200000	11/3/91	125.00	135.31
6	Ms. Lucy Doe	1 University Place	Chicago	IL	300000	11/3/91	576.89	624.48
7	Mr. George Doe	700 East 22nd St.	New York	NY	150000	11/4/91	210.00	227.33
8	Ms. Suzi Sunshine	2 Sparkle St.	Boston	MA	145678	11/4/91	210.50	227.87
9	Dr. Jane Smyth	10 Medical Row	New York	NY	123456	11/5/91	145.67	157.69
10	Ms. Elsie Cow	45 Milkmaid Dr.	Freehold	NY	234567	11/6/91	101.98	110.39
11	Ms. Mary Johnson	10 Park Ave.	Ft. Lee	NJ	118000	11/6/91	128.98	139.62

Figure 13.1. The parts of a database.

Computed Field

A field containing formulas or functions is a **computed field**. For example, in Figure 13.1 the Total field contains a formula to compute the amount of the sale plus the tax.

Field Name

A **field name** identifies the data stored in each field. The first row of a database must contain the field names, and each column in the database must have a field name. Field names can contain up to 255 characters, and must be text constants. If field names contain numbers, the numbers must be formatted as text. Do not use formulas, blank cells, logical values, or error values as field names. If you do not follow these rules, the database will not perform its operations correctly. In Figure 13.1, Name, Street, City, State, Zip, Date of Sale, Amount of Sale and Total are all field names.

Creating a Database

The first step in creating a database is planning. Your original goal may be to send a mailing to everyone on the list, but some day you might want to extract parts of the list for limited mailings. You might want to sort the list by city, state, zip code, date, or amount spent. All of these considerations should be taken into account when planning your database. You must use a separate field for each item you might want to use to sort the database. For example, if you think that you might someday want to sort by last names, you should create separate fields for first and last names. Let's create the sample database shown in Figure 13.1.

1. Enter the field names in the first row of the area that will become a database.

2. Enter the records in each row of the database directly below the field names. Each record in our database contains eight fields. These fields can contain numbers, text, or formulas. The data is entered exactly as you would enter it into a worksheet. In the first Total field, enter a formula to compute 8.25 percent of the Amount of Sale, and add this figure to the Amount of Sale *(=G2*.0825+G2)*. Leave the rest of the fields in this column blank for now.

3. Select all of the fields you want to include in the range. You must include the field names, and should have an extra blank row below the last record in the database.

4. Click on Data in the menu bar to open the Data menu, as shown in Figure 13.2.

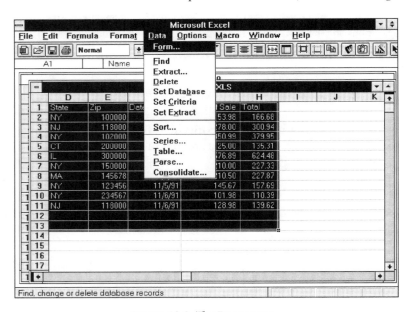

Figure 13.2. The Data menu.

5. Click on Set Database to define the database range. Excel automatically names the database range as Database.

Editing and Formatting a Database

You can edit or format a database using any of the editing or formatting features that are available for worksheets. For example, you can change the data in fields, copy or cut data, change formatting styles, and so on. Chapters 4 and 6 give detailed information on worksheet editing features, and Chapter 5 explains formatting features in Excel. For example, to copy the formula in cell H2 to the rest of the cells in column H:

1. Select cell H2.
2. Click on Edit in the menu bar.
3. Click on Copy.
4. Select the range to which you wish to copy the formula. In this case, it is cell H3 to cell H10.
5. Click on Paste. The formula for the total is now copied into each field in the column.

Adding Database Records

When you add records to a database, you must be careful to insert them within the defined range. This means that you must either add records between rows of existing data, or include a blank record at the end of the database. Otherwise, you must redefine the range each time you add records or the information will not be included in your database. To add a record to a database:

1. Select a row heading within the defined range of the database, preferably a blank record at the end.
2. Click on Edit.
3. Click on Insert.

You have added a blank record to the database within the defined database range. When you enter data in the fields in this record, all of the information you entered will be included in all of the operations of the database.

Adding Database Fields

When you add fields (that is, new columns) to a database, you must either add the columns inside the defined range or redefine the database range. This is one reason why planning is important. To add a field within the defined range of a database:

1. Click on the column heading where you want to add a field.
2. Click on Edit in the menu bar.
3. Click on Insert.

The field is added to the database.

Deleting Database Records

To delete a database record:

1. Click on the row heading of the record you want to delete.
2. Click on Edit in the menu bar.
3. Click on Delete.

The record is deleted from the database.

Deleting Database Fields

When you delete a field from a database, you must delete the entire column, including the field name.

1. Click on the column heading of the field you want to delete.
2. Click on Edit in the menu bar.
3. Click on Delete.

Be careful when deleting database fields that contain values used in formulas. All of the rules concerning worksheet formulas and functions apply to databases.

N O T E

Using Data Forms to Maintain Your Database

A **data form** is a dialog box Excel creates by using the field names in your database. It allows you to view one record at a time, change, add, or delete records from your database, and find specific records in your database based on criteria you supply. You can use the data form supplied by Excel, or you can create a custom data form, although this operation goes beyond the scope of this book. If you want to create custom dialog boxes, we suggest you continue on to an advanced book once you have mastered the basic features of Excel. To see the data form Excel created for your current database:

1. Click on Data in the menu bar.
2. Click on Form. The Data Form dialog box Excel created for this defined database range is displayed in Figure 13.3.

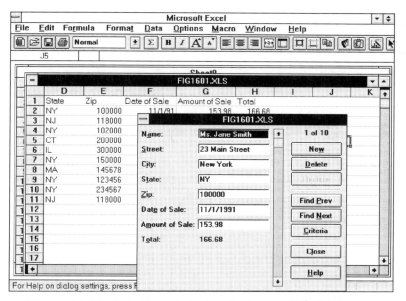

Figure 13.3. The Data Form dialog box for Frills and Thrills' database.

The parts of a data form are as follows:

- **Control box**. The control box lets you to move or close the Data Form dialog box.
- **Title bar**. The title bar shows you the name of the worksheet containing the currently defined database.
- **Field names**. The field names are the field names in your database.
- **Fields**. The fields column in the dialog box contains the data for each field of the displayed record in your database. The data form defaults to the first record in your database when you open it.
- **Fields with text boxes**. Fields with text boxes contain data that can be edited using the data form.
- **Fields without text boxes**. Fields without text boxes indicate fields that you cannot edit while using the data form, such as fields that are the result of a formula, or that are locked while the worksheet is protected.
- **Scroll bar**. The scroll bar allows you to scroll through the records quickly and shows your approximate position in the database.
- **Record number indicator**. The record number indicator tells you which record is currently displayed and how many records there are in the entire database. Blank records at the end of the database are not counted. The record number indicator changes its message to *New Record* when you scroll to the first blank record after the last nonblank record in the database.
- **Command buttons**. The command buttons in the data form are explained later in this chapter.

N O T E

If your database contains more fields than the data form can display, you will not be able to view the remaining fields, and you will not be able to edit the information in those fields or add data to them when adding a new record.

Editing Records Using Data Forms

You can use a data form to edit the data in certain fields in any of the records in your database. You cannot edit computed fields or fields that are protected. To edit a record:

1. Open the worksheet containing the database you want to edit.
2. Click on Data in the menu bar.
3. Click on Form to display the Data Form dialog box.
4. Scroll to each record you want to edit and make the desired changes.
5. Click on Close.

N O T E

Changes to a record are permanently saved as soon as you move to a new record. If you have not yet moved to a new record, you can undo the changes by clicking on the Restore command button. If you have moved to a new record, the changes have been saved and you will have to re-edit the record to restore its original contents.

Adding Records Using Data Forms

The New command button in the data form allows you to add new records to the database. To do this:

1. Open the worksheet containing the database you want to use.
2. Click on Data in the menu bar.
3. Click on Form to display the Data Form dialog box.
4. Click on New. Excel scrolls to the first blank record at the end of the database. You can also scroll past the last record in the database. If no blank record exists, Excel will add one. The record number indicator changes its message to *New Record*.
5. Enter the data in the first field of the record. To move to the next field, either click on the field using the mouse, or press Tab.
6. Continue until you have finished entering all of the data, and then press Enter. The record is added to the database and a new blank record is displayed.
7. Repeat steps 2 and 3 to add as many records as you wish.
8. Click on Close when you have finished adding records.

N O T E

If there is data in the row below the defined range, Excel will display a message telling you there is no room to add a new record at the bottom of the database. You must either move or delete the data that is in the way in order to add more records. You cannot enter data in a computed field. Excel automatically copies the formula to the new record.

Defining Criteria in Data Forms

You can define **criteria** that are used to find records in a database. Criteria are the instructions you use to tell Excel which records you want to find. For example, you could tell Excel to find all of the records in the current database with an amount of sale greater than $200. You could tell Excel to find all of the records in the State field whose contents are equal to "NY." You could tell Excel to find all of the records in the database where the contents of the Amount of Sale field is greater than or equal to 200 *and* the contents of the State field are equal to NY, as shown in Figure 13.4.

N O T E

When you search for records in a data form you can specify only one criterion for each field. If you want to search for more than one criterion in a field—such as all of the records that contain either NY or MA in the state field—you must specify a criteria range in your worksheet and use the Set Criteria command. You must also use the Set Criteria command to search for records that meet criteria that are based on a formula. The Set Criteria command is discussed later in this chapter.

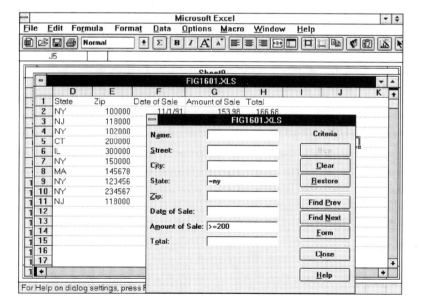

Figure 13.4. Defining criteria for finding records.

When you are using a data form to find records, you are using **comparison criteria**. Comparison criteria are used to find records whose field contents either match or fall within the limits you specify. Criterion names must be the names of the fields in which you are searching. For example, in Figure 13.4, the criterion name is State and the criteria is "ny."

N O T E

Text used as a criterion is not case-sensitive. For example, in Figure 13.4 the criterion for State is "ny." This criterion will find all of the records that contain "NY," "ny," "Ny," or "nY" in the State field.

You can search the database for records that match a series of characters or a quantity.

Using Matching Character String Criteria

To search for a series of characters, simply enter the text, numbers, or logical values you want to match in a specified field. Excel will find all of the records whose contents begin with or exactly match the text, numbers, or logical values you entered for the specified field.

You can use the DOS wildcards * and ? to search for matching character strings. For example, you could type *sm?th* to locate all records in the current database that end with "sm?th." The question mark represents a single letter. The asterisk tells Excel to find any characters in the Name field in any record that precede the letters "sm?th." The ? tells Excel to find the letters "sm" and "th" and any single character between the letters "sm" and "th". You would locate the records for Ms. Jane Smith and Dr. Jane Smyth. When you search for matching characters strings, Excel assumes there is an asterisk (*) at the end of the text you enter as a criterion. For example, if your criterion name is State and you type in "new," Excel will locate all of the records whose State fields begin with the word new, such as "New York" and "New Jersey."

If the text you wish to find actually contains an asterisk (*) or question mark (?), precede the text with a tilde (~). This indicates to Excel that you are searching for a character and not using a DOS wildcard.

Using Comparison Criteria

In addition to searching a database for matching character strings, you can also search for criteria whose data falls within specified limits by typing a comparison operator in front of the value. For example, you could search for all records whose Amount of Sales fields are greater than or equal to 200 by typing *>=200*. The following table shows the six comparison operators available to you:

Operator	Meaning
=	Equal to
>	Greater than
<	Less than
>=	Greater than or equal to
<=	Less than or equal to
<>	Not equal to

If you use an equal sign (=) with nothing after it, you will locate only blank fields. If you use a "not equal to" operator (<>) with nothing after it, you will locate only nonblank fields.

N O T E

If there are many records you want to search, do not use a data form. Use criteria defined on your worksheet with the Set Criteria command, which is covered later in this chapter. The criteria you use in a data form does not replace the criteria you defined on your worksheet with the Set Criteria command.

Finding Records Using Data Forms

To find records that match the criteria you specify:

1. Open the worksheet containing the database you want to search.

2. Click on Data in the menu bar.

3. Click on Form to display the Data Form dialog box.

4. Click on Criteria. The Data Form dialog box changes to accept criteria, as shown in Figure 13.4. The record number indicator changes its message to *Criteria*. The fields are blank. The New button is dimmed, the Delete button changes to the Clear button, and the Criteria button changes to the Form button.

5. Type the criteria you want in the blank text boxes next to the field names. If you want to select all of the records for that field, leave the text box blank.

6. To search forward in the database and display the first record that matches the criteria, click on Find Next. To search backward and display the last record that matches the criteria, click on Find Prev. If there are no matching records in the direction in which you are searching, Excel will beep and the last matching record remains selected. If there are no matching records at all, the last selected record is displayed. Note that when you click on Find Next or Find Prev and a matching record is found, you are returned to the regular data form. To return to the criteria form, click on Criteria.

7. To return to the regular data form without searching for any records, click on Form. When you have returned to the regular data form, you can use Find Next and Find Prev to search for matching records. The criteria you have selected are still in effect

and you will not be able to use the Find Next and Find Prev buttons to move between any records other than those matching the criteria. You can move throughout the database and display records that do not match the criteria by using the scroll bar. To return to the criteria form, click on Criteria.

8. The Clear button clears all existing criteria.

9. The Restore button restore the last existing criteria.

10. Click on Close to clear the existing criteria and exit both the criteria form and the regular data form.

When you select criteria and click on Form, the criteria you selected are still in effect. If you want to clear the criteria and return to the regular data form, click on Clear. If you want to clear the criteria and exit both the criteria form and the regular data form, click on Close.

N O T E

Deleting Records Using Data Forms

To delete a record from a database:

1. Open the worksheet containing the database.

2. Click on Data in the menu bar.

3. Click on Form to display the Data Form dialog box.

4. Display the record you want to delete. You can use the scroll bar or you can specify criteria to locate the record or records you want to delete.

5. Click on Delete. Excel will display a message asking you to confirm the deletion.

6. Click on OK. The current record and all of its data are deleted. All of the records following the deleted record will be moved up to fill the empty space left by the deleted record.

You cannot undo a delete command in a data form. Before you confirm a deletion, be certain you want to delete all of the information contained in the record.

WARNING

Using Find Next and Find Prev

The Find Next button searches forward through your database and finds and displays each successive record that matches your criteria until you reach the end of the database. If your criteria range is blank, Find Next displays the next record in the database.

The Find Prev button searches backward through your database and finds and displays each successive record matching your criteria until you reach the beginning of the database. If your criteria range is blank, Find Prev displays the previous record in the database.

Moving Around Data Forms

The following table shows the mouse actions and keyboard selections you can use to move around a data form.

To	With mouse	With keyboard
Select a field	Click on the field	Press Alt+the underlined letter in the field name
Choose a command button	Click on the button	Press Alt+the underlined letter in the button
Move to the same field in the next record	Click the down arrow in the scroll bar	Press Down Arrow
Move to the same field in the previous record	Click the up arrow in the scroll bar	Press Up Arrow
Move to the next editable field in the record	—	Press Tab
Move to the first editable previous field in the record	—	Press Shift+Tab
Move to the first field in the next record	—	Press Enter
Move to the first field in the previous record	—	Press Shift+Enter
Move to the same field ten records forward	Click below the scroll box	Press PgDn
Move to the same field ten records back	Click above the scroll box	Press PgUp
Move to the new record	Drag the scroll box	Press Ctrl+PgDn
Move to the first record	Drag the scroll box to the top of the scroll bar	Press Ctrl+PgUp
Move within a field	Click the location	Press Home; End; or Right/Left Arrow
Delete the previous character	—	Press Backspace
Delete the selected text or the next character	—	Press Delete
Select within a field	Drag the mouse through the selection	Press Shift+Home, Shift+End, Shift+Left Arrow, or Shift+Right Arrow

Sorting a Database

Once you have created your database, you can use it to sort your data. You can sort rows or columns in any database range. You have the choice of sorting either alphabetically or numerically, in ascending or descending order.

Sorting a Database Using One Sort Key

When you sort a database in Excel you must select at least one **sort key**. When you are sorting by rows, the sort key specifies which column to sort by. When you are sorting by columns, the sort key specifies which row to sort by. You can specify as many as three sort keys at a time. When you sort by more than one key, the first sort key is the primary key; the data will be sorted by that specification first. Cells that have the same data in them when sorted by the primary sort key will be sorted within themselves by the secondary sort key. For instance, if the Name column were the primary sort key and the First Names column were the secondary sort key, all of the Smiths would be sorted by first name.

If you identify only one sort key, rows or columns with duplicate data entries in that key will be left in the order in which they were found. For example, if you sort the database in Figure 13.1 by name and do not select any other sort key, the database will look like the one shown in Figure 13.5.

	A	B	C	D	E	F	G	H
1	Name	Street	City	State	Zip	Date of Sale	Amount of Sale	Total
2	Dr. Jane Smyth	10 Medical Row	New York	NY	123456	11/5/91	145.67	157.69
3	Mr. George Doe	700 East 22nd St.	New York	NY	150000	11/4/91	210.00	227.33
4	Ms. Elise Jones	23 Summit Drive	New York	NY	102000	11/2/91	350.99	379.95
5	Ms. Elsie Cow	45 Milkmaid Dr.	Freehold	NY	234567	11/6/91	101.98	110.39
6	Ms. Jane Smith	23 Main Street	New York	NY	100000	11/1/91	153.98	166.68
7	Ms. Lucy Doe	1 University Place	Chicago	IL	300000	11/3/91	576.89	624.48
8	Ms. Mary Johnson	10 Park Ave.	Ft. Lee	NJ	118000	11/2/91	278.00	300.94
9	Ms. Mary Johnson	10 Park Ave.	Ft. Lee	NJ	118000	11/6/91	128.98	139.62
10	Ms. Priscilla Smith	23 Elm Street	Greenwich	CT	200000	11/3/91	125.00	135.31
11	Ms. Suzi Sunshine	2 Sparkle St.	Boston	MA	145678	11/4/91	210.50	227.87

Figure 13.5. A database sorted by name.

To sort a database using one sort key:

1. Open the worksheet containing the database you want to sort.

2. Select the range inside the defined database range you want to sort. You do not have to select the entire database range. Everything inside the range you select will be sorted. Any fields not included in the sort range will not be affected by the sort.

3. Click on Data in the menu bar.

4. Click on Sort. The Sort dialog box is displayed, as shown in Figure 13.6.

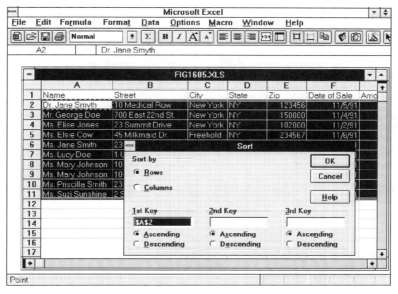

Figure 13.6. The Sort dialog box.

5. You want to keep the rows in your database intact, so select the Rows option. To keep the columns intact, select the Columns option.

6. You are going to sort by name. In the 1st Key text box, enter the address of any cell in the Name column.

7. Select Ascending.

8. Click on OK.

You will notice that all of the names in the database are in alphabetical order and that the two entries for Ms. Mary Johnson have been left in their original order.

You must select a range that includes all data that belongs together. For example, if you selected only D2:D11 from Figure 13.1 to be sorted, all of the data in the State field would be sorted, but none of the data in any of the other fields would be affected. This would ruin the database, since none of the rest of the information in the row would have been moved.

WARNING

In such a scenario, row 2 would contain the following information: cell A2, *Ms. Jane Smith;* cell B2, *23 Main Street;* cell C2, *New York;* cell D2, *CT;* cell E2, *10000;* cell F2, *11/1/91;* cell G2, *153.98;* and cell H2, *166.68.* If this were done to an actual database, there would be no way to know who lived in what state except by painful manual reconstruction of the data.

In this scenario, if you had selected all of the cells that belonged together, all of the data would have been reordered along with the data in the State field. A2:H11 is the needed range here.

N O T E Do not include field names as part of a range to be sorted. The field names for a database must always be in the top row of the database. Always save your worksheet before you sort, in case you make a fatal error while sorting. You can undo a sort immediately after it has finished by using the Undo key.

Sorting a Database Using Multiple Sort Keys

If you sort the database first by name and then by amount of sale, the database will look like the one shown in Figure 13.7.

	A	B	C	D	E	F	G	H
1	Name	Street	City	State	Zip	Date of Sale	Amount of Sale	Total
2	Dr. Jane Smyth	10 Medical Row	New York	NY	123456	11/5/91	145.67	157.69
3	Mr. George Doe	700 East 22nd St.	New York	NY	150000	11/4/91	210.00	227.33
4	Ms. Elise Jones	23 Summit Drive	New York	NY	102000	11/2/91	350.99	379.95
5	Ms. Elsie Cow	45 Milkmaid Dr.	Freehold	NY	234567	11/6/91	101.98	110.39
6	Ms. Jane Smith	23 Main Street	New York	NY	100000	11/1/91	153.98	166.68
7	Ms. Lucy Doe	1 University Place	Chicago	IL	300000	11/3/91	576.89	624.48
8	Ms. Mary Johnson	10 Park Ave.	Ft. Lee	NJ	118000	11/6/91	128.98	139.62
9	Ms. Mary Johnson	10 Park Ave.	Ft. Lee	NJ	118000	11/2/91	278.00	300.94
10	Ms. Priscilla Smith	23 Elm Street	Greenwich	CT	200000	11/3/91	125.00	135.31
11	Ms. Suzi Sunshine	2 Sparkle St.	Boston	MA	145678	11/4/91	210.50	227.87

Figure 13.7. A database sorted by name and amount of sale.

To sort by more than one key:

1. Open the worksheet containing the database you want to sort.
2. Select the range inside the defined database range you want to sort. You do not have to select the entire database range. Everything inside the range you select will be sorted. Any fields not included in the sort range will not be affected by the sort. Select A2:H11 as your range.
3. Click on Data in the menu bar.
4. Click on Sort to display the Sort dialog box.
5. You want to keep the rows in your database intact, so select the Rows option. To keep the columns intact, select the Columns option.
6. You are going to sort first by name and then by amount of sale. In the 1st Key text box, enter the address of any cell in the Name column. In the 2nd Key text box, enter the address of any cell in the Amount of Sale column.
7. Select Ascending for each sort key.
8. Click on OK.

Now, not only are all of the names in the database in alphabetical order, the entries for Ms. Mary Johnson have been reorganized so that the amount of sale entries are in numerical order.

Ascending Sort Order

For each sort key you identify, you must indicate whether you want to sort the column or row in ascending or descending order. In ascending order, Excel sorts from top to bottom for rows and from left to right for columns. Excel follows a specific sort order if you specify ascending order:

◆ **Numbers**. Sorts from the largest negative number to the largest positive number.

◆ **Text**. Text sorts in Excel are not case-sensitive. Numbers that are entered as text values are sorted as text (5 would come *after* 138, for example). Numbers that are entered as numeric values are sorted before text values. Figure 13.8 shows how the database looks when it is sorted by street.

	A	B	C	D	E	Date of Sale	Amount of Sale	Total
1	Name	Street	City	State	Zip	Date of Sale	Amount of Sale	Total
2	Ms. Lucy Doe	1 University Place	Chicago	IL	300000	11/3/91	576.89	624.48
3	Dr. Jane Smyth	10 Medical Row	New York	NY	123456	11/5/91	145.67	157.69
4	Ms. Mary Johnson	10 Park Ave.	Ft. Lee	NJ	118000	11/6/91	128.98	139.62
5	Ms. Mary Johnson	10 Park Ave.	Ft. Lee	NJ	118000	11/2/91	278.00	300.94
6	Ms. Suzi Sunshine	2 Sparkle St.	Boston	MA	145678	11/4/91	210.50	227.87
7	Ms. Priscilla Smith	23 Elm Street	Greenwich	CT	200000	11/3/91	125.00	135.31
8	Ms. Jane Smith	23 Main Street	New York	NY	100000	11/1/91	153.98	166.68
9	Ms. Elise Jones	23 Summit Drive	New York	NY	102000	11/2/91	350.99	379.95
10	Ms. Elsie Cow	45 Milkmaid Dr.	Freehold	NY	234567	11/6/91	101.98	110.39
11	Mr. George Doe	700 East 22nd St.	New York	NY	150000	11/4/91	210.00	227.33

Figure 13.8. The database sorted by street.

Since all of the numbers in the State field are entered as text values, the field is sorted alphabetically and not numerically. Text is sorted in the following ascending order: 0 1 2 3 4 5 6 7 8 9 Space ! " # $ % & " ( ) * + , - . / : ; < = > ? @ [\ } ^ _ ` { | } ~ A B C D E F G H I J K L M N O P Q R S T U V W X Y Z

◆ **Logical Values**. False values come before true values.

◆ **Error Values**. Error values are equal.

◆ **Blanks**. Blanks are always sorted last.

Descending Sort Order

If you specify descending order, Excel reverses the order of everything except blanks. Blanks are always sorted last. The sort order is as follows:

- ◆ **Error Values**. Error values are equal.
- ◆ **Logical Values**. True values come before False values.
- ◆ **Text**. Text sorts in Excel are not case-sensitive. Numbers that are entered as text values are sorted as text (5 would come *after* 138, for example). Numbers that are entered as numeric values are sorted before text values. Since all of the numbers in the State field in Figure 13.8 are entered as text values, the field is sorted alphabetically and not numerically. Text is sorted in the following descending order: Z Y X W V U T S R Q P O N M L K J I H G F E D C B A ~ } | { ' _ ^] \ [@ ? > = < ; : / . - , + *) (" & % $ # " ! Space 9 8 7 6 5 4 3 2 1 0
- ◆ **Numbers**. Sorts from the largest positive number to the largest negative number.
- ◆ **Blanks**. Blanks are always sorted last.

N O T E Be sure that you have entered the numbers in a row or column either as text values or as all numeric values. If not, for ascending sorts, Excel will sort numbers entered as numeric values before it sorts numbers as text values, and for descending sorts, Excel will sort the numbers entered as text values before sorting numbers entered as numeric values.

Using Names in Sort Key Text Boxes

If you have defined names for your ranges, you can type a defined name instead of a cell address in the 1st, 2nd, and 3rd Key text boxes. The cell in the upper-left corner of the named range will be the address in the key text box. For example, if you selected cells D2:D11 and defined the name of the range as City, you could type City in the 1st, 2nd, or 3rd Key text box. Cell D2 would be used as the sort key.

Using a Criteria Range

You have already learned how to find records in a data form by setting criteria. This method limits you to locating records that contain only one criterion for each field. You cannot search for multiple criteria. For example, you cannot search for records in which the Amount of Sale is greater than $100 and less than $200. You cannot search for records that meet criteria that are based on a formula. You cannot search for and extract the records that match your specified criteria. To do all of this you must use a criteria range in your worksheet and use the Set Criteria command.

You can search for two types of criteria when you use a criteria range: comparison criteria and computed criteria. **Comparison criteria** allows you to find records in which the contents of the specified fields either match or fall within the criteria limits. For example, you could search for all records in which the contents of the Amount of Sale field are between $100 and $150. You used this type of criteria to search for records in a data form earlier in this chapter. The other type of criteria is **computed criteria**. Computed criteria are used to find records that meet specified criteria based on a formula. For example, if your database contains a field for the Amount of Sale and a field for the Tax Rate for each state, and you want all of the records in which the Amount of Sale plus the Tax Rate is equal to or greater than $200, you would use computed criteria and enter this formula:

```
=Amount of Sale*Tax Rate+Amount of Sale>=200
```

Excel will find all of the records where the amount of sale plus the tax rate is greated than 200.

Setting Up and Defining a Criteria Range for Comparison Criteria

Setting up a criteria range is basically the same as setting up a database. To set up a criteria range:

1. Select a row in the worksheet where you want to enter the field names that contain the criteria for which you wish to search. These names are called the **criteria names**.

2. Enter the criteria you want to search for in the rows beneath the field names. Use the same syntax and rules discussed earlier in this chapter to define criteria in data forms. You can search for several criteria at the same time. For example, if your database contains fields for states and sales, you could create a criteria range that will search for all sales greater than $50 in the state of New York, as shown in Figure 13.9.

   You can select records that match any combination of AND or OR relationships. For example, you can search for all of the records whose state is New York AND whose sales are greater than 50, or you can search for all of the records whose state is New York OR whose sales are greater than 50. Excel recognizes an AND or OR condition by the position of the criteria in your criteria range. To select criteria using the AND relation, you must enter the criteria in the same row, as shown in Figure 13.9. If the AND relation applies to the same field name—for example, all records in the state of New York AND all records with sales greater than 50 AND sales less than 100—you must enter the field name twice, as shown in Figure 13.10. If you want to find all of the records in the database that contain the state of New York OR the state of New Jersey, you must enter the criteria in different rows under the same field name, as shown in Figure 13.11.

3. Select the range that contains the criteria names and criteria.
4. Click on Data in the menu bar.
5. Click on Set Criteria.

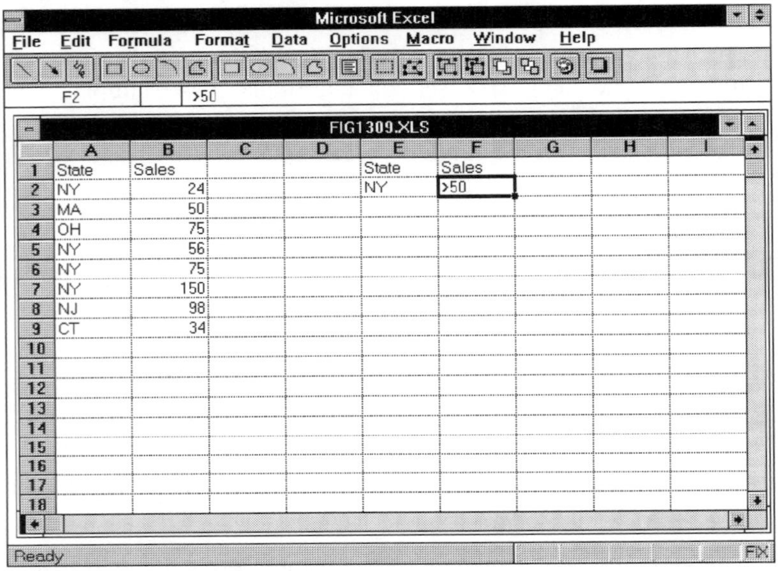

Figure 13.9. A criteria range to search for all sales in New York greater than $50.

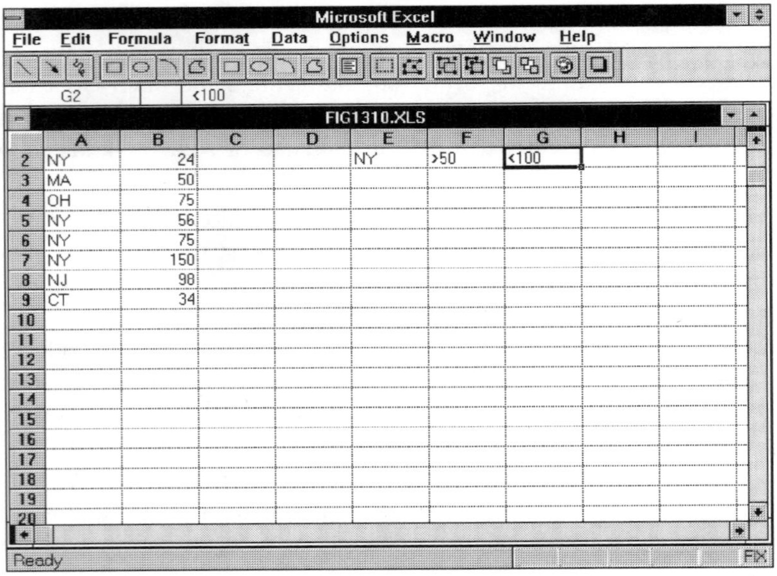

Figure 13.10. A criteria range using an AND relation in the same field.

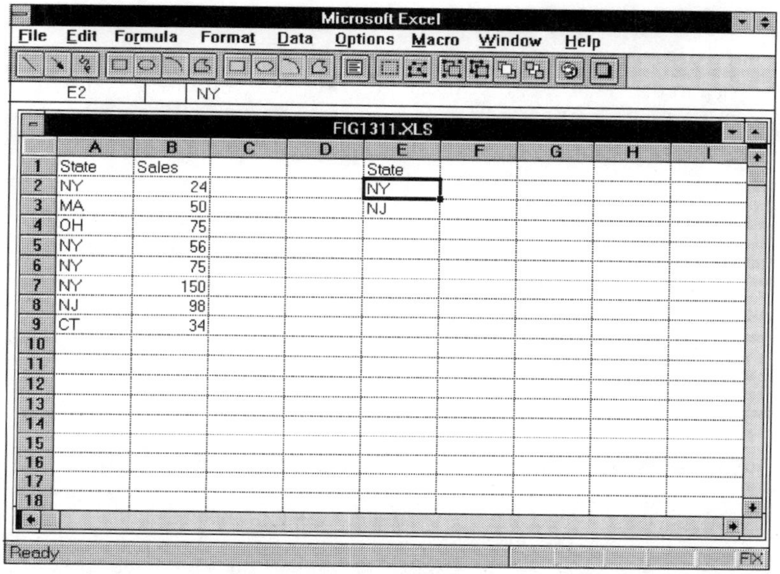

Figure 13.11. A criteria range using an OR relation in the same field.

Setting Up and Defining a Criteria Range for Computed Criteria

When you set up a criteria range for computed criteria, you enter a formula instead of a constant value as your criteria. The criteria formula must refer to values contained in one or more fields in your database. All criteria formulas compare the resulting value of the formula to another value, and must produce either a TRUE or FALSE value. For example, if cell A1 contains the value $25 and cell B1 contains the value $30 the criteria formula A1+B1>50 will produce the logical value TRUE, since the sum of $25 and $30 is greater than $50. To set up a criteria:

1. Select a row in the worksheet where you want to enter the names to indicate the criteria for which you wish to search. These names are called the **criteria names**. Unlike entering criteria names for comparison criteria, you *cannot* enter field names for your criteria names when you search records for computed criteria. When Excel encounters field names used as criteria names in the first row of a criteria range, it automatically assumes that you are searching for comparison criteria. For example, if you want to find all of the records in a database where the amount of sale plus the tax is greater than $200, you would enter the formula *=sales*tax+sales>200,* and your criteria name could be *Totals.*

2. Enter the criteria you want to search for in the rows beneath the criteria names. A computed criteria formula can use either field names or the relative reference of the first record in the database. If you use an absolute reference, Excel will evaluate only the record referred to by the absolute reference, and will not search the rest of the database for records that match your computed criteria. For example, if you have the field names *Sales* and *Tax*, and the database records containing the values for these fields begins in cells A7 and B7, to find all of the records whose sales plus tax is greater than $200, you could enter either *=Sales*Tax+Sales>200* or *=A7*B7+A7>200*, to search the entire database for all records that match this computed criteria. To search for multiple criteria using computed criteria, you can use the AND and OR functions in your formulas. For example, to search for all of the records for the states of New York OR New Jersey, you would enter *=OR(State="NY",State="NJ")*, as shown in the formula bar in Figure 13.12.

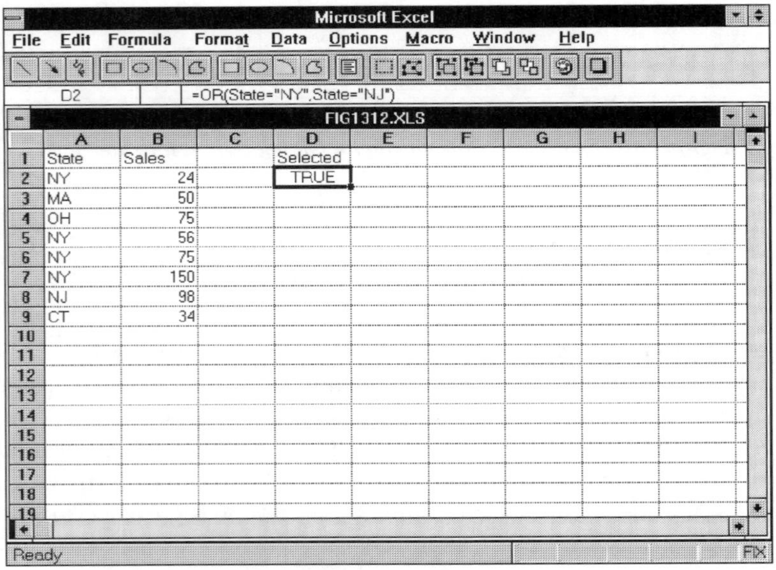

Figure 13.12. A formula to search for multiple criteria in the formula bar.

3. Select the range that contains the criteria names and the criteria.
4. Click on Data in the menu bar.
5. Click on Set Criteria.

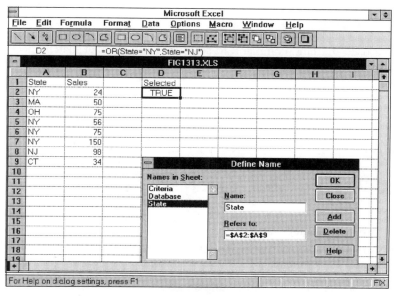

Figure 13.13. The field name State defined.

If you enter field names as your criteria, you must first define them, using the Define Names command in the Formula menu. The range you define must contain all of the fields you wish to search. If a field is not included in the defined range, Excel will ignore the field when it searches for the field name criteria. Figure 13.13 shows the field name State defined.

Finding Records that Match a Criteria Range

When you have set your criteria and defined your range, you can search through the database for all of the records that match the criteria. If the active cell is outside the database when you begin your search, Excel selects the first record in the database that matches the criteria; if the active cell in located inside the database, Excel selects the first record below the active cell that matches the criteria.

1. Click on Data in the menu bar.
2. Click on Find.
3. Excel has selected the first record in the database that matches the specified criteria.
4. Use your Up and Down arrow keys or the scroll boxes to scroll backward and forward through the database to each record that matches the specified criteria. If you have reached the last matching record and continue to scroll, Excel will beep and will remain on the last selected record.

Exiting the Find Command

Once you have used the Find command to search for records that match specified criteria, you must exit the command in order to access all of the records in your database. To exit the Find command:

1. Click on Data in the menu bar.
2. Click on Exit Find.

You can now access all of the records in your database.

Extracting Records that Match Specified Criteria

When you set your criteria and define your criteria range, you can elect to extract the records that match the specified criteria and copy them to another section of your worksheet. In order to do this, you must set an **extract range**. You can copy any or all of the fields in your database. To set and copy your data to an extract range:

1. Define both the database and criteria ranges.
2. Enter the exact names of the fields you want to extract in a row on the worksheet. These names must exactly match the field names in your database. Only the fields whose names are included in the extract range will be copied into the extract range.
3. Select either a range that contains the field names or a range that contains the field names and the cells into which the extracted data will be copied. If you select a range that contains both field names and cells to copy the extracted data into, only as much data as will fit into the selected cells will be copied. Any data that does not fit in the selected range will not be copied, and Excel will display a message informing you that the extract range is full. If this happens you must either make the extract range larger or select a range that contains only the field names (Excel will copy all matching records when only the field names are selected as the extract range).
4. Click on Data in the menu bar.
5. Click on Set Extract.
6. Click on Data in the menu bar.
7. Click on Extract. If you do not want to extract duplicate records, select the Unique Records Only check box.

The records that match the specified criteria have been copied to the rows below the field names you entered.

WARNING

When you copy data to an extract range, all of the data in the cells included in the extract range are replaced by the data that has been copied. If you selected only field names as your extract range, the cells below the field names to the bottom of the worksheet are cleared, whether data is copied into them or not. Be very careful about the placement of your extract range. You cannot Undo an Extract command.

Deleting Records that Match the Specified Criteria

You can simultaneously delete all of the records in your database that match the specified criteria.

1. Define your database and criteria ranges.
2. Click on Data in the menu bar.
3. Click on Delete. Excel displays a message informing you that matching records will be permanently deleted from the database.
4. Click on OK.

All of the records that match the specified criteria will be deleted.

WARNING

Save your database before using the Delete command. You cannot Undo the Delete command. If you save your worksheet and then discover that you made a mistake defining the criteria range and deleting your data, you can exit the worksheet without saving and retain your original data.

Creating a Chart Using a Database Range

Once you have defined your database range, you can create a chart using the data included in the database range. If you have extracted data from your database and want to use the data in the extracted database, select the range you want to include in the chart, click on Data in the menu bar, and click on Set Database to define a new database range. To create a chart using a database range:

1. Select your database range.
2. Click on Options in the menu bar.
3. Click on Toolbars to display the Toolbars dialog box.
4. Select Chart and click on Show to display the Chart toolbar in the bottom of your application window.
5. Click on the ChartWizard. Follow the steps in the ChartWizard to create your chart. Charts are discussed in detail in Chapter 12.

Review Exercises for Chapter 13

◆ Review the parts of a database.

◆ Add at least five records to the Frills and Thrills sample database.

◆ Use some of the editing and formatting features that you have been using in your worksheets in your sample database.

◆ Delete the five records you have added to your database.

◆ Open the data form for the database and identify its parts.

◆ Practice moving around the data form using either the mouse or the keyboard.

◆ Use your imagination to create several criteria and search for the records with matching items in your database.

◆ Sort the database using one sort key.

◆ Sort the database using two or three sort keys.

◆ Define a comparison criteria range using more than one value in a field.

◆ Define a computed criteria range.

◆ Extract records from your database that match a criteria range.

Before You Go On...

Before you go on to the next chapter you should be familiar with the parts of a database. You should be able to create and edit a database. You should know how to add records to a database without having to redefine the database range. You should be able to identify the parts of a data form. You should be able to add, delete, and edit records in a data form. You should feel confident in your ability to use comparison criteria to search for records in a database. You should be able to move around in a data form using either the mouse or the keyboard. You should be able to sort a database using one, two, or three sort keys. You should be familiar with the difference between comparison and computed criteria. You should be able to set up and define comparison and computed criteria ranges. You should know how to find records using specified criteria, extract records that match the criteria in a criteria range, and delete records that match specific criteria.

Chapter **14**

ENHANCING PRESENTATIONS WITH GRAPHICS AND SLIDES

What You Will Learn in This Chapter

- ◆ How to work with graphic objects
- ◆ How to use object groups
- ◆ How to turn your work into pictures
- ◆ How to create and run a slide show

361

Unlike so many other spreadsheet or worksheet programs, Excel has gone beyond the concept of simple number crunching and worksheet presentation. We live in a much more visual age, and the growth of the computer industry has made possible graphic and design presentations that would have been prohibitively expensive even ten years ago. Excel has been a forerunner in this field. You have already seen the exciting charts you can produce from your worksheets. In this chapter you are going to learn how to use graphic objects to further enhance your worksheets, and how to create slide shows to present your work. You will need a mouse to work with the features in this chapter.

We will cover only the basic graphic shapes and objects in this chapter. This is really a very exciting feature of Excel, and it actually deserves its own book to do it justice. However, even with just an introduction to the subject, you will be surprised at what you can accomplish. If you plan to use this feature to create complex presentations, or if you are the artistic type who cannot resist improving the aesthetics of any task you undertake, we suggest you invest in an advanced user's manual in which the subject is covered in more detail.

We will not be creating any new documents in this chapter; however, it would be a good idea to create some simple graphic objects to practice working with.

Drawing Graphic Objects with the Toolbar

You can use the tools in the drawing toolbar to create lines, ovals, rectangles, arcs, and polygons. You can also create freehand drawings and filled shapes. The shapes you create with the drawing tools are known as **graphic objects**. Figure 14.1 shows the drawing toolbar with all of the tools identified. If you have never tried drawing with a mouse before, you might find the process a bit cumbersome. Keep at it—you'll get the knack eventually. If you have worked with other drawing programs, such as Paintbrush, you will find it very easy to create graphic objects in Excel.

Shapes are transparent or filled shapes depending on the tool used. For example, to create a transparent oval, select the oval tool. To create a filled oval, select the filled oval tool. Later in this chapter, you will learn how to fill shapes with colors and patterns.

Drawing Lines and Shapes

Let's start off by drawing simple shapes. You must have the drawing toolbar displayed.

1. Click on the line tool. The mouse pointer changes shape to a cross-hair pointer.
2. Place the pointer where you want to begin drawing a line.
3. Drag with the mouse until the line is at the position and angle you want.
4. Release the mouse button. The line has been drawn.

Practice creating other shapes using the unfilled oval, rectangle, and arc tools in the drawing toolbar. To restrict lines to horizontal, vertical, or 45-degree angles, hold down the Shift key while you draw. To change the oval tool to a circle tool, or the rectangle tool to a square tool, hold down the Shift key while you draw.

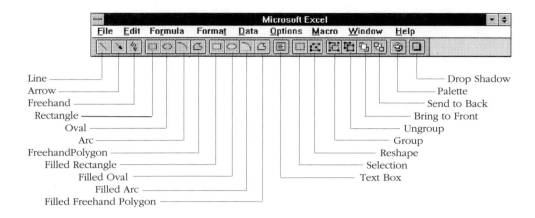

Figure 14.1. The Drawing toolbar.

You learned how to use the text box tool and the arrow tool in Chapter 6. Refer to that chapter, if necessary, to refresh your memory on how to use these tools.

You can align graphic objects with gridlines in a worksheet by holding down the Alt key while drawing.

When you select a tool by double-clicking on it, the tool stays selected until you deselect it by clicking on it again, selecting another tool, or clicking on another part of the worksheet without dragging. This makes it easy to draw the same shape over and over. To draw multiple lines, rectangles, and so forth:

1. Double-click on the tool you want to use to create the shape.
2. Draw the first graphic object.
3. Release the mouse button. The tool is still selected and you can move to another location on the worksheet.
4. Draw additional shapes with the same tool.
5. When you are finished, deselect the tool.

Creating a Drawing with the Freehand Tool

You can draw your own freehand shapes and drawings using the freehand tool. To draw in a continuous line, click on the tool and start drawing. When you release the mouse button, the tool will be deselected.

To keep the tool selected so that you can continue drawing even after releasing the mouse button, double-click on the freehand tool. The tool will stay selected until you click on it again, select another tool, or double-click in another location on the worksheet.

To create a freehand drawing:

1. Click on the freehand tool.

2. Place the cross-hair pointer where you want to start the drawing and click.

3. Drag to create the drawing you want.

4. When you are finished, release the mouse button.

Creating a Drawing with the Freehand Polygon Tool

A polygon is simply a flat plane enclosed by many angles. You can create a polygon with the freehand polygon tool or with the freehand tool. To draw a polygon with straight lines or a combination of straight lines and freehand lines, you should use the freehand polygon tool. If your drawing is comprised of all freehand lines you should use the freehand tool, as described in the previous section.

Drawing Straight Lines with the Freehand Polygon Tool

To draw straight lines with the freehand polygon tool:

1. Click on the freehand polygon tool.

2. Place the cross-hair mouse pointer where you want to begin drawing and click.

3. Without pressing the mouse button, move the mouse in the direction you want to draw the line. As you move the mouse the line will be drawn. Move the mouse to where you want the next line to begin.

4. Click to form a vortex of the polygon and begin the next line.

5. Move the mouse in the direction you want to draw the next line.

6. Repeat steps 4 and 5 until the polygon is complete.

7. Double-click to end the drawing or, if the last line closes the polygon, click at the location where you began the drawing.

Drawing a Combination of Straight Lines and Freehand Lines with the Freehand Polygon Tool

1. Click on the freehand polygon tool.

2. Place the cross-hair mouse pointer where you want to begin drawing.

3. To draw freehand, drag the mouse as you draw.

4. To draw straight lines, click where you want to begin and, without pressing down on the mouse button, move the mouse to draw the line. To draw another line, click and draw the next line.

5. To switch from a straight line to a freehand line, drag the mouse. To switch from a freehand line to a straight line, release the mouse button and move the mouse to draw the line. When you are finished, click to end the line.

6. Double-click to end the drawing or, if the last line closes the polygon, click where you began the drawing.

Selecting, Moving, and Sizing Graphic Objects

Once you have drawn or imported a graphic object, you can move or size it. To move or size a graphic object, you must first select it. When you select a graphic object, small black squares called **handles** appear on the border of the object, as shown in Figure 14.2. The handles are attached to a frame. For a rectangle or line, the frame is the actual border of the graphic. For an arc, polygon or oval, the frame is an invisible rectangle surrounding the object.

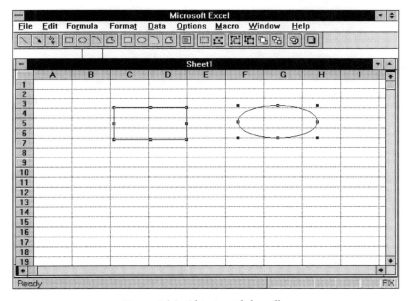

Figure 14.2. Objects with handles.

You can select an object by clicking on it or by using the selection tool. You can select an object only when the mouse pointer is in the shape of an arrow.

Selecting a Graphic Object with the Mouse Pointer

To select a graphic object with the mouse pointer:

1. Bring the arrow mouse pointer to the border of the graphic object.
2. Click on the object.
3. The object is selected if it is surrounded by handles. If you do not see handles, the object is not selected. Try again, making sure the pointer is in the shape of an arrow before you click.

Selecting Multiple Graphic Objects with the Mouse

To select multiple graphic objects with the mouse pointer:

1. Bring the arrow mouse pointer to the border of the first graphic object you want to select.

2. Click on the object.

3. The object is selected if it is surrounded by handles. If you do not see handles, the object is not selected. Try again, making sure the pointer is in the shape of an arrow before you click.

4. Holding down the Ctrl key, repeat steps 1 and 2 for each object you want to select.

Selecting Multiple Graphic Objects in One Area with the Selection Tool

Use the selection tool to select multiple graphic objects in an area.

1. Click on the Selection tool.

2. Bring the cross-hair mouse pointer to one corner of the area that contains the objects you want to select.

3. Drag with the mouse, creating a large rectangle around all of the objects you want to select. An object must be entirely enclosed in the selection rectangle to be selected.

4. Release the mouse button. All of the objects in the selection rectangle are selected.

5. To deselect the selection tool, click on it again.

Selecting Graphic Objects in Multiple Areas with the Selection Tool

You can also use the selection tool to select graphic objects in multiple areas:

1. Click on the Selection tool.

2. Bring the cross-hair mouse pointer to one corner of the first area containing the objects you want to select.

3. Drag with the mouse, creating a large rectangle until all of the objects you want to select in the first area are enclosed in the rectangle. An object must be entirely enclosed in the selection rectangle to be selected.

4. Release the mouse button. All of the objects in the selection rectangle are selected.

5. To select objects in additional areas, hold down the Ctrl key and repeat steps 2 through 4.

6. To deselect the selection tool, click on it again.

Selecting All Graphic Objects in a Worksheet

You can select all of the graphic objects in a worksheet at once:

1. Click on Formula in the menu bar to open the Formula menu.
2. Click on Select Special to display the Select Special dialog box, shown in Figure 14.3.

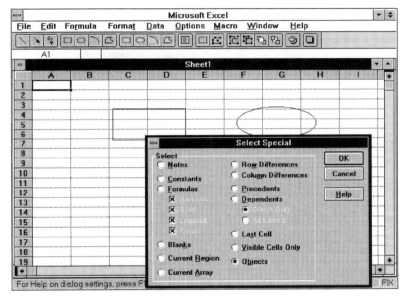

Figure 14.3. The Select Special dialog box.

3. Select Objects in the Select options box.
4. Click on OK. All of the graphic objects have been selected.

N O T E

When you select one graphic object, the object's number and type appear in the formula bar. For instance, note that in Figure 14.4, the first rectangle object is selected, and *Rectangle 1* appears in the upper-left corner of the formula bar.

Removing a Graphic Object from a Selection

If you have selected only one graphic object, you can deselect it by selecting another object or by clicking on another location in the worksheet.

If you have selected more than one graphic object, you can remove one or more objects from the selection. To remove an object from the selection, hold down the Ctrl key and click on the graphic object you want to deselect.

To remove a group of objects from a selection, click on the selection tool. While holding down the Ctrl key, enclose the objects you want to deselect in the selection rectangle.

Using Object Groups

If you are working with large numbers of graphic objects, you can create **object groups**. Objects that are grouped together can be moved, sized, edited, and formatted as a group. If you want to work with an individual object that is part of a group, you must first ungroup it.

Creating an Object Group

To group graphic objects:

1. Select the objects you want to group together.
2. Click on the group tool, **or** choose the Group command in the Format menu.

Ungrouping Graphic Objects

To ungroup graphic objects:

1. Select the grouped objects you want to ungroup.
2. Click the ungroup tool, **or** choose the Ungroup command in the Format menu.

Moving, Sizing, and Deleting Graphic Objects

Graphic objects can be cell-oriented or page-oriented. If an object is attached to its underlying cell or cells, it will be moved or sized when the cell is moved or sized. Graphics that are unattached to a cell or cells are page-oriented, and will remain in place even if the underlying cells are moved or sized. Objects can also be attached so that they move with their underlying cells, but do not change size if the size of the cells changes.

When an object is moved and sized with its underlying cells, it maintains the position and size of the upper-left corner and lower-right corner of the underlying cells. When an object is moved but not sized with its underlying cells, it is positioned with the upper-left corner of the underlying cells.

All objects that are not imported from other applications are initially formatted to move and size with their underlying cells.

Attaching and Unattaching Objects from Their Cells

To attach or unattach objects from their cells:

1. Select the object you want to attach or unattach.
2. Click on Format in the menu bar to open the Format menu.
3. Click on Object Properties. The Object Properties dialog box is displayed, as shown in Figure 14.4.
4. Select the option you want.
5. Click on OK.

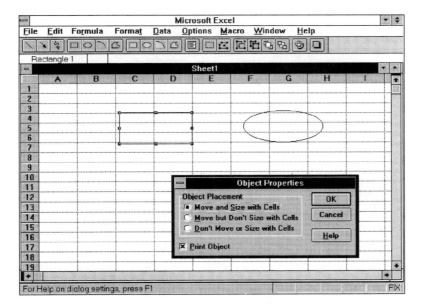

Figure 14.4. The Object Properties dialog box.

An attached object moves only when the cell it is attached to is moved. Using the Cut or Copy commands to move the contents of a cell will not affect the object, since these commands affect only the cell contents, not the cell structure.

N O T E

Sizing a Graphic Object

You size a graphic object by dragging its handles. If more than one object is selected, all of the selected objects will be sized proportionately. If you size one object in an object group, all of the objects in the group will be sized.

Graphic handles appear in the corners and on the sides of the frame of a graphic object, as shown in Figure 14.2. To size an object vertically or horizontally, drag the handles that appear on the sides of the object. To drag an object in both directions at once, drag a corner handle.

N O T E

Lines and arrows have only two handles, one at each end of the object.

To size a graphic object:

1. Select the object you want to size.
2. Position the mouse pointer (it should be in the shape of a double-headed arrow) over a handle.
3. Drag the handle to size the object. To proportionally size an object, hold down the Shift key while you drag a corner handle.

Moving a Graphic Object

To move a graphic object, drag the object to a new location or use the Cut and Paste command. Using Cut and Paste gives you more control over where you place the object.

To move a graphic object by dragging:

1. Select the object you want to move.
2. Position the arrow mouse pointer on the border of the object.
3. Drag the object to its new location. To move the object horizontally or vertically, hold down the Shift key while you drag.

To move a graphic object using the Cut and Paste command:

1. Select the object you want to move.
2. Click on Edit in the menu bar to open the Edit menu.
3. Click on Cut. The object is moved to the Windows Clipboard.
4. Select the cell to which you want to move the object.
5. Click on Edit in the menu bar to open the Edit menu.
6. Click on Paste. The object is pasted from the Clipboard to its new location.

N O T E

When moving or copying an object, you can align the object to a cell gridline by holding down the Alt key while dragging the object.

Copying a Graphic Object

You can copy a graphic object by dragging or by using the Copy and Paste commands.

To copy an object by dragging:

1. Select the object you want to copy.
2. Position the arrow mouse pointer on the border of the graphic object.
3. While holding down the Ctrl key, drag the object to its new location. To drag vertically or horizontally, hold down the Ctrl and Shift keys while you drag.

To copy a graphic object with the Copy and Paste command:

1. Select the object you want to copy.
2. Click on Edit in the menu bar to open the Edit menu.
3. Click on Copy. The object is copied to the Windows Clipboard.
4. Select the cell to which you want to copy the object.
5. Click on Edit in the menu bar to reopen the Edit menu.
6. Click on Paste. The object is pasted from the Clipboard to its new location.

N O T E

Sometimes when you create, move, or size graphic objects, they will overlap. If an object is completely covered, select the object overlapping it and click on the send to back tool. The overlapped object will come to the forefront. If an object is partially covered, select the object you want to bring to the forefront, and click on the bring to front tool.

Deleting a Graphic Object

To delete a graphic object:

1. Select the object you want to delete.
2. Click on Edit in the menu bar to open the Edit menu.
3. To clear the object completely, click on Clear.

To move the object into the Clipboard, click on Cut. The object can then be pasted to another location in the document.

You can undo the deletion immediately after deleting:

1. Click on Edit in the menu bar to open the Edit menu.
2. Click on Undo.

Formatting and Editing Graphic Objects

Editing most graphic objects is very simple—you can change the size or placement of the object by sizing or moving the graphic. However, graphics created using the freehand tool or freehand polygon tool are a little more complex to edit, since it is often necessary to reshape only sections of the drawing. This is done using the reshape tool. When you select the reshape tool, selection handles appear at close intervals along the freehand line and at the beginning and end of each straight line. You can reshape the drawing at any of the handles.

Editing Polygons and Freehand Drawings

To edit a polygon or freehand drawing:

1. Select the drawing you want to edit.
2. Click on the reshape tool. Selection handles appear at close intervals along the drawing.
3. Bring the cross-hair mouse pointer to the first location you want to reshape on the drawing.
4. Drag the handle to reshape the drawing. To delete a vertex in a polygon, hold down the Shift key and click the vertex handle. To add a vertex to a polygon, hold down the Shift key, position the mouse on a line of the polygon, and drag the pointer to the location where you want the new vertex.
5. Repeat steps 3 to 4 until you have finished reshaping the drawing.
6. Click on the reshape tool to deselect it.

Formatting Graphic Objects

You can format an object's borders and fill it with different colors or patterns. You can format both transparent and filled objects.

To format an object:

1. Bring the arrow mouse pointer to the border of the object you want to format and double-click. The Patterns dialog box is displayed, as shown in Figure 14.5 (the Patterns dialog box is covered in detail in Chapter 5).
2. In the Border options box, select the border options you want to apply to the object.
3. In the Fill options box, select the fill options you want to apply to the object. The Sample box in the lower-right corner of the dialog box will display the object with the selected options.
4. Click on OK. The selected graphic object has been formatted with your choices.

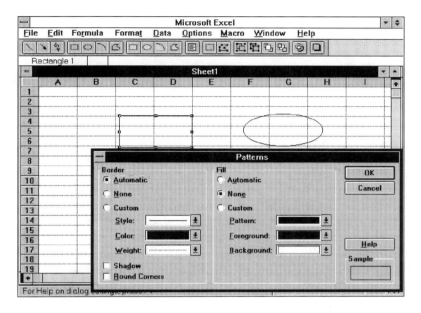

Figure 14.5. The Patterns dialog box.

You can also use the color tool to change the color of an object:

1. Select the object whose color you want to change.
2. Click on the color tool until the object becomes the color you want.
3. To return to previous colors in the color tool, hold down the Shft key while you click on it.

Printing Graphic Objects

You can determine which graphic objects, if any, will print when the worksheet is printed. If you print a graphic object that has been formatted with colors or patterns, the colors and patterns will print only if your printer is capable of supporting them.

To print objects with a worksheet:

1. Select the objects you want to print.
2. Click on Format in the menu bar to open the Format menu.
3. Click on Object Properties to display the Object Properties dialog box.
4. Select Print Object.
5. Click on OK. The selected objects will print.

To print a worksheet without graphic objects:

1. Select the objects you do not want to print.
2. Click on Format in the menu bar to open the Format menu.
3. Click on Object Properties to display the Object Properties dialog box.
4. Clear the Print Object check box.
5. Click on OK. The selected objects will not print.

Creating Pictures

You can create pictures from charts, cells, or graphic objects and then copy the pictures to different locations in a worksheet or to a different worksheet.

When you copy a chart as a picture, the chart is not linked to its original source data on the worksheet. You can copy an embedded chart or a chart document as a picture.

When you copy a picture of a linked cell, you can link the picture so that it automatically updates when you update the data. Both the data and the cell format will be updated.

You can create a picture to appear as it does on the screen or as it would print. If you decide to have the picture appear as it would print, the formatting and colors will be changed to reflect the formatting and colors supported by the printer that was selected when the picture was created.

You create a picture using the Picture Copy command. The picture is then pasted to another location in the worksheet or in another worksheet.

After a picture is pasted in a worksheet, it can be moved or sized using the same techniques for moving and sizing any graphic objects.

You can import graphics from other applications or export graphics from Excel to other applications. Excel will accept graphics from and import graphics to any application that can support the Clipboard picture and bitmap formats. Consult your Windows manual for more information about acceptable formats. Once the graphic is in the Clipboard, it can be pasted in Excel with the Paste command.

Copying a Chart, Cell, or Object to a Picture

To copy a chart, cell, or object to a picture:

1. Select the chart, cell(s) or object you want to copy.
2. Hold down the Shift key and Click on Edit in the menu bar to open the Edit menu.
3. Click on Copy Picture. The Copy Picture dialog box appears, as shown in Figure 14.6.
3. Select from the following options:

   ◆ To copy the graphic as it appears on screen, choose As Shown On Screen in the Appearance box.

◆ To copy the graphic as it would be printed, choose As Shown When Printed in the Appearance box.

◆ To create the picture as a bitmapped image, choose Bitmap in the Format box. A **bitmapped** image is comprised of **pixels**, or dots. This means that the picture will not necessarily scale proportionately when you size it.

◆ To create the picture as a picture image, choose Picture in the Format box. A **picture image** is a line drawing that will scale proportionately when the picture is sized.

4. Choose OK. The picture has been copied to the Clipboard.

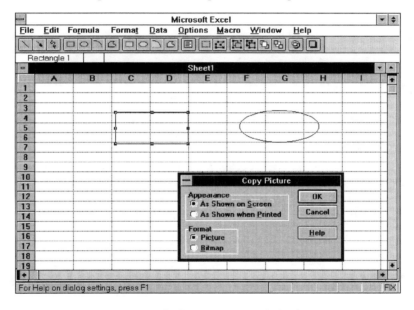

Figure 14.6. The Copy Picture dialog box.

Pasting a Picture

Once you have created a picture, you can paste it to a different worksheet, or to another location in the same worksheet.

To paste the picture:

1. Click on the location where you want to paste the picture.

2. Click on Edit in the menu bar to open the Edit menu.

3. Click on Paste. The picture is pasted in the new location.

To copy and paste a linked cell to a picture:

1. Select the cells you want to copy.
2. Click on Edit in the menu bar to open the Edit menu.
3. Click on Copy.
4. Select the location where you want to paste the cells.
5. Hold down the Shift key and click on Edit in the menu bar to open the Edit menu.
6. Choose Paste Picture Link.

N O T E

To paste a picture into another application, switch to the application and follow that application's instructions for copying graphics from the Clipboard.

Creating Slide Shows

Slide shows are an exciting new feature in Excel 4.0 that allow you to really jazz up your presentations. You can select data or graphics, incorporate them into a slide show, and then show the slides on a computer screen. This is a great accompaniment to any presentation, and is much more efficient and cost-effective than having your graphs, worksheets, and so forth turned into transparencies or other display devices. You can even use sounds in your slides if you are using Windows 3.1 or Windows 3.0 with Multimedia Extensions 1.0 or later.

Slides are pasted from the Clipboard into a slide show template. To open the template:

1. Click on File in the menu bar to open the File menu.
2. Click on New to display the New dialog box.
3. Select Slides. Click on OK to open a slide show template, as shown in Figure 14.7.

Creating a Slide From a Range of Cells

You can create a slide from a cell or a range in a worksheet. If you do not want the gridlines to show in the slide, turn them off using the Options Display command before copying the cell or range. Before you start, open the slide show template. To create a slide from a range:

1. Select the cell or range you want to use in the slide.
2. Click on the copy tool in the Standard toolbar or click on the Copy command in the Edit menu.
3. Switch to the slide show template.
4. Choose the Paste Slide button. The slide is pasted into the template, and the Edit Slide dialog box is displayed, as shown in Figure 14.8.

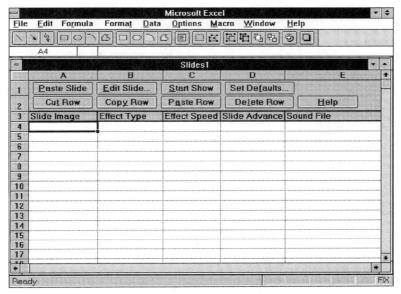

Figure 14.7. The Slide Show template.

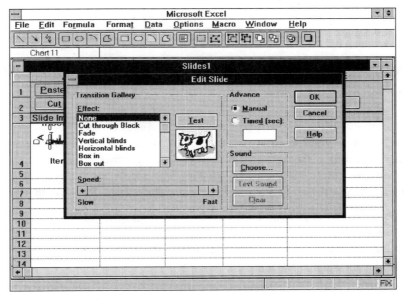

Figure 14.8. The Edit Slide dialog box.

5. Select from the following options:

- ◆ **Effect**. You can choose the effect you want during the transition from one slide to the next. Clicking on the Test button will show you the results of each choice.

- ◆ **Speed**. This choice allows you to control the speed of the transition effect. Use the scroll arrows or move the scroll box to speed up or slow down the transition effect.

- ◆ **Advance**. This choice allows you to choose between manual and timed advancement between slides. If you choose manual, you can advance the slide by clicking the left mouse button or pressing the Spacebar. If you choose timed, the slides will automatically advance at the timed intervals (in seconds) that you enter in the Timed text box.

- ◆ **Sound**. If your system is capable of using the sound feature (see above for requirements), you can use the sound option to import and record sounds to be used during the transition between slides.

6. Choose OK.

The image is pasted into the template and the options to be used with the image in the slide show are selected. A picture of the range of cells selected is pasted into Column A of the template as a slide. Columns B, C, D and E contain information about how the slide is to be used in the slide show.

Creating a Slide Show from an Embedded Chart or a Graphic

You can use embedded charts, chart documents, or graphics in a slide show. You can copy an embedded chart or graphic into the Clipboard by selecting the range of cells under the chart or graphic and then using the copy tool or Copy command to copy the data to the Clipboard. However, an easier and more effective way is to copy the chart or graphic as a picture using the Copy Picture command. To create a slide from charts or graphics:

1. Select the range of cells under the embedded chart or graphic and click on the copy tool or select Copy from the Edit menu. **Or,** select the chart or graphic and, while holding down the Shift key, select the Copy Picture command from the Edit menu.

2. Switch to the slide show template.

3. Choose the Paste Slide button. The slide is pasted into the template and the Edit Slide dialog box is displayed, as shown in Figure 14.8.

4. Select the options you want in the Edit Slide dialog box.

5. Choose OK.

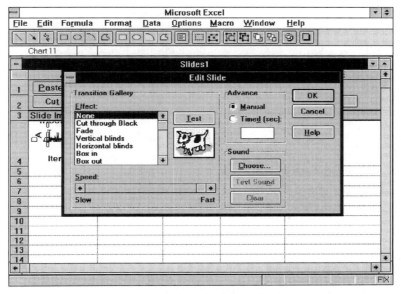

Figure 14.8. The Edit Slide dialog box.

N O T E

Do not use the Cut command to copy the data into the Clipboard. The graphic you use must remain in its original position in the worksheet in order to be used as a slide.

Changing a Slide Show's Defaults

To change a slide show's defaults, click on the Set Defaults button in the template. The Set Defaults dialog box is displayed; it provides you with the same choices as the Edit Slide dialog box. The choices you make will affect any new slides you create.

Editing, Moving, Copying, or Deleting Slides

You can edit the attributes of any slide in a slide show, or move, copy, or delete slides.

Editing a Slide

When you edit a slide, you can change the transition effects in the Edit Slide dialog box. To edit a slide:

1. On the slide show template, select any cell in the row that contains the slide you want to edit.

2. Click on the Edit Slide button to display the Edit Slide dialog box.

3. Choose the options you want in the slide.

4. Click on OK. The new options have been applied to the slide.

Moving a Slide

You can rearrange the order of slides by moving them. To move a slide:

1. On the slide show template, select any cell in the row that contains the slide you want to move.

2. Click on the Cut Row button.

3. Select the row above which you want to insert the slide.

4. Choose the Paste Row button. The slide is pasted above the currently selected row.

Copying a Slide

You can repeat a slide by copying it to another location in the slide show. To copy a slide:

1. On the slide show template, select any cell in the row that contains the slide you want to copy.

2. Click on the Copy Row button.

3. Select the row above which you want to copy the slide.

4. Click on the Paste Row button. The slide is pasted above the currently selected row.

Deleting a Slide

To delete a slide:

1. On the slide show template, select any cell in the row that contains the slide you want to delete.

2. Click on the Delete Row button. The slide is deleted.

Running, Saving, and Opening a Slide Show

When you run a slide show, you can choose to run it only once or have it repeat in a continuous loop until you stop it. You can also choose with which slide to start the show. To run a slide show:

1. On the slide show template, click on the Start Show button. The Start Show dialog box is displayed, as shown in Figure 14.9.

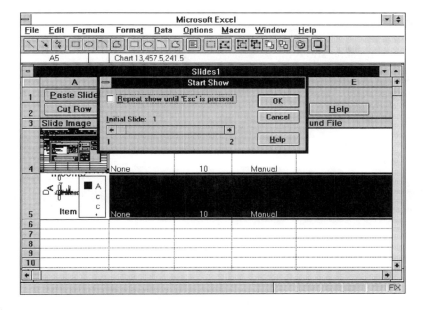

Figure 14.9. The Start Show dialog box.

If you want the show to run in a continuous loop until you stop it, select the Repeat Show Until 'Esc' is Pressed box. If you want to begin with a slide other than the first one, use the Initial Slide bar to select the slide with which you want to begin the show.

2. Select OK. The show will begin running. If you have selected a manual transition in the Edit Slide dialog box, click the left mouse button or press the Spacebar to advance to the next slide.

To interrupt the slide show at any time, press the Esc key. The Slide Show Options dialog box is displayed. Select the options you want.

Saving a Slide Show

To save a slide show:

1. Switch to the slide show template.
2. Click on File in the menu bar to open the File menu.
3. Click on Save to display the Save As dialog box.
4. Give the slide show a name. Excel will automatically add an .XLS extension to slide show documents.
5. Click on OK.

Opening an Existing Slide Show

To open an existing slide show:

1. Click on File in the menu bar to open the File menu.
2. Select the slide show you want to open from the file list.
3. Click on OK to open the slide show.

Review Exercises for Chapter 14

- ◆ Create a series of graphic objects on a new worksheet. Practice moving and sizing the objects.
- ◆ Draw a polygon using the freehand polygon tool. The polygon should have straight lines and freehand lines. Practice editing the polygon. Change the border and fill the polygon with a pattern.
- ◆ Create a slide show using the charts you created in Chapter 12. Copy the charts to pictures before you paste them into the slide show template. Run the slide show on your monitor. Change the transition options between the slides and run the show again.

Before You Go On...

Before you go on to the next chapter you should be familiar with the basics of creating and using graphics. You should be able to copy cells, ranges, charts, and objects to pictures, and you should be able to create, edit, and run a slide show. At this point you should also have a clear understanding of all of the Excel features covered in the book and how they interact with one another.

Chapter 15

USING EXCEL 4.0 WITH MICROSOFT WINDOWS

What You Will Learn in This Chapter

- How to use the Windows Program Manager to track your open applications
- How to switch between two, three, or more open applications
- How to access DOS while in Windows
- Multitasking in Windows
- How to close all open applications in Windows
- How to check for available memory
- What to do when you get an *Unrecoverable Application Error* message

Windows is known as a **graphical user interface** program. This means that instead of having to memorize DOS commands to do things like access a software program, you can click on an icon with your mouse. Excel 4.0 is designed the same way. Instead of having to memorize keystrokes to accomplish a task, you can click on either the menu bar or the tool bars to access features. Because using a mouse is faster than using the keyboard, you can accomplish most tasks very quickly. You can even cut, copy, and paste text at the flick of a click!

Excel 4.0 must be used with Windows. It is not necessary for you to be a Windows expert, but there are certain features you should be familiar with so that you can take advantage of the Windows environment. You should be familiar with the Windows Program Manager: you should know how to switch between Excel and Windows, how to switch between Excel and other applications, how to access DOS from Windows, and how to run applications in background.

Windows Program Manager

When you access Windows you are automatically in the Program Manager. The Program Manager is the area of Windows where you maintain the group windows that contain the icons you use to access your applications. Another one of the Program Manager's jobs is to keep track of all of the applications you are running at one time. When you open Excel 4.0, the Program Manager adds the application to its Task List. When you open another application while you are still in Excel, it adds the new application to the list. To see how the Program Manager works:

1. Double-click on the Excel icon to execute the program. You are now in the Excel worksheet document window.
2. Press Ctrl+Esc. The Program Manager Task List will pop up on your screen.
3. Double-click on Program Manager. You are back in the Program Manager window.
4. Double-click on Dialog Editor in the Excel program group window. The Dialog Editor is displayed in your window.
5. Press Ctrl+Esc. The Program Manager Task List is displayed on the screen. Listed are Microsoft Excel, Program Manager, and Dialog Editor, as shown in Figure 15.1. The Program Manager Task List tells you at a glance what applications are running.
6. Double-click on Microsoft Excel to return to Excel.

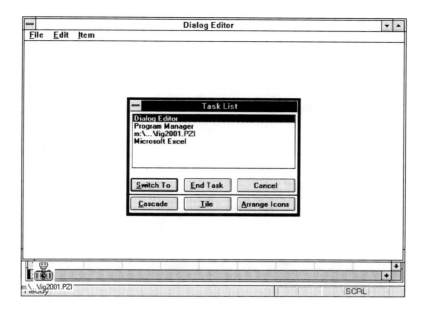

Figure 15.1. The Program Manager Task List.

Switching Between Two Open Applications

To move back and forth between two open applications (for example, Excel and the Dialog Editor):

1. Open the first application.
2. Press Ctrl+Esc to access the Program Manager Task List.
3. Click twice on Program Manager.
4. Open the second application.
5. Press Ctrl+Esc to return to the Program Manager.
6. Double-click on your first application.
7. To switch back and forth between the two applications without using the Program Manager, press Alt+Tab.

Switching Between More Than Two Open Applications

You can, of course, have more than two applications active at the same time in Windows. You can open as many applications as the memory in your computer will allow.

If you have three or more applications open, you cannot use Alt+Tab to switch between them; this works only when switching between the last two applications you accessed. If you do not want to have to go through the Program Manager every time you switch to another program, there is another way. Say, for instance, that you have opened Microsoft Excel, the Excel Dialog Editor, and Excel Q+E. You are currently in the Excel document window and you want to switch to the Dialog Editor.

1. Open your first application (Microsoft Excel).
2. Click on the minimize button in the application window, as shown in Figure 15.2. You are in back in the Program Manager and there is a Microsoft Excel icon at the bottom of your screen, as shown in Figure 15.3.

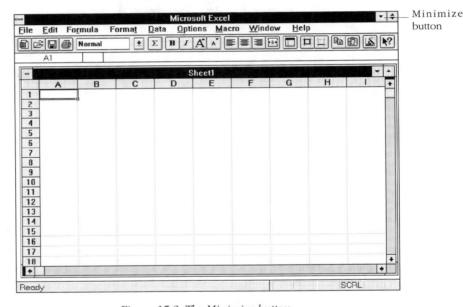

Figure 15.2. The Minimize button.

3. Double-click on Dialog Editor in the Microsoft Excel program group window.
4. When you have finished using the Dialog Editor, click on the minimize button. You are back in the Program Manager and you now have two icons at the bottom of your screen, Microsoft Excel and the Dialog Editor.
5. Double-click on Q+E in the Microsoft Excel program group window.
6. When you are finished using Q+E, click on the minimize button. You are back in the Program Manager and you now have three icons at the bottom of your screen.
7. Double-click on the Microsoft Excel icon. You are now in Microsoft Excel.

You can continue to minimize your applications and select them in the Program Manager by double-clicking on the program icons. You can also use the Alt+Esc key combination to rotate between open applications.

1. Double-click on the Microsoft Excel icon to return the program to a full window (or, if it is no longer open, open it from the Microsoft Excel program group in the Program Manager).

2. Open the Dialog Editor and Q+E the same way.

3. Press Alt+Esc. You have rotated to another open application.

4. Continue to press Alt+Esc to rotate through all of your open applications.

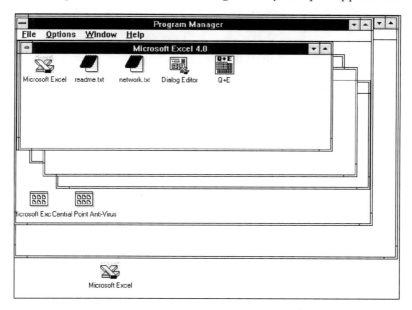

Figure 15.3. The Microsoft Excel icon at the bottom of the Program Manager screen.

Accessing DOS from Windows

Occasionally you will need to access DOS from within Windows. You can do this from any application you are currently in. To access DOS:

1. Click on the minimize button in your window or use the Alt+Esc key combination to return to the Program Manager.

2. Click on Main to open the Main program group.

3. Double-click on the DOS prompt icon.

4. Perform whatever DOS tasks you need to perform.

To return to the Windows Program Manager:

1. Type Exit and press Enter.

2. Double-click on the program icon or, if you did not minimize the window, press Alt+Esc to rotate the open applications.

Multitasking in Windows

Performing several tasks simultaneously on your computer is referred to as **multitasking**. If you want to multitask, you must have at least a 386 computer (your CPU chip is an 80386). If you have a 386 computer, your multitasking capabilities are limited only by the amount of memory your computer has available for each task. As an example of multitasking, assume you have a large database and you are going to sort and select several hundred names and addresses for a mailing while, at the same time, you need to generate your end-of-the-month bills. To add insult to injury you also have a worksheet that must be in the mailbox for the last pickup of the day—one hour from now.

If your computer has enough memory available, you can go into your database program, establish your sort and select criteria, and then, while the database is sorting and selecting, you can switch to your billing program. You can give your billing program the information it needs to generate the bills and send them to the printer. You can then switch to Microsoft Excel and begin to type your worksheet. While you are working on the worksheet, the database is sorting and selecting and the billing program is printing out your bills. By the time you have finished your worksheet and have dropped it in the mailbox, your database is sorted, your bills are printed, and you can take a well-deserved break!

Exiting Applications

You should exit all open applications before you exit Windows. If you try to exit Windows while applications are still open, you will receive an error message. There are several ways to exit open applications:

1. You can exit an application while it is in the active window using the normal commands to exit the program.

2. You can exit an application from the Program Manager Task List. Select the application and click on End Task.

3. You can exit an application while it is minimized to an icon. Click on the icon and select Close.

Memory Problems

Each application you open while you are in Windows uses memory (RAM). In addition, memory is also used by DOS and Windows. You can check to see how much memory you have available in the Windows Program Manager. Click on Help in the menu bar to open the Help menu. Click on About Program Manager. A dialog box will appear telling you what mode you are running in and how much RAM is still available for use. If you are operating Windows on a 386 computer and have more than 2 megabytes of RAM, you should not encounter memory problems often. Windows should automatically manage and allocate enough memory for each application up to the limits of your RAM. If you are constantly getting messages that tell you there is not enough memory to run an application, you will probably have to add more RAM to your computer. If you are running non-Windows applications (programs not designed to be used in Windows), check your Windows manual to find out how to adjust memory allocation in the program information files (PIFs).

Windows Swap File

Windows has a feature called Swap File, which uses available hard drive space when Windows needs more memory. Instead of holding an application in RAM, Windows writes it to the hard drive, thereby freeing up memory for another application. There are two kinds of swap files: temporary and permanent. If you use the Swap File feature, be sure to periodically erase the files from your hard drive, since they take up a great deal of space. For more information on swap files, consult your Windows manual.

Unrecoverable Application Error Messages

Any time you are working in a Windows application you might get an Unrecoverable Application Error message. When this happens, you should exit all open applications, exit Windows, and reboot your computer. You should reboot whenever you receive this message, even if the problem seems to have resolved itself and everything appears to be running normally.

Review Exercises for Chapter 15

- ◆ Open Microsoft Excel from within Windows.
- ◆ Use Ctrl+Esc to access the Program Manager.
- ◆ Open another application.
- ◆ Use Alt+Tab to move between the two programs.
- ◆ Open another application.
- ◆ Use program icons or Alt+Esc to switch between the applications.
- ◆ Go to DOS from the Program Manager.
- ◆ Type Exit and return to Windows.
- ◆ Exit all open applications.

Congratulations!

You have completed the last chapter of *Teach Yourself... Excel 4.0*. You should now be able to enjoy the many exciting features the program offers.

Appendix A

INSTALLATION AND CONFIGURATION

This appendix details the requirements necessary to run Excel 4.0, and explains how to install the program on your computer, and how to configure it for your special needs.

System Requirements

Excel 4.0 for Windows will run on any Industry Standard Architecture (ISA) computer such as an IBM PC/AT or compatible, or any Micro Channel Architecture (MCA) computer, such as an IBM Personal System/2 or compatible, as long as the computer is capable of running Microsoft Windows, version 3.0 or later (at least a 20826 or higher processor). Your video card and monitor should be capable of supporting graphics (EGA, VGA, or Hercules graphics card).

Hard Disk Requirements

You must have a hard disk to run Excel 4.0. It will not run off of floppy disks. Your hard disk must have at least 5 megabytes of free space to install the program (full program installation requires 11 megabytes of free space). Although you can store documents on floppy disks, it is advisable to keep them on the hard disk, which means that you should have enough additional space to store your files. When you run the Setup program to install Excel 4.0, you will receive a message telling you how much space is required to run the program, and how much space is available on your hard disk. If you do not have enough space left, you will have to delete files in order to free up space.

Floppy Disk Requirements

You must have at least one floppy disk drive to install the program from disks. The program is shipped with high-density disks. It is available on low-density disks, but they must be specially ordered from Microsoft.

Memory Requirements

In order to run Excel 4.0, you must also run Microsoft Windows and DOS. The minimum memory allocation for all of these programs is 2 megabytes. If you have any other programs running at the same time, or if you plan to multitask, you should have at least 4 megabytes of RAM in your computer. If you run out of memory while trying to use an application, Windows will prompt you with an Insufficient Memory error message.

Mouse Requirements

You should have a mouse to work with Excel 4.0. Some features of the program will not work without one (such as toolbars). Excel will automatically recognize your mouse when the program is installed.

Software Requirements

To run Excel 4.0, you must have Microsoft Windows, version 3.0 or later, running in standard or enhanced mode. You must also have Microsoft or IBM DOS, version 3.0 or later.

Installing Excel 4.0

Before you install Excel 4.0, you must be running Microsoft Windows on your computer. Windows must be running in standard or enhanced mode.

When you install Excel 4.0, a Microsoft Excel 4.0 program group will be set up in the

Windows Program Manager. To install Microsoft Excel 4.0:

1. Start Microsoft Windows in standard or enhanced mode.
2. Insert the Excel 4.0 disk labeled *Setup* in drive A or B.
3. Click on File in the menu bar of the Program Manager to open the File menu.
4. Choose Run.
5. Type *a:setup* or *b:setup* (depending upon which floppy drive you are using).
6. Press Enter.
7. Choose Complete, Custom, or Minimum setup (this book does not cover Network installation).

    ◆ **Complete Setup**. When you choose Complete Setup, Excel and all of the optional files and groups are installed in the default directory you choose.

    ◆ **Custom Setup**. When you choose Custom Setup, you can choose which of the optional files or groups you wish to install. Optional files that are not installed can be installed later if they are needed.

    ◆ **Minimum Setup**. When you choose Minimum Setup, only the files needed to run Excel are installed. None of the optional files will be installed. Choose this option only if you need to save space on your hard drive.

8. Excel will ask for each disk it needs and will guide you through the rest of the installation.

Printers

Printers used in Excel are installed in Microsoft Windows. Excel will automatically identify and use any printer that has been installed in Windows. To install a printer in Windows:

1. Click on Window in the menu bar to open the Window menu.
2. Click on Main to open the Main group window.
3. Double click on Control Panel.
4. Double click on Printers to display the Printers dialog box.
5. Click on Add Printers. The Printers dialog box expands to include a List of Printers list box. If you have never installed a printer in Windows, the List of Printers list box will automatically be included in the Printers dialog box.
6. Select your printer from the list.
7. Click on Install. You will probably be asked to insert a Windows program disk into the A drive so that Windows can copy the printer driver from the disk to your hard drive.
8. Once the printer driver is installed, click on the Configure button to display the Configure dialog box.

9. Click on the I/O printer port you are using. The default is LPT1.

10. Click on OK to return to the Printer dialog box. The name of the port you selected appears to the right of the printer name.

11. Click on Configure to display the Configure dialog box.

12. Click on Setup to display the Setup dialog box containing the name of your printer and printer port selection.

13. Since each printer driver can be used with more than one type of printer, you must tell Windows exactly what printer you will be using. Open the Printer drop-down list and select the name of your printer.

14. The rest of the options in the Setup dialog box allow you to change the default settings for your printer and to install print cartridges and soft fonts for your computer if it is capable of using them. The options available to you are determined by your printer. All of the possible options are:

    ◆ **Paper Source**. If your printer has more than one tray, you can select the default printer bin. You can also select whether the paper will be fed manually or by tractor feed. The choices available to you will vary depending upon the printer you are using.

    ◆ **Paper Size**. The default is for 8.5-by-11 inch paper. You can change this default size. Windows has seven papers sizes available.

    ◆ **Memory**. This option allows you to tell Windows how much memory your printer has. Windows will automatically choose the default memory for your printer.

    ◆ **Orientation**. This option allows you to choose whether the default paper orientation for your printer will be portrait or landscape.

    ◆ **Cartridges**. The Cartridges box lists all of the possible font cartridges you can use for your printer, and tells you how many cartridges you can plug into your printer at the same time. If your printer has only one cartridge, click on the name of the cartridge in the list box. If your printer has two cartridges plugged into it, select both cartridges by holding down the Shift key and clicking on the names. These fonts will appear in the Font dialog box in Excel.

    ◆ **Graphics Resolution**. If your printer is capable of printing graphics in more than one resolution, you can choose low resolution (the printout quality is not as good, but printing is faster) or high resolution.

    ◆ **Copies**. This option controls the number of copies of each page you print. The default is 1.

    ◆ **Fonts**. When you click on the Fonts button, the Fonts Installer dialog box is displayed. If you want to add soft fonts to your printer's capabilities, you must have first installed them on the computer. Once they are installed, you can configure the Windows printer driver to recognize them.

To add a font, click on Add Fonts to display the Add Fonts dialog box. You will be asked to insert a disk or to tell Excel the path where the soft fonts are located. A list of available fonts appears in the Source list box on the left of the Font Installer dialog box. Select the font you want Windows to recognize, and click on Add. The Add Fonts dialog box is displayed with a default directory path for the font you are adding. Unless you have a reason to change the default, accept it and click on OK. You will be prompted if the directory does not exist. Confirm that you want Windows to create the directory. The font now appears in the list box on the right side of the Font Installer dialog box. Continue to add each font you want to use in Windows. You must tell Windows whether you want to download the font with each print job or have the font present when printing begins.

If you want to download the font with each print job, you don't have to do anything. This is the default selection for each font. If you want to have one or more fonts present when printing begins, you will have to change the default. In the Font Installer dialog box, select the font you want to be present when the print job begins. Click on Permanent. Continue selecting fonts and clicking on Permanent until you have selected all of the fonts you want to be present when printing begins. Click on Exit. The Download Options dialog box is displayed. Select both options and click on OK. The fonts you have selected as permanent will be downloaded to your printer and will remain in the printer's memory until you turn the printer off. Each time you turn on your computer and printer, the fonts will automatically be downloaded. The advantage of choosing to have fonts automatically downloaded is that you do not have to wait for the font to download every time you print. However, you must have enough memory in your printer to hold all of the fonts that you select this way. The fonts you have selected will now appear in the Excel Font dialog box.

◆ **Options**. Some printers have additional options available. These options are dependent upon the printer.

Using Startup Switches

Startup switches allow you to start Excel and open a document at the same time, change to a different directory when you start Excel, open a file as read only, or prevent Excel from creating the default SHEET1.XLS worksheet. You can type the startup switch every time you start Excel, or you can change the Excel icon in the Excel group window and have the startup switch automatically execute when you start Excel. The syntax used to tell Excel to use a startup switch is as follows:

Syntax	**To Accomplish**
excel.exe filename	Opens a specific file. For example, excel.exe incjan.xls tells Excel to open the incjan.xls worksheet when the program is started. If the file you want to open is in a different directory than Excel, you must include the entire path and filename. For example, if the incjan.xls worksheet is located in the C:\INCOME directory, you would type excel.exe c:\income\incjan.xls to start Excel and open the incjan.xls at the same time.
excel.exe /r filename	Opens a specific file as read only. If the file you want to open as read only is in a different directory than Excel, you must include the entire path and filename. For example, if the incjan.xls worksheet is located in the C:\INCOME directory, you would type excel.exe r/ c:\income\incjan.xls to start Excel and open the incjan.xls worksheet as read only at the same time.
excel.exe /p directory path	Specifies a different default directory than Excel. For example, to change the default directory (the directory that Excel uses when you start the program) to C:\INCOME instead of C:\EXCEL, you would type excel.exe /p c:\income
excel.exe /e	Stops Excel from creating the default SHEET1.XLS worksheet when you start the program.

Using a Startup Switch Occasionally

If you want to start Excel and use a startup switch occasionally, you can do so from Windows:

1. Click on File in the menu bar to open the File menu.
2. Click on Run to display the Run dialog box.
3. In the Command Line text box, type the full path for Excel plus the startup switch you want to use. For example, to change the default directory from C:\EXCEL to C:\INCOME, you would type *c:\excel\ excel.exe /p c:\income.*
4. Click on OK.

Excel will start using the startup switch you specified.

Using a Startup Switch Permanently

You can make any of the startup switches permanent. This way, every time you start Excel, it will use the startup switch you have specified, and you will not have to type the command. You must change the Excel icon's properties in Windows to make a startup switch permanent:

1. Click on Window in the Program Manager menu bar to open the Window menu.
2. Click on Excel 4.0.
3. In the Excel group window, click once on Microsoft Excel.
4. Click on File in the Program Manager menu bar to open the File menu.
5. Click on Properties to display the Properties dialog box.
6. Add the startup switch you want to use in the Command Line text box. For example, to start Excel without the SHEET1.XLS worksheet, you would edit the Command Line text box to read: *c:\excel\excel.exe /e.*

Appendix **B**

CONVERSION

Files created by programs other than Excel and Lotus 1-2-3 cannot be read by Excel for Windows. Before any files created by other programs can be used in Excel for Windows, they must be opened and converted into an Excel form. Excel has come up with a very simple conversion process, and has made it equally easy to convert an Excel file to another format.

Converting a File to an Excel Format

1. Click on File in the menu bar to open the File menu.
2. Click on Open to display the Open dialog box.
3. Type the path and filename of the file you want to open and convert.
4. If the file you want to open has been converted into a text format, choose the Text button in the Open dialog box. The Text File Options dialog box is displayed, with a choice of delimiter characters you can use to divide the text into cells. Each line in a text file represents one row. Data within each row is divided into cells based upon the delimiter character used in the text. For example, data exported from dBase

401

(where the database records include two fields, firstname and lastname) as comma delimited text looks like this:

```
"Phyllis","Romanski"
"Susan","Rothenberg"
```

Each row contains the data for two fields. The data is surrounded by quotation marks (" ") and each field is separated by a comma (,). When the data is imported into Excel as comma-delimited text, the data in each row will be separated into cells and columns depending upon the location of the comma. *Phyllis* would be located in cell A1, *Romanski* in cell B1, *Susan* in cell A2, and *Rothenberg* in cell B2. In the Column Delimiter box, select the delimiter character that was used to separate data in the text. If you select None, the data will not be separated into cells and columns and you will have to parse the data after it is imported. Parsing is discussed later in this appendix. If the delimiter character is not listed, select the Custom option and type the delimiter character in the Custom text box.

5. Click on OK.
6. Your file is now in the document window.
7. Click on File in the menu bar to open the File menu.
8. Click on Save As to display the Save As dialog box.
9. Choose Normal in the Save File As Type drop-down box.
10. Type in the new path and filename for your file.
11. Choose OK.

The file has been saved in an Excel format.

Converting Excel Files to Another Format

To convert Excel files to another format:

1. Click on File in the menu bar to open the File menu.
2. Click on Save As to display the Save As dialog box.
3. Type the name of the file you want to save in the File Name text box.
4. In the Save File As Type drop-down box, select the format you want to use for your file.
5. Click on OK.

If you want to export cells as space-delimited text (text with spaces separating the fields), you must use the Flat File add-in macro. Exporting cells as space-delimited text is discussed later in this chapter.

N O T E

The following table shows a list of formats for which Excel opens and saves documents.

Format	Type of document
Normal	Microsoft Excel version 4.0
Template	Microsoft Excel version 4.0 template
Excel 3.0	Microsoft Excel version 3.0
Excel 2.x	Microsoft Excel for Windows version 2.1, Microsoft Excel for the Macintosh version 2.2, or Microsoft Excel for OS/2 version 2.2
SYLK	Symbolic link format (Microsoft Multiplan)
Text	ANSI text for Windows, Text for DOS or the Macintosh
CSV	Comma separated values (comma-delimited text); ANSI text for Windows, Text for DOS or the Macintosh
WKS	Lotus 1-2-3 release 1A
WK1	Lotus 1-2-3 release 2.x
FMT	Formatting information in the WYSIWYG add-in for Lotus 1-2-3 release 2.x (opened or saved as a WK1 file)
WK3	Lotus 1-2-3 release 3.x and Lotus 1-2-3 for Windows
FM3	Formatting information for Lotus 1-2-3 for Windows and for the WYSIWYG add-in for Lotus 1-2-3 release 3.1 (opened or saved as a WK3 file version 4.0)
DIF	Data interchange format (VisiCalc)
DBF 2	dBase II
DBF 3	dBase III
DBF 4	dBase IV

Parsing Imported Text into Cells and Columns

If you import text data into Excel and do not use a delimiter character to separate the data into cells and columns, all of the data in each row will be imported as one cell entry, and will be one column wide. You must **parse**, or separate, the data into separate cells and columns. Excel has two different methods of parsing data, depending upon whether the imported data contains spaces to fill fields and make all the entries in that field the same length, or whether the field lengths are variable.

Parsing Data with Matching Field Lengths

To parse data with matching field lengths:

1. Select the range that contains the data you want to parse. The range can include any amount of rows, but can be only one column wide.
2. Click on Data in the menu bar to open the Data menu.
3. Click on Parse to display the Parse dialog box. The Parse Line text box shows the contents of the first cell in the range with brackets ([]) inserted in the text to show where text will be separated. All of the characters enclosed in a set of brackets will be placed together in a cell. The parse settings for the first cell will be used for all of the rows in the selected range. If you do not want the parse settings for the first cell to be used for every row in the range, you must parse using the Flat File macro, as explained in the next section in this chapter.
4. Edit the brackets to enclose the characters you want to keep together. Excel will separate the fields depending upon the number of characters enclosed in each set of brackets. For example, the Parse Line text *[cats] [dogs] [totals]* will separate the data into three cells; each of the first two cells will contain four characters, and the last cell will contain six characters. The data in every row in the selected range will be separated, with four characters in each of the first two cells, and six characters in the third cell. To remove all brackets, choose the Clear button. To return the brackets to their original position, choose the Guess button.
5. In the Destination text box, type the address of the cell where you want to place the first field of parsed data. Additional rows of parsed data will be placed in the rows below the destination cell.
6. Click on OK.

Parsing Data with Variable Length Fields

If the data you imported does not have the same length for all of the entries in a field, or if you want each row to be treated independently, you must use the Flat File add-in macro provided by Excel to parse your data. This macro places each logical word in its own cell.

1. Open the FLATFILE.XLA add-in macro. This file is located in the Library directory of Excel.
2. Select the range that contains the data you want to parse. The range can include any number of rows, but can be only one column wide.
3. Click on Data in the menu bar to open the Data menu.
4. Click on Smart Parse to display the Smart Parse dialog box.
5. Under Column Delimiter, select the option you want to use to separate the text in the selected range. For example, if you select Blank Space [ ], Excel will separate

each group of characters that is separated by one or more spaces into a separate cell. This action will apply to every selected row in the range.

6. Select the Remove Extra Blank Spaces check box if you want to remove extra blank spaces between words.

7. Click on OK.

N O T E

When you parse data, Excel fills the cells to the right of the destination column until all of the data has been separated. If there is data in those cells, it will be overwritten.

Exporting Cells as Space-Delimited Text

If you want to export your data into a text file in which data is separated by spaces instead of tabs or commas, you must use the Flat File add-in macro. The macro will export only the number of characters in a column equal to the whole number (or number rounded to the lower whole number) of the column width. For example, if the width of column A is 14.5, only the first 14 characters in the column will be exported. If you want any characters included in the last .5 width of the column, you must increase your column width to 15.

1. Open the FLATFILE.XLA add-in macro.

2. Select the adjacent range that contains the data you want to export as space-delimited text.

3. Click on Data in the menu bar to open the Data menu.

4. Click on Export to display the Export dialog box.

5. In the To File Name text box, type the name of the text file you want to create.

6. Select the Retain Cell Formats check box if you want the exported data to retain the alignment and number formats of the selected cells. If you select this option, one extra space will be inserted in the text between columns. If you do not want to retain the alignment and number formats, clear the Retain Cell Formats check box. When the Retain Cell Formats check box is cleared, no extra spaces are inserted in the text between columns.

7. Click on Export.

Your data has been exported as a text file with spaces separating the text between columns.

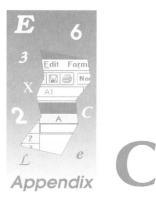

MICROSOFT EXCEL AND LOTUS 1-2-3

If you are a Lotus 1-2-3 user who has just switched to Excel, or if a friend has given you a Lotus 1-2-3 worksheet and you want to use it in Excel, you are in luck! Opening and using a Lotus worksheet in Excel is almost as simple as opening an Excel worksheet. When you open the worksheet, Excel automatically recognizes the Lotus formats and imports the worksheet into Excel. Lotus macros created on a Lotus worksheet can also be run on a worksheet imported into Excel.

Opening Lotus 1-2-3 Worksheets

To open a Lotus 1-2-3 Worksheet:

1. Click on File in the menu bar.
2. Click on Open to display the Open dialog box.
3. In the List Files of Type box, select Lotus 1-2-3 files.
4. If the worksheet you want to open is not in the current directory, select the drive or directory where the worksheet is located in either the Drives or Directories drop-down box, and click on OK. **Or,** type the full path for the location of the Lotus worksheet in the File Name text box and click on OK.
5. Select the Lotus worksheet you want to open in the File Name list box.
6. Click on OK.
7. If you see a message informing you that a formula was not imported, click on OK. Excel will substitute the result of a formula for any formula that cannot be imported.

When you open a Lotus worksheet in Excel, Alternate Formula Entry and Alternate Expression Evaluation are automatically turned on. Alternate Formula Entry means that any formula or function entered in a Lotus worksheet is automatically translated into an Excel formula or function, and formulas automatically reapply names or revert names to references. When Alternate Expression Evaluation is turned on, Excel calculates formulas and database criteria according to Lotus rules.

N O T E

If the Lotus worksheet you imported has an associated .FMT or .FM3 file to provide for WYSIWYG (What-You-See-Is-What-You-Get) formatting, it will automatically be opened with the worksheet. The file must have the same name, and be in the same directory, as the Lotus worksheet.

Saving Lotus Worksheets as Excel Worksheets

1. Click on File in the menu bar.
2. Click on Save As to display the Save As dialog box.
3. Change the Save File as Type to Normal.
4. In the File Name text box, type the path and name of the file.
5. Click on OK.

NOTE

When you save a Lotus worksheet containing macros as an Excel worksheet, you can continue to run the macros on the Excel worksheet.

Importing and Exporting

Exporting Excel Worksheets to Lotus 1-2-3

You can save your Excel worksheets in a Lotus format. Embedded charts will be saved with the .FMT and .FM3 files. Any features in your Excel worksheet that are not supported by Lotus, such as graphic objects, will not be saved in a Lotus format. To export your worksheet:

1. Click on File in the menu bar.
2. Click on Save As to display the Save As dialog box.
3. Change the Save File as Type to the Lotus format you want.
4. In the File Name text box, type the path and name of the file.
5. Click on OK.
6. If you see a message informing you that a formula was not imported, click on OK. Usually, Excel will substitute the value of the formula in the Lotus file.

When you save an Excel worksheet in a Lotus format, all of the formatting is automatically saved in an .FMT or .FM3 file. The .FMT or .FM3 file will have the same name, and be located in the same directory, as the Lotus worksheet.

The following is a list of Lotus 1-2-3 formats from and to which Excel can import and export worksheets.

Lotus 1-2-3 Release	File Format
1A	WKS
2.0, 2,01, 2.2	WK1
2.3	WK1, FMT
3.0	WK3
3.1, 3.1+, 1-2-3/W	WK3, FM3

When you open a Lotus worksheet in Excel, the associated .FMT or .FM3 file is automatically opened. Drop shadows and objects drawn on top of charts will not import, and double underlines and wide underlines appear as single underlines in Excel. Even though an .FMT or .FM3 file is automatically saved when you save a Lotus worksheet in Excel, you can save only the first eight styles and the first eight fonts you use on the worksheet.

Importing Text Files

To import a text file from Lotus to Excel:

1. Click on File in the menu bar.
2. Click on Open to display the Open dialog box.
3. Select the file you want to open.
4. Click on the Text button. The Text File Options dialog box is displayed.
5. Select the character that tells Excel how the text is to be **parsed**, or separated, into columns. If the character you want to use does not exist, select the Custom option button and type the character you want. If you select None, all of the text will be placed in one column when the file is opened in Excel.
6. Click on OK in the Text File Options dialog box.
7. Click on OK in the Open dialog box. The text file, parsed to your specifications, is opened in Excel.

Importing Macro and Range Names

If a macro name exists on a Lotus worksheet imported into Excel, Excel imports all of the range names and their references for that worksheet, and automatically turns on Alternate Formula Entry.

Importing and Exporting Formulas

Excel attempts to import and export all formulas in Lotus and Excel worksheets. If Excel finds a formula it cannot import or export, it substitutes the result of the formula.

Importing and Exporting 3-D Worksheets

When you open a .WK3 file in Excel, 3-D worksheets are imported as a workbook file. If the .WK# file is a single-sheet file, it will open as a .WK3 file, and will not convert to a workbook file. Excel exports workbooks as multiple-sheet .WK3 files.

Importing Cell Comments

In a .WK3 file, any characters following a semicolon in a formula are imported by Excel as a text note.

Importing and Exporting Numbers and Labels

Excel imports and exports all numbers and labels.

Importing and Exporting References

Any Excel formula that contains a reference to multiple nonadjacent selections will not be exported. Functions that produce references as a result are not exported to Lotus 1A. The Excel intersection (space) and union (.) operators will not export to Lotus. Excel substitutes the value of the formula for formulas that contain these operators.

When you save an Excel worksheet to a Lotus format, any references to rows beyond 2048 (for .WKS format) or 8192 (for .WK1 and .WK3 formats) wrap to the top of the worksheet. For example, if you save a reference to row 2049 in a .WKS format, the reference changes to A1 in Lotus.

Importing and Exporting External References

Lotus 1-2-3 releases 1A and 2.01 do not support file linking (external references). Any Excel worksheet formula containing these references is not exported to .WKS or .WK! formats. Usually, Excel substitutes the value of the formula.

Importing and Exporting Logical Values

Excel True and False functions change to the Lotus 1-2-3 functions @True and @False, and vice versa.

Importing and Exporting Error Values

The Excel constant error value #N/A is exported to Lotus as the @NA function. All other constant error values are exported as @ERR. The Lotus @ERR function is imported to Excel as #VALUE!, and the @NA error function is imported as #N/A.

Exporting Named Ranges

Lotus does not support named constant values or named formulas. As a result, they are not exported by Excel. Instead, formulas that use those names will contain the constant or formula, enclosed in parentheses if necessary.

Importing and Exporting Operators

The following table shows the operators used by Excel and Lotus in descending order of evaluation.

Excel Operators	Lotus Operators
AND, OR, NOT functions	
+ or – (unary)	∧
∧	+ or - (unary)
* or /	* or /
+ or -	+ or -
&	= < > <= >= <>
= < > <= >= <>	#NOT# (unary)
	#AND# #OR#
	& (Release 2.0 or later)

In Lotus, the exponentiation operator (∧) is evaluated before the negation operator (–). In Excel negation is evaluated first. Thus, the formula =–2∧4 produces the value –16 in Lotus and 16 in Excel. To circumvent this problem, use parentheses to force the correct order of evaluation.

Importing and Exporting Tables

The formulas and values in the top row and left column of a table, as well as the values within the table, are imported to and exported from Excel. If you want Excel to automatically calculate the tables, you will probably have to identify them as tables again. To do this, use the Table command on the Data menu.

Lotus 1-2-3 Release 3.0 has 3-D tables that contain 3-D indexes and lookups. Only the values of these tables are imported to Excel.

Importing and Exporting Databases

The Excel database, criteria, and extract ranges are all imported to and exported from Excel. There are minor differences in the ways Excel and Lotus interpret database criteria. However, when you open a Lotus worksheet in Excel, Alternate Expression Evaluation is automatically turned on, and database criteria are evaluated according the Lotus rules.

Excel database functions DPRODUCT and DCOUNTA have no equivalent in Lotus. The Lotus function @DQUERY has no equivalent in Excel. When Excel imports or exports these functions, the values resulting from the functions are substituted for the functions themselves.

Importing and Exporting Number Formats

The following table shows how Excel imports Lotus number formats.

Lotus Format	Excel Format
*/-	General_)
Comma, 0 decimals	#,##0_);(#,##0)
Comma, 2 decimals	#,##0.00_);(#,##0.00)
Currency, 2 decimals	$#,##0.00_);($#,##0.00)
Date1 (dd-mmm-yy)	d-mmm-yy
Date2 (dd-mmm)	d-mmm
Date3 (mmm-yy)	mmm-yy
Fixed, 0 decimals	0
Fixed, 2 decimals	0.00
General	General_)
Hidden (Release 2.0 or later)	;;
Percent, 0 decimals	0%
Percent, 2 decimals	0.00%
Scientific, 0 decimal	0E+00_)
Scientific, 2 decimals	0.00E+00
Text	General_)

Importing and Exporting Alignment Formats

Right, Left, Center, and Fill alignments are imported to and exported from Excel. When they are exported to Lotus, all nontext cells are right-aligned.

Importing and Exporting Cell Protection

Protected cells are imported to and exported from Excel. Hidden formulas in Excel are visible when they are exported to Lotus.

Importing and Exporting Calculation Options

Automatic and manual calculation remains the same when imported to and exported from Excel. If calculation is set to Automatic Except Tables in the Calculation Options dialog box, it changes to automatic when it is exported to Lotus.

Linking Lotus and Excel Worksheets

You can link values from a Lotus worksheet to an Excel worksheet without importing the Lotus worksheet into Excel. To link values from a Lotus worksheet to an Excel worksheet:

1. Open both the Lotus and Excel worksheets.
2. Switch to the Lotus worksheet.
3. Select the cell or range containing the data you want to link to the Excel worksheet.
4. Click on Edit in the menu bar.
5. Click on Copy.
6. Switch to the Excel worksheet.
7. Select the cell or the upper-left corner of the range you want to contain the linked data.
8. Click on Edit in the menu bar.
9. Click on Paste Link. A formula is entered in each cell that links the worksheets.

When you change the data in your Lotus worksheet, the linked cells are automatically updated when you open the Excel worksheet.

NOTE

If you try to edit one or more of the cells in the Excel worksheet into which you pasted linked data from a Lotus worksheet, you will receive a message informing you that you cannot change part of an array. If you want to be able to clear or move individual cells, you must copy and link each cell individually.

Running Lotus Macros in Excel

You can open your Lotus worksheet in Excel and run the macros contained on that worksheet. You can open any Lotus file format (.WKS, .WK1, or .WK3) in Excel and run Lotus macros with menu commands, functions, keywords, and advanced macro commands that are compatible with Lotus 1-2-3 release 2.01 and some Release 2.2 functionality.

The name you assigned your macro in Lotus is defined in Excel as a Lotus macro name. You can run any macro that is assigned a name consisting of a backslash (\) followed by a single letter. Excel assigns a lowercase letter to each macro name. Excel does not support range names that begin with a backslash. Therefore, you can edit your Lotus macros in Excel, but you cannot create new Lotus macros in Excel. If you save your Lotus worksheet in an Excel format, you can continue to run the Lotus macros imported with the worksheet. To run a Lotus macro in Excel:

1. Click on File in the menu bar.
2. Click on Open to display the Open dialog box.

3. In the File Name text box, type the path and filename of the Lotus worksheet you want to open.

4. Click on OK.

5. Press Ctrl+the letter of the macro name.

Excel will run your macro. While your macro is running, MI (Macro Interpreter) appears in the status bar. If your macro contains a (?) command, MI Pause appears in the status bar until you press Enter, at which time the macro will continue.

Excel does not understand and does not run macros that contain menu commands specific to Lotus release 2.2 and later, such as /File Admin. Lotus add-ins are not supported by Excel. Remove any occurrence of keystrokes or command names that attach, start ,or use a Lotus add-in. When you run a Lotus macro in Excel, the macro cannot end in a menu. If **N O T E** the macro ends in a menu you will be prompted and the macro will terminate. Macros can, however, end in a prompt for information.

Translating Lotus Macros into Excel Macros

You can use the Macro Translation Assistant to translate Lotus macros into Excel macros. The Macro Translation Assistant cannot translate Excel macros into Lotus macros. To use the Macro Translation Assistant to translate a Lotus macro:

1. Click on the Control Menu in the Excel application window.

2. Click on Run to display the Run dialog box.

3. Select the Macro Translator option button.

4. Click on OK. The Macro Translation Assistant window is displayed.

5. Click on Translate in the menu bar to open the Translate menu.

6. Select Lotus 1-2-3. The Select Source Sheet list box appears.

7. Select the Lotus worksheet containing the macros you want to translate.

8. Click on OK. The Select Macro(s) To Translate list box appears.

9. Select the macro you want to translate.

10. Click on OK.

If the Macro Translation Assistant cannot translate a function, it inserts a message describing the action performed by the function. You must replace it with an Excel function that performs the same action.

If you enable the Verbose check box in the Select Macros To Translate dialog box, Excel copies the original macro into the translated macro. This is helpful if there is a problem with the translated macro, since you also have a copy of the original to act as a guide.

N O T E

Running Translated Lotus Macros

1. Click on File in the menu bar.
2. Click on Open to display the Open dialog box.
3. Select the macro sheet containing the macro you want to run.
4. Click on OK.
5. Click on Macro in the menu bar.
6. Click on Run to display the Run Macro dialog box.
7. Select the macro you want to run.
8. Click on OK.

Specifying Default Lotus Worksheet Settings in Excel

You can enter statements in the EXCEL4.INI file to customize some of the default settings used by Excel. The EXCEL4.INI file is a text file and can be edited with a text editor or word processor, or by using the DOS line editor. You must, however, save the file as a text file without any formatting when you are finished editing it.

You can change the way Excel opens and saves Lotus worksheets by changing the elements in the EXCEL4.INI file. You set the defaults by specifying different values for the statements listed in the EXCEL4.INI file. After you have changed the file, you must exit Excel and restart the program for the changes to take effect.

The following statements and default values are automatically entered into the [WK? Settings] section of the EXCEL4.INI file when you install Excel. The [WK? Settings] section controls the opening and saving of Lotus worksheets in Excel.

◆ **WYSIWYG_Save=1**. This statement specifies whether or not you want an .FMT or .FM3 file to be saved when you save its associated Lotus file. The default is yes. To change the default to no and ignore all .FMT or .FM3 files when you save a Lotus worksheet, change the default value in the WYSIWYG_Save statement to 0 (WYSIWYG_Save=0).

◆ **Load_Chart_Wnd=1**. This statement specifies how Lotus charts are created when an associated Lotus chart is opened in Excel. The default in Excel is to automatically create charts. To change the default, change the value to 0 (Load_Chart_Wnd=0).

◆ **AFE=2**. This statement specifies how Lotus range names are imported when a Lotus worksheet is opened in Excel. By default, Excel turns on alternate formula entry only if a macro name exists on the Lotus worksheet you open. To specify that the alternate formula entry always be turned on, change the statement to AFE=1. To specify that alternate formula entry never be automatically turned on, change the statement to AFE=0.

◆ **Monospace=1**. This statement specifies the default font for your imported worksheet. The default font for Lotus worksheets is 10 point Courier. If you want to change the default to the normal Excel default font, change the statement to Monospace=0.

◆ **Gridlines=0**. This statement specifies whether or not gridlines are displayed when you open a Lotus worksheet in Excel. By default, Excel does not display gridlines. If you want gridlines, change the Gridlines statement to Gridlines=1.

If you want to change global settings in Excel, refer to Appendix A.

Appendix **D**

THE WINDOWS FILE MANAGER

The Windows File Manager allows you to list all of your directories and subdirectories; list the files in a specified directory; delete, copy, move, and rename files; and create and change directories. The File Manager also allows you to open files in Excel, print files, and search one or more directories for files containing specified words or phrases. You can access the File Manager by clicking on the File Manager icon in the Main program group in the Windows Program Manager.

Using the File Manager

To access the File Manager from your Excel document window:

1. Press Ctrl+Esc to access the Windows Task List.
2. Double-click on Program Manager.
3. Click on Window in the Program Manager menu bar.
4. Click on Main to access the Main program group.
5. Double-click on File Manager.

A directory tree is displayed listing all of the files, directories, and subdirectories in the root directory of your hard drive (C:\).

Changing Directories

To change from the root directory to another directory (such as EXCEL), double-click on the directory or subdirectory you wish to access. A listing of all of the files and subdirectories in the C:\EXCEL directory appears on your directory tree.

Opening Files

To open an Excel file when the file is located in the same directory as the program files, first change the directory to EXCEL, then simply double-click on the file name. Excel will open, and the file will be displayed in the document window.

To open an Excel file when the file is located in a subdirectory of the directory containing the program files, first change directories so that the file you wish to open is in the directory tree, then double-click on the filename. Excel is started up and the file you opened is displayed in the Excel document window.

To open an Excel file from the File Manager, when the file is not located in the directory that contains the program files or in a subdirectory of that directory:

1. Click on the file you wish to open.
2. Click on File in the File Manager menu bar.
3. Click on Run to display the Run dialog box.
4. Type the full path and name of the executable file (the main program file). If you installed Excel using the standard installation, type *C:\EXCEL\EXCEL.EXE*. Excel appears on your screen. The document window contains the default worksheet document window.
5. Click on File in the Excel menu bar.
6. Click on Open to display a list of the files in the directory you chose.
7. Double-click on the file you wish to open.

When you save a file that has been opened in a changed directory, Excel will automatically save it to the same directory.

WARNING

If you have accessed the File Manager while Excel is active, do not open an Excel file from the File Manager. Doing so will execute Excel twice, making two versions of the program active at the same time. This is a recipe for confusion and trouble.

Creating Directories

You will usually want to create more than one directory in order to organize your files logically. Generally, file directories are located as subdirectories under the directory containing the program files. Creating all of your data subdirectories in the same directory will save you the trouble of having to search for them. If you have been working your way consecutively through this book, you have created several documents, which are probably located in your EXCEL directory. Create a separate directory named DATA for them now; later we will use the File Manager to move all of them to their new home. To create a new directory from within the File Manager:

1. Double-click on Excel. A list of all of the files and subdirectories in the EXCEL directory appears on your directory tree.
2. Click on Create Directory to display the Create Directory dialog box.
3. The Current Directory should be C:\EXCEL. If so, just type *Data* in the New Directory text box. If the Current Dir. is not C:\EXCEL, type *C:\EXCEL\DATA* in the New Directory text box.
5. Select OK.

The new subdirectory name now appears in the current directory tree.

N O T E

Path and directory names are not case-sensitive. You can type them in uppercase or lowercase, or any combination of the two.

The usual method of naming directories is by category. For example, a student might create a directory called SCHOOL and another called PERSONAL. An accountant with several clients might create directories such as CLIENT1, CLIENT2, CLIENT3, and so on. You cannot use spaces or more than eight characters in a directory name. If you try to enter a space in a directory name, the File Manager will replace it with an underline; if you try to use more than eight letters, the File Manager will shorten your directory name. For example, CLIENT 1 would become CLIENT_1, and LITIGATION would become LITIGATI.

Deleting Files

Eventually you will want to delete files from your computer. It is amazing how quickly they can multiply and how much space they will take up. To delete a file from a directory:

1. Make sure you are in the correct directory. If you are not, change directories.
2. From the directory tree, select the file you want to delete.

3. Click on File.

4. Click on Delete to display the Delete dialog box. The file you have selected will be listed in the Delete text box. If the wrong filename is listed, either backspace over the name and type in the correct filename, or choose Cancel and select the correct file.

5. Choose Delete. The file disappears from the list in the directory tree, and has been deleted.

Once you have deleted a file or files, you cannot undo the action. Be certain that you are deleting the correct file, and that you won't need it again.

N O T E

Deleting Several Files at Once

1. From the directory tree, select the files you want to delete.

2. If you want to delete a group of files that are in consecutive order, click on the first file you wish to select; then hold down the Shift key, point to the last file you wish to select, and click. All of the files, from the first one you chose to the last, will be selected.

3. If you want to delete a group of files that are not in consecutive order, click on the first file you wish to select, hold down the Ctrl key, and click on all other files you wish to select.

4. Click on File.

5. Click on Delete to display the Delete dialog box.

6. Select Delete.

You can select all of your files at once by using the Select All feature. To access this feature click on File, then on Select All. If you change your mind, click on File, then click on Unselect All.

N O T E

Deleting an Entire Directory

The File Manager allows you to delete an entire directory and all of its files in one operation. To delete a directory and all of its files:

1. Select the directory you want to delete in the directory tree.

2. Click on File in the menu bar.

3. Click on Delete. The Delete dialog box is displayed and the name of the directory appears in the Delete text box.

4. Click on OK. A confirmation box is displayed asking you to confirm deletion of the directory and all of its files.

5. Click on Yes.

WARNING

Use this feature with great care. Even with special software, recovering a deleted directory is difficult—and may be impossible.

Copying Files

Before you can copy a file, you must know the path that describes the location of the place you want to copy it to. If you are not certain of the path, use the directory tree. To copy a file to a floppy disk, you do not need to know an entire path, but only the drive designation. If you have only one floppy drive, the drive designation is A. If you have two floppy drives, the one on the top is called A and the one on the bottom is called B. Floppy disks can be divided into directories just as a hard drive can, but because they hold so little data, it is rarely necessary.

When you copy a file, it exists in two places—the original location and the location to which it is copied. To copy a document you have created from the C:\EXCEL directory into your new DATA directory:

1. If you are not already in the C:\EXCEL directory, use the directory tree to change directories.

2. Select one of the documents you have typed.

3. Click on File.

4. Click on Copy to display the Copy dialog box. The Copy dialog box should contain the correct path, and the From Text box should contain the name of the file you want to copy.

5. In the To text box, type *C:\EXCEL\DATA*. You do not need to type the name of the file. Windows will copy the file into the DATA directory using exactly the same name. If the directory you are copying the file into already has a file with that name, Windows will prompt you before copying. You can copy a file and give it another name by typing the name you want it to have in the To text box. If you have a file named INCOME.XLS and want to copy it into your C:\EXCEL\DATA directory and call it INCOME91.XLS, you would type *C:\EXCEL\DATA\INCOME91.XLS*.

6. Choose Copy.

You have now copied a file into your DATA directory.

Copying Several Files at Once

1. Select the files you want to copy in the directory tree.
2. If you want to copy a group of files that are in consecutive order, click on the first file you wish to select; then hold down the Shift key, point to the last file you wish to select, and click. All of the files, from the first one you chose to the last, will be selected.
3. If you want to copy a group of files that are not in consecutive order, click on the first file you wish to copy, hold down the Ctrl key, and click on all of the other files you wish to copy.
4. Click on File.
5. Click on Copy to display the Copy dialog box.
6. Click on Copy.

You can select all of your files at once by using the Select All feature. To access this feature, click on File, then on Select All. If you change your mind, click on File, then on Unselect All.

N O T E

Copying Directories and All of Their Files

When you copy a directory in the File Manager, you also copy all of the files the directory contains. To copy an entire directory:

1. Select the directory you want to copy.
2. Click on File in the menu bar.
3. Click on Copy to display the Copy dialog box.
4. Enter the path to which you want to copy the directory.
5. Click on OK.

Moving Files

When you move a file, you take it from one location and put it in another. The Move feature lets you move a file, or move and rename it simultaneously. Let's move one of the files you created in C:\EXCEL.

1. If you are not in the C:\EXCEL directory, use the directory tree to change directories.
2. Select the file you want to move. Be very careful. If you move an Excel program file, the program may not operate properly. Select a file you created.

3. Click on File.

4. Click on Move to display the Move dialog box. The path is listed in the Move dialog box and the name of the file you selected is listed in the From text box.

5. In the To text box, type *C:\EXCEL\DATA*.

6. Choose Move. If you have another file in the DATA directory with the same name, Windows will prompt you. To move and rename a file, type the following in the To text box: *C:\EXCEL\DATA\filename*.

The file disappears from the directory tree. If you change your directory to C:\EXCEL\DATA, you will see it listed there.

Moving Several Files at Once

To move several files at once:

1. Use the directory tree to access the directory you want.

2. If you want to copy a group of files that are in consecutive order, click on the first file you wish to select; then hold down the Shift key, point to the last file you wish to select, and click. All of the files, from the first one you chose to the last, will be selected.

3. If you want to copy a group of files that are not in consecutive order, click on the first file you wish to copy, hold down the Ctrl key, and click on all of the other files you wish to copy.

4. Click on File.

5. Click on Move to display the Move dialog box. All of the files you selected will be listed in the From text box.

6. In the To text box, type the path you want to move the files to.

7. Choose Move. If you have another file in the new directory with the same name, Windows will prompt you.

You can select all of the directory's files at once by using the Select All feature. To access this feature, click on File, then on Select All. If you change your mind, click on File, then on Unselect All.

N O T E

Moving Directories and All of Their Files

When you move an entire directory in the File Manager, all of the files in the directory are automatically moved with it. To move an entire directory:

1. Select the directory you want to move.

2. Click on File in the menu bar.

3. Click on Move to display the Move dialog box.

4. In the To text box, type the path to which you want to move the directory.

5. Click on Move. Windows will keep you informed as to the progress of the procedure.

6. When the directory and all of its files have been moved, you will be asked whether you want to delete the original directory. If you say Yes, the directory is removed from the directory tree. If you say No, the directory remains in the directory tree, but it is empty.

Renaming Files

To rename a file:

1. If you are not in the C:\EXCEL directory, use the directory tree to change directories.

2. Select the file you want to rename. Be very careful. If you rename an Excel program file, the program will not operate properly. Select a file you have created.

3. Click on File.

4. Click on Rename to display the Rename dialog box. The path is listed in the Rename dialog box, and the name of the file you selected is listed in the From text box.

5. In the To text box, type the new name of the file.

6. Choose Rename. If you have another file in the directory with the same name, Windows will prompt you.

Your file has been renamed.

Changing File Attributes

The Change Attributes command in the File Manager allows you to change the attributes of a file or group of files. To set or change the attributes for your files:

1. Select the file(s) whose attributes you want to change.

2. Click on File in the menu bar.

3. Click on Change Attributes to display the Change Attributes dialog box. You can enable any or all of the attributes below:

   ◆ **Read Only**. Files marked as Read Only will not allow users to make changes to the file.

   ◆ **Archive**. If enabled, the Archive attribute indicates that the file has been modified.

   ◆ **Hidden**. This attribute hides the file from both DOS directory listings and from the File Manager directory window.

   ◆ **System**. This attribute tells DOS and Windows that the file is a DOS operating system file. These files are usually hidden as well.

Printing Files

File Manager allows you to print a file or group of files. You may print only DOS text files or Windows files. To print a file:

1. Use the directory tree to choose the directory you want.
2. Click on File.
3. If you want to print a group of files that are in consecutive order, click on the first file you wish to select; then hold down the Shift key, point to the last file you wish to select, and click. All of the files, from the first one you chose to the last, will be selected.
4. If you want to print a group of files that are not in consecutive order, click on the first file you wish to print, hold down the Ctrl key, and click on all of the other files you wish to print.
5. Click on Print to display the Print dialog box. The path of the file(s) is listed in the Print dialog box, and the name of the file(s) is listed in Print text box.
6. Choose Print.

To print a file that is not in the current directory tree:

1. Click on File.
2. Click on Print to display the Print dialog box.
3. In the Print text box, type in the path and name of the file you want to print.
4. Choose Print.

Running Other Programs from the File Manager

The File Manager Run command permits you to execute other programs from within the File Manager. When you exit another program, you will be back in the File Manager. In order to use this feature, your computer must have enough memory—at least two megabytes of RAM—to run more than one program at a time. To run another program from File Manager:

1. Click on File.
2. Click on Run to display the Run dialog box.
3. If you are not in the directory containing the program files for the program you wish to execute, type in the Command Line text box the full path and filename (including extension) of the executable file for the program you want to run.
4. If you are in the directory containing the program files for the program you wish to execute, type the name of the executable file in the Command Line text box.
5. Choose OK.

Or, use the directory tree to change to the directory containing the program file, then double-click on the program execute file.

Using the Associate Feature

The File Manager Associate feature allows you to create an association between a program and a group of files with the same file extension. Every time you open a file that has the associated extension, you will open the application to which it belongs. To create an association:

1. Select the directory containing the file for which you want to create an association (it does not have to be in either the same directory or a subdirectory of the program executable file).

2. Click on File in the menu bar.

3. Click on Associate to display the Associate dialog box.

4. In the Associate text box, type the full path and name of the executable program.

5. Click on OK.

Using the Search Feature

The File Manager Search feature allows you to search for documents in a drive, one or several directories, or a selected list. You can search by filename or you can use a combination of characters and DOS wildcards. This is extremely useful when you want to retrieve a document and you can remember only part of the name, when you have several documents with almost exactly the same name and have forgotten which is which, or when you cannot remember to what directory you saved a document.

Searching for Documents

The Search command in the File menu allows you to search all of your directories to locate a file that matches a specified pattern. If you want to search for a document or documents in one of your Excel directories:

1. Use the directory tree to change your directory to C:\EXCEL.

2. If you know the directory the document is in, double-click on the directory.

3. In the Search For text box, type in the name of the file you want to locate. If you are looking for a group of files, you can use a DOS wildcard to identify them. For information concerning DOS wildcards, consult your DOS manual.

4. The File Manager will search the directory you are currently in, as well as all of its subdirectories. If Search Entire Disk is enabled, the File Manager will search the entire drive.

5. Choose OK.

When the File Manager has completed its search, a Search Results window is displayed listing all of the files that match the search criteria.

Using the Disk Feature

The File Manager Disk feature handles all of the operations necessary to copy and format floppy disks.

Copying from One Floppy to Another

1. Select the drive containing the disk whose contents you want to copy.
2. Click on Disk in the menu bar.
3. Click on Copy Diskette. You will be prompted for each step in the disk-copy process.

If you have one disk drive, you can use the Copy Diskette command only if both the source diskette and the target diskette are the same kind of floppy disk—either high density or double density.

N O T E

Assigning Disk Labels

You can assign or change the volume labels on your floppy or hard disks using the File Manager's Label Disk command:

1. Select the drive whose volume label you want to change or to which you want to assign a volume label.
2. Click on Disk in the menu bar.
3. Click on Label Disk to display the Label Disk dialog box.
4. In the Label text box, type in the new label for the disk.
5. Click on OK.

Formatting Floppy Disks

To format a floppy disk:

1. Click on Disk in the menu bar.
2. Click on Format Diskette. If you have more than one floppy disk drive, a dialog box is displayed asking you to select either drive A or drive B.
3. The Format Diskette dialog box is displayed asking you to confirm that you want to format the floppy disk in the selected drive. Click on Format.
4. Another dialog box is displayed asking you to choose whether the disk you are formatting is high density or double density. If you do not select High Capacity (high density), the disk will be formatted as double density (360 kilobytes for 5.25-inch

disks, and 720 kilobytes for 3.5-inch disks). If you want to create a system disk (one that can start the computer if the hard drive fails) while you are formatting, select Make System Disk.

5. Click on OK. Windows will keep you informed of the progress of the formatting procedure.

Expanding and Collapsing Directory Levels

If you look closely at the file folders in the directory tree window, you will notice that some of the folders have a plus sign (+) on them, some have a minus sign (–), and some are blank. File folders with plus signs are directories that have subdirectories not shown in the directory tree. A minus sign indicates that all of the directory's subdirectories are showing. If the file folder is blank, the directory has no subdirectories. You can instruct the File Manager to show one subdirectory level, to show all of the branches (or subdirectories) in a directory, or to show all of the subdirectories on the entire disk. To expand and collapse directory levels:

1. Click once on any directory that has a plus or minus sign on its file folder. If the file folder has a plus sign, the directory will branch one level with each click. If the file folder has a minus sign, the directory will collapse one level with each click. **Or,** select the directory you want and click on Tree in the menu bar.

2. Select Expand One Level to show the next directory level (subdirectory) of the selected directory.

3. Select Expand Branch to see all of the subdirectories of the selected directory.

4. Select Expand All to display all of the branches for every directory on the disk.

5. Select Collapse Branch or click on the root directory in the directory window to collapse all of the branches.

6. To return to the directory window default, select Expand One Level.

Using the View Menu

The File Manager View menu allows you to change the layout of the directory window. The following commands are available:

◆ **Name**. Shows the names of directories and files in the directory window.

◆ **Other**. This choice opens the View Other dialog box. You can add information about size, last modification date and time, and/or file attributes to the directory. If you enable Set System Default, the chosen options will apply to all directory windows in every Windows session.

◆ **File Details**. Shows all available information for the directory and files, including name, size, last modification date and time, and file attributes for each file.

- **By Name**. This choice sorts files alphabetically by filename.
- **By Type**. This choice sorts files alphabetically by extension, and then alphabetically by filename. Directories are listed first and then files.
- **Sort by**. This option opens the Sort By dialog box, which allows you to sort files by name, type, size, or last modification date. If you enable Set System Default, the chosen option will apply to all directory windows in every Windows session.
- **Include**. This choice opens the Include dialog box, which allows you to specify the items displayed in the directory window: name, directories, programs, documents, other files, and hidden/system files. If you enable Set System Default, the chosen items will apply to all directory windows in every Windows session.
- **Replace on Open**. Replaces the contents of the active directory window every time you open a new directory.

Using the Options Menu

Use the File Manager Options menu to customize some File Manager settings.

Changing Confirmation Settings

To prevent you from accidentally deleting or overwriting files, the File Manager automatically asks you to confirm that you want these actions to occur. To change the confirmation settings:

1. Click on Options in the menu bar.
2. Click on Confirmation to display the Confirmation dialog box. You can enable any or all of the confirmation settings.
   a. If you enable Confirm on Delete, a confirmation box will ask for an OK to delete files. This box is enabled by default.
   b. If you enable Confirm on Subtree Delete, a confirmation box will ask for an OK to delete directories. This box is enabled by default.
   c. If you enable Confirm on Replace, a confirmation box will ask for an OK before it overwrites an existing file. This box is enabled by default.
   d. If you enable Confirm on Mouse Operation, a confirmation box will ask for an OK every time you try to copy, delete, or move files or directories using a mouse.
3. When you have made your selections in the Confirmation dialog box, click on OK.

Using Lower Case

When you enable Lower Case in the Options menu, you change the information displayed in all windows to lowercase letters.

Setting the Status Bar

When you enable Status Bar in the Options menu, the status bar is displayed in the lower-left corner of the File Manager window.

Minimize on Use

When you enable Minimize on Use in the Options menu, you shrink the File Manager to an icon whenever you run an application.

KEYBOARD COMMANDS

The following keyboard commands can be used with Excel 4.0. Keys that must be pressed at the same time are separated by a plus sign (+). Keys that must be pressed sequentially are separated by a comma (,).

Help Keys

To	Press these keys
Switch to Help window	F1
Switch to context-sensitive Help	Shift+F1

Moving and Selecting

To	Press these keys
Move left, right, up, or down	Arrow keys
Move to the beginning of a row	Home
Move up one window	Page Up
Move left one window	Ctrl+Page Up
Move down one window	Page Down
Move right one window	Ctrl+Page Down
Move to the beginning of the worksheet	Ctrl+Home
Move to the lower-right corner of the Worksheet	Ctrl+End
Move to the edge of the data block in the direction of the arrow key	Ctrl+Arrow key or End, Arrow key
Move to the last cell in the current row	End, Enter
Select the entire row	Shift+Spacebar
Select the entire column	Ctrl+Spacebar
Select the entire worksheet except objects, if a cell is selected; select all objects on a worksheet, if an object is selected	Ctrl+Shift+Spacebar
Extend the selection left, right, up, or down	Shift+Arrow key
Extend the selection to the edge of the data block, in the direction of the arrow key	Ctrl+Shift+Arrow key or End, Shift+Arrow key

continued...

...from previous page

To	Press these keys
Extend the selection to the last cell in the current row	End, Shift+Enter
Extend the selection to the beginning of the row	Shift+Home
Extend the selection up one window	Shift+Page Up
Extend the selection down one window	Shift+Page Down
Extend the selection left one window	Ctrl+Shift+Page Up
Extend the selection right one window	Ctrl+Shift+Page Down
Turn Extend mode on or off	F8
Turn Add mode on or off (for nonadjacent selections)	Shift+F8
Select the current data block	Ctrl+Shift+*
Go to a specific cell or range	F5
Find a cell with specific contents	Shift+F5
Find the next cell	F7
Find the previous cell	Shift+F7
Turn End mode on or off	End

Moving Within a Selection

To	Press these keys
Move down one cell in the selection	Enter
Move up one cell in the selection	Shift+Enter
Move right one cell in the selection	Tab
Move left one cell in the selection	Shift+Tab
Move to the next corner of the range area	Ctrl+Period
Move to the next range within nonadjacent selections	Ctrl+Tab

continued...

...from previous page

To	Press these keys
Move to the previous range within nonadjacent selections	Ctrl+Shift+Tab
Collapse the selection to the active cell	Shift+Backspace

Scrolling Through a Document

To	Press these keys
Scroll one row up or down or one column left or right	Arrow keys
Scroll up one window	Page Up
Scroll down one window	Page Down
Scroll left one window	Ctrl+Page Up
Scroll right one window	Ctrl+Page Down
Make the cell in the upper-left corner of the window active	Home
Make the cell in the lower-right corner of the window active	End

Selecting Items in Charts

To	Press these keys
Select the next item	Right Arrow
Select the previous item	Left Arrow
Select the next class of items	Up Arrow
Select the previous class of items	Down Arrow

Editing

To	Press these keys
Activate the formula bar	F2
Carry out an action	Enter
Cancel an action	Esc
Repeat the last action	Alt+Enter
Undo the last action	Ctrl+Z or Alt+Backspace
Insert cells	Ctrl+Shift+Plus Sign
Delete the selection	Ctrl+Hyphen
Clear the selection	Delete
Clear formulas	Ctrl+Delete
Cut the selection	Ctrl+X or Shift+Delete
Copy the selection	Ctrl+C or Ctrl+Insert
Paste the selection	Ctrl+V or Shift+Insert
Delete the preceding character in the formula bar, or activate and clear the formula bar when a cell is selected	Backspace
Edit a cell note	Shift+F2
Paste a name into a formula	F3
Paste a function into a formula	Shift+F3
Define a name	Ctrl+F3
Create names from cell text	Ctrl+Shift+F3
Calculate all documents	F9 or Ctrl+=
Calculate the active document	Shift+F9
Insert the AutoSum formula	Alt+=
Fill right	Ctrl+R or Ctrl+Shift+>
Fill down	Ctrl+D or Ctrl+Shift+<

Formatting

To	Press these keys
Select the style box	Ctrl+S
Apply the general number format	Ctrl+Shift+~
Apply the currency format with two decimal places (negative numbers appear in parentheses)	Ctrl+Shift+$
Apply the percentage format with no decimal places	Ctrl+Shift+%
Apply the exponential number format with two decimal places	Ctrl+Shift+^
Apply the date format with day, month, and year	Ctrl+Shift+#
Apply the time format with the hour and minute, and indicating A.M. or P.M.	Ctrl+Shift+@
Apply the two-decimal-place format with commas	Ctrl+Shift+!
Apply the outline border	Ctrl+Shift+&
Remove all borders	Ctrl+Shift+_ (underline)
Apply Normal font	Ctrl+1
Apply or remove bold	Ctrl+B
Apply or remove italic	Ctrl+I
Apply or remove underline	Ctrl+U
Apply or remove strikeout	Ctrl+5
Hide rows	Ctrl+9
Unhide rows	Ctrl+Shift+(
Hide columns	Ctrl+0 (zero)
Unhide columns	Ctrl+Shift+)

Working in the Formula Bar

To	Press these keys
Activate the formula bar	F2
Insert the current date in the formula bar	Ctrl+;
Insert the current time in the formula bar	Ctrl+Shift+:
Copy the value from the cell above the active cell into the formula bar	Ctrl+Shift+" (double straight quote)
Copy the formula from the cell above the active cell into the formula bar	Ctrl+' (apostrophe)
Fill the selection with the formula	Ctrl+Enter
Enter the formula as an array formula	Ctrl+Shift+Enter
Move one character up, down, left, or right	Arrow keys
Move to the start of the line	Home
Convert a reference from relative to absolute, from absolute to mixed, or from mixed back to relative	F4
Insert a line break in the formula bar	Alt+Enter
Insert a tab in the formula bar	Ctrl+Tab
Point to a selection in a worksheet after you have typed an operator in the formula bar	Arrow keys
Paste the argument to a function you are entering in the formula bar	Ctrl+A

Working with Files

To	Press these keys
Create a new worksheet	Alt+Shift+F1
Create a new chart	Alt+F1

continued...

...from previous page

To	Press these keys
Create a new macro sheet	Alt+Ctrl+F1
Save the active file with the Save As command on the File menu	Alt+F2
Save the active file with the Save command on the File menu	Alt+Shift+F2
Open an existing file	Alt+Ctrl+F2
Print the active file	Alt+Ctrl+Shift+F2
Quit Excel	Alt+F4
Close the active document window	Ctrl+F4

Working with Application and Document Windows

To	Press these keys
Select the menu bar	Alt or F10
Select a shortcut menu	Shift +F10
Select the application Control menu	Alt+Spacebar
Select the document Control menu	Alt+Hyphen
Move the document window	Ctrl+F7, Arrow keys
Size the document window	Ctrl+F8, Arrow keys
Maximize or zoom the document window	Ctrl+F10
Minimize the document window	Ctrl+F9
Restore the document window	Ctrl+F5
Close the document window	Ctrl+F4
Switch to the next open document window	Ctrl+F6
Switch to the previous open document window	Ctrl+Shift+F6
Switch to the next document in the workbook	Alt+Page Down

continued...

...from previous page

To	Press these keys
Switch to the previous document in the workbook	Alt+Page Up
Move to the next pane	F6
Move to the previous pane	Shift+F6
Show the Info window	Ctrl+F2
Quit Excel	Alt+F4

Working in the Data Form

To	Press these keys
Select a field	Alt+key for underlined field-name letter
Choose a command button	Alt+key for underlined button letter
Move to the same field in the next record	Down Arrow
Move to the same field in the previous record	Up Arrow
Move to the next field that you can edit in the record	Tab
Move to the previous field that you can edit in the record	Shift+Tab
Move to the first field in the next record	Enter
Move to the firs field in the previous record	Shift+Enter
Move to the same field 10 records forward	Page Down
Move to the same field 10 records back	Page Up
Move to the new record	Ctrl+Page Down
Move to the first record	Ctrl+Page Up
Move within a field	Home; End; Left or Right Arrow
Delete the previous character	Backspace
Delete the selected text or the next character	Delete

continued...

...from previous page

To	Press these keys
Select within a field	Shift+Home; Shift+End; Shift+Left Arrow; or Shift+Right Arrow

Finding Records in a Database

Before using these keys, choose the Find command in the Data menu.

To	Press these keys
Find the next matching record	Down Arrow
Find the previous matching record	Up Arrow
Find the next matching record at least one window down from the selection	Page Down
Find the previous matching record at least one window up from the selection	Page Up

Outlining

To	Press these keys
Demote a row or column	Alt+Shift+Right Arrow
Promote a row or column	Alt+Shift+Left Arrow
Hide or display outline symbols	Ctrl+8

Changing the Display

To	Press these keys
Switch between displaying values and displaying formulas	Ctrl+' (single left quotation mark)
Switch between displaying all objects, displaying placeholders, and hiding all objects	Ctrl+6
Switch display of outline symbols on and off	Ctrl+8

Viewing a Document in Print Preview in Actual Size

To	Press these keys
Move left, right, up, or down	Arrow keys
Move to the left of the page	Ctrl+Left Arrow or Home
Move to the right of the page	Ctrl+Right Arrow or End
Move to the top of the page	Ctrl+Up Arrow
Move to the bottom of the page	Ctrl+Down Arrow
Move to the upper-left corner of the page	Ctrl+Home
Move to the lower-right corner of the page	Ctrl+End
Move to the next page	N
Move to the previous page	P

Viewing a Document in Print Preview in Full Page Size

To	Press these keys
Move to the first page	Home
Move to the last page	End
Move to the next page	Down Arrow
Move to the previous page	Up Arrow

Command Shortcut Keys

The following keys can be used to bypass menu commands and dialog box options.

Menu	Command (dialog box option)	Keys
Edit	Clear (selection)	Delete
Edit	Clear (formulas)	Ctrl+Delete

continued...

...from previous page

Menu	Command (dialog box option)	Keys
Edit	Copy	Ctrl+C
Edit	Cut	Ctrl+X
Edit	Delete	Ctrl+Hyphen
Edit	Fill Down	Ctrl+D or Ctrl+Shift+<
Edit	Fill Right	Ctrl+R or Ctrl+Shift+>
Edit	Insert	Ctrl+Shift+Plus Sign
Edit	Paste	Ctrl+V
Edit	Repeat	Alt+Enter
Edit	Undo	Ctrl+Z
File	New (Worksheet)	Alt+Shift+F1
File	New (Macro Sheet)	Alt+Ctrl+F1
File	New (Chart)	Alt+F1
File	Open	Alt+Ctrl+F2
File	Print	Alt+Ctrl+Shift+F2
File	Exit/Quit	Alt+F4
File	Save	Alt+Shift+F2
File	Save As	Alt+F2
Format	Border (Outline)	Ctrl+Shift+&
Format	Border (removes all borders)	Ctrl+Shift+_ (underline)
Format	Column Width (Hide)	Ctrl+0 (zero)
Format	Column Width (Unhide)	Ctrl+Shift+)
Format	Font—normal	Ctrl+1
Format	Font—bold toggle	Ctrl+B
Format	Font—italic toggle	Ctrl+I
Format	Font—underline toggle	Ctrl+U
Format	Font—strikeout toggle	Ctrl+5

continued...

...from previous page

Menu	Command (dialog box option)	Keys
Format	Number (General format)	Ctrl+Shift+~
Format	Number (#,##0.00 format)	Ctrl+Shift+!
Format	Number (h:mm AM/PM format)	Ctrl+Shift+@
Format	Number (d-mmm-yy format)	Ctrl+Shift+#
Format	Number [$#,##0.00_);($#,##0.00) format	Ctrl+Shift+$
Format	Number (0% format)	Ctrl+Shift+%
Format	Number (0.00E+00 format)	Ctrl+Shift+^
Format	Row Height (Hide)	Ctrl+9
Format	Row Height (Unhide)	Ctrl+Shift+(
Formula	Create Names	Ctrl+Shift+F3
Formula	Define Name	Ctrl+F3
Formula	Find (opens dialog box)	Shift+F5
Formula	Find (finds next)	F7
Formula	Find (finds previous)	Shift+F7
Formula	Goto	F5
Formula	Note	Shift+F2
Formula	Paste Function	Shift+F3
Formula	Paste Name	F3
Formula	Reference	F4
Formula	Select Special (Notes)	Ctrl+Shift+?

SYMBOLS USED IN CREATING CUSTOM FORMATS

Each custom format you create can contain up to three number sections and one text section. Sections are separated by semicolons. If you create only one section, all selected cells use the custom format determined by that section. If you create two sections, the custom format of the first section is used if the number is positive or is zero, and the custom format of the second section is used if the number is negative. If you create three number sections, the custom format of the first section is used if the number is positive, the custom format of the second section is used if the number is negative, and the custom format of the third section is used for zeros. If you create three sections and the last section is a text format code, the first section applies if the number is positive or a zero, the second section applies if the number is negative, and the third section applies if the cell contains text.

0 (zero)

This is a digit placeholder. It determines how many digits will be displayed.

If the number has fewer digits before or after the decimal point than the format code has, Excel will display the extra zeros. For example, your format code is 00.00 and you enter the number 5, it would be displayed as 05.00—because you had four zeros in the format code, your number would be displayed with four digits.

If a number has more digits to the right of the decimal point than the format code has, the number is rounded to as many decimal places as there are zeros to the right of the decimal point in the format code. If there are no zeros to the right of the decimal point in the format code and the number contains a decimal, the number is rounded to the nearest whole number.

If a number has more digits to the left of the decimal point than the format code has, Excel displays the extra digits. For example, if your format code is 0 and your number is 10, the entire number is displayed.

 # (number symbol)

The Number Symbol is also a digit placeholder. It works the same as the zero with one exception: if the number has fewer digits before or after the decimal point than the format code has, Excel will *not* display the extra zeros.

? (question mark)

The question mark is a digit placeholder. It works the same as the zero with one exception: if the number has fewer digits before or after the decimal point than the format code has, Excel will *not* display the extra zeros, but will align the decimal points in all numbers using this symbol.

The question mark is also used to display fractions with varying numbers of digits.

. (period)

In Excel the period functions as a decimal point. It determines how many digits (0, #, or ?) are displayed to the left and right of the decimal point. If the format code contains number symbols or question marks, Excel begins numbers that are less than one with a decimal point. If you do not want this to happen, use zero as your first-digit placeholder to the left of the decimal point.

% (percentage sign)

Excel multiplies the number by 100 and adds the percentage character to the number.

$ - + / ( ) : space

These symbols tell Excel to display these characters when they are contained in the format code.

, (comma)	The comma is used as a thousands separator. Excel displays thousands separated by commas if the format code contains a comma surrounded by zeros or number symbols. A comma following a digit placeholder scales the number back by a thousand. Two commas following a digit placeholder scale the number back by a million. For example, the format code *0,* would display 5,000 as 5.
E- E+ e– e+	These symbols are used in scientific format codes. If a format code contains a zero or a number symbol to the right of an E- E+ e- or e+, Excel displays the number in scientific format and displays an E or e. The number of digit placeholders to the right determines the exponent's number of digits. An E– or e– will display a minus sign by negative exponents. An e+ or e+ will display a plus sign beside positive exponents and a minus sign beside negative exponents.
/ (slash mark)	The slash mark tells Excel to display the character in the format code that immediately follows the slash mark. The slash mark is not displayed. You can also surround your character with double quotation marks (" ") to achieve the same result. Excel will insert the slash mark for you if you enter any of the following characters: ! ∧ & ' ' ~ {} = or <>.
* (asterisk)	The asterisk tells Excel to repeat the next character in the format code until the entire cell is filled. You can have only one asterisk in any section of a format code.
_ (underline)	The underline symbol tells Excel to skip the width of the next character in the format code. This is used mostly to align positive and negative numbers when the negative numbers are enclosed in parenthesis.
" " (double quotes)	Double quote marks tell Excel to display whatever text is inside them in the format code.
@	This is a text placeholder. It tells Excel either to display text that is included in the format code, or to display text that is already in the cell when you apply the number format. The text placeholder cannot be the first symbol in a format code; it must be preceded by at least one number section.
m	A single *m* displays the month without leading zeros. For example, January will be displayed as 1, not 01. If this symbol immediately follows h or hh, it displays the minute and not the month.

mm	This symbol displays the year as a four-digit number. For example, 1992 will be display as 1992.
mmm	This symbol displays the month in text form using the first three letters of the month. For example, April will be displayed as Apr.
mmmm	This symbol displays the month in full in text form. For example, February will be displayed as February.
d	This symbol displays the day as a number without leading zeros.
dd	This symbol displays the day as a number with leading zeros if the day has only one digit (08). If the day has two digits, it will not be displayed with leading zeros.
ddd	This symbol displays the day in text form using its first three letters. For example, Wednesday will be displayed as Wed.
dddd	This symbol displays the day in full in text form. For example, Thursday will be displayed as Thursday.
yy	This symbol displays the year as a two-digit number. For example, 1992 will be displayed as 92.
yyyy	This symbol displays the year as a four-digit number. For example, 1992 will be displayed as 1992.
h	This symbol displays the hour as a number without leading zeros. If the format code contains an AM or PM designation, the hour is based on the 12-hour clock. If the format code does not contain an AM or PM designation, the hour is based on the 24-hour clock (Navy time).
hh	This symbol displays the hour as a number with leading zeros. If the format code contains an AM or PM designation, the hour is based on the 12-hour clock. If the format code does not contain an AM or PM designation, the hour is based on the 24-hour clock.
m	This symbol displays the minute as a number without leading zeros if it immediately follows the h or hh symbol.
mm	This symbol displays the minute as a number with leading zeros if it immediately follows the h or hh symbol.
s	This symbol displays the second as a number without leading zeros. It follows the h or hh symbol and the m or mm symbol.

ss	This symbol displays the second as a number with leading zeros. It follows the h or hhsymbol and the m or mm symbol.
AM, am, PM, pm, A, P, a, p	This symbol displays the hour using a 12-hour clock. AM, am, A, or a is used to display the hours from midnight until noon. PM, pm, P, or p is used to display the hours from noon until midnight.
[BLACK]	Displays the characters in the cell in black. This symbol requires a color monitor.
[BLUE]	Displays the characters in the cell in blue. This symbol requires a color monitor.
[CYAN]	Displays the characters in the cell in cyan. This symbol requires a color monitor.
[GREEN]	Displays the characters in the cell in green. This symbol requires a color monitor.
[MAGENTA]	Displays the characters in the cell in magenta. This symbol requires a color monitor.
[RED]	Displays the characters in the cell in red. This symbol requires a color monitor.
[WHITE]	Displays the characters in the cell as white. This symbol requires a color monitor.
[YELLOW]	Displays the characters in the cell as yellow. This symbol requires a color monitor.
[COLOR n]	Displays the corresponding color in the color palette. This symbol requires a color monitor.
[condition value]	In this symbol the condition may be any one of the following: < > = >+ <= <>. The value may be any number. This symbol allows you to set your own criteria for each section of a format code. For example, [>500] $#,##0.00_); #,##0.00_) will format all cells with entries greater than 500 with a dollar sign and two decimal places, and all of the rest of the cells containing numeric values with two decimal places and no dollar sign.

INDEX

Symbols

& (ampersand), as text operator, 219-221
* (asterisk)
  to indicate sound notes, 172; for multiplication, 30; as wildcard, 83, 255, 344
\ (backslash), 254
^ (carat), 30
✓ (checkmark), 13
: (colon)
  in functions, 65; as reference operator, 221
, (comma)
  in array constants, 229; in functions, 65
{ } (curved brackets), 227, 229
$ (dollar sign)
  for absolute references, 68, 192; for currency, 94
... (ellipses), 13
= (equal sign)
  as comparison operator, 345; for external references, 192; in formulas, 30, 220; in functions, 65
! (exclamation point)
  in external references, 192; in paths for source data, 203, 204
> (greater-than sign), 345
< (less-than sign), 345
– (minus sign), 30
(number sign), 97, 105
( ) (parentheses), in formulas, 218
% (percent sign)
  in entering numbers, 94; as operand, 30
. (period)
  in functions, 65; as union operator, 222
+ (plus sign), 30
? (question mark), as wildcard, 83, 344
" " (quotation marks), 221
' (single quotation mark)
  in external references, 192; for numeric text values, 27, 92
/ (slash)
  as default key for menu bar or Help, 177 ; for division, 30
~ (tilde), 83, 344